MICROSOFT® WORKS® 3.0
ON THE IBM-PC

JANET R. WILSON
SEATTLE UNIVERSITY

PRENTICE HALL
Englewood Cliffs, NJ 07632

Library of Congress Cataloging-in-Publication Data

Wilson, Janet R. (Janet Ruth), 1949 -
    Microsoft Works 3.0 on the IBM-PC / Janet R. Wilson.
        p.   cm.
    Includes index.
    ISBN 0-13-012709-4 (pbk.)
    1. IBM Personal Computer — Programming. 2. Microsoft Works.
  I. Title
  QA76.8.I2594W542   1993   92-32809
  005.369—dc20   CIP

Acquisition editor: Elizabeth Kendall

Development/production editor: Deborah Brennan
Interior designer: Deborah Brennan
Cover designer: Bruce Kenselaar

Prepress buyer: Ilene Levy
Manufacturing buyer: Ed O'Dougherty
Scheduler: Leslie Coward

© 1993 by Prentice-Hall, Inc.
A Simon & Schuster Company
Englewood Cliffs, New Jersey 07632

Printed in the United States of America

10   9   8   7   6

ISBN 0-13-012709-4

Prentice Hall International (UK) Limited, *London*
Prentice Hall of Australia Pty. Limited, *Sydney*
Prentice Hall Canada Inc., *Toronto*
Prentice Hall Hispanoamericana, S.A., *Mexico*
Prentice Hall of India Private Limited, *New Delhi*
Prentice Hall of Japan, Inc., *Tokyo*
Simon & Schuster Asia Pte. Ltd., *Singapore*
Editora Prentice Hall do Brasil, Ltda., *Rio de Janeiro*

PART 1   INTRODUCTION

CHAPTER 1 MICROCOMPUTER CONCEPTS   1

Computer System Components 2
The Keyboard 4
Review Questions 7

CHAPTER 2 OPERATING SYSTEMS   9

Starting the Computer 10
DOS Commands 12
Guided Tutorial 22
Review Questions 26
Hands-on Exercises 28
      Exercise 1 28

CHAPTER 3 AN OVERVIEW OF WORKS   29

Getting Started 30
Guided Tutorial 35
Review Questions 37
Hands-on Exercises 37
      Exercise 1 37

PART 2   THE WORD PROCESSOR TOOL

CHAPTER 4 CREATING DOCUMENTS   39

Creating a Document 40
Character Formatting 52
Saving a Document 54
Exiting Works 54
Opening an Existing Document 55
Printing the Document 56
Guided Tutorial 59
Review Questions 62
Hands-on Exercises 65
      Exercise 1 65
      Exercise 2 66

CHAPTER 5 ADVANCED FORMATTING   67

Creating a New File 68
Changing the Fonts 76
Works Toolbar Features 79
Guided Tutorial 81
Review Questions 83
Hands-on Exercises 85
      Exercise 1 85
      Exercise 2 85

CHAPTER 6 BUILT-IN WORD PROCESSING ASSISTANCE — 87

Searching For and Replacing Text 88
Using Special Commands in Text 92
Checking for Spelling Errors 96
Using the Thesaurus 100
Guided Tutorial 102
Review Questions 105
Hands-on Exercises 107
    Exercise 1 107
    Exercise 2 109

CHAPTER 7 REVISING TEXT — 111

Making Modifications to a Document 112
Guided Tutorial 117
Review Questions 118
Hands-on Exercises 119
    Exercise 1 119
    Exercise 2 119

CHAPTER 8 PAGE DESIGN — 121

Adjusting the Margins 122
Changing Tab Settings 124
Determining Page Breaks 131
Creating Headers and Footers 133
Reviewing Printer Setup 138
Creating Footnotes 140
Using Bookmarks 144
Adding Borders 147
Printing Options for Multipage Documents 149
Guided Tutorial 151
Review Questions 157
Hands-on Exercises 159
    Exercise 1 159
    Exercise 2 159

CHAPTER 9 WORKS WINDOWS AND OTHER ACCESSORIES — 163

Viewing Works Settings 164
Creating a Template 166
Using Works Windows 168
Using Works Other Accessories 175
Using WorksWizard 180
Guided Tutorial 182
Review Questions 184
Hands-on Exercises 185
    Exercise 1 185
    Exercise 2 185

Exercise 3 188
Exercise 4 190

PART 3　THE SPREADSHEET TOOL

CHAPTER 10　CREATING A SPREADSHEET　191

Creating a Spreadsheet 192
Editing Cells...201
Saving a Spreadsheet..203
Closing a Spreadsheet and Exiting Works 204
Guided Tutorial...205
Review Questions..207
Hands-On Exercises...208
　　　Exercise 1 208
　　　Exercise 2 209

CHAPTER 11　FORMULAS　211

Using Formulas 212
Guided Tutorial...219
Review Questions..220
Hands-on Exercises 221
　　　Exercise 1 221
　　　Exercise 2 222

CHAPTER 12　EDITING A SPREADSHEET　223

Using Relative Cell Addresses 224
Using Absolute Cell Addresses 227
Moving a Range of Cells 228
Viewing Cell Addresses...228
Inserting and Deleting Rows or Columns 229
Removing a Range of Cells..232
Guided Tutorial...233
Review Questions..236
Hands-On Exercises...237
　　　Exercise 1 237
　　　Exercise 2 238

CHAPTER 13　FORMATTING　239

Changing the Character Formats.....................................240
Creating Headers and Footers 246
Previewing the Spreadsheet 247
Inserting Page Breaks 247
Deleting Page Breaks 248
Changing the Margins 249
Printing the Spreadsheet..249
Guided Tutorial...251

Review Questions...253
Hands-On Exercises...253
     Exercise 1...254
     Exercise 2...256

CHAPTER 14 INCREASED SPREADSHEET POWER   **257**

Inserting Date and Time 258
Freezing Titles..259
Changing the Time Format 260
Calculating the Dates or Times...............................261
Entering a Series..262
Using Range Names 264
Sorting Contents of Cells 266
Guided Tutorial..268
Review Questions...269
Hands-On Exercises...270
     Copying a spreadsheet.................................270
     Exercise 1...270
     Exercise 2...276
     Exercise 3...278
     Exercise 4...279
     Exercise 5...281

PART 4   **THE CHARTING TOOL**

CHAPTER 15 CHARTS   **283**

Creating Charts...286
Making Modifications...288
Naming a Chart..294
Printing a Chart...304
Guided Tutorial..306
Review Questions...309
Hands-On Exercises...310
     Exercise 1...310
     Exercise 2...311

PART 5   **THE DATABASE TOOL**

CHAPTER 16 DATABASE DESIGN   **313**

Creating a Database...314
Editing a Database 321
Editing in Form View 326
Adding a Label to a Form 328
Adding Notes to a Form 328
Formatting a Database 330
Guided Tutorial..337

Review Questions 341
Hands-on Exercises 342
    Exercise 1 342
    Exercise 2 344

CHAPTER 17   SORTING AND QUERYING   345

Sorting Records 346
Querying a Database 347
Searching Through a File 352
Guided Tutorial 356
Review Questions 359
Hands-On Exercises 361
    Exercise 1 361
    Exercise 2 362

CHAPTER 18   REPORTS   363

Creating a Report 366
Creating a Custom Report..369
Guided Tutorial 380
Review Questions 383
Hands-On Exercises 385
    Exercise 1 385
    Exercise 2 386

CHAPTER 19   FORM LETTERS AND MAILING LABELS   387

Creating a Form Document..388
Merging and Printing the Form Letter 391
Creating Mailing Labels 391
Guided Tutorial 396
Review Questions 398
Hands-On Exercises 399
    Exercise 1 399
    Exercise 2 401

PART 6   THE COMMUNICATIONS TOOL

CHAPTER 20   APPLYING COMMUNICATIONS FUNCTIONS   403

Beginning Communications 404
Guided Tutorial 415

PART 7   INTEGRATED PRACTICE

CHAPTER 21   INTEGRATED DOCUMENTS   417

Transferring Information Among Tools 418
Integrated Project 1   The Premium Art Gallery, Part 1 420
Integrated Project 2   The Premium Art Gallery, Part 2 434
Integrated Project 3   Northwest Fund Raisers............................438

Integrated Project 4 King County Environmental
                      Support Group 446
Integrated Project 5 Hobby Shop 453
Integrated Project 6 Perennial Plant Shop
                      and Information Center 458

APPENDIX I   INSTALLING WORKS   467

APPENDIX II   GLOSSARY OF TERMS   469

PREFACE

Microcomputers have become commonplace in many schools, offices, and other organizations. The software available for microcomputers is found in vast quantities and ranges of applications. Clearly, the most common application programs found in the educational setting are those for word processing, spreadsheet, and database functions. Microsoft® Corporation has developed a powerful application called Works that does all of these functions and also includes a communications tool. Works is not only powerful, it is easy to learn. The use of drop-down menus, two- or three-keystroke commands, and a limited number of commands to perform complex operations makes Works easy to understand. Understanding any application program is one of the first obstacles a user must tackle. Works quickly eliminates any fears through the use of commands that are easy to use whether accessing them from the keyboard or using a mouse.

PURPOSE

This book provides you with step-by-step instructions on performing basic to sophisticated procedures using Microsoft® Works. As you work through the book, you are creating, modifying, and editing actual documents. All Works' commands are introduced while working on a document, just as you would in any session with Works that you were doing independently. In addition, tutorial documents and practice exercises are included at the end of every chapter.

The instructions and practice documents include a wide variety of formats. There are word processing documents, newsletters, and form documents (which are merged with database files). There are database files that require formulas and are used to compile reports. Queries, sorts, and searches are used on database files. Spreadsheets are created and many types of formulas, searches, and sorts are performed on various spreadsheet formats. A guideline for using communications capabilities is given in detail in Part 6.

Microsoft® Works 3.0 on the IBM-PC is designed for use at a variety of levels. The user with no previous Works' exposure can start at the beginning of the book and follow the step-by-step instructions through all of Works' features. An intermediate or advanced user could begin at any appropriate chapter and follow the guidelines for more specific features.

REQUIREMENTS

This book assumes that you have minimum experience in using a personal computer. It is not necessary to have experience using a software application program. Complete guidelines are given for starting the computer, and steps for the installation of Works are included in Appendix I. You should have some background in the basics of the personal computer system. If necessary, review your system manual to identify the parts of your computer, such as the disk drives, monitor, design of the keyboard (although an introduction to the keyboard is included in this book), and the memory capacity of the computer. You should also be aware of the type of printer in use and how it operates.

BOOK ORGANIZATION

The book is divided into seven parts. Each part covers a particular Works tool, background topic, or exercise set. Part I provides a brief overview of PC basics including instruction in some of the more common DOS commands. Parts II - VI give students an in-depth examination of the five principle applications within Works — word processing, spreadsheets, charting, databases, and communication. Finally, all five tools are tied together in a contextualized, hands-on manner in Part VII, Integrated Practice.

The following supplements are also available to complement the *Microsoft Works 3.0* text:

- **Instructor's Manual with a data disk.** The data disk includes many of the documents presented in the text and can be used in class to save inputting time. The symbol to the left is used throughout the text to indicate those documents which are included on the Instructor's data disk.

- **Test Manager (3.5" and 5.25" disks)**. The manager is a test-generating package that allows instructors to customize the test questions contained in the Instructor's Manual. The instructor can edit, delete, add to, or change the order of the questions to suit his or her particular needs.

CHAPTER FEATURES

OBJECTIVES

A list of objectives is included at the beginning of each chapter. They summarize the features covered in the chapter.

PREVIEW

A preview is included at the beginning of each chapter. It contains an overview of the features and commands to be covered in the chapter, their uses, and how they may be applied.

PRESENTATION/PRACTICE

All instructions are given as numbered steps. These steps guide the user through completing a word processing document, spreadsheet, or database file. They are also used to perform modifications, edits, and other features available using each Works tool. In this way, a document is completed using each of the features in the chapter objectives.

GUIDED TUTORIAL

All of the features covered in a chapter are used to complete an extensive step-by-step practice document. This is an additional reinforcement of Works functions presented in an integrated, contextualized manner.

REVIEW QUESTIONS

Review questions are included at the end of each chapter. They include questions on most of the commands discussed throughout the previous chapter. When the questions are answered, they serve as a guideline for completing the practice documents and offer a reference for students as they complete the exercises and as they work on documents independently.

HANDS-ON EXERCISES

The hands-on documents are a key component of the book. They give the needed extra practice using commands covered in each chapter. Usually at least two exercises are included at the end of every chapter. These are best done independently using the book and screen reference tools.

ACKNOWLEDGMENTS

Many people have been involved in making this book possible. I would like to thank Liz Kendall for her insights and knowledge of the textbook business and for the communication she had with the educational community. That communication resulted in many excellent ideas that were implemented in the final manuscript.

I would also like to thank Debbie Brennan at Regents/Prentice Hall for her involvement and supervision of the production of the book, and Stephen Hartner for his help in laying out the pages. They turned a plain keystroke manuscript into a beautiful presentation of text, images, and instructions. They are appreciated and have a wonderful talent.

The many reviewers who gave of their time and expertise are also appreciated. The reviews from colleagues resulted in extremely helpful suggestions, most of which are implemented into the final product.

The manuscript was keystroke tested and reviewed by **Nancy J. McPhee**, Green River Community College, **Norman P. Hahn**, Thomas Nelson Community College, and **Elyse Duffy**. This is a time-consuming effort and requires great attention and care to detail. It was very helpful to have other sets of eyes looking at the manuscript and to receive their professional input.

The following reviewers are also to be thanked.

Elvira Hromek, Morton College

D. Lavern Jones, Thomas Nelson Community College

Larry Lozuk, Baylor University

Alan Rowland, Indiana Vocational Technical College, Indianapolis

Eugene M. Spiess, Indiana Vocational Technical College, Indianapolis

Erin Carney, Public Relations Department, and **Jon Grande**, Product Manager, both at Microsoft® Corporation were responsible for expediting the Works beta copies when needed and for keeping us updated on changes in the software.

The marketing staff at Regents/Prentice Hall is to be commended as well. It is their efforts that sell and promote a book. In addition, local area sales representatives have the final task of promoting the book on site at schools and campuses. They do an outstanding and tough job and are to be congratulated for being among the most visible and knowledgeable sales representatives I have met.

The time involved in producing a textbook must ultimately take the understanding of those around the author. I wish to thank my husband, **Patrick Randle**, for his encouragement and understanding and for simply being there. And, last but not least, **Triscuit** the cat, for sleeping in the chair behind me, many hours at end, purring her comforting song.

1 MICROCOMPUTER CONCEPTS

Objectives

- Identify computer system components.

- Distinguish between hardware and software components.

- Become familiar with the standard keyboard.

PREVIEW ⟫⟩→

The combination of Microsoft Works and your microcomputer provides you with a powerful tool in today's business world. Together they allow you to write and edit letters, customize form letters, perform calculations, make charts and graph and organize information for easy retrieval in a variety of formats.

This book is designed to show you how to make the most of your computer and Microsoft Works in an easy-to-follow, step-by-step fashion. Before learning the details of Works, however, you should have a firm understanding of some basic computer concepts. A solid foundation in the basics will help to make Works and in fact, any application program, easier to master.

COMPUTER SYSTEM COMPONENTS

A microcomputer system is made up of a number of smaller pieces. Some of these pieces are mechanical in nature; that is, they have moving parts like the mechanism that pops your floppy disks out of the drive. The most central pieces, however, are electronic. That means they work by means of impulses running through silicon chips, which are connected with wires. The combination of electronic and mechanical pieces makes up what is referred to as **hardware**. Hardware is the tangible part of your computer, the part you can touch. There are a number of hardware components in any microcomputer system. Some of these are the **central processing unit (CPU)**, **keyboard**, **monitor**, **hard disk drive**, **diskette drive**, and **printer**. All of these are discussed in detail below.

All of the electromechanical parts of the computer are useless without the direction of computer programs. These programs, or computer code, are called **software**. Software may be stored on your system's computer chips or on floppy disks depending on its purpose. One type of software common to all microcomputers is **system software** or **operating system.** System software contains instructions that coordinate the various parts of the computer system to make it run rapidly and efficiently. System software programs are the necessary component (much like the fuel in an airplane) that allows the computer to operate. One of the most common type of system software programs used with IBM computers and IBM compatible computers is DOS (Disk Operating System). The **operating system** software programs are critical to supervision of the computer's work. In Chapter 2 you will learn more about both of these operating systems.

Besides system software, there are other software programs that are designed to perform specific job-related tasks such as word processing, spreadsheet, and database design. These types of programs are often called **application software.** Microsoft Works is an example of application software. It is common to store the application software program on the hard drive; however, it is also possible to run the application from a floppy diskette. This diskette is often called the **program disk**.

Files are what you create with your application software programs. With Works, for example, each file is a specific document that you have prepared, such as a letter, spreadsheet, or database file of addresses. You may wish to store these files on a separate diskette, which would then be your **data disk.** You can give each file a name that will help you remember what it contains and help you locate it among a group of files stored on the data disk.

THE HARDWARE COMPONENTS

All computer systems contain the same basic components:

- Microprocessor (or processor)
- Memory
- Monitor
- Keyboard
- Printer
- Secondary storage

If you were to open up the system unit of your computer and look inside, you would basically see hardware—silicon chips and wire. Two parts in this area are the **central processing unit (CPU)** and the **memory**. Both the CPU and memory are contained on silicon chips. The CPU is often referred to as the *brain* of the computer system. This is a good analogy, because the CPU literally controls the functions of the system and coordinates its activities—transmitting and receiving data through electrical impulses.

Memory

A microcomputer system has two kinds of memory: read only memory (**ROM**) and random access memory (**RAM**). These memory components are also contained on silicon chips. ROM contains programs that are installed by the manufacturer. ROM generally can be read (the information can be used by the computer) but cannot be written to (data cannot be stored over it). These program instructions are necessary for many of the functions of the computer. RAM temporarily holds all program instructions and data used by the CPU. These instructions are stored electronically. The operating system is loaded into RAM memory when the computer is first turned on. An application program such as Works is stored in RAM temporarily as are the data from files on which you are working.

The monitor

The monitor resembles a TV screen. You can see your document on this screen as you type in Works. The monitor is a visual display of your interaction with the computer. It is therefore an **output device**. Instructions from the application program appear on the screen so that you can make decisions about what step to perform next. You can also check the results of revisions you have made to a document. You input from the keyboard, and then see the results of the input on the screen. The display or output on monitor screens is usually either **monochrome** (one color) or **color** (multiple colors). Quality of the image on the screen may vary depending on the type of monitor you have. EGA, Enhanced Graphics Adapter, and VGA, Variable Graphics Array, are two of the most common monitors.

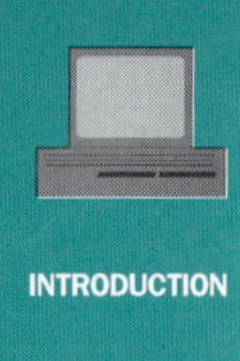

The printer

The printer is also an **output** device. Your computer communicates with your printer through a cable connection, much like your keyboard communicates with the computer. There are many types of printers ranging from daisy-wheel to dot matrix to ink jet to laser printer. Your instructor can tell you more about the printer you will be using and how to communicate with it.

The paper output from your printer is called **hard copy** because it is in a tangible form. The opposite of hard copy is **soft copy.** The image on your screen is a good example of soft copy. Soft copy is temporary, but it it also considered output.

SECONDARY STORAGE

FIGURE 1-1
TWO COMMON TYPES
OF DISKETTES

Earlier in this chapter you learned about the internal memory in your computer called random access memory or RAM. RAM storage is temporary. When the power is turned off, everything contained in RAM is erased. For this reason, most data are stored semipermanently on a **secondary storage medium**. A secondary storage medium is commonly some kind of **magnetic disk,** such as one of those shown in Figure 1-1, or a rigid **hard disk.** They come as dual- or high-density and single or double sided. More storage space is available on a high-density, double sided diskette.

Secondary storage devices, such as a hard disk drive or diskette drive, are the hardware components that write data to, or read data from, either the hard disk or the diskette. These devices are slower than RAM since they contain mechanical parts. Hard disks and diskettes are discussed in depth later in this chapter.

THE KEYBOARD

The keyboard is an input device. It is used to put data into the computer. There are a variety of keyboard styles and sizes available with computer systems. All keyboards, however, have several major features in common. They all have the standard alphabetic and numeric character keys in the center of the keyboard. The keyboard is connected to the computer by a cable so that messages are sent directly to the computer's memory when keys are pressed. When you are typing a document or entering other data, the **cursor** appears on the screen at the point where your next character will be inserted. The cursor is usually a flashing square or dash on the screen, and it moves as you enter characters or numeric figures.

Most keyboards also contain a numeric keypad. The numeric keypad may be used as a calculator and the numbers on the keypad frequently double as **cursor movement keys**, often called **Arrow keys**. The switch between the numeric mode and the cursor movement keys usually is done using a key called the **Num Lock** key, located near the numeric keypad as shown in Figure 1-2. The figure shows an IBM-compatible keyboard. Although your keyboard design may vary somewhat, the function of the named keys will not.

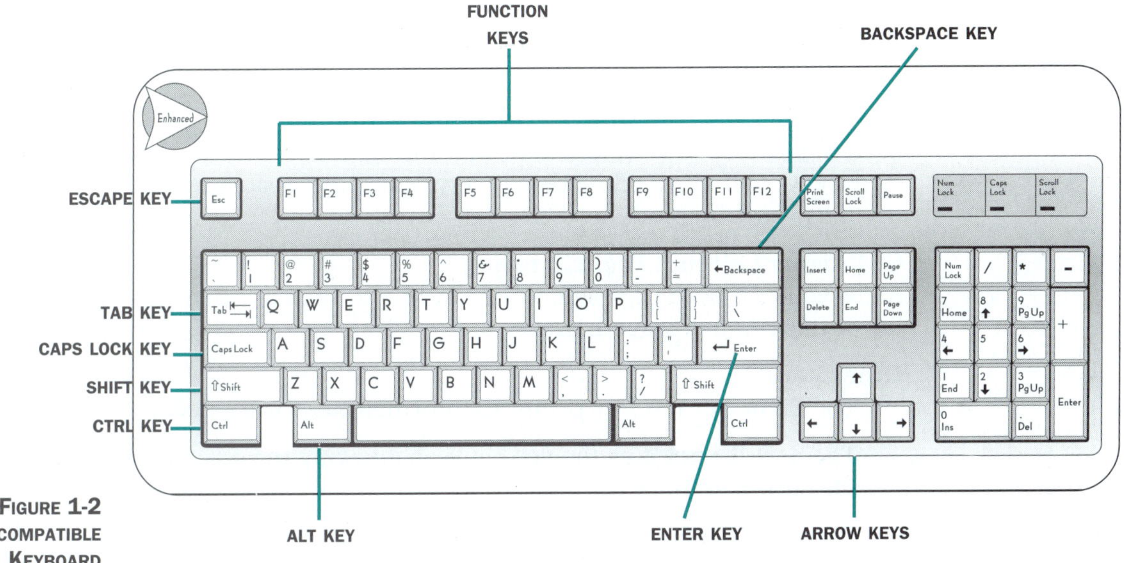

FIGURE 1-2
IBM -COMPATIBLE KEYBOARD

Function keys
Used for quick access to frequently used functions. Different programs may assign different functions to each key.

The Esc key
Returns to the document, previous menu, or from a menu to the opening screen. Escapes from the current menu or dialog box.

The Tab key
Moves to the next tab, field, or cell or moves back one field or cell (depending on whether you are using the word processor, database, or spreadsheet tool) when used with the Shift key.

The Ctrl key
Used in combination with other keys to provide a secondary function to those keys.

The Shift key
Used to create uppercase lettering or to access a key's secondary function.

The Caps Lock key
Switches the keypad between upper- and lowercase letters.

The Alt key
Like the Ctrl key, it is used in combination with other keys to provide a secondary function. In Works, the Alt key is used to access the menu from the keyboard.

The Enter key
Used to select an option, end an operation, terminate a paragraph, or insert a line in a report specification or script.

The Backspace key
Erases text to the left of the cursor. Also erases the current field (database) or cell (spreadsheet).

Alt/Backspace
Undoes an unwanted editing change in a word processor, or clears the field or cell contents in the database or spreadsheet.

The Arrow keys
Used to move up, down, left, and right through a document. The left and right arrow keys will move one screen at a time in the spreadsheet and database tools when used in combination with other keys.

Ctrl/Arrow Left and Right arrows
Allow you to move one selection left and right, such as one word in word processing or one cell in a spreadsheet.

Other keys
The **Print Screen key** prints all information on the screen.

The **Scroll Lock key** toggles between allowing the screen image to move or the cursor to move through a document.

The **Page Up** key redisplays the previous screen in a word processing document, spreadsheet, or a database file.

The **Page Down** key redisplays the next screen in a word processing document, spreadsheet, or database file.

The **Delete** key deletes above the cursor position.

The **End** key moves to the end of a file, field, or image.

The **Hom**e key moves to the beginning of a file, field, or image.

When using the keyboard to make menu selections in Works, the **Alt** key is often combined with another letter key. For example, **Help** may be reached by pressing **F1** or by pressing **Alt/H/H** (holding the **Alt** key down, pressing **H,** and then **H** again). Reaching menu options is sometimes achieved by pressing **Alt** and the first character of the menu option. When a character or menu command is highlighted (or shown in bold or a color), press **Alt** and the highlighted character to reach that command. More information will be provided about the use of the **Alt** key as you begin creating documents.

REVIEW QUESTIONS

1. Locate each of the following on your keyboard.

   a. function keys   h. Num Lock key
   b. Esc key   i. Alt key
   c. Return or Enter key   j. Ctrl key
   d. Backspace key   k. Arrow keys
   e. Shift keys   l. Tab key
   f. Del key   m. Caps Lock key
   g. Numeric keypad

Fill in the BEST answer for each item.

2. A computer system contains both ________ and __________ parts.

3. Written programs stored on the hardware or on a diskette are called ____________.

4. Programs that do useful tasks for end users (like you) of computers are called (two words) ____________ __________.

5. The disk on which application software is contained is called the __________________ disk.

6. The material you create with an application program is organized into ________.

7. Match each of the following definitions to the appropriate hardware component.

   a. Secondary storage
   b. RAM memory
   c. Keyboard
   d. Printer
   e. Microprocessor
   f. Monitor

   ______ An output device used to create hard copy

   ______ Where documents can be saved permanently without concern about power failure

   ______ An input device used to send messages to the computer

   ______ The internal temporary storage section of a microcomputer

   ______ The CPU (central processing unit)

   ______ The screen where output is displayed on a microcomputer

Choose the BEST answer to the following items.

8. A diskette and a hard disk are examples of:

    a. RAM
    b. Memory
    c. Secondary storage media
    d. Primary storage media

9. The Shift, Ctrl, or Alt keys:

    a. Work only by themselves and perform no other function
    b. Work by pressing them in conjunction with the spacebar
    c. Work by pressing them in conjunction with another key
    d. Work by pressing two of them together

10. The Del key removes text:

    a. To the left of the cursor
    b. Only at the cursor position
    c. To the right of the cursor
    d. At the cursor position

11. Works is an example of:

    a. System software
    b. Programming languages
    c. Application software
    d. Programs stored permanently in ROM

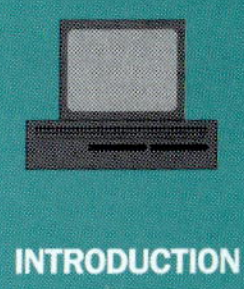

Objectives

- Identify dual- and hard disk systems.

- Learn about drive configurations.

- Understand some basic **DOS** commands.

PREVIEW ▶▶▶

An operating system is a set of programs that tells a computer system how to control resources, execute programs, and manage data. Application programs such as Works could not run on the computer without the operating system to guide them. When the DOS operating system is present, a symbol called the **prompt** appears on the screen. Depending on the type of computer in use (hard drive or dual-disk drives), the symbol will vary. It is, however, usually a letter of the alphabet, such as:

    `A:\>`   (on a dual-disk system)

    or

    `C:\>`   (on a hard disk system)

(This prompt may vary somewhat in appearance from the samples shown here.)

The system prompts are usually a letter of the alphabet, such as A, B, or C, followed by a greater than symbol (>). When you see one of these prompts, you are at the operating system and are ready to give system commands or to load an application program into memory (RAM).

The operating systems common to IBM-type personal computers are MS-DOS (Microsoft Disk Operating System) or PC-DOS (Personal Computer Disk Operating System). In this book, the operating system is referred to simply as DOS.

DOS programs are stored on one or more diskettes and are usually purchased with the computer system. There are many programs stored on the DOS disk(s). They contain instructions for invoking certain commands that the user can access. You could read an entire book about all of the commands you can invoke using DOS; however, in this guide, you will learn only a few of the most commonly used commands—those you can start using immediately. First, you need to identify the kind of computer you are using and the location of DOS.

When using a hard disk system, DOS will probably be in a directory of its own. A **directory** is a collection of files given a unique name, such as the DOS directory, where all DOS files are located, more on this later.

STARTING THE COMPUTER

As mentioned, a computer system has several hardware components. One of the components you are now familiar with is RAM (random access memory). Some DOS programs are necessary for the operation of an application program such as Works. They are loaded automatically when the system is turned on when using a hard disk system, and when the DOS disk is inserted in drive A and the system is turned on when using a dual-disk system. These DOS programs must be stored in RAM prior to accessing an application program. Because the size of memory is limited, only the files needed for normal operation are loaded. These files are often referred to as **internal** or **resident** files. Other files that are not needed for the everyday operation of the computer are not loaded into memory and are referred to as **external** or **transient** files. Occasionally, you may need to access the external files by invoking a command. If, when using a DOS command, you receive a message similar to "bad command..." you have attempted to use an external DOS command and your DOS is not available. Insert your DOS disk (dual-disk system) or change to the DOS directory (hard disk system).

DRIVE CONFIGURATIONS

There are two kinds of disk drives: diskette drives and hard disk drives. Figure 2-1 shows the possible drive configurations that come with IBM PCs and IBM-compatible systems. Compatible systems are manufactured by companies other than IBM, but can use the same operating system and applications.

The configurations shown in Figure 2-1 are:

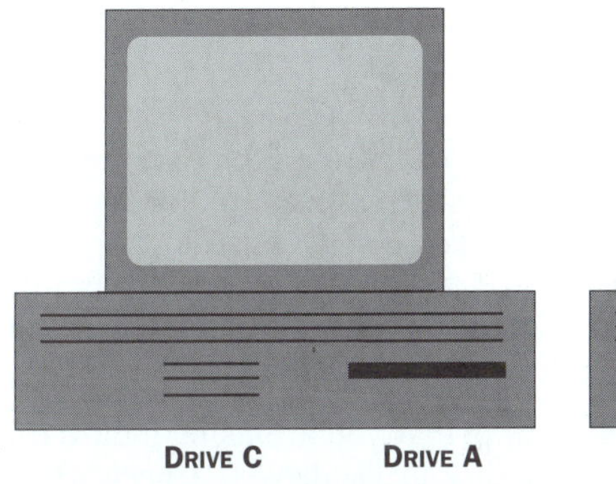

A personal computer with a hard disk (drive C) and a diskette drive (drive A).

A dual-disk drive system (drives A and B).

A single diskette drive system (drive A) with one diskette slot.

A system with a hard drive (drive C) and two diskette slots (drives A and B).

**FIGURE 2-1
DISK DRIVE
CONFIGURATIONS**

The most common configurations are either the hard disk drive with two diskette drives or the hard disk system with one diskette drive. These two types of systems are discussed in this chapter. You may also be using a dual-disk drive system. However, as software programs add more features and functionality, it is often necessary to use a hard disk system simply because of the size limitations of floppy diskettes and the slower access times. Generally speaking, when using a dual-disk system, first DOS and then the application program will be inserted into drive A, and your data disk (the disk containing the files you have created and want to save) will be located in drive B. When using a hard disk and one or two diskette drive system, your program and DOS files may be stored permanently on the hard drive, and your data (document) files will be saved on a diskette (the data disk) in drive A.

There are two other possibilities concerning your diskette drives. Depending upon the type of drive(s) installed in the computer, your computer may use either 5 1/4-inch or 3 1/2-inch diskettes.

DOS COMMANDS

Once you are at the system prompt, you are ready to type DOS or system commands. As mentioned earlier, those covered in this book are but a few of the many commands you can invoke using DOS. They are, however, some of the commands used most frequently, and you will want to be familiar with them for future use. You can view some of these commands by looking at a list of files contained in the DOS directory or on the DOS disk.

These instructions will assume that you are using a hard disk system and that Works is stored on the hard disk drive, drive C. Check with your instructor or lab manager if your system is configured differently.

USE DOS COMMANDS

1. START   at the hard disk system prompt, C:\>

2. TYPE   **DIR**

3. PRESS   **Enter**

A list of the directories and files contained on the hard disk appears. The DOS files may be contained in a directory of a different name with the system you are using. If you do not see a DOS directory (shown on the screen as DOS <DIR>), check with your instructor or lab manager to locate the name of the correct directory before doing step 4. Dual-disk users will not need to change to a DOS subdirectory; they will see information on the A drive at the top of the screen rather than the C drive information.

4. TYPE	**CD\DOS**	

This command will switch to the DOS directory.

5. PRESS	**Enter**	

You will see a DOS directory prompt similar to the following:
`C:\DOS>`

6. TYPE	**DIR** and press **Enter**	

You will see a directory similar to the partial one shown in Figure 2-2. Do not worry if you see a long list of file names, some of which scrolled off the screen. The names shown in the example may have scrolled up the screen. View the file names that are visible when reading through the next instructions.

```
Volume in drive C has no label
Directory of C:\DOS\>

COMMAND    COM    23210    3-07-85    2:23p
ANSI       SYS    1651     3-07-85    2:23p
ASSIGN     COM    1509     3-07-85    2:23p
  .
  .
  .

     48 file(s)   14336 bytes free
```


Look closely at your list of DOS files. The name of the file contains two parts—shown in the first and second columns on your screen. The first part is the file name; the second part is the file extension. Looking at the example in Figure 2-2, the first file name is COMMAND and its file extension is COM. The file name is written as COMMAND.COM. The file name and extension appear differently when listed in a directory than when you type them. In typing, the period is used to show separation between the file name and its extension. File names are one to eight characters in length, and it is *IMPORTANT* to remember when creating file names that they may contain numbers or characters but *NOT* spaces. The file extensions are always zero to three characters (or numbers) in length, with three characters most common. Extension names are also optional. They are used with files to identify the type of file and are either entered automatically by the program in use or by the user.

The middle column shown in Figure 2-2 and on your directory contains the total number of bytes used in the file. The fourth and fifth columns show the date and time the file was created or last modified. You can see the advantage of knowing the date and time of file modification. When you look at this directory, the direc-

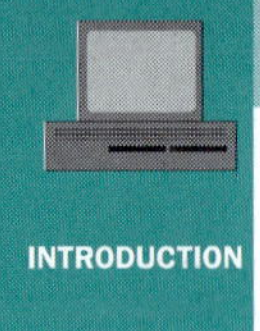

tory of your data disk, or another disk directory, the format will be similar. At the bottom of your list of files is a message showing the total number of files in your DOS directory and the total number of bytes free on the hard disk. Dual-disk users will see the total number of files and the total number of bytes free on their DOS disk.

You can use different variations of the DIR command to see a copy of a directory. At your system prompt, you could type

```
DIR/W
```

to see a copy of the directory across the width of your screen. This command eliminates some of the file information, however. Only the filename and extension are displayed, so that more files can be displayed across the screen. The information at the bottom of the screen (total files and bytes free) will remain the same.

As you may have noticed, when the directory gets too long, some of the files may disappear from the screen. To view only a screen or page of files at a time, you could type

```
DIR/P
```

at the system prompt. A message will appear at the bottom of the screen telling you to "Press any key to continue..." when you are ready to view the next page.

THE FORMAT COMMAND

The FORMAT command is one of the most used and most important of the DOS commands. It is used every time you buy a new blank diskette. The FORMAT command is used to prepare a new diskette for receiving files. It sets up a directory, marks off sectors (storage areas), and tests the tracks on the surface of the diskette to be sure that data can be stored on them. The tracks are similar to the grooves in a record, and the sectors are divisions similar to pieces in a pie. The sectors and tracks are designated storage areas on the surface of the disk.

You need to format the diskette only once. If you give the FORMAT command to a diskette containing data documents, it will erase the contents of the diskette. If you want to do this, use FORMAT; otherwise, be very careful to use it only with new diskettes.

FORMAT (DUAL-DISK SYSTEM)

1. INSERT — a new diskette in drive B (usually on the right or bottom) with the label up and the open slot to the back of the drive (or in the direction of the arrow on the 3 1/2- inch diskette). Be sure the DOS diskette is in drive A.

2. CLOSE — the drive doors.

At the A:\>

3. TYPE — **FORMAT B:**

Note: You may use either upper- or lowercase letters. In this book upper-
case letters are used for clarity.

4. PRESS   Enter

A message appears asking you to place a blank diskette in
drive B. The message will then ask you to press any key or the
Enter key (depending on your DOS version) when you are sure
that the diskette has been inserted correctly .

5. PRESS   Enter or any key (whichever you are asked to do by the screen
message)

You will hear a whirring sound and will see the light next to the
B drive turn on. Wait until the formatting process is complete

6. PRESS   Enter at a message asking about a volume label (if necessary).

The following message appears

```
Format another (Y/N)?
```

7. PRESS   N for No

8. PRESS   Enter

The system prompt appears.

FORMAT (HARD DISK SYSTEM)

At the system prompt (C:\DOS>),

1. TYPE   FORMAT A:

2. PRESS   Enter
(message OK)

3. INSERT   the new floppy disk into drive A, if necessary

4. PRESS   Enter or any key when the diskette is ready

You will hear a whirring or clicking sound and see the light next
to drive A turn on. Wait until the formatting process is complete.

5. PRESS   Enter when asked about the volume label (if necessary)

the following message appears

```
Format another (Y/N)?
```

6. PRESS   N for No

7. PRESS   Enter to return to the system prompt (C:\DOS>)

8. TYPE   CD .. or **CD**

9. PRESS   Enter

This action will return you to the root directory, C:\>.

Note: At this point you could turn your computer off and boot again at the next session. You are ready to turn your computer off when you have returned to the system prompt (A> on a dual-disk system or C> on a hard disk system). These prompts will always be your starting and ending messages. You should always see a system prompt when the system is correctly booted, and you should always see one when you have finished using the computer before turning the system off.

The Format /V option

The Format/V option will format a disk and ask for a name for the diskette (volume). For example,

```
Format a:/v
```

would prompt you for a name for the current diskette. You could enter your name or another personal label for the diskette that you are formatting. This is a way to uniquely identify your disk.

Note: If using DOS 5.0 or higher, this message appears automatically

THE ACTIVE DRIVE

A prompt showing on the screen, such as A> or C>, displays your **active** (or logged) **drive.** When you use commands such as the DIR command to see the contents of the drive, you are looking at the contents of the active drive. You can view the contents of other drives (for example, drive B on a dual-disk system or drive A on a hard disk system) by giving another command.

Note: From this point on, it will be assumed that you know that if you are using a hard disk system, your formatted disk (later to contain your data documents) will be in drive A, and that if you are using a dual-disk system, your formatted disk will be in drive B. It will also be assumed that you know that you are operating from drive C with a hard disk system. If you are using a dual-disk drive, substitute drive A for drive C.

THE ACTIVE DRIVE (HARD DISK SYSTEM)

From drive C and with a formatted disk in drive A,

1. **TYPE**   **DIR A:**   (B: if using a dual-disk system)

2. **PRESS**   **Enter**

At this time there are no data documents, so you will not see files in the disk directory. It will be blank and a message will appear stating "File not found."

When you give the command above, you remain logged onto drive C. This means that after the directory information is displayed, you are returned to the original system prompt (C:\>). You also have the option of changing the active drive and thus changing the prompt.

At the C prompt, C:\>

1. TYPE   **A:**

2. PRESS   **Enter**

An A> appears. You have now changed the active or logged drive. At this point you can look at the directory of the drive by typing DIR and pressing Enter.

CHANGE THE ACTIVE DRIVE

1. TYPE   **C:** (A: if using a dual-disk system)

2. PRESS   **Enter**

This will return you to the original active disk drive.

THE COPY COMMAND

One of the most useful DOS commands is the **COPY** command. You use the COPY command to copy files from one disk to another. You have the option of copying one, some, or all of your disk files. There are many reasons why you may want to make copies from one disk to another. You may want to transfer a file to another disk containing related files, or you may simply want to make a backup copy of a file. If you are making backup copies to another disk, and that disk is new, you will need to be sure that it is formatted. If you are copying to a disk that already contains some files, all you need to do is give the COPY command.

Before you use the COPY command, you need to be at the system prompt (either A for a dual-disk system or C for a hard disk system or at any other active drive). The COPY command is an **internal** DOS command, so you do not use the system (or DOS) files.

For this exercise you will copy one of the DOS files to your formatted disk. This is for practice purposes only, and you will be instructed to erase the file at the end of this exercise. In general, the COPY command should not be used on copyrighted software such as DOS.

COPYING

AT C:\>

1. INSERT your formatted data disk in drive A (hard disk) or in drive B (dual disk)

2. TYPE **COPY COMMAND.COM A:** (use **B:** instead when using a dual-disk system)

Note: *COMMAND.COM is one of the files on your DOS disk. You can view this file by giving the DIR command.*

This command copies the file COMMAND.COM from the logged drive (A or C in this case) to the disk in drive B or A. Note also that the file name includes the extension. When you are copying from one disk to another, be sure to include the entire name, with the period separating the file name and the file's extension.

If you make an error in the spacing or typing of file names before you have pressed Enter, simply backspace to correct the error and retype it.

3. PRESS **Enter** when the line is correctly typed

A message will appear when the copying process is complete. It will say, **1 File(s) copied**.

At times you may want to copy more than one file. Suppose, for example, that you wanted to copy all files with the extension of .COM to another disk. (A more likely possibility might be that you would want to copy all Works files with an extension of .WPS, which you might enter when you save some of your Works word processing documents. For this exercise, though, you will practice by copying the .COM files from the DOS disk directory.)

At C:\>

4. TYPE **COPY *.COM A:** (or **B:** with a dual-disk system)

5. PRESS **Enter**

This command copies all files from the default drive and directory (C) to the data disk in A with file name extensions of COM. The asterisk (*) is recognized as a **wildcard** or **global character** and will thus pick all files with the extension COM regardless of the file name.

If you wrote a command like the one above but changed the position of the asterisk (*), you could copy all *like* file names with different extensions, such as

```
COPY LETTER.*  A:
```

One other variation of this command is

```
COPY *.* A:
```

As with the other commands, the asterisk (*) is a global character, and in this command will copy all files regardless of the file name or the extension.

As you practice more with creating and saving documents, you will become more comfortable with organizing your documents by extension names. For example, you may want all memos to have an extension of MEM or all letters to have an extension of LET. The possibilities of one to three-character extensions are limited only to the combinations of letters and figures you can arrange in three characters. You may also choose to let Works add extensions automatically. Three character extensions are added for the type of document saved, such as Word processor, (WPS), or Spreadsheet, (WKS).

HE DISKCOPY COMMAND

The DISKCOPY command is similar to the COPY *.* command in that it copies all files from one disk to another. There are, however, some major differences between the two commands. The DISKCOPY command erases the contents of the target disk (the disk in drive A or B). It also formats the target disk before copying files. These could be either good or bad features, depending on how you look at them. Use the DISKCOPY command when you have a new disk, unformatted, onto which you want to copy the entire contents of another disk. Be careful NOT to use this command to copy files onto a disk with contents you want to save. For that function, use the COPY command.

The DISKCOPY command also copies all of the features of the disk, including bad sectors or tracks. It makes an exact mirror image of the the source disk (the one you are copying from) to the target disk. If you think the source disk may be bad, copy necessary files to another disk using the COPY command. When copying, also be certain you are copying from like disk to like disk. In other words, the disks must be labeled the same, such as double sided/double density or single sided/double density, and so on.

In the following steps, it is assumed that you will be copying from one drive to another. A common use of the DISKCOPY command is to copy a disk, such as the data disk, to a second disk as a backup copy. In this case you would insert the disk containing the files in drive A and the disk to be copied to in drive B of a dual-disk or hard disk system.

The DISKCOPY command is an **external** command, so you need to work from DOS before using the command.

DISKCOPY (DUAL DISK ONLY)

1. **INSERT** the DOS disk into drive A
2. **INSERT** the data disk (formatted disk) into drive B
3. **TYPE** **DISKCOPY A: B:**
4. **PRESS** **Enter** when the line is typed correctly

> You will see a message on the screen that asks you to be sure that the source (disk you are copying from) and target (disk you are copying to) disks are in the correct location and then to press Enter or any key (depending on the DOS version) when ready.
>
> **5. PRESS** **Enter** or any key (whichever you are asked to do by the screen message)
>
> Wait while the contents of the disk are copied. When the process is finished, a message will appear asking whether you want to copy another.
>
> **6. TYPE** **N** for No (to the message asking whether you want to copy another)
>
> If you wish, you can now view the contents of the disk in drive A or B by typing either DIR A: or DIR B: at the system prompt. You will see that the DOS disk has been copied onto the disk in drive B.

THE ERASE COMMAND

The ERASE command will erase one, some, or all files from a disk. The ERASE command needs to be used with caution. Be certain that you want to erase files *permanently* before using this command.

This command is useful for erasing unwanted files from your disk. Sometimes files are accidentally saved under different but similar file names when the contents of the files are exactly the same. Occasionally a data file is accidentally save on the DOS disk. In these instances, you can erase the unwanted files from the disk and thus *clean* the disk so that you have more room to save files you create in the future.

The ERASE command is an **internal** command so you do not need to be at a DOS prompt or have the DOS disk inserted in drive A to give this command. It will also have the same effect if you give it from an A, B, or a C system prompt.

With your data disk (now containing DOS files) in drive A (hard disk system), do the following. First, look at the directory,

ERASE		
1. TYPE	**DIR A:** (B: if using a dual-disk system)	
2. PRESS	**Enter**	
	You can see that one of your files is the COMMAND.COM file. Practice erasing this file by typing the following command:	
3. TYPE	**ERASE A:COMMAND.COM** (Be sure to include the A:)	
4. PRESS	**Enter**	

A file is erased and C:\> reappears. Once again, the asterisk (*) command can act as a global command so that you can erase selected files. You could substitute the * for the file name or file extension and thus erase groups of files. Similarly, the *.* command will erase all files.

5. TYPE   **ERASE A:*.***   (Be sure to include the A:)

6. PRESS   **Enter**

The screen will ask

```
Are you sure (Y/N)?
```

7. PRESS   **Y** for yes

8. PRESS   **Enter**

Note: *It cannot be stressed enough that caution must be used when employing the ERASE command. Use it primarily for erasing individual files that are no longer of use to you. If you want to erase the contents of the disk, be sure to check every filename before doing so. Once the ERASE command is executed, the files will be erased. If you erase files by mistake, check with your instructor to see if they can be restored. You may also substitute ERASE with DELETE.*

THE /S FORMAT COMMAND

Use the /S command to copy system files to a floppy disk. Doing so will allow you to boot the system from the floppy disk. Files are often copied onto a program disk or data disk so that one disk may be used to both boot and run the program or to boot and store documents.

With the data disk in Drive A or B,

1. TYPE   **FORMAT/S**

2. PRESS   **Enter**

3. FOLLOW   the system messages as with other format commands.

From now on, you may use this disk to boot a dual-disk system.

GUIDED TUTORIAL

WHAT YOU'LL DO

- Format a blank disk.
- View directories.
- Practice other DOS commands.

WHAT YOU'LL NEED

One blank floppy disk

HOW TO DO IT

With the system on and a C:\> prompt (hard disk system) or A:\> (dual-disk system) visible on the screen,

1. INSERT   a blank floppy disk into drive A (hard disk system) or drive B (dual-disk system).

    Note: *If using a dual-disk system, be sure that the DOS disk is in drive A.*

       At the system prompt (C:\> or A:\>)

2. TYPE   **DIR** and **PRESS Enter**.

    A list of the files on drive C or A is displayed. Because dir was typed alone (without other conditions such as dir/w for viewing files across the width of the screen), all files appear in one long column. The list of files may have scrolled off the screen so that you are now viewing the end of the list.

    This format shows all information about the files on this drive. When viewing the list for drive C, some of the names may be directories. There should be a directory called Works, for example; one called DOS; and so on. Directories contain grouped files for individual programs or applications.

3. TYPE   **DIR/W** and **PRESS Enter**.

    All of the directories (with a hard disk) and/or files (with both a dual-disk and a hard disk system) are now visible on the screen. In some cases there may be too many directories or files to view them all at once; however, normally this command allows all directory names and file names to appear on the screen at one time. This is the advantage of the dir/w command. The disadvantage of this command is that less information is available. The size, date last modified, and time last modified are not available. The dir/w command is useful when all you wish to see are the filenames and extensions or the names of the directories.

4. **TYPE**   **DIR/P** and press **Enter**.

All files and/or directories and size and modification information is available, but only one screen if information is displayed.

5. **PRESS**   **any key** to view the next page of files and directories.

6. **CONTINUE** pressing any key until the system prompt reappears.

You have now viewed the files on the hard disk or on the DOS disk in drive A. The disk in drive A or B will now be formatted. Once formatted, it may be used to store documents created using Works or any other DOS-compatible program.

At the C:\> (hard disk) or A:\> (dual-disk) system prompt,

7. **TYPE**   **FORMAT A:** (or **B**: with a dual-disk system).

Note: *You may also use the Format a:/v option if you wish to add a label to your diskette. This is not necessary when using DOS 5.0 or higher.*

8. **PRESS**   **Enter**.

Since the new disk is already inserted into drive A or drive B,

9. **PRESS**   **Enter** again.

The formatting process begins. WAIT until the format process is complete.

10. **PRESS**   **Enter** again to bypass the volume label message if necessary

When the message

```
Format Another (Y/N)?
```

appears,

11. **TYPE**   **N** for No and press **Enter**.

The format is complete.

Note: *When using a hard disk system, it is not necessary to switch to the DOS directory for the format command to be in effect. Any system prompt will work. When using a dual-disk system, remember that the DOS disk must be in drive A.*

VIEWING THE DIRECTORY

With a formatted disk in drive A or B, you can now view its directory. At this time, no files will be present; however, you may still practice moving from one drive to another and viewing directories.

At C:\> or A:\>

1. TYPE   **A:** (hard disk) or **B:** (dual disk).

2. PRESS   **Enter.**

The prompt for the new active drive (A or B) appears.

3. TYPE   **DIR** and press **Enter.**

No files are available for viewing at this time; however, when you have saved files on the formatted disk, you may view them using this command.

At the A:\> or B:\> prompt

4. TYPE   **C:** or **A:** and press **Enter.**

If using a dual-disk system, take the DOS disk out of drive A and insert the Works program disk. Close the drive door if necessary.

HARD DISK USERS ONLY

At the C:\>

1. TYPE   **CD WORKS** and press **Enter.**

The Works directory prompt appears, C:\WORKS>.

2. TYPE   **CD ..** or **CD** and press **Enter.**

The cd.. command moves you back one level at a time. The cd\ command will move you directly to the root directory, C:\>.

3. TYPE   **CD WORKS** to move to the Works directory again.

4. TYPE   **DIR** and press **Enter.**

5. READ   through the list of files.

6. TYPE   **DIR/W** and read through the list of files again.

7. TYPE   **CD** to move back to the root directory, C:\>.

8. TYPE   **DIR A:** to view the A directory while maintaining drive C as active.

9. CONTINUE   to the Review Questions.

DUAL-DISK USERS

At A:\> and with the Works program disk in drive A,

1. **TYPE**   **DIR** and press **Enter**.
2. **READ**   through the files.
3. **TYPE**   **DIR/W** and press **Enter**.
4. **READ**   through the files.
5. **TYPE**   **B:** and press **Enter**.
6. **TYPE**   **DIR** and press **Enter**.
7. **TYPE**   **A:** and press **Enter**.
8. **TYPE**   **DIR B:** and press **Enter**.

   This allows you to view the directory of drive B while maintaining the active drive as A.

9. **CONTINUE**   to the chapter review.

REVIEW QUESTIONS

Fill in the BEST answer for each item.

1. The operating system common to the IBM personal computer is ____________.

2. There are many ____________ stored on the DOS disk(s).

3. DOS programs necessary for everyday operation of a computer are stored in ________ whenever the computer is being used.

4. Some DOS files that are not necessary for normal computer operation are referred to as ____________ because they remain on the DOS disk until needed.

5. DOS files may be described as either ____________ or ____________.

6. The DOS disk must be in the drive of a dual-disk system before using ____________ DOS commands.

7. The disk drive configuration on the computer you are using is ____________.

8. Your DOS files are usually located in drive ______.

9. Your data disk is usually located in drive ______.

10. Your diskette size is ____________.

    (This question is for **dual-disk users only**.)

Choose the BEST answer to the following questions.

11. Which of the following is the correct procedure to follow to start up ("boot") your system (dual-disk users only)?

    a. Insert the DOS disk into drive A with the label facing down and the slot to the back; close the drive door; turn on the computer.
    b. Insert DOS into drive A with the label facing up and the slot to the back; close the drive door; turn on the computer.
    c. Turn on the computer; insert DOS into drive A; close the drive door.
    d. None of the above.

12. The DISKCOPY command is best used to

a.   Make an identical copy of all files on a disk
b.   Copy files from the source disk and save files on the target disk
c.   Format a disk
d.   Copy selected files only

13. To view a directory of files on a disk, type

a.   DIR and press Enter
b.   DIR/W and press Enter
c.   DIR A: and press Enter (or DIR B: with a dual-disk)
d.   Any of the above
e.   None of the above

14. A directory shows which of the following:

a.   The filename, extension, size of the file, and date and time of its creation
b.   The filename, extension, and size only
c.   The filename, extension, and date only
d.   The filename, size, date, and type of system used

15. The command DIR/P does which of the following?

a.   Prints a copy of the directory
b.   Prints a page of the directory
c.   Shows a page of the directory
d.   Prints the size of the directory

True (T) or False (F)?

16. _____   The FORMAT command is used primarily to prepare a new disk for receiving data files.

17. _____   Accidentally formatting a disk would not erase the disk contents.

18. _____   The A, B, or C prompt displays the "active" drive.

19. _____   The COPY command is most frequently used to copy single files at a time from one disk to another.

20. _____   The DISKCOPY command is frequently used to copy the entire contents of one disk to another without losing the contents of the target disk.

HANDS-ON EXERCISES 

EXERCISE 1

For additional practice:

1. Format a blank disk (you may reformat the one used in the instructions).

2. Practice moving from one directory to another, such as from the C:\> root directory to the Works directory or the DOS directory when using a hard disk or from drive A to drive B when using a dual-disk system.

3. Practice viewing the files in a directory.

4. Practice the copy and erase commands or any other DOS commands covered in this chapter as necessary.

Objectives

- Start Works from a dual-disk or hard disk system.

- Identify the components of Works menus and dialog boxes.

- Make menu selections.

- Get help.

- Exit Works.

PREVIEW ▶▶▶➡

In this chapter you will learn how to start Works on your PC. Instructions are included for both hard disk and dual-disk systems. Included also are instructions for using the Works menu system and moving around the opening screen. It will be assumed that you are somewhat familiar with the PC at this point and that you are fairly comfortable with the use of the keyboard and the location of the keys. If necessary, review Chapters 1 and 2.

GETTING STARTED

From a hard disk system

For complete instructions on installing Works on a hard disk system, see Appendix I. The following instructions assume that the program is installed and that you are ready to begin learning Works.

If you are storing documents on a floppy disk, the formatted disk should be inserted in drive A or drive B, depending on your system. These instructions will assume that the disk drive is drive A, since this is the most common. Where drive A is referenced, change to B if your system uses B for the floppy drive. Be sure that the disk is formatted. If you need instructions in formatting the disk, check the DOS manual or refer to Chapter 2. These instructions will also assume that the Works program is stored in a directory called **Works**. Check with your instructor or other lab managers if you have difficulty locating the Works directory or think it is stored under a different name.

With the system turned on,

STARTING WORKS (HARD DISK SYSTEM)

1. **INSERT**   a formatted floppy disk into drive A

Note: *Do Step 1 only if you are storing data documents on a floppy and not on the hard disk.*

At the C:\> prompt,

2. **TYPE**   **CD WORKS**

3. **PRESS**   **Enter**

At the C:\WORKS> prompt,

4. **TYPE**   **WORKS**

5. **PRESS**   **Enter**

You will now see a screen similar to the one shown in Figure 3-1.

From a dual-disk system

If your computer is not turned on, insert DOS into drive A and turn the computer on. Enter the date and time and press **Enter** so that the A prompt is on the screen.

STARTING WORKS (DUAL DISK SYSTEM)

1. **INSERT**   **Works** into drive A

2. **INSERT**   a formatted blank disk into drive B (for the data documents)

   At the A:\> system prompt,

3. **TYPE**   **WORKS**

4. **PRESS**   **Enter**

   You will see a screen similar to the one shown in Figure 3-1.

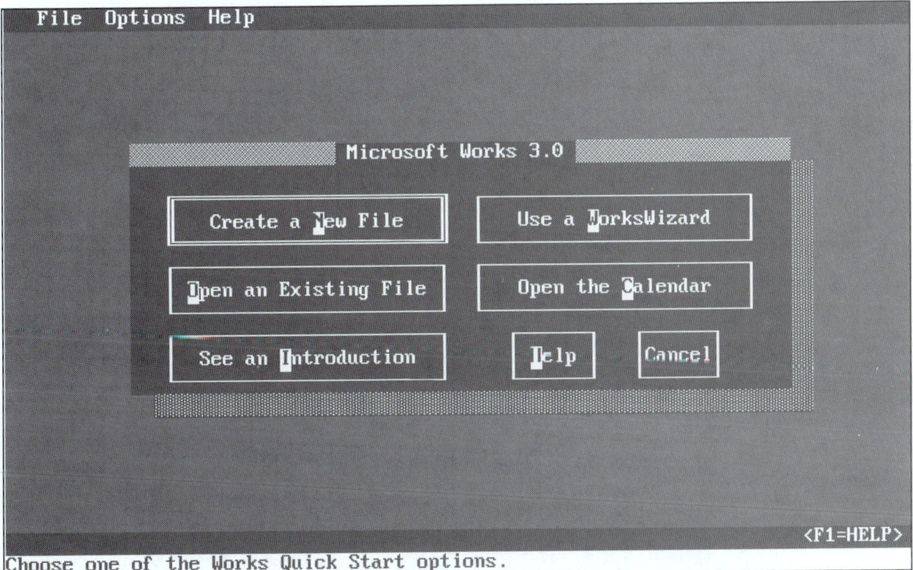

FIGURE 3-1
OPENING SCREEN

QUICK START OPTIONS

The Quick Start options appearing in the dialog box are used to move quickly into a new file, open an existing file, or make another choice without accessing the menus. When you are familiar with Works, using these options makes it faster to access a frequently used Works tool directly without working through multiple menu options. A click of the button with the mouse is all that is necessary.

QUICKSTART

1. CHOOSE **Cancel** by clicking the mouse button on the option, pressing the Tab key or the Arrow keys to move to Cancel and then pressing **Enter**.

The list of **File** menu options is showing and the first option, **Create New File,** is highlighted. The menu titles at the top of the screen comprise the menu bar. The list of options, such as those shown under the **File** menu, are called commands. Each of the options is a Works command that tells Works what to do next. When a command has a string of dots following it, called ellipsis, it indicates that this command will display a dialog box if selected. Dialog boxes contain additional options.

2. CHOOSE **Create New File** by pointing and clicking the left mouse button once on the option, pressing N, or by pressing Enter. (The desired choice is already highlighted.)

Note: *There are three ways to make menu selections. In this book, the mouse button is mentioned first since it is the method most often used for making selections and is often easier and faster than other methods; however, you should be aware that the keyboard may also be used. Selections are made by pointing and clicking on the desired menu command; pressing the highlighted letter in the command; or by pressing the Down or Up Arrow keys, highlighting the option, and pressing Enter. Use whichever method is easiest for you.*

The **Create New File** dialog box appears in the middle of the screen as shown in Figure 3-2.

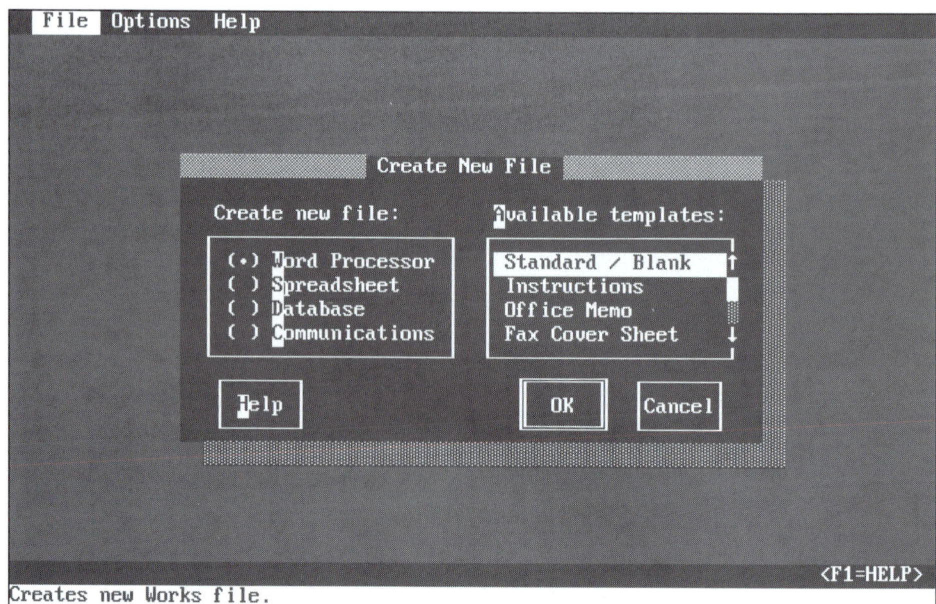

FIGURE 3-2
DIALOG BOX
DISPLAYED WHEN
USING THE CREATE
NEW FILE COMMAND

A dialog box is a type of form where many selections may be made and you check off or fill in the requirements. As you are making selections from menus and dialog boxes in Works, note the various ways in which you make selections. Sometimes you will enter characters, at other times you will check off boxes, and so on. All of these are options within the dialog box.

The options shown on your screen and in Figure 3-2 are in an option box on the left and a list box on the right. The mouse or keyboard are used to make selections from the option box; the keyboard or mouse are used to make selections from the list box. Selections are made by pressing the **Tab** key to move from one option box to another, the Arrow keys to move from one option within a box to another, or the mouse button to click on the desired option. An example of an option box follows.

```
(*)  Normal        (  )  Superscript        (  )  Subscript
```

OPTION BOX

Another type of dialog box is a text box. A text box requires that you respond by giving a typed request as in the following example.

```
New alarm:

   Message:        [.................................]

   Date:           [.................................]

   Time:           [.................................]
```

TEXT BOX

In this box, a typed response is requested to the **Message**, **Date**, and **Time** options.

One other type of response is required of users in a dialog box. It is the option of completing or canceling a command and is usually shown in the lower right corner of the box. In the dialog box on your screen and in Figure 3-2, this option is the **Cancel** option, usually referred to as a *button*; it appears in the lower right corner of the box.

To cancel this dialog box,

3.	CLICK	**once** on the **Cancel** button
	OR	
	PRESS	**Esc**
	OR	
	PRESS	the **Tab** key to highlight the **Cancel** button and press **Enter**
		You are returned to the opening screen. No menu options are shown; however, using the mouse button or keyboard at this time would pull one of the menu command lists down.

MAKING MENU SELECTIONS

You can move from menu to menu by either using the **Left** and **Right Arrow** keys, or by clicking the mouse button once on the menu title.

MAKE MENU SELECTIONS

1.	MOVE	to the **Options** menu by pressing the left mouse button once anywhere on the word Options or by pressing **Alt/O**

Note: *Menus are reached by pressing Alt and the first initial of the menu title or by using the directional (Arrow) keys and pressing Enter. This instruction is also given to you on the message line at the bottom of the screen.*

2.	MOVE	to the **Help** menu by clicking on the menu title with the left mouse button or by pressing the **Right Arrow** key
3.	PRESS	the **Down Arrow** key and note that the message line at the bottom of the screen displays information about each of the menu options as they are highlighted
4.	CHOOSE	**Exit Works** from the **File** menu and continue to the tutorials and Review Questions

WHAT YOU'LL DO

- Start Works.
- Step through various drop down menus.
- Create a new file.
- Exit from Works.

HOW TO DO IT

HARD DISK USERS

At C:\>,

1. **TYPE**   **CD WORKS** to switch to the Works directory
2. **PRESS**   **Enter**
3. **TYPE**   **WORKS** and press **Enter** to load Works into memory

DUAL-DISK USERS

At A:\> and with the Works program disk in drive A,

1. **TYPE**   **WORKS** to load the Works program into memory

ALL USERS

1. **VIEW**   the "quick start" options that appear on the screen.
2. **CHOOSE**   **Cancel** at this time by clicking the left mouse button on the Cancel button, tabbing to the **Cancel** button and pressing Enter, or by pressing **Esc**

   The **File** menu commands drop down automatically when the "quick start" box is closed.
3. **PRESS**   the **Right Arrow** key once to move to the Options menu
4. **PRESS**   the **Right Arrow** key once to move to the Help menu
5. **CLICK**   the **Left Mouse** button once on the menu title **Options**
6. **CLICK**   the **Mouse** button once on the menu title **File**
7. **PRESS**   **Esc** to turn off the drop down menus
8. **PRESS**   **Alt/F** to pull down the **File** menu
9. **PRESS**   **Esc** to turn off the **File** menu
10. **PRESS**   **Alt/O** to pull down the **Options** menu
11. **PRESS**   **Esc** and then **Alt/H**

12.	MOVE	to the **File** menu
13.	PRESS	**Enter** if **Create New File** is highlighted (press **N** if it is not)
14.	PRESS	the **Tab** key to move through the options available with the Word Processor selected
15.	KEEP	pressing the **Tab** key until you return to the **Create new file** box
16.	CLICK	the **mouse** button once on the **Cancel** button
17.	CLICK	the **mouse** button once on the **File** menu
18.	CHOOSE	**Exit Works**

REVIEW QUESTIONS

1. List each of the steps used to start Works from the system you are using.

2. Explain briefly each of the following.

   a. Dialog box

   b. Option box

   c. Message line

   d. Text box

3. List three ways to make menu selections in Works.

4. List two or more ways to move through Works dialog boxes.

HANDS-ON EXERCISES

EXERCISE 1

1. Load Works into memory.

2. Cancel the "quick start" options box.

3. Click anywhere on the blank area of the screen to close the **File** commands.

4. Display the **Help** commands.

5. Move to the **Options** menu. What are the selectable options?

6. Choose the **File** menu. What does the message line say?

7. Move to the **Options** menu and then back to the **File** menu. What does the message line say?

8. Choose **Exit Works** when finished.

4 CREATING DOCUMENTS

Objectives

- Create a document.

- Identify parts of the Works screen.

- Enter text.

- Move the cursor.

- Show All Characters Option.

- Format paragraphs.

- Format characters.

- Save a document.

- Exit Works.

- Open a document.

- Print a document.

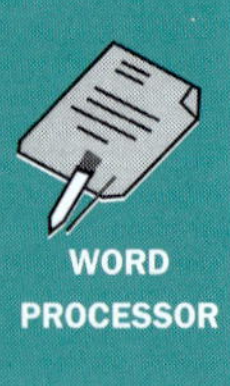

PREVIEW ⟫⟫➡

The true benefit of Works lies not in the fact that each of the applications is easy to use and contains many powerful functions, but in the fact that moving from one application to another is like moving from one document to another within a single application. In this chapter you will learn to create a document using the word processing tool in Works. This will give you a feeling for how easy it is to create and modify several word processing documents as well as how to move through Works' menu structure.

As you progress through this book, additional functions will be introduced and more practice documents will be available for reinforcement. You should work through all instructions and practice exercises to fully understand and be able to utilize the power of Works and learn the full power of an integrated program such as Works.

Word processing tools are used to create business documents that are usually straight text. Documents commonly used with this type of tool are manuscripts, merged letters, memos, and so on. Quite often businesses want other information in word processing documents. This information may be graphs, charts, spreadsheets, and other images that help to supplement the information in a document. When using application programs other than a fully integrated one such as Works, it is often a cumbersome process to export and import files from one application to another. It also usually requires learning an entirely new program with a new set of keystrokes and commands. With Works, the same menu structure and commands that are applied in word processing are also applied in the spreadsheet, database, and communications tools. Learning one set of commands is, in other words, great preparation to moving into a new tool, such as spreadsheet. Most of the keystrokes and commands are similar in appearance so the learning time is kept to a minimum. In this chapter, you begin by creating the shell for an integrated document. In this case it is the word processing document.

CREATING A DOCUMENT

You will begin by creating a manuscript. This manuscript and documents relating to it contain information about a charter boat business. The business, Puget Sound Charters, charters small to medium-sized boats in the greater Seattle area in the Pacific Northwest. The boats are primarily for individual and company dinner cruises. As you work through the book, you will learn much about the charter business including keeping track of clients in a database file, sales in spreadsheet documents, and writing promotional documents in word processing. Your first document will be a notice promoting reduced costs on trip tickets.

CREATE A DOCUMENT

From the "quick start" box,

1. **CHOOSE** **Create New File**... by clicking the mouse button once on the command or by pressing **N**

At the new command box, you have a choice of choosing any one of the applications available in Works. Word Processor is selected automatically.

2. **CLICK** **OK** or press Enter

The screen shown in Figure 4-1 appears.

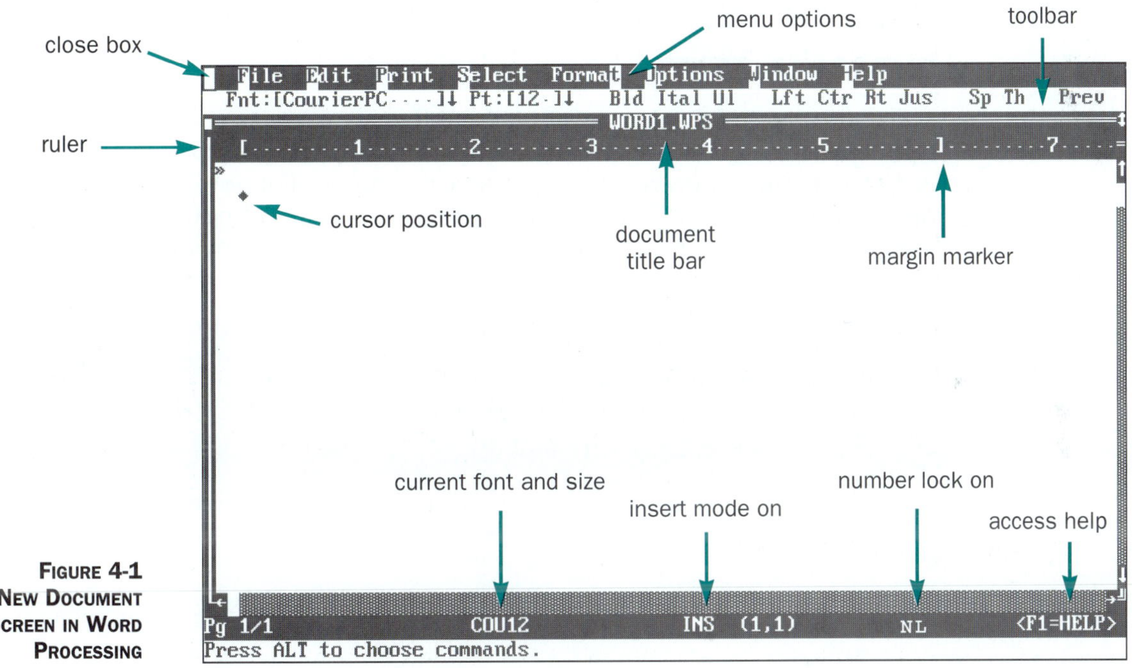

FIGURE 4-1
NEW DOCUMENT
SCREEN IN WORD
PROCESSING

From this screen you can begin creating new documents. At the top of the screen is the menu bar showing each of the menu options available when you are in a word processing document. These options will be discussed throughout Part 2 as new word processing commands are reviewed. This new document shows the title WORD1.WPS in the title bar. WORD1.WPS is the default name for the first word processing document created in a session. You can change the name through the **File** menu commands. In each of the corners of the screen are scroll bars. The scroll bars allow you to move quickly from left to right and forward and backward in a document when using the mouse. Clicking and dragging the mouse button on one of the scroll bar arrows scrolls through the document. Look at Figure 4-1 so that you identify each component on your screen.

THE WORKS SCREEN

Before typing the first document, look at the ruler line. Notice that the ruler line contains two brackets, [   ], one at the zero position ([ ) and one at the 6.0 position ( ]). These brackets indicate the left and right margins of a document. The default width for a word processing document is 6 inches. As you type, text reaching the right bracket ( ]) will automatically wrap to the next line without pressing the **Enter** key. This is referred to as *word wrap*—text wrapping to the next line.

Also note the lower left corner of the status line. It tells you that you are on page 1 of 1 in this document (Pg 1/1). As you create additional pages in later exercises, these numbers could change. A change to Pg 2/2 would indicate that you are on page 2 of a two-page document. In the center of the status line is the default character font and pitch, COU12, PIC12, or another (Courier 12 pitch or Pica 12 pitch). The font and pitch may vary from system to system. INS indicates that you are in Insert mode, NL shows that the Num Lock key is on, and <F1=Help> accesses the Help menu.

ENTERING TEXT

You will be typing the document on the following page. As you type, use the **Backspace** key to erase characters to the left of the cursor position and the **Del** or Delete key to remove characters above the cursor. For now, do not worry about other errors. Press the **Enter** key only at the end of short lines or at the end of a paragraph. Within a paragraph, let the text wrap to the following line.

ENTER TEXT

1. TYPE   the following document. Do not worry if the right margin aligns differently from that shown, and **do not** type the hyphens shown in the example.

```
PROMOTIONAL OFFER

Next month Puget Sound Charters will offer two- and
three-hour cruise tickets to all persons who visit one
of our charter boats at any of their Puget Sound loca-
tions. Tickets will be available at reduced prices dur-
ing the entire month and will include brunch and dinner
cruises.

The locations for visiting the boats are:

Kirkland on Lake Washington
Lake Union in downtown Seattle
Seward Park on Lake Washington
   and
Shilshoe in Ballard

Drop in for a visit and learn about all of our cruising
schedules.
```

MOVING THE CURSOR

Works contains shortcuts for moving the cursor throughout a document. It is important that before beginning, you become familiar with cursor movements. Table 4-1 contains the keys used to move to a location in a document. Read through the table and practice using each of the movements in the document you have just created. At first, you may refer to the table as you are learning and practicing how to move quickly to locations within the document; however, do practice them. They save time and increase efficiency when used regularly.

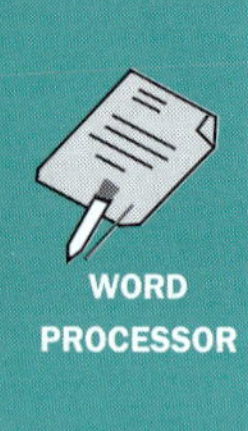

PRESS	TO MOVE TO
Left Arrow key	One character left
Right Arrow key	One character right
Up Arrow key	One line up
Down Arrow key	One line down
Ctrl/Left Arrow key	Left one word
Ctrl/Right Arrow key	Right one word
Ctrl/Up Arrow key	One paragraph up
Ctrl/Down Arrow key	One paragraph down
Home key	Beginning of the line
End key	End of the line
Ctrl/Home	Beginning of the document
Ctrl/End	End of the document
Page Up	One window up
Page Down	One window down
Ctrl/Page Up	Beginning of the window
Ctrl/Page Down	End of the window

**TABLE 4-1
CURSOR
MOVEMENTS**

PARAGRAPH FORMATTING

There are many ways to format text. In this exercise you will learn some basic paragraph formatting functions, such as centering text. Before beginning paragraph formats, it is important to distinquish between two command formats used in word processing tools. They are Character and Paragraph formatting. Character formatting includes any command that affects the appearance of the individual characters in the document, such as adding bold or italic formats to text. Paragraph formatting is a format that affects all text prior to a paragraph marker. When centering text, the center command is carried with the paragraph marker at the end of the line. For example, you could give a center command to an entire paragraph or to a single line, depending on where the paragraph marker is displayed. The marker is displayed at the point where you pressed the Enter key (also called a hard return). If you wanted to center several lines in a heading where the Enter key had been pressed at the end of each line, you could select all lines and then give the center command. In this exercise, you will practice both techniques — positioning the cursor anywhere in a paragraph to format it and selecting multiple paragraphs for formatting.

CENTERING TEXT

CENTER TEXT

1. **POSITION**   the cursor anywhere in the word PROMOTIONAL at the top of the document (click the mouse button on the word or press **Ctrl/Home**)

2. **PRESS**   **Ctrl/C** (hold down the **Ctrl** key and press **C**)

The line is centered.

Note: *You could also choose **Format** and **Center** by pressing **Alt/T** to reach the **Format** menu commands and then pressing **C** for **Center**, or by clicking the mouse button on the **Format** menu option and then on the **Center** command. Throughout this book, where commands are performed faster by using key combinations, they will be used; however, use whichever method is easier for you.*

SELECTING BLOCKS OF TEXT

Blocks of text are selected so that special commands may be applied to all text that is highlighted. Selecting text is one of the most useful commands in word processing and other applications. It saves time when formatting large blocks of text. By selecting the text, you can give the command once and affect the entire block of text.

SELECT TEXT

1. **POSITION**   the cursor under the **K** in Kirkland in the list of locations (click the mouse button or use the Arrow keys)

2. **PRESS**   **F8** to turn on the **EXT** (extend) mode

   Note: *EXT appears in the right corner of the status line at the bottom of the screen.*

When the EXT mode is on, you can begin to select blocks of text.

3. **PRESS**   the **Down Arrow** key five times or hold the mouse button down and drag the highlight through the last line in the locations, Shilshoe in Ballard

4. **PRESS**   **Ctrl/C**

When finished, deseelct the blocks of text.

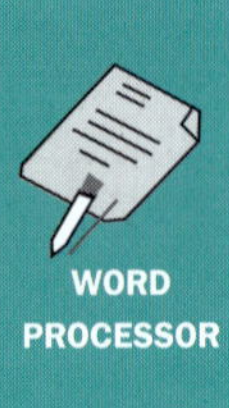

5. PRESS   any **Arrow** key to deselect the centered text or click the mouse button once anywhere on the screen

All lines are centered.

Note: *When using a mouse, it is not necessary to turn on the* **EXT** *mode using the* **F8** *key. Select text by clicking and dragging the mouse button.*

Other options available when selecting text are shown in Table 4-2. This table shows how text is selected by using a few keystrokes or by clicking and dragging the mouse button. Review the options in the table. Although you may need to reference this table when practicing selections, memorizing the commands saves time because text is selected often during word processing applications.

PRESS F8	TO SELECT
Two times	a word
Three times	a sentence
Four times	a paragraph
Five times	the entire document

OR

Click the and drag the mouse button until the text is selected as follows (press Esc to turn off the EXT mode, if necessary):

CLICK	TO SELECT
Right button	a word
Left button in left window margin	a line
Right button in left margin	a paragraph
Both buttons in left margin	entire document

**TABLE 4-2
SELECTING BLOCKS
OF TEXT**

MAKING CORRECTIONS IN TEXT

The **Backspace** key has been used to delete characters to the left of the cursor. The **Delete** (or **Del**) key has been used to delete text above the cursor position. As you type text, any new text is inserted between characters automatically . In other words, existing text is pushed to the right of the cursor position. You can also use a command from the **Options** menu that allows you to type over text. When a block of text is selected using the **F8** key and the **Typing Replaces Selection** command is chosen, you can type over existing text, replacing the old text.

MAKE CORRECTIONS

1. **POSITION** the cursor in the space immediately following the word **offer** in the first line of this document

2. **PRESS** the **Spacebar** once to insert a blank space

3. **TYPE** **a one-time only** and press the **Spacebar**

   Note: *All text is pushed to the right of the cursor.*

4. **CHOOSE** the **Options** menu

5. **CHOOSE** **Typing Replaces Selection** (if you go back to the Options menu, a dot should appear to the left of the command to show that this option is active)

6. **SELECT** the word **tickets** in the second line of the document (click the right mouse button once on **tickets**)

7. **TYPE** **package** followed by a space

The typing replaces the selected word.

Note: *You may also press the Insert key to toggle between insert and overtype modes. With Insert on, text is pushed to the right. With Insert off, you may select text and then type new text over it, thus replacing the old block of text.*

Use this option whenever you want to replace existing text with new text. Choose the option again to return to the automatic insert mode where inserted text is pushed to the right of the cursor position.

SEPARATING AND MERGING PARAGRAPHS

You can separate paragraphs by pressing the **Enter** key to insert a paragraph mark, or merge two paragraphs by pressing the **Del** or **Backspace** key to delete the paragraph mark separating the paragraphs.

Turn on **Show All Characters** from the **Show** command in the **Options** menu to see the paragraph marks, tabs, spaces, and so on. These characters will not print when the document is printed, but are useful to see when editing text.

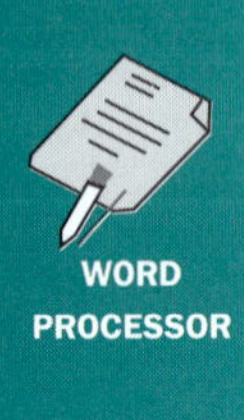

SEPARATE AND MERGE PARAGRAPHS

1. **CHOOSE**   **Typing Replaces Selection** from the **Options** menu to turn off the option

2. **POSITION**   the cursor on the **T** in Tickets in the last sentence of the first paragraph

3. **PRESS**   **Enter** twice

A new paragraph is formed.

With the cursor on the **T** of Tickets at the beginning of this new paragraph,

4. **PRESS**   the **Backspace** key twice

The two paragraphs are merged.

INDENTING THE FIRST LINE OF A PARAGRAPH

When in a Works workspace, such as the document space now on your screen, the automatic insert mode is on. To indent the paragraphs in this document, all that is necessary is to press the **Tab** key. Text to the right of the cursor position will be pushed to the right.

INDENT FIRST LINE OF PARAGRAPH

1. **POSITION**   the cursor under the **N** in Next in the first paragraph

2. **PRESS**   the **Tab** key once

The paragraph is indented and other lines in the paragraph are realigned automatically.

3. **INDENT**   all other paragraphs in the text: those beginning with **The** and **Drop**.

Note: *To remove a tab, position the cursor on the first character of the paragraph and press the **Backspace** key.*

JUSTIFYING A PARAGRAPH

A justified paragraph shows text on both the left and right margins aligned or even. The default for the right margin is ragged, as is now showing on your screen. The default for the left margin is aligned. You can center all lines in a paragraph, leave them ragged, or justify them. To justify the first paragraph in this document, the cursor is positioned anywhere within the paragraph and then a command is invoked that will make the right margin aligned like the left.

JUSTIFY A PARAGRAPH

1. **POSITION**   the cursor anywhere in the first paragraph

2. **CHOOSE**   the **Format** menu option by pressing **Alt/T** or clicking once on **Format**

3. **PRESS**   **J** for Justified or click the mouse button once on **Justified**

Note: *You could also press **Ctrl/J** when the paragraph is selected. Using the menu option shows you that commands are available both through the menu options and through use of keystrokes. The abbreviated command (such as **Ctrl/J**) is used most of the time in this book; however, for practice in reaching menu commands, the menu option method will also be discussed.*

The right margin is now justified.

REVIEWING PARAGRAPH ALIGNMENTS

You have used the justify and center paragraph alignment commands in this document. Paragraphs can also be right aligned. To review all of these alignments and the keys used to change the formatting, the centered lines in this document will be rearranged temporarily.

REVIEW PARAGRAPH ALIGNMENTS

1. **POSITION**   the cursor on the **K** in Kirkland, the first of the centered lines

2. **PRESS**   **F8** to turn on the **EXT** mode

3. **PRESS**   the **Down Arrow** key five times to highlight the centered text or click and drag the mouse button until the next five lines are highlighted

4. **PRACTICE**   the following paragraph alignments with the highlighted text and note the appearance of each as the keys are pressed.

FOR THIS ALIGNMENT	PRESS
Left-aligned	Ctrl/L
Right-aligned	Ctrl/R
Centered	Ctrl/C
Justified	Ctrl/J

> *Note:*   When **Ctrl/J** is pressed, the text will appear leftaligned. This is due to the short lines in the body of the text. If the text reached the right margin, it would be aligned on the right just as in the first paragraph of this document.

5.   **RETURN**   the text to the centered position (**Ctrl/C**).

6.   **PRESS**   any **Arrow** key or click the mouse button once to remove the highlight

DOUBLE SPACING TEXT

Changing the line spacing in text is also part of paragraph formatting. Text can be changed to double spacing or back to single spacing in two steps by using the shortcut method or by selecting text and using the **Format** menu commands. As with other paragraph format commands, the setting for line spacing is carried with the paragraph marker at the end of a paragraph. As in justifying a paragraph, when using paragraph formats on a single paragraph, it is not necessary to select the paragraph first; the cursor need only be positioned anywhere in the paragraph.

DOUBLE SPACE (MENU COMMANDS)

1.   **POSITION**   the cursor anywhere in the first paragraph

2.   **CHOOSE**   **Format** by either pressing **Alt/T** or by clicking the mouse button once on **Format**

After briefly reading through the list of options available,

3.   **PRESS**   **D** for Double Space or click the mouse button once on **Double Space**

The first paragraph is now double spaced.

DOUBLE SPACE (SHORTCUT)

1.   **POSITION**   the cursor anywhere in the first paragraph

2.   **PRESS**   **Ctrl/1** to change the paragraph back to single space

3.   **PRESS**   **Ctrl/2** to change the paragraph to double space

4.   **RETURN**   the text to single space

CUSTOMIZING LINE SPACING

You can change the line spacing in a document to a space different from the standard commands available through the **Format** menu. This is done through the **Indents & Spacing** dialog box. Many line settings are available from this dialog box. When you know what multiple settings you want to arrange for a new document, it is often faster to go directly to the dialog box rather then invoking several keystroke combinations.

CUSTOMIZE LINE SPACE

1. POSITION the cursor under the **K** in Kirkland in the centered text

2. SELECT the next five lines by pressing **F8** and the **Down Arrow** key five times or by clicking and dragging the mouse button through the lines

3. CHOOSE the **Format** menu by pressing **Alt/T** for Format or clicking the mouse button once on **Format**

4. PRESS A for the **Indents & Spacing** dialog box or by clicking the mouse button once on this command

A dialog box similar to Figure 4-2 appears.

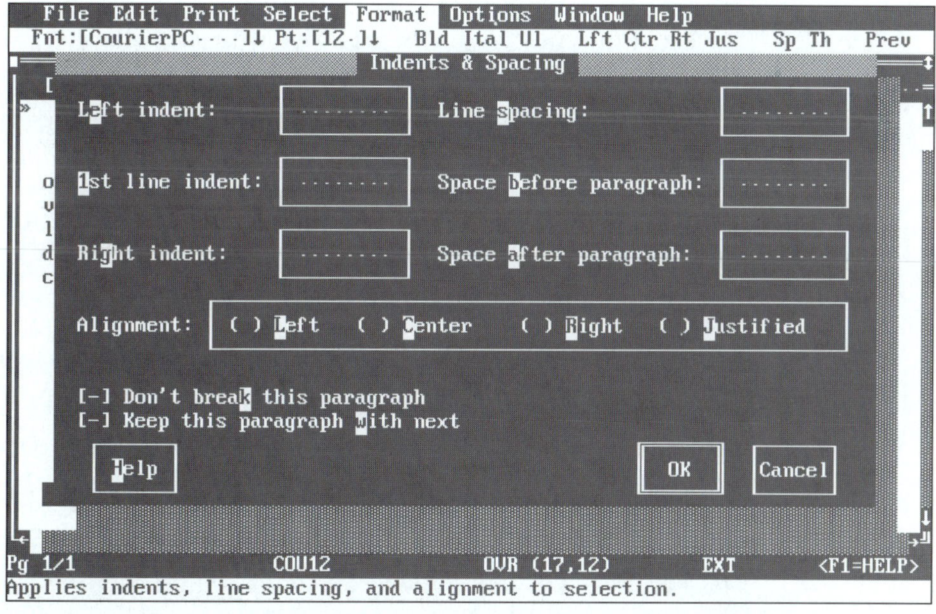

FIGURE 4-2
INDENTS & SPACING
DIALOG BOX

This box contains some of the commands already used in this chapter. They include those listed in the **Alignment** box: **Left**, **Center**, **Right**, and **Justified**. If desired, you could open this dialog box and use the **Arrow** keys to change the

selections. Other options included in this dialog box deal with changing the alignment of specific lines of text or paragraphs. The default for this indentation is zero (0). Later in this chapter you will learn how to make changes to the indentation of paragraphs. For now, leave these settings blank.

Line spacing can also be changed using this box. Generally, this dialog box is accessed when you want to change the spacing or other settings to specific settings that are not available by choosing **Format** menu commands.

5. POSITION	the cursor in the text box opposite **Line spacing:** (press the **Arrow** keys or use the **Tab** key or press **Alt** and the highlighted letter)
6. TYPE	**1.75** as the line spacing for the selected block of centered text
7. PRESS	**Enter** to accept the changes or click on **OK** with the mouse button
Note:	*You could also position the cursor on* **OK** *and then press* **Enter**; *however, just pressing* **Enter** *when all selections are made will also accept the changes.*

CHARACTER FORMATTING

Character formatting includes any changes made to individual characters. Unlike paragraph formatting, character formatting is not carried with the paragraph marker at the end of a line. It is carried with each character or all characters selected prior to assigning a format.

There are two ways to apply character formats to text. One is to give a command prior to typing text, and the second is to apply the formatting after the text is typed. Character formats include **bold** text, <u>underlined</u> text, *italicized* text, and others. Commands may be given from the keyboard or from menu options. Both methods are discussed; however, the combination keystrokes are the primary focus because they are faster and easier to use.

FORMAT A CHARACTER

1. POSITION	the cursor under the **P** in PROMOTIONAL in the heading
2. SELECT	the heading by pressing **F8** and the **Down Arrow** key once
3. PRESS	**Ctrl/B** (hold down the **Ctrl** key and press **B**)
4. PRESS	the **Down Arrow** key once to turn off the selection or click the mouse button once anywhere in the document

The heading now appears in bold print.

USING THE FORMAT MENU

You can also assign formats from the **Format** menu (**Alt/T**).

FORMAT WITH FORMAT MENU

1. POSITION the cursor under the **P** in Puget Sound Charters in the first line

2. SELECT the entire title, **Puget Sound Charters**

*Note: Press **F8** or use the mouse button to select as described previously and as shown in Table 4-2.*

3. CHOOSE the **Format** menu

*Note: Press **Alt/T** or click the mouse button once on **Format***

The **Format** commands include those for assigning character formats to text. Right now the title of the company is selected and any format could be assigned to it. For this exercise, *Italic* character format will be assigned.

4. CHOOSE **Italic**

*Note: Press **I** or move to **Italic** with the **Arrow** keys and press **Enter**. You could also click the mouse button once on the Italic command. From now on in the instructions, it will be assumed that you are comfortable with making selections. Refer to tables and previous instructions if you have any questions about making menu choices or selecting text. Detailed instruction will be given only when new techniques are used.*

5. PRESS the **Down Arrow** key or click the mouse button once to remove the highlight

The company title is now shown in color, bold, or italic, depending on whether you are in graphics or text mode (which is explained in a later chapter) and whether or not you have a color monitor.

6. To complete character formatting, select and assign formats to the following blocks of text. Use either the menu options or keystrokes for each as shown in the following chart. To return any text to plain type, select it and choose **Plain text** from the **Format** menu or press **Ctrl/Spacebar** and use the **Arrow** keys to deselect the text.

CHARACTER STYLE	TEXT TO SELECT
underline (Ctrl/U)	two- and three-hour cruise
bold (Ctrl/B)	Kirkland
bold	Lake Union
bold	Seward Park
bold	Shilshoe

SAVING A DOCUMENT

Proofread the document carefully and use the **Delete** and **Backspace** keys to make any corrections. Check all of the paragraph and character formatting. When all changes are correct, save the document.

SAVE A DOCUMENT

1. CHOOSE   the **File** menu
2. CHOOSE   the **Save As...** command

Since this is the first time the document has been saved, the **Save** command could also have been used. On the first save, the **Save** command will show this dialog box for naming the document. After the first save, however, the **Save** command or **Alt F/S** will save the revisions of a document without accessing a dialog box. The **Save As** command may be used to name a document for the first time and must be used to save the document under a different name or to a different drive.

> Note: If you are saving the data documents to a floppy disk or in a different directory, switch to that directory or to drive A or B before saving the document. See your instructor for instructions, if necessary.

3. TYPE   **CH4PR1** as the name of this document

> Note: The document name stands for **Chapter 4, Practice Document 1**.

4. PRESS   **Enter** to accept the name or click the mouse button once on **OK**

The document is saved and the new name appears in the title bar at the top of the window along with the extension **.WPS**. See **About the Dialog Box**, which follows, for more information.

EXITING WORKS

You can exit Works directly from a document by choosing the **Exit Works** command from the **File** menu.

EXIT WORKS

1. CHOOSE   the **File** menu and press **X** to **Exit Works** or click the mouse button on this option

OPENING AN EXISTING DOCUMENT

In the exercises that follow, it will be assumed that you are now familiar with using the mouse or making selections from the keyboard; therefore, instructions to *choose* a menu or command or *select* text will be used.

OPEN AN EXISTING DOCUMENT

1. **LOAD**   onto Works from the Works directory prompt, **Works>**

2. **CHOOSE**   **Open an Existing File** from the "quick start" options box by clicking the mouse button on the option or by pressing **O**

A dialog box similar to that shown in Figure 4-3 appears.

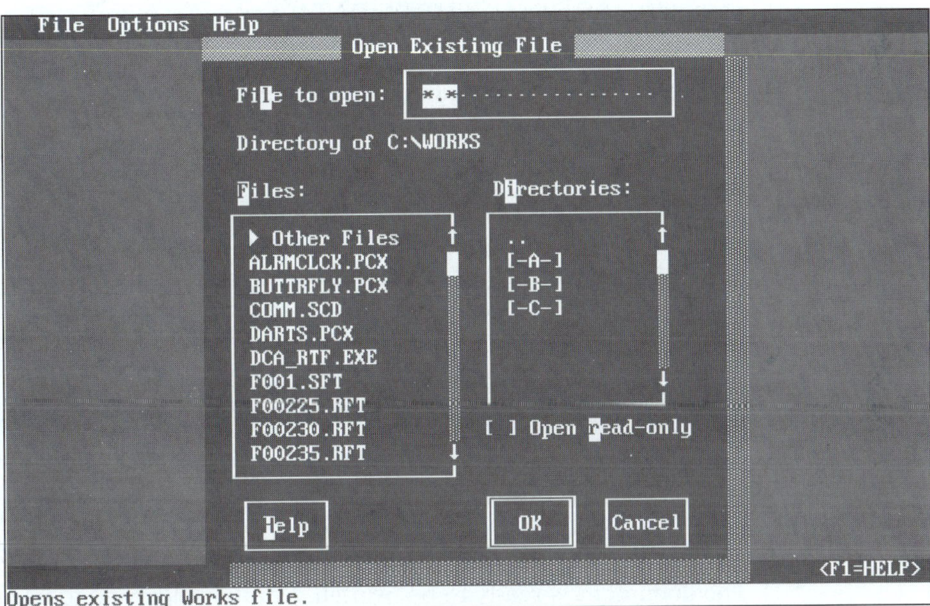

FIGURE 4-3
OPEN DIALOG BOX

Note: *Your dialog box may show only one document, CH4PR1.WPS, in Word Processing. How many documents appear in the list box will depend on how many you have created and whether or not the tutorial is loaded. In any case, the only document you need to be concerned with at this time is the one you have created in this chapter, CH4PR1.WPS.*

ABOUT THE DIALOG BOX

The options available through this dialog box include either choosing a file name from the list or typing the filename in the **File to open:** text box. Notice that the Directory of **C:\WORKS** sets the current directory path (if using a hard disk sys-

tem or **A:\WORKS** if using a dual-disk system). The documents you have been saving may be in this directory with the Works files, in a separate directory on the hard disk, or in a directory on a floppy disk in drive A or B.

As documents are saved, Works automatically assigns a file extension. An extension is a three-character ending to the name you assign to a file. In the list of word processing documents in this dialog box, the documents end with **.WPS**, which stands for "word processing" and is assigned to all word processing documents. You may assign your own three-character extension to a file if you wish. Later in the practice exercises, you will assign extensions such as **.PR1** to identify a document as practice document 1. When you assign a file extension, Works does not assign the **.WPS** extension. All spreadsheet documents are assigned **.WKS** for "worksheet." All database documents are assigned **.WDB** for Works "database." As with word processing, you may assign your own ending at any time. Use the scroll bar on the right of each of the list boxes to move quickly through the list of documents (as the list increases).

The directory path is set in the **File to open:** text box. You can either type in the path name such as **C:\WORKS\DATA**, or choose a directory from the **Directories** list box.

The **Open read-only** option lets you open a file for reading only. No editing changes may be made when this option is used.

> **3. CHOOSE** the correct directory containing your documents from the **Directories** list box or locate your data disk directory
>
> **4. CHOOSE** **CH4PR1** as the file to open
>
> *Note:* *When using the keyboard, highlight the name and press* **Enter**; *when using a mouse, click the mouse button twice on the document name.*

PRINTING THE DOCUMENT

The document is ready to be printed. You have learned to use both paragraph and character formats. Paragraph formatting was used to center the heading and the lines in the middle of the document. It was also used to justify the right margin. Character formats were used in the heading to add bold text to the heading. Italic character format was used to emphasize the name of the company in the first line. Underlining was used in the length of the cruises in the first paragraph. Now practice previewing and then printing the document so that you can see the final results.

PREVIEWING THE DOCUMENT

Among the commands found in the **Print** menu is the **Preview** option. **Preview** is useful for viewing the document exactly as it will look in print. This command saves time printing multiple copies of a document for proofing.

PREVIEW THE DOCUMENT

1. CHOOSE   the **Print** menu

2. CHOOSE   **Preview** from the **Print** menu

3. CHOOSE   **Preview** again from the dialog box that appears

A picture of your document appears. This image shows the exact placement of the printed text on the page. If there is something you would like to change, you can do so at this time by pressing **ESC** to cancel the preview and print process. If the document looks correct, you have other options, as shown in the box to the left of the document. These options include pressing **PgUp** or **PgDn** for the preceding or following page (used when the document is more than one page long), or pressing **P** to continue and print the document.

4. PRESS   **P** to print the document

Note: *Make sure that you are on-line to the printer and that the on-line light is on or the printer is in the ready mode as necessary.*

SELECTING THE CORRECT PRINTER

You may also need to select from more than one printer for your environment. Ask your instructor or lab monitor about doing this. If you are on-line to the wrong printer, your document may look different from what you expect.

PRINTING WITHOUT PREVIEWING

You can also print the document without previewing it first, although it is strongly recommended that you use the preview command whenever it is desirable to learn how the hard copy will appear on the page. To print without previewing the document, use the **Print** command from the **Print** menu.

PRINT WITHOUT PREVIEW

1. CHOOSE   the **Print** menu

2. CHOOSE   the **Print** command

The dialog box shown in Figure 4-4 appears.

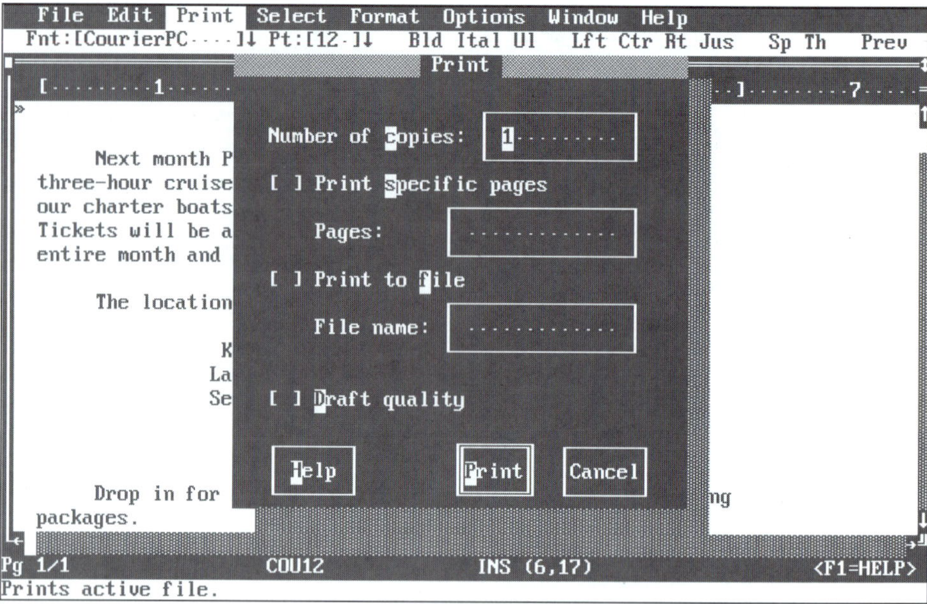

FIGURE 4-4
PRINT DIALOG BOX

From this dialog box as with the Print Preview Dialog box, you have the option of printing multiple copies, printing specific pages of a long document, sending the output to a file rather than the printer, or printing a draft-quality document. These options are discussed in further detail in Chapter 5.

3. **CHOOSE** **Cancel** at this time to return to your document workspace

4. **CHOOSE** **Close** from the **File** menu to close this document or click the mouse button once on the close box in the upper left corner of the document

5. **QUIT** or **CONTINUE** to the tutorial and review.

GUIDED TUTORIAL

WHAT YOU'LL DO

- Practice editing commands.
- Format characters and paragraphs.
- Create new files; open existing ones.

```
¶
¶
¶
Today's Date¶
¶
¶
¶
¶
Ms. Rebecca Barnes¶
1907 Seventh Avenue S. E.¶
Bellevue, WA 98005¶
¶
Dear Ms. Barnes:¶
¶
It has come to my attention that you are interested in
exploring job opportunities with Data Enterprises.¶
¶
We are currently seeking applicants for a position as Junior
Programmer in our EDS department. This position offers a com-
petitive salary with flexible working hours. In addition to
training, we offer successful employees a full range of
opportunities for professional development.¶
¶
If you would like more information on this challenging posi-
tion which is now open, please contact me.¶
¶
I shall look forward to hearing from you.¶
¶
Sincerely yours,¶
¶
¶
¶
George Bellfield¶
Personnel Manager¶
```

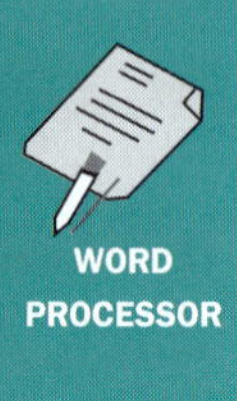

WORD PROCESSOR

INSTRUCTOR'S DATA DISK

HOW TO DO IT

1. **RETRIEVE** the letter on the preceding page from the instructor's data disk. The name of the document on disk is **CH4TUT**. The name of the document stands for **Tutorial, Chapter 4, Document 1.**

2. **SELECT** the words **interested in** in the first paragraph using one of the following methods:

    a) Drag the mouse button through the text.

    b) Position the cursor under the first letter of the first word and press F8 two times and **Ctrl/Right Arrow** key twice.

3. **PRESS** the **Delete** key to remove the words

4. **POSITION** the cursor under the **I** in In at the beginning of the last sentence in the second paragraph

5. **PRESS** the **Enter** key twice to create a new paragraph

6. **POSITION** the cursor under the **I** in the last paragraph

7. **PRESS** the **Backspace** key twice to merge the two paragraphs and the **Spacebar** twice to add space between the sentences

8. **POSITION** the cursor in the first paragraph

9. **CHOOSE** the **Format** menu by clicking once on the menu name or press **Alt/T**

10. **CLICK** the mouse button on the **Justified** command or press **J** to justify the right margin

11. **SELECT** and justify all remaining paragraphs in the document (justify the remaining paragraphs all at one time)

12. **POSITION** the cursor in the space immediately following the word **development** at the end of the third paragraph

13. **PRESS** the **Spacebar** twice and type the text in the following box; press the **Tab** key twice to indent each line.

```
Seminars are regularly offered in:

        Employee Relations
        Management Training
        Job Satisfaction
        Retirement Planning
        and more
```

14. SELECT   all of the indented lines by dragging the mouse button through the text or by using the **F8** key

15. PRESS   **Ctrl/2** to doublespace the text

  Note: *You could also set the spacing using the **Double Space** command or the **Indents & Spacing** command from the **Format** menu.*

16. SELECT   the company name, **Data Enterprises**, in the first paragraph

17. CHOOSE   the **Format** menu

18. CHOOSE   **Bold** as the character format by pressing **B** or by clicking the mouse button on the **Bold** command or by pressing the **Down Arrow** key and then pressing **Enter**

19. SELECT   the words **Junior Programmer**, in the second paragraph

20. CHOOSE   **Italic** from the **Format** menu

21. CHOOSE   the **File** menu by clicking on the menu name or by pressing **Alt/F**

22. CHOOSE   **Save As** by clicking the mouse button on the command or by pressing **A**

23. CHOOSE   the correct directory from the **Directories** list box

24. TYPE   **CH4TUT** as the document name (it may appear in the box already)

25. PRESS   **Enter** or choose OK

  Note: *The **Save** and **Save As** commands may both be used to save the document for the first time. Either one will prompt you for the name of the document. When saving the document under a new name, use the **Save As** command.*

26. CHOOSE   **Exit Works** from the **File** menu

27. SIGN   onto Works again.

28. CHOOSE   **Open an Existing File** from the "quick start" box

29. CHOOSE   the correct directory from the **Directories** list box by clicking on the directory name twice with the mouse button or by selecting the name and pressing **Enter**

30. CLICK   the mouse button twice on the document **CH4TUT.WPS** to open it

31. CHOOSE   **Print** from the **Print** menu (press **Alt/P** to reach the Print menu or click the mouse button on the menu name; press Enter or P for Print)

32. PRESS   **Enter** or click OK with the mouse button

When the document is printed,

33. CHOOSE   **Exit Works** from the **File** menu

REVIEW QUESTIONS

1. Which of the following is the correct command for starting a new document?

   a. New
   b. Create New File
   c. New File
   d. Create

2. Which of the following is a correct method for selecting text using the mouse button?

   a. Point and drag through the text
   b. Clicking the right mouse button once
   c. Clicking the right mouse button more than once
   d. All of the above

3. Which of the following moves the cursor to the beginning of the document?

   a. Ctrl/Right Arrow key
   b. Ctrl/PgUp
   c. Ctrl/Up Arrow key
   d. Ctrl/Home

4. Which of the following moves the cursor down one window?

   a. Page Down
   b. Ctrl/Down Arrow key
   c. Ctrl/End
   d. End

5. List two ways to center text.

6. Which of the following keystrokes will select a sentence?

   a. Pressing F8 once
   b. Pressing F8 twice
   c. Ppressing F8 three times
   d. Pressing F8 four times

7. _______ The **Typing Replaces Selection** command allows text to be pushed to the right when new text is typed between words.

8. _______ Paragraphs are separated by positioning the cursor at the beginning of the new paragraph and pressing the **Enter** key twice.

9. _______ A justified paragraph is one that is aligned on both the left and right
margins.

10. _______ A right justified paragraph is one that is aligned on both the left and
right margins.

11. Match each of the following phrases to the correct command.

_____ The keystrokes used to left align text

_____ The keystrokes used to double space text

_____ The keystrokes used to single space text

_____ The keystrokes used to reach the Format menu

_____ The keystrokes used to format text in bold

a. Ctrl/1
b. Ctrl/B
c. Ctrl/S
d. Alt/T
e. Ctrl/L
f. Ctrl/2

12. The _________________ or ___________ commands may be used to save a document for the first time.

13. The _________________ command is used to save a document under a new
name.

14. The _________________ command is used to save a document for the second
and subsequent times, thus overwriting the previous copy.

15. The ________________ command from the ________________ menu is used to
leave Works and return to DOS.

16. The ______________________________ command is used to open an existing document.

17. Which of the following commands is used to look at the document as it will print?

    a. **Print** from the **Print** menu
    b. **Print Preview** from the **Print** menu
    c. **Preview** from the **Preview** menu
    d. **Preview** from the **Print** menu

18. Which of the following shows ways to close a document?

    a. The **Close** command from the **File** menu
    b. The **Exit** command from the **File** menu
    c. The **Close** box in the upper left corner of the window
    d. All of the above

HANDS-ON EXERCISES 

EXERCISE 1

1. Write a one-page resume about yourself and your qualifications. At this time, do not be concerned about the alignment. Use the following format as a guideline. When listing skills, use a few words that really focus on your experience, such as:

   Four years of part-time work
   Excellent work record
   Training in accounting

Keep each skill on a single line. Leave space after the address and prior to education and experience.

```
NAME
ADDRESS
CITY STATE  ZIP
QUALIFICATIONS
Skill 1
Skill 2
Skill 3
.

.

.
EDUCATION
School 1
School 2
.

.

.
EXPERIENCE
Job or experience 1
Job or experience 2
HOBBIES AND SPECIAL INTERESTS
Activity 1
Activity 2
.

.

.
```

2. Save the resume as **CH4HO1** for **Chapter 4, Hands-on Exercise 1**.

3. Select and center the three lines of the heading: the Name, Address, and City lines.

4. Select and set in bold each of the main headings on the left margin: Qualifications, and so on.

5. If some of the text is in paragraph format, select it and justify the right margin.

6. Select each of the lines in the Qualifications section and change the line spacing to 1.5 inches (Hint: use the **Format** menu).

7. Proof, preview, and save the document again.

EXERCISE 2

1. Use the word processor tool to complete a homework assignment or other project.

Objectives

- Format prior to typing text.

- Create indented paragraphs.

- Remove or changing indents.

- Create custom paragraph indents.

- Change fonts.

PREVIEW ⟫➡

You have created, saved, and printed a document using the Works word processing tool. You have applied some of the basic functions of word processing to make the document's appearance more distinctive. The next document you will create will contain additional paragraph formats. You can also apply formats that will adjust the margins of paragraphs and the indentation of lines within a paragraph, such as indenting the first line or indenting an entire left margin of a paragraph, and so on.

This document will also use commands for copying and moving text from one location to another within a document. Works also contains commands for undoing editing changes and for permanently deleting text. At the end of this exercise, in the tutotial you will have additional practice using all of the commands you have learned so far.

CREATING A NEW FILE

CREATE A NEW FILE

From the opening Works' screen,

1. CHOOSE   the **File** menu (**Alt/F** or click the mouse button on File)

2. CHOOSE   **Create New File...**
(or choose Create New File from the"quick start" box)

3. CHOOSE   **Word Processor** by pressing **Enter** or clicking the mouse button once on this option

A new empty working space appears.

CENTERING A HEADING PRIOR TO TYPING TEXT

In the previous document, you learned how to center a heading after it was typed. In this document, you will learn how formatting commands can be applied prior to typing text. After applying this method, you can choose which option is most comfortable for you to use on a regular basis. Often, giving the commands prior to typing is faster and easier. Text does not need to be selected and the command applied. A simple command before and after is all that is needed.

CENTER A HEAD BEFORE TYPING

With the cursor at the top of the working space,

1. **PRESS**   Ctrl/C

The cursor is positioned in the center of the document between the left and right margins.

2. **TYPE**   the heading lines as shown in the following box. Press the **Caps Lock** key to type the heading in all capital letters. Press **Enter** twice after the first and second lines of text. The second and third lines of text will automatically be centered.

```
PUGET SOUND CHARTERS

AGENDA FOR MARKETING MEETING

NOVEMBER 20, 1992
```

3. **PRESS**   **Enter** three times after the date line
4. **PRESS**   Ctrl/L

The cursor is returned to the left margin and paragraph formatting is returned to normal. Holding the **Ctrl** key down and pressing **L** changes the paragraph format to left aligned.

WORD PROCESSOR

CONTINUING THE DOCUMENT

CONTINUE THE DOCUMENT

1. TYPE the following partial text. Turn off Caps Lock, if necessary. Stop one space after the last word, *at*. Do not worry about the alignment and do not use hyphens.

```
     This agenda contains a list of items to be discussed at
the next marketing meeting. Please read through each item
carefully prior to the meeting. If you have any additional
comments, suggestions, or questions, be prepared to discuss
them at the meeting.
     The meeting will be held promptly at
```

2. PRESS **Ctrl/B** to begin bold print

3. TYPE **2 p.m. in the conference room**.

4. PRESS **Ctrl/spacebar** to turn off the character formatting

5. TYPE the remainder of this paragraph as shown in the following box. Press the **Spacebar** twice at the end of this sentence.

```
Please bring progress reports with you.
```

CREATING INDENTED PARAGRAPHS

Indented paragraphs are used to create paragraphs that are indented on the left margin, the right margin, or both. They include hanging indents, which are itemized paragraphs or enumerated items within a document, such as the instructions and step-by-step exercises in this book. You can use Works' commands to have text indent automatically on a left margin that is indented. A typical standard indented paragraph is set at 0.5 inch; however, you can decide on any width for the indention using the **Indents & Spacing** command from the **Format** menu.

To indent all lines of a paragraph

All lines of a paragraph are indented using the **Left indent** option in the **Indents & Spacing** dialog box. This option will indent all paragraphs from the cursor downward until the setting is changed again.

CREATE AN INDENTED PARAGRAPH

1. **POSITION** the cursor two lines below the last paragraph in this document (press **Enter** twice after the last sentence)

2. **CHOOSE** the **Format** menu

3. **CHOOSE** the **Indents & Spacing** command

4. **TYPE** **0.5** in the **Left indent** text box as shown below

   Note: *The "0" does not need to be deleted. As soon as the 0.5 is typed, the zero will be erased automatically.*

```
Left indent:        [0.5........]
```

Left indent will wrap all text in a paragraph to 0.5 inch from the left margin. Other options available for paragraph indents from this dialog box include a **1st line indent**

5. **PRESS** **Enter** when finished or click OK

The cursor has moved in 0.5 inch from the left margin, and the ruler line at the top of the document shows the left margin marker ([), 0.5 inch in from zero (0).

Note: *This exercise used the **Indents & Spacing** dialog box. There is, however, another shortcut method for indenting the left of a paragraph. Pressing **Ctrl/N** for a nested paragraph will indent it 0.5 inch each time it is pressed. **Ctrl/G** will adjust the paragraph to the left for each time it is pressed.*

6. TYPE   the following text as shown in the box. Do not worry if the right margin wraps differently from that shown.

```
The following items are carried over from the two previous
marketing meetings. No firm decisions have been made about
which approach would be most suitable for the upcoming sales
campaign; however, after the success of recent months, an
approach similar to last quarter's might prove successful
again.
```

The left edge of the paragraph wraps automatically 0.5 inch from the left margin.

7. PRESS   the **Enter** key twice at the end of the paragraph

REMOVING OR CHANGING INDENTS

After the **Enter** key is pressed, the indention remains. It will remain until the 0.5 inch setting is returned to zero (or another setting) in the **Indents & Spacing** dialog box.

REMOVE OR CHANGE INDENTS

1. **CHOOSE**   the **Format** menu
2. **CHOOSE**   **Indents & Spacing**
3. **TYPE**   **0** in the **Left indent:** text box
4. **PRESS**   **Enter** or click the mouse button on OK

The cursor is returned to the left margin setting of zero (0).

> *Note:*   *This change removed the indention. If you wanted, you could simply change the number of the indent or add a right indent option. After the **Enter** key is pressed at the end of the indented paragraph, any new settings will be in effect with the paragraph marker to the right of the cursor position.*

CREATING A HANGING INDENT

Hanging indents are used for enumerated items, such as 1, 2, 3, and so on. As with the left indent, hanging indents need to wrap a set amount of spaces in from the left margin. With hanging indents, however, the first line is set to the left of all other lines in the paragraph. The **Ctrl/H** key combination is used to create hanging indents that are 0.5 inch in from the left margin. The **Ctrl/G** key combination is used to backspace one indent setting. If paragraphs are to be indented more than 0.5 inch from the left margin, **Ctrl/H** is pressed two or three times, and so on. **Ctrl/G** moves the setting back 0.5 inch for each time **Ctrl/H** was pressed.

CREATE A HANGING INDENT

For practice,

1. **LOOK**   at the ruler line. Notice that the left margin symbol is on zero ([).
2. **PRESS**   **Ctrl/H** for a 0.5 hanging indent

Note the change in the ruler line. The left margin marker is now at 0.5 inch.

3. **PRESS**   **Ctrl/H** one more time

The left margin marker is now at 1.0.

4. **PRESS**   **Ctrl/G** one time   .

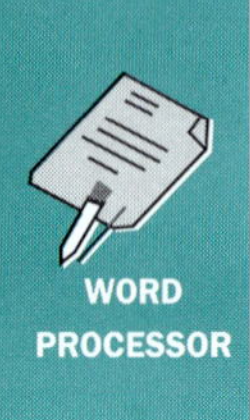

The marker is now at 0.5.

5. **PRESS**   **Ctrl/G** one more time

The marker is back at 0.

6. **PRESS**   **Ctrl/H** twice so that the left indent marker is at 1.0 and the cursor is at 0.5 (shown as I on the ruler line)

7. **TYPE**   **1.** (including the period)

8. **PRESS**   the **Tab** key to move to the 1.0 position on the ruler line

9. **TYPE**   the text shown in the box that follows.

```
 1. Open house and drawing for a discount on any weekday
    brunch cruise.
```

10. **PRESS**   the **Enter** key twice

11. **CONTINUE**   typing the remaining itemized list in the following box. Let the text wrap automatically on the right margin to the next line. Press the **Enter** key twice after each paragraph.

```
 2. Free dinner tickets and a 10 percent discount on pur-
    chases of additional tickets prior to March 1.

 3. Free dinner or brunch tickets to the first 100 persons
    visiting one of our boats during the next two weeks.

 4. Discount on all brunch and dinner tickets during the
    next quarter. Discount amount to be determined.

 5. Discount on dinner cruises for persons purchasing more
    than five tickets during the quarter.
```

12. **PRESS**   **Enter** twice at the end of the last paragraph

13. **PRESS**   **Ctrl/G** twice to return the indent to the left margin

SAVING THE DOCUMENT

<table>
<tr><td colspan="3">SAVE THE DOCUMENT</td></tr>
</table>

Save this document as **CH5PR1**.

1.	CHOOSE	the **File** menu
2.	CHOOSE	**Save As** or choose **Save** since this is the first save of this document
3.	CHOOSE	the correct directory if storing documents on a floppy disk in drive **A** or **B**
4.	TYPE	**CH5PR1** in the **Save file as:** text box
5.	PRESS	**Enter** or click OK

CREATING CUSTOM INDENTS

The default setting for hanging indents is 0.5 inch. This is also the default for all tab positions when the **Tab** key is pressed. The indent can be adjusted through the **Indents & Spacing** command in the **Format** menu. This command was used previously to indent an entire paragraph 0.5 inch. As mentioned, however, 0.5 inch is not the only setting. You can set the indent to any position on the ruler line. Once the setting is changed in the **Indents & Spacing** dialog box, it remains in effect from the position of the cursor through the following paragraph marker.

Custom changes are made when the measurements are changed in the **Left indent** box and in the **1st line indent** box. The left indent measurement is entered as a positive number. It indicates where the left margin will fall. The 1st line indent indicates how far to the left the first line will appear. It is entered as a negative number. For example, you could enter 2.0 as the left indent and -1.0 as the 1st line indent. This would show the left margin at position 2.0 on the ruler line and the first line at 1.0 on the ruler line (-1.0 from 2.0).

<table>
<tr><td colspan="3">CREATE CUSTOM INDENTS</td></tr>
</table>

1.	SELECT	items 1 through 5 so that they are all highlighted
2.	CHOOSE	the **Format** menu
3.	CHOOSE	**Indents & Spacing**
4.	TYPE	**2.0** in the **Left indent** box
	Note:	*Press the Tab key to move from box to box or click the mouse button.*
5.	TYPE	**-1.0** in the **1st line** indent box
6.	PRESS	**Enter** or click OK

The itemized numbers now appear at 1, and the left margin of the list appears at 2.0 on the ruler line.

CHANGING AN INDENT

You can change the indent back to its original setting or to another setting by adjusting the ruler lines positions in the **Indents & Spacing** dialog box. For example, the original 0.5 indent for the numbers and 1.0 for the left paragraph could be done by typing 1.0 in the **Left indent** box and -0.5 in the **1st line indent** box. The **Ctrl/G** key combination can also be used as it was when adjusting the position of hanging indents.

CHANGE AN INDENT

With all hanging indent paragraphs highlighted,

1. PRESS   **Ctrl/G** three times

Remember that **Ctrl/G** moves paragraphs 0.5 inch each time it is pressed.

2. PRESS   **Ctrl/H** to create the hanging indent

The paragraphs are back to the original hanging indent position of 0.5 for the numbers and 1.0 for the left margin.

CHANGING THE FONTS

In the previous chapter, you learned how to use the character formatting commands by changing text to bold, italic, underline, and so on. Another form of character formatting is changing the font and print size. This is done through the **Font & Style** command in the **Format** menu. Some of these commands will be applied to this document.

CHANGE THE FONTS

1. POSITION   the cursor under the first line of the main heading of this document, **PUGET SOUND CHARTERS**

2. SELECT   the title

3. CHOOSE   **Format**

4. CHOOSE   **Font & Style...**

The dialog box appears as shown in Figure 5-1.

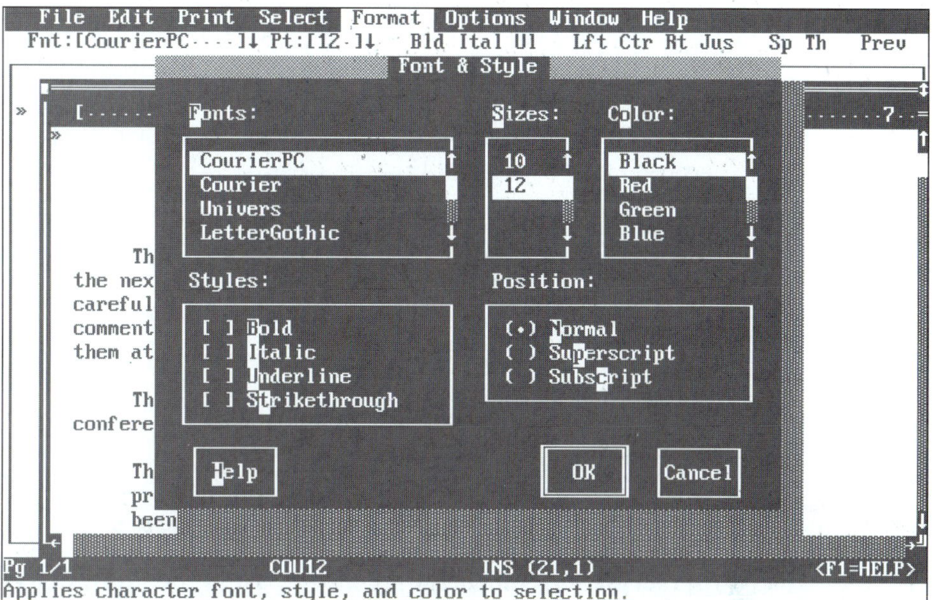

FIGURE 5-1
FONT & STYLE
DIALOG BOX

From this dialog box additions can be made to some of the character styles used previously, such as bold, italic, and underline. In the check box for **Styles**, another option, **Strikethrough**, is also available. **Strikethrough** is used to draw a line through text and is most commonly used to show editing changes where it is necessary to see the text, yet show it blocked out with a single line. It is usually used to show text that will later be deleted.

The **Fonts** list box contains fonts available with your printer. They may vary from those shown in Figure 5-1. If using a mouse, you can scroll through the list by clicking on the Up or Down Arrow (↑ ↓) in the scroll bar on the right side of this box. Otherwise use the **Arrow** keys.

Using either the **Arrow** keys or the mouse,

5. SCROLL   through the list and look at the various font styles your program has available

As you move through the font selections, notice the **Sizes** box to the right. It shows a list of the size or sizes of fonts that are available with the font selection that is highlighted.

6. CHOOSE   **HELV** or another font if that is not available

Notice that 14 is the only number in the **Sizes** box. This font style is available only in 14 point. The default size for text in a working space is 12 point Courier; therefore, the 14-point Helvetica selection will print a slightly larger

size letter than the regular Courier type. The larger the size number, the larger the individual characters will appear. If more than one size is listed in the **Sizes** box, pressing the **Right Arrow** key once or clicking the mouse button in the **Sizes** box would position the cursor in the **Sizes** box. A selection could then be made by highlighting the desired point size.

7. CHOOSE   **Bold** from the **Styles** options

8. PRESS   **Enter** or click OK

The text size does not change on the screen, but may be seen in **Print Preview**.

USING SUPERSCRIPT OR SUBSCRIPT

Superscript and **Subscript** are also a part of the **Font & Style** dialog box. **Superscript** moves text up from the line of type. It is often used for footnotes. It may also be used for bullets (a small **o**) entered to make a paragraph or body of text stand out. **Subscript** moves the text down from the line. Either the superscript or subscript may also be used in writing mathematical formulas.

In this exercise, the numbers that are itemizing the hanging indent paragraphs will be removed and superscripted bullets will be inserted in their place.

USE SUPER- OR SUBSCRIPT

1. SELECT   **Typing Replaces Selection** from the **Options** menu

2. SELECT   the number **1** in the first hanging indent

3. CHOOSE   the **Format** menu

4. CHOOSE   **Font & Style** from the **Position** box

5. CHOOSE   **Superscript**

6. PRESS   **Enter** or click OK

The number changes color.

7. TYPE   a small **o** to replace the 1 with an ^{o} or "bullet"

8. DELETE   the **period** by pressing the **Del** or **Delete** key

9. REPEAT   steps 2 through 8 for the remaining numbers so that all are replaced by superscripted bullets.

    Note: *You may also use the shortcut method by pressing **Ctrl/+** [use the **Shift** key and the **equals (=)** key for the plus sign] for superscript. Use **Ctrl/=** for subscript.*

VIEW THE FONT AND NUMBER CHANGE

Use **Print Preview** to view the changes made to the document.

1. CHOOSE **Print**
2. CHOOSE **Preview**
3. CHOOSE **Preview** again

You can see the change in the main heading font size and style as well as the raised bullets.

4. PRESS **ESC** to return to the workspace
5. SAVE this document as **CH5PR2**

WORKS TOOLBAR FEATURES

Font styles and character and paragraph formats may be applied quickly using Works Toolbar. The Toolbar appears across the top of the window and looks like the one shown in Figure 5-2.

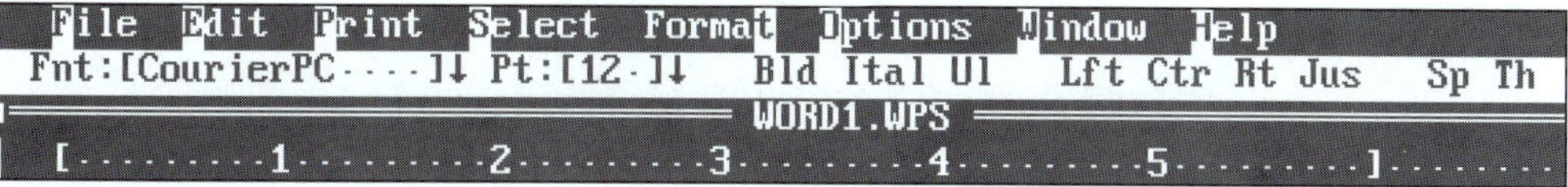

FIGURE 5-2
WORKS TOOLBAR

Clicking on the arrow to the right of the font list box (**Fnt:**) will produce a list of fonts available with your system. Clicking on the arrow to the right of the points (Size) list box (**Pt:**) will show the sizes available with a given font. In addition, the following options are available by clicking on them with the mouse.

Bold print	Bld
Italic print	Ital
Underline	Ul
Left paragraph alignment	Lft
Center alignment	Ctr
Right alignment	Rt
Justified alignment	Jus

Spelling (**Sp**) and Thesaurus (**Th**) (discussed in Chapter 6) may be accessed quickly using the Toolbar. Print Preview (**Prev**) is also available.

WORD PROCESSOR

USE WORKS TOOLBAR

1. **CLICK** the mouse button once on **Prev** to access Print Preview

2. **PRESS** **Esc** when finished

3. **POSITION** the cursor anywhere in the first line of the heading

Notice that the Toolbar shows **Bld** and **Ctr** (bold and center) highlighted.

4. **SELECT** all of the first line in the heading

5. **CLICK** **once** on Bld

6. **CLICK** **Lft** for left alignment

7. **CLICK** the mouse anywhere in the document to note the change in the heading

Notice also that the **Lft** button is now highlighted; however, the **Bld** and **Ctr** buttons are not.

8. **SELECT** all of the first line again

9. **CLICK** **once** on **Bld** and **once** on **Ctr** to bold and center the line again

10. **POSITION** the cursor anywhere in the first paragraph

11. **CLICK** **once** on the **Jus** button to justify the paragraph

12. **CLICK** **once** on the **Rt** button

13. **CLICK** **once** again on the **Lft** button to left align the paragraph

14. **SELECT** any word in the first paragraph

Notice that the font (**Fnt**) and point (**Pt**) sizes are shown on the left of the Toolbar.

15. **POINT** and drag through the list of fonts available

16. **POINT** and drag through the list of points available

17. **RETURN** to the normal font and point size if necessary

Use the Toolbar whenever you find it most convenient. Throughout this text, menu commands and dialog box options are discussed in detail; however, you may on occasion find it easier to access the Toolbar for quick changes when working with documents.

Text may be formatted from the Toolbar just as when using menus — either before or after typing text. To turn a format off, select the text and click on the Toolbar button again.

18. **SAVE** the document again and stop or continue to the tutorial and reviews.

GUIDED TUTORIAL

WHAT YOU'LL DO

- Practice hanging indents.
- Change font and print styles.
- Type over text.
- Create super- and subscripts.

HOW TO DO IT

INSTRUCTOR'S DATA DISK

1. CREATE the following document or retrieve it from the instructor's data disk. It is called **CH5TUT** for **Chapter 5 Tutorial.** Do not worry if the right margin aligns differently from that shown in the example.

2. PRESS the **Enter** key six times before typing **TO**; two times after **TO** and **FROM**, one time after **DATE**, and three times after **SUBJECT**, as shown in the example.

3. Let the text wrap on the right margin when typing the body of the document.

```
TO:         Roberta Melbourne

FROM:       (your name)

DATE:       (current date)
SUBJECT:    Word processing slides


Here are the word processing slides you requested. A check
for $25, to cover processing and duplication, may be sent
directly to me. Note that I have added a few slides to the
series since the program at the recent Arizona Computer
Education meeting. They are:

I do not have a script for the slides. If you have
questions about any of them, please drop me a line or give
me a call. Note that I have numbered the slides. If you
have a question, you can refer to them by number.
```

WORD PROCESSOR

  4. POSITION the cursor one line down from the top of the document.

  5. PRESS **Ctrl/C** and **Ctrl/B** to turn on the center and bold commands

  6. TYPE **MEMORANDUM** in all CAPS

  7. POSITION the cursor under the **S** in SUBJECT

  8. PRESS the **Enter** key once to move SUBJECT down a line

  9. POSITION the cursor after the colon (:) at the end of the first paragraph.

10. PRESS **Enter** twice to add blank lines between the paragraphs

11. PRESS **Ctrl/H** twice to create a hanging indent at 1.0 inch (press **Ctrl/G** to reduce the indent if an error is made)

12. TYPE **1.**

13. PRESS the **Tab** key

14. TYPE the text shown in the following box.

```
1.   New software products.
2.   New computer monitors.
3.   Upgrades in laser printers.
4.   Advances in software products.
```

15. SAVE the document as **CH5TUT**. Be sure to save to the correct drive/directory.

16. SELECT **MEMORANDUM** at the top of the document

17. CHOOSE **Font & Style** from the **Format** menu

18. CHOOSE **Helvetica** or another font, different from the one in use, from the **Fonts** list box on the Toolbar. Choose size 14 if available.

19. PRESS **Enter** or click OK

20. FORMAT each of the headings in the memo (TO, FROM, and so on) in the same font .

21. PRESS the **Insert** key.

22. POSITION the cursor inder the number **1.** from the itemized list

23. TYPE a small **o** to replace the number

24. SELECT the small **o**

25. PRESS **Ctrl/Shift +** (on the +/= key) to superscript the **o**

26. DELETE the period following the **o**

27. CHANGE the remaining itemized numbers to superscripted bullets

28. PRESS the **Insert** key to return to Insert mode.

29. PROOF and save the document again

30. PREVIEW and print a copy of the document

REVIEW QUESTIONS

1. Which of the following menus is used to create a new document?

   a. Format
   b. Edit
   c. File
   d. Select

2. List the three main types of documents that can be created using Works.

3. Which of the following is the correct set of keystrokes to use when centering a heading?

   a. Alt/C
   b. Shift/C
   c. Shift/+C
   d. Ctrl/C

4. What keys are used to position the cursor on the left margin after a center command is given?

5. Which of the following shows the correct procedure for bolding text after it has been typed?

   a. Select the text and press Ctrl/B
   b. Select the text and press Alt/B
   c. Press Ctrl/B and then select the text; press Ctrl/N when finished
   d. Press Ctrl/B before and after the text

6. Which of the following commands turns off the character formatting (such as bold or underline)?

   a. Ctrl/O
   b. Ctrl/L
   c. Ctrl/Spacebar
   d. Ctrl/N

7. _____ The **Indents & Spacing** dialog box from the **Format** menu may be used to create itemized paragraphs.

8. _____ The **Ctrl/G** keystroke combination is used to move the left margin marker to the right when creating indented paragraphs.

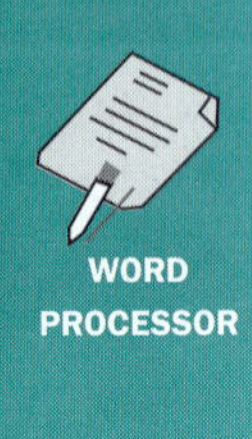

9. _____ The **Font & Style** dialog box is accessed through the **Edit** menu.

10. _____ Text may be super- or subscripted by using one of two methods.

11. The _______________ dialog box allows you to change the position, size, and style of text.

12. The _______________ command in the _______________ menu allows you to see changes to the document without printing it first.

13. List several features found on the Works Toolbar.

14. How is formatting turned off from the Toolbar?

HANDS-ON EXERCISES

EXERCISE 1

1. Open the resume you created in Exercise Chapter 4, **CH4HO1**.

2. Bullet and create hanging indents for each of the jobs you have listed and/or each of the schools you have attended. Superscript the bullets.

3. Change the font and style of other blocks of text to make the resume more attractive. Do not use more than two fonts throughout.

4. Proof and revise the resume as necessary.

5. Preview and print a copy.

EXERCISE 2

1. Retrieve the data document **CH5HO2** from the instructor's data disk.

2. Format all side headings (text appearing on a line alone and prior to a paragraph) in italic and bold.

3. Type the company name at the top of the document. Center and set the heading in bold prior to typing it.

4. Select all itemized text and change to a left indent of 1.5 and a first line indent of -0.5 so that the first line starts at 1.0.

5. Preview and save the document again.

6. Print a copy.

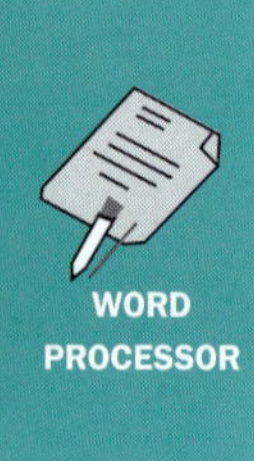
WORD
PROCESSOR

6 BUILT-IN WORD PROCESSING ASSISTANCE

Objectives

- Search and replace text.

- Search for and replace special characters.

- Use insert special commands in text.

- Check for spelling errors.

- Use the thesaurus.

PREVIEW »»

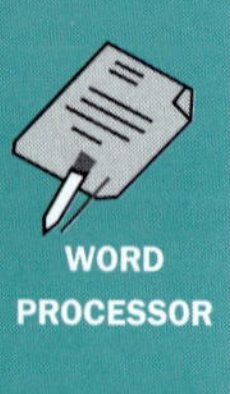

One of the most useful features in Works is the built-in assistance commands. These commands let you search for and replace existing text, hyphenate text, check spelling, and use a thesaurus. These are useful tools available to you from the early stages of learning Works. It is helpful at any time to use an automatic spell program. Hyphenation is useful in both long and short documents. It allows for an even right margin and the hyphenation of long words that would otherwise wrap to the next line. The Thesaurus option gives you a tool used to select alternate words when composing text. In long documents, search and replace is useful for locating repeat occurrences of words or for locating specific words or symbols that would take time to locate if scrolling through the document.

SEARCHING FOR AND REPLACING TEXT

The **Search** command is used to locate specific text. Usually, the text is a word in a long document. Without a search function, it would take a great deal of time to search for specific text in a long document. For example, suppose that you wanted to locate a specific date in a 15-page document that contained many dates. If you had no idea of the page on which the date was located, it would take time to scroll through each page looking for the exact date. With the **Search** command, you can type in the word for which you are searching (it may also be a phrase or symbol), and Works will quickly locate it for you. It takes only a few moments.

When the **Replace** command is used, text can be located and then replaced with other text. For example, if a date occurred several times throughout a long document and the date needed to be changed wherever it occurred, the **Replace** command could be used to locate every occurrence and replace it with the new date — all within a matter of moments.

SEARCHING FOR TEXT

When Works is searching for text, it does so from the cursor position forward in the document. Works can also search through specific blocks of text. If a paragraph is selected and the **Search** command is given, only the block of text selected will be searched. If you need to search through the entire document, be sure to position the cursor at the beginning of the document.

SEARCH FOR TEXT

1.	SIGN	onto the program if necessary
2.	OPEN	the document **CH5PR2** which you created in Chapter 5; or retrieve it from the instructor's data disk.
	Note:	*Be sure to change directories if opening the document from drive A or B*
3.	POSITION	the cursor at the beginning of the document (**Ctrl/Home**) if necessary

4. CHOOSE   the **Select** menu

5. CHOOSE   **Search**

The dialog box shown in Figure 6-1 appears.

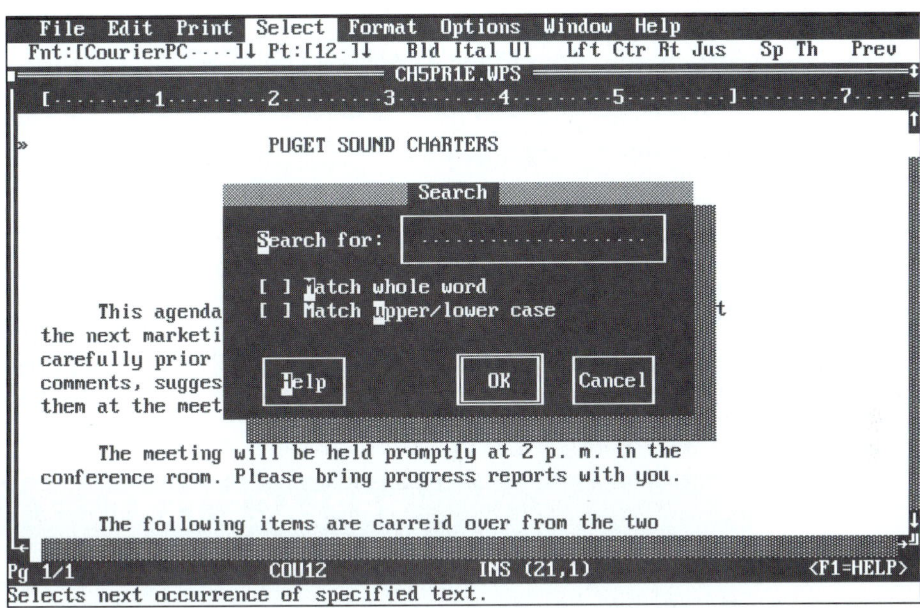

FIGURE 6-1
SEARCH DIALOG BOX

In the **Search for** text box, you enter the text for which you are searching. There are a few ways in which you can designate the exact text. In the text box, you can type alphanumeric text. You can also search for phrases and include the spaces between words when doing so.

The option **Match whole word** allows you to search for whole words only. For example, if you are searching for the word **the**, Works would also find *the*ater and *the*se. If you choose the **Match whole word** option, however, Works will locate only the whole-word occurrences that are exact word matches.

The option **Match upper/lower case** locates the exact uppercase match in words. When this selection is not made, upper- and lowercase occurrences of the word will be found.

Comment concerning dialog boxes

If you are using the keyboard to make selections in a dialog box, you can either use the **Arrow** keys to move to an option or you can press **Alt** and the highlighted character. In Figure 6-1, the **S** in **Search**, the **M** in **Match**, and the **u** in **upper** are shown in a white highlight. Pressing the **Alt** key and the letter would also give you that option.

WORD PROCESSOR

6. **TYPE** **Please bring** as the phrase for which you are searching

7. **PRESS** **Enter** or click OK

Please bring is highlighted. Although this is a short document, you can perhaps see the advantage of this function if you were searching for a phrase in a very long document.

8. **PRESS** the **Right Arrow** key once

9. **PRESS** the **Spacebar** once to add a blank space between words

10. **TYPE** this week's

11. **POSITION** the cursor at the beginning of the document

REPLACING TEXT

Replacing text is just like searching for it only with an option added that replaced the text located with new text. You can either replace all occurrences or select which occurrences should be replaced.

REPLACE TEXT

1. **CHOOSE** **Select**

2. **CHOOSE** **Replace**

The dialog box in Figure 6-2 appears.

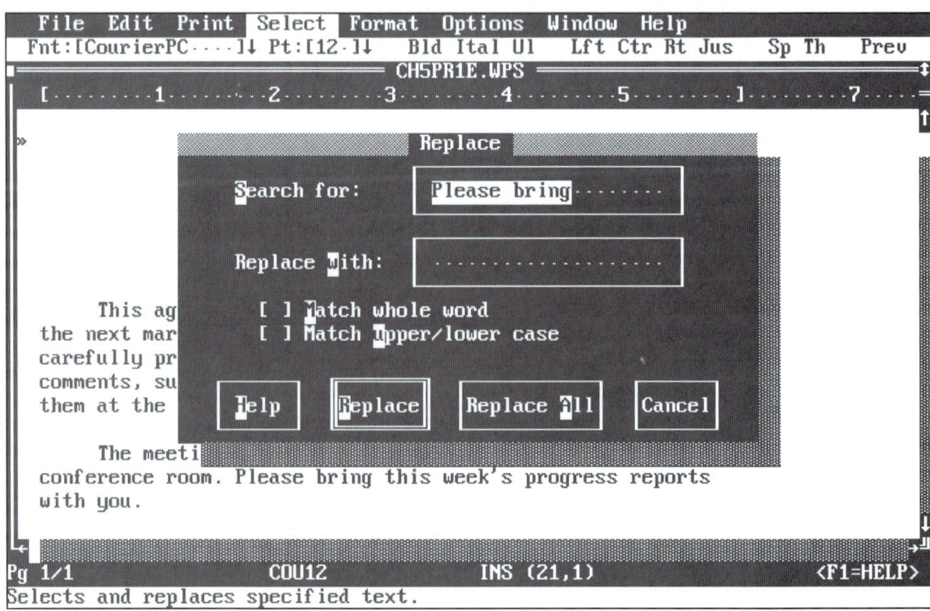

FIGURE 6-2
REPLACE DIALOG
BOX

90

Note: *The last phrase or word for which you were searching automatically appears in the **Search for** box. As soon as you type a new word or phrase, this one will be removed. You do not need to re-position the cursor.*

3. TYPE   **weekday** as the word for which you are searching

Other options in this box include those found in the **Search** dialog box, **Match whole word** and **Match upper/lower case**. Also included are options to **replace**, **replace all**, **help**, or **cancel**. The **replace** option will pause at each occurrence of the word and display a response box asking whether or not the word should be replaced. In other words, it gives you the option of replacing the occurrence that is highlighted or not replacing it. Choosing the **Replace All** option would automatically replace all occurrences throughout the book.

4. TYPE   **weekend** in the **Replace with** box

Note: *You can move to this box by pressing the **Down Arrow** key or by pressing **Alt/W**, since w is the highlighted character. In some dialog boxes only the highlighted letter needs to be pressed; in others, the Alt key is required. It is required here because you are moving from a text box and Works would recognize a letter as part of the text, In this instance, you may also click the mouse button once in the box.*

5. CHOOSE   **Replace**

6. CHOOSE   **Yes** to replace the occurrence of the word that is selected at the top of the screen

A box appears stating that there are no more occurrences of the word in this document. If this word appeared in other locations in the document, Works would stop at each one to ask for confirmation.

7. PRESS   **Enter** or click OK

8. POSITION   the cursor at the top of the document.

SEARCHING FOR SPECIAL CHARACTERS

Searching for and replacing text can include special characters as well as text. Most of the time you will use these commands to locate or replace blocks of text; however, you may want to locate special characters within the body of a document, such as a tab mark or a paragraph mark, and replace it with another character.

As well as special symbols in text, you can also search for white space. White space is any combination of spaces, tab marks, and nonbreaking spaces (those that will not break at the end of a page). Table 6-1 lists the keystrokes that are used in either the **Search** or **Replace** dialog box to locate special symbols and characters. As you use Works more extensively, you will have chances to use one or more of these options. If the options, such as hyphens and page breaks, are unfamiliar at this time, they will become familiar later.

WORD PROCESSOR

TYPE THIS	TO SEARCH FOR OR REPLACE THIS
^t	Tab mark
^p	Paragraph mark
^n	End-of-line mark
^d	Manual page-break mark
^s	Non-breaking space
^-	Optional hyphen
^~	Non-breaking hyphen
^^	Caret (^)
^?	Question mark (?)
^# (# is an ASCII number)	Any ASCII character
^w	White space
?	Any character

TABLE 6-1
SPECIAL
CHARACTERS USED
IN SEARCHING

USING SPECIAL COMMANDS IN TEXT

Special characters options are found in the **Insert Special Character** dialog box in the **Edit** menu. There are several other options in this box that will also be discussed.

USE SPECIAL COMMANDS

With the cursor at the beginning of the document,

1. **CHOOSE** the **Edit** menu
2. **CHOOSE** **Insert Special Character**

The following dialog box appears.

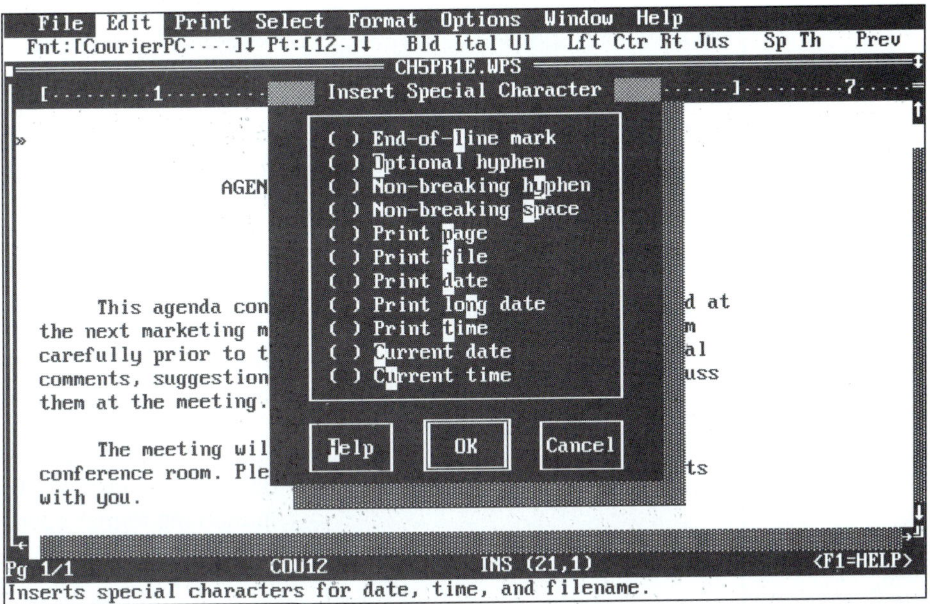

FIGURE 6-3
INSERT SPECIAL
CHARACTER DIALOG
BOX

From this box, the options listed in Table 6-2 are available. Frequently used keystrokes (shown in parentheses) may be pressed while in the document.

OPTION	FUNCTION
End-of-line mark	Inserts a marker designating the end of a line. The following text will be moved to the next line down. Tables and multi-line headers and footers could be entered as one paragraph containing markers where a line ends. This option saves space within a document.
Optional hyphen	Inserts an optional hyphen that does not appear on the screen unless the Options Show All Characters command is used. An optional hyphen designates how words are to be hyphenated if they occur at the end of a line.
Non-breaking hyphen	Inserts a non-breaking hyphen. This option keeps hyphenated words from being separated at the end of a line. These hyphens are displayed on the screen.

Non-breaking space	Inserts a non-breaking space. This option keeps two words together on a line.
Print page (Ctrl/P)	Inserts a page number placeholder. When the document is printed, the page number is inserted.
Print file (Ctrl/F)	Inserts a file name placeholder. When the document is printed, the file name is printed.
Print date (Ctrl/D)	Inserts a date placeholder. When the document is printed, the date is printed.
Print long date	Inserts the long-date placeholder. When the document is printed, Works prints the date in the long format spelling out the month, date, and year.
Print time (Ctrl/T)	Inserts the time placeholder. Works prints the time when the document is printed.
Current date	Inserts the current date.
Current time	Inserts the current time.

**TABLE 6-2
INSERT SPECIAL
OPTIONS**

3. CHOOSE   Cancel at this time

To insert an optional hyphen

In this exercise, the position of words in your document may vary. For that reason, you will first insert an optional hyphen. The word may or may not then separate on the line at the point of the insertion. If it does, you will see a change on the screen. If it does not, you can see the change by making a selection from the **Options** menu.

INSERT AN OPTIONAL HYPHEN

1. POSITION   the cursor under the **f** in the word **carefully** in the first paragraph

This is a word that could be hyphenated if it were on the right margin when the document is printed.

2. CHOOSE   the **Edit** menu

3. CHOOSE   **Insert Special Character**

4. CHOOSE   **Optional hyphen**

5. PRESS   **Enter** or click OK

If the word could be hyphenated after *care*, and the word *care* moved to the preceding line, you will see the break now on the screen. This is an optional hyphen; if it is not in a position to be hyphenated at this time, you will not see a change on the screen.

SHOW OPTIONAL HYPHEN ON SCREEN

1. CHOOSE   **Options**

2. CHOOSE   **Show**

3. CHOOSE   **Show All Characters** to turn on the show all characters mode if necessary

4. PRESS   **Enter** or click OK

Optional hyphens may be used on any words that may need hyphenating and that would otherwise be carried to the following line. If there is not enough room to hyphenate the word between the end of the line and the right margin marker, the word will be carried to the next line. The optional hyphen looks like a regular hyphen when **Show All Characters** is turned on.

5. CHOOSE   **Show** from the **Options** menu

6. CHOOSE   **Show All Characters** again to remove the **X** and turn the option off

7. PRESS   or click OK

USING OTHER *INSERT SPECIAL* COMMANDS

In the following exercise, you will add a few more features to the current document using other commands from the **Insert Special Characters** dialog box. Once you have practiced these, practice using any of the other commands in the dialog box on other documents.

USE OTHER *INSERT SPECIAL* COMMANDS

1. POSITION   the cursor at the beginning of the document

2. PRESS   the **Enter** key twice

3. PRESS   the **Up Arrow** key twice to move up into the blank space above the heading

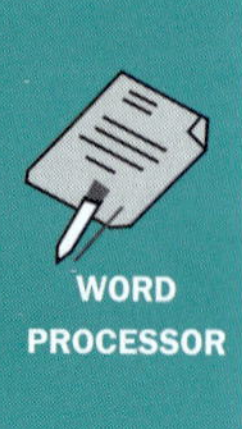

4.	**PRESS**	**Ctrl/L** to position the cursor on the left margin
5.	**CHOOSE**	the **Edit** menu
6.	**CHOOSE**	**Insert Special Characters**
7.	**CHOOSE**	**Current Date**
8.	**PRESS**	**Enter** or click OK

The current date is inserted on the left margin at the top of the document.

9.	**SAVE**	this document again as **CH6PR1**.

CHECKING FOR SPELLING ERRORS

Works contains a built-in dictionary that may be used to check for spelling errors, words with incorrect capitalization, words that are incorrectly hyphenated, and words that are repeated, such as **an an**. When Works thinks it has located an incorrect word, it stops, highlights the word, and offers you the chance to type the correct word, change all occurrences of the misspelled word, see suggestions for the correct spelling, and more.

When checking the spelling of a document, you also have the option of adding to the dictionary the words that Works does not recognize. The options available will be discussed further when the dialog box is on the screen.

CHECK FOR SPELLING ERRORS

1.	**OPEN**	a new word processor document space.
	Note:	*Leave the current document, **CH6PR1**, open also. The new document will open and the old document will remain on the screen. You will be able to see the names of both documents at the top of the screen. When new documents are open, they are stacked on top of each other much like documents stacked on a desk. Works' windows are discussed in more detail n Chapter 9.*

2.	**TYPE**	the following document (spelling errors and all); or retrieve it from the instructor's data disk. The document name is **CH6PR2**.

HISTORY OF PUGET SOUND CHARTERS

Puget Sound Charters was founded in early 1980. The compeny opened its doors to the public in February with a pormotional campagne offering free dinner cruises and an open house held on the the second Saturday of the month.

The first shop was located in teh old part of town, on First and Madeson. The showroom was capible of holding approxamately 15 boats and was convenently located for heavy foot traffic. Tourists, business personnel, and shoppers were regular customers in teh store.

With the advent of addisional construction and highrises, however, the location became less accessable. A decision was made in early 1989 to move to the north of town. The new location has proven to have even better acss. Parking is avalable and the population base north of town provides a heavy flow of customers.

3. **SAVE** the document as **CH6PR2** if you have just typed it

4. **POSITION** the cursor at the beginning of the document if necessary

5. **CHOOSE** **Options**

6. **CHOOSE** **Check Spelling**

Note: *You could also click on **Sp** from the Toolbar to reach the Spelling dialog box.*

The dialog box shown in Figure 6-4 appears.

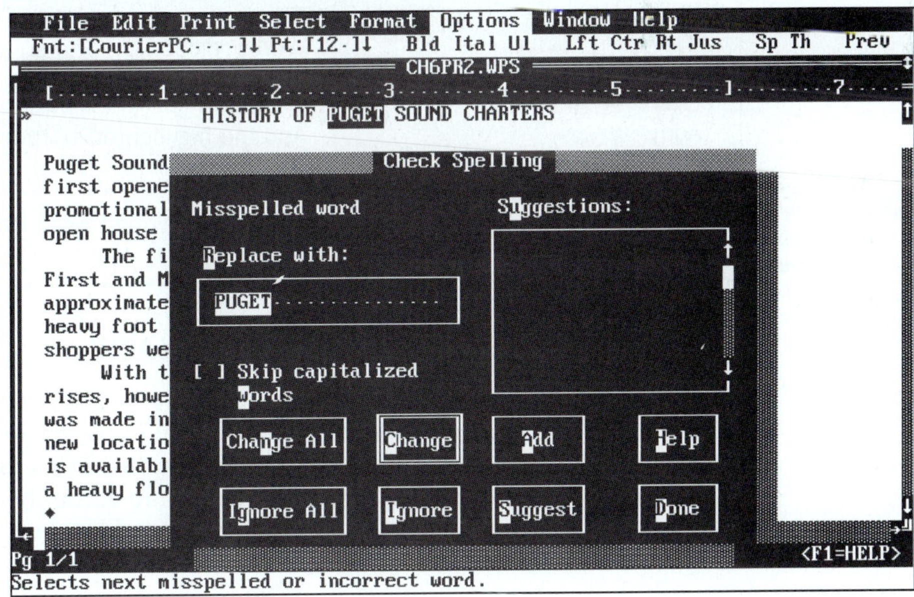

FIGURE 6-4
THE CHECK SPELLING DIALOG BOX

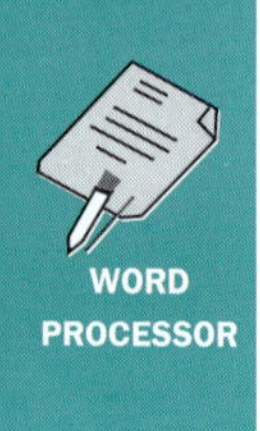

The dialog box offers the options shown in Table 6-3.

THIS OPTION	WILL DO THIS
Replace with: [word.........................]	Replace the highlighted word with this one if the Enter key is pressed.
[ ] Skip capitalized words	Skip over words that are shown in all caps or that begin with a capital letter. This is most useful if you want to skip names of cities, states, or other proper names.
[Change All]	Change all occurrences of the incorrect word throughout the document to the suggested word in the Replace with box. This word is either the one suggested by Works or the one selected by you after choosing the Suggest option.
[Ignore All]	Ignore all occurrences of the word. This is useful for words that are not included in the dictionary but that are spelled correctly.
[Change]	Perform the same function as pressing the Enter key when replacing a word.
[Ignore]	Ignore the first occurrence of the word but will stop at any other occurrence later in the document.
[Suggest]	Show a list of suggestions contained in the Works' dictionary. The suggestions will appear in the Suggestions list box.
[Add]	Add the highlighted word to the Works' dictionary.
[Done]	Cancel the Works' Spell Check.

TABLE 6-3
CHECK SPELLING
DIALOG BOX
OPTIONS

ADDING A WORD TO THE DICTIONARY

The first word that is not in the Works' dictionary is PUGET. This is not a common word and is most often used by those living in the Pacific Northwest. For that reason, it is not in the Works' dictionary. Suppose this word were one that you wanted to use over and over again. This would certainly be the case with the Puget Sound Charters company. In this case it would be best to add it to the dictionary so that Works does not stop at the word in every new document.

ADD A WORD TO THE DICTIONARY

1. CHOOSE **Add** from the selection at the bottom of the dialog box by either using the Arrow keys to move to the [Add] option or clicking once on [Add] or pressing **Alt/A**

Next Works stops again at the word Puget. It does not recognize this word because it is in upper- and lowercase lettering rather than all capitals.

2. ADD the word **Puget** to the dictionary as you did in step 1.

Works stops at **compeny** next.

3. CHOOSE the **Suggest** option (click once on the option or press **Alt/S**)

A list of suggestions appears in the **Suggestions** box. This list shows what Works thinks are possibilities for the correct spelling of the highlighted word. The word **company** also appears in the **Replace with** box.

4. CHOOSE **company** by pressing **Enter**, clicking the mouse button twice on the correct word, or choosing **Change**

At the word **pormotional**,

5. CHOOSE **Suggest** and make the correct selection

At the word **campagne**,

6. CHOOSE **Suggest** and make the correct selection

At **the the**,

7. CHOOSE **Change** to replace the two words with a single occurrence

At the word **teh**,

8. CHOOSE **Suggest** and make the correct selection

9. CONTINUE making selections using the **Suggest** option for the following words:

Madeson
capible
approxamately
convenently

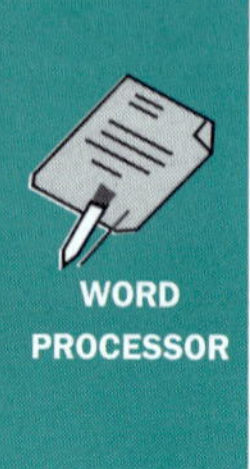

When the word **teh** is highlighted a second time, Works automatically inserts the correct spelling, the, in the **Replace with** text box. This word was corrected once previously in the document, and now the dictionary recognizes it again.

10. PRESS **Enter** to accept the **Replace with** suggestion for the correct spelling of **the**

On the word **addisional**,

11. TYPE **additional** in the **Replace with** box

   Note: *You could use the Suggest option again; however, sometimes Works cannot locate a word and it is necessary to type it in from the keyboard.*

12. PRESS **Enter**

At the word **highrises**,

13. CHOOSE **Suggest**

Works offers a suggestion that includes a hyphen; however, this word does not show the word in plural, so it will need to be typed in from the keyboard.

14. TYPE **high-rises** in the **Replace with** box
15. CHOOSE **Enter**

At the word **accessable**,

16. CHOOSE **Suggest**
17. CHOOSE the correct spelling
18. COMPLETE the spell check and choose **OK** or press Enter when finished.
19. SAVE the document again

USING THE THESAURUS

A thesaurus aids in composing text. It contains synonyms — words with the same meaning as a word you are using. When writing documents, suggestions for alternate words can be made using the Thesaurus command from the Options menu.

USE THE THESAURUS

1. **SELECT**   the word **location** in the third paragraph

2. **CHOOSE**   the **Options** menu

3. **CHOOSE**   **Thesaurus**

   Note: *You could also use the Toolbar option, Th, to reach the Thesaurus dialog box.*

4. **CHOOSE**   **Suggest**

The dialog box shown in Figure 6-5 appears.

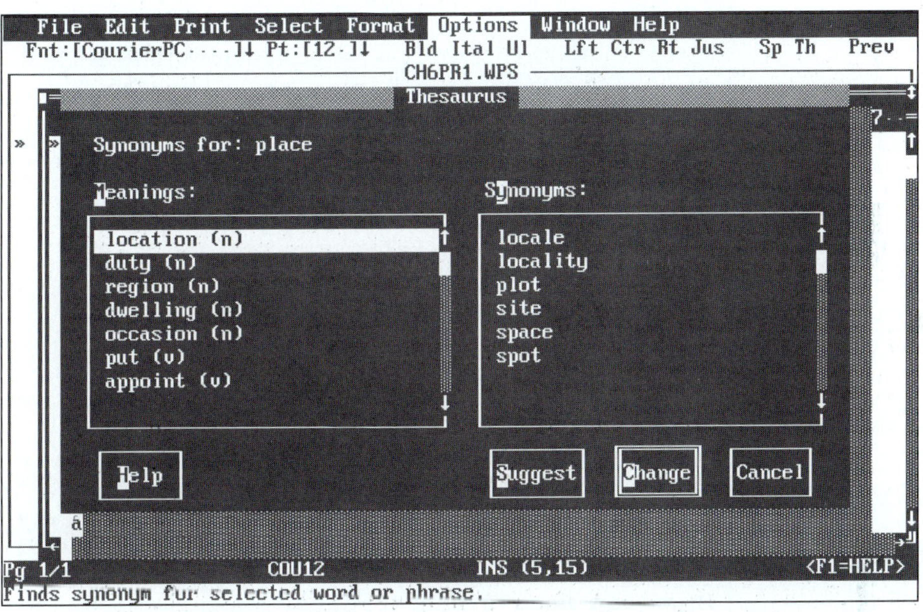

FIGURE 6-5
THESAURUS DIALOG
BOX

The **Meanings** box on the left of the screen shows the meanings and corresponding part of speech for the selected word. The **Synonym** box on the right shows a list of possible alternate words. A selection is made in the box to the right and the **Enter** key pressed, or the **Change** option is chosen. You can also **Cancel** the dialog box and return to the document with the word unchanged.

5. **CHOOSE**   **site** as the new word by selecting it and pressing **Enter**, clicking on the word twice with the mouse button, or choosing **Change**

You are returned to your document, and the word is changed.

6. **SAVE**   this document again as **CH6PR2**. **QUIT** or **CONTINUE** to the Tutorial.

GUIDED TUTORIAL

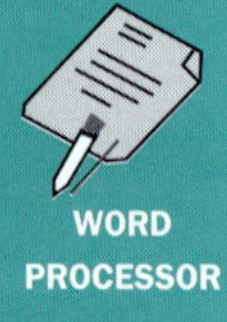

WHAT YOU'LL DO

- Practice search and replace.
- Use the spell checker and thesaurus.
- Insert special characters.

HOW TO DO IT

1. CREATE the document shown in the following box. This document is on the instructor's data disk. You will be performing a spelling check prior to printing the document.

Do not worry if the alignment is different from that shown. Bold where shown. Press the Tab key twice after To and once after From and Subject. Press the Enter key twice at the end of each line in the heading of the memo; press Enter three times after Subject.

<pre>
                    PUGET SOUND CHARTERS

To: All Staff

From: Management

Subject: Upcoming Cruise Events
</pre>

The following evening cruises are scheduled for this weekend. Please review them carefully. If there is any question about your responsibility with a cruise, please call the office.

Hawaiian Luau Dinner Cruise

This cruise will include a lei greeting at the top of the gangway. Dark green will be the color theme. Pineapples will be on each of the tables. The staff should wear Aloha shirts, shorts, tennis shoes, and leis (available from management). Taped Hawaiian music will play in the background. Pictures will be taken on the pier. The cruise will depart at exactly 7 p.m. and conclude at 10:30 p.m.

Washington State Association for Educational Development

Nothing special on this cruise. It will be the standard evening cruise from 7 to 10 p.m. It will include the beef and turkey breast buffet, Northwest salmon, and assorted salads, rices, and potatoes. Music will include the Puget Sound Charters theme song and the Broadway Hits show by the staff. The cruise will include dancing from 8:30 to 10:00 p.m.

2. **SAVE** the document as **CH6TUT**.

3. **POSITION** the cursor at the beginning of the document. Choose **Search** from the **Select** menu.

Note: *Positioning the cursor at the beginning of the document is not necessary. It is sometimes more convenient. When the cursor is in any other position or close to the end of the document, the spelling check will stop and ask if you wish to start at the beginning of the document. Repositioning the cursor prior to the spelling check may save time. You should practice both methods and use whichever you find more convenient.*

4. **TYPE** **this weekend** in the **Search for** box.

5. **PRESS** **Enter** or choose OK.

6. **CHANGE** the format to italicwhen the words are located.

7. **POSITION** the cursor at the top of the document (**Ctrl/Home**).

8. **CHOOSE** **Replace** from the **Select** menu.

9. **TYPE** **pier** in the **Search for** box.

10. **TYPE** **upper deck** in the **Replace with** box.

11. **CHOOSE** **Replace**.

12. **SAY** **Yes** to the **Replace** box that appears and choose **OK** or press Enter when the next box appears.

13. **POSITION** the cursor at the top of the document.

14. **CHOOSE** **Search** from the **Select** menu.

15. **TYPE** caret p (^p) in the **Search for** box to search for paragraph markers.

16. **PRESS** **Enter** or choose OK.

The cursor stops at the first paragraph marker after the main heading. You may repeat the search command quickly by pressing the **F7** key.

17. **PRESS** **F7** until you reach the paragraph marker just above **Hawaiian Luau Dinner Cruise**.

18. **PRESS** the **Enter** key twice to add blank lines.

19. **PRESS** **F7** to move to the blank line above the next bold sideheading and add an additional blank line.

20. **POSITION** the cursor at the top of the document.

21. **CHOOSE** **Insert Special Characters** from the **Edit** menu.

22. **CHOOSE** **Print date** and **OK** to print the date at the top of the document. A marker, *date*, will appear.

When the document is printed, the current date will print at the position of the marker.

23. **PRESS** **Enter** twice to move the main heading down

24. **RUN** a spelling check on this document.

25. **USE** the thesaurus to find a new meaning for the word **responsibility** in the first paragraph. Select the word and then use the thesaurus command to locate alternative words.

26. **SAVE** the document again.

27. **PREVIEW** the document using Print Preview, and print a copy.

REVIEW QUESTIONS

1. The _______________ command from the _____________ menu is used to locate text or characters in a document.

2. The _______________ command from the _____________ menu is used to locate and change text or characters in a document.

3. The **Match whole word** command is used to do which of the following?
   a. Match to all words containing the letters in the **Search for** box
   b. Match the exact upper- and lowercase lettering from the **Search for** box
   c. Match the exact lettering (upper or lower case) in the **Search for** box
   d. None of the above

4. _____ The **Replace** command in the dialog box, used when replacing text, will replace all occurrences of the text in the **Search for** box.

5. _____ Each occurrence of the text in the **Search for** box may be confirmed when being replaced.

6. _____ When searching for special characters, the character itself is typed into the **Search for** box.

7. The _______________ command from the _______________ menu is used to insert special characters in a document.

8. List at least three options which are considered special characters. What appears on the screen when each is used?

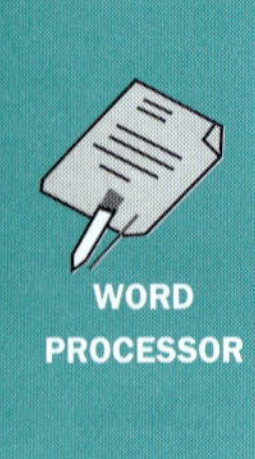

9. Match each of the following phrases to the correct option from the **Check Spelling** dialog box.

_______   Used to replace the word with the text in the Replace with box

_______   Used to bypass the change for this occurrence of the highlighted word only

_______   Used to ask for possible correct spellings of the highlighted word

_______   Used to include the word in the dictionary

    a. Add
    b. Done
    c. Change
    d. Ignore
    e. Suggest

10. Briefly describe the function of the thesaurus command.

HANDS-ON EXERCISES 

EXERCISE 1

1. Retrieve the document shown on the following page from the instructor's data disk. It is **CH6HO1A**. Add the following formats to the disk as shown.

   Centered and underlined main heading.

   Bold print for the company names in the first paragraph only.

   Hanging indent for the itemized text.

   Hanging indent to 1.0 for the last paragraph.

   Using a bullet and superscript on the last paragraph.

Note: *Create the bullet by typing a small o. Superscript this character. Do not worry if your margins align differently from those shown.*

CONTRACT

This contract will confirm the agreement between **Puget Sound Charters** and **Lake Union Caterers** covering the handling of all catering duties on cruises during the next year. **Lake Union Caterers** will provide brunch and dinner meals according to the following terms and conditions agreed upon by both parties.

The terms and conditions are set forth as follows:

1. Puget Sound Charters hereby commissions Lake Union Caterers to prepare brunch and dinner cruises for all scheduled cruises during the next calendar year.

2. All conditions to this contract shall be agreed upon by both parties. Puget Sound Charters will maintain the right to cancel this contract if Lake Union Caterers fails to provide services set in this contract.

3. Catering shall include a full brunch buffet each Saturday and Sunday unless otherwise specified. It shall further include dinner meals Tuesday through Friday unless otherwise specified by Puget Sound Charters.

4. In consideration of the services to be provided by Lake Union Caterers, Puget Sound Charters will pay them at a rate of $25 per meal.

    - This agreement shall be in effect as of January 1, 1991, and will continue through December 31, 1991 or until the contract is terminated by one of the parties.

---

2. Run a spell check on the document.

3. Position the cursor under any words containing three or more syllables on the right margin. Insert an optional hyphen in these words.

4. Double space the first paragraph in the contract.

5. Use a special character marker to insert the current date at the top of the document — centered two lines above the main heading.

6. Use the thesaurus to find better words for the following:

    duties in the first paragraph

    conditions in the line above itemized paragraph 1

    specified in the first sentence in itemized paragraph 3

7. Save the document as **CH6HO1B**.

8. Preview and print a copy of the document.

EXERCISE 2

1. Open the document **CH6HO1B**.which you created in Exercise 1; or retrieve it from the Instructor's data disk.

2. Search for the occurrence of Puget Sound Charters in the first itemized paragraph. When located, bold the company title. Use the Search command again to locate the next occurrence and bold it. Continue this process until all remaining occurrences of the company name are in bold print.

3. Use the same procedure as that used in step 2 to bold all occurrences of the name of the catering company, Lake Union Caterers.

4. Justify the right margin for the entire contract.

5. Insert a time marker at the top of the document just under the date.

6. Search for and replace all occurrences of the word **contract** (including the heading), and change this word to **agreement**. Be sure that the upper- and lowercase remains the same as when used the first time.

7. Use **Show** from the **Options** menu to view the optional hyphens in this document. Add any additional optional hyphens where long words might be divided on the right margin.

8. Save the revised document under a new name, **CH6HO2**.

9. Preview the document prior to printing.

10. Print a copy.

WORD
PROCESSOR

Objectives

- Undo an edit.

- Move blocks of text.

- Copy blocks of text.

- Copy character and paragraph formats.

WORD PROCESSOR

PREVIEW »»➡

In this chapter, additional commands used to revise text are covered. In addition to using the **Backspace** key and the **Delete** key to remove text, blocks of text can be selected and then deleted. Deleted text can be retrieved using an **Undo** command found in the **Edit** menu. The **Undo** command retrieves text that was removed or undoes other editing changes when it is applied immediately after the change.

Also found in the **Edit** menu are commands for moving blocks of text, copying blocks of text, and a copy special command. Each of these commands will increase your efficiency when creating and modifying documents.

MAKING MODIFICATIONS TO A DOCUMENT

Documents are frequently modified. With the use of programs such as Works, they are modified perhaps more often. Making changes to a document with Works is easy and fast. Blocks of text can be removed quickly. Text can be copied from one location to another or formatted as learned in Chapter 6. One bonus of having access to such a tool is that text is often better written and is presented in an attractive format.

In the following exercises, you will learn to remove blocks of text, undo editing changes, and use other special Works commands for making modifications to documents.

UNDOING AN EDIT

Text that has been deleted accidentally can be retrieved using the **Undo** command from the **Edit** menu. This command is used to retrieve deleted text. If it is not applied immediately after the deletion, however, the text is permanently removed and cannot be retrieved.

UNDO AN EDIT

INSTRUCTOR'S DATA DISK

1. OPEN   the marketing agenda document, **CH6PR1**; or retrieve it from the Instructor's data disk.

2. SELECT   the entire first paragraph using the mouse or **F8** key

3. PRESS   the **Delete** key

The paragraph is removed.

4. CHOOSE   the **Edit** menu

The first command in this menu is **Undo**.

5. PRESS **Enter** to choose **Undo** or click the mouse button once on the command

  Note: *Alt/Backspace will also undo an editing error.*

The text is replaced.

If any other edits are performed between the deletion and the use of the Undo command, the most recent edit will be the one recovered.

MOVING A BLOCK OF TEXT

When a block of text is moved, it is removed from the original location and inserted into a new location. All that is required is selecting the text, choosing the **Move** command from the **Edit** menu, positioning the cursor in the new location, and pressing the **Enter** key. It's as simple as that.

MOVE A BLOCK OF TEXT

1. SELECT the second paragraph which begins, **The meeting will ...**

2. CHOOSE **Move** from the **Edit** menu

  Note: *You can also press F3.*

3. POSITION the cursor in the blank line below the last bulleted paragraph

4. PRESS **Enter** to insert the block of text

COPYING A BLOCK OF TEXT

When a block of text is copied, it remains in the original position and is inserted into a new position. It may be inserted as many times as needed.

COPY A BLOCK OF TEXT

1. POSITION the cursor in the space immediately to the right of the last paragraph in the document

2. PRESS the **spacebar** twice to add two blank spaces

3. TYPE the text in the box below.

```
Bring your suggestions to the meeting. Jot them down in the
area provided at the bottom of this agenda.
```

4. **PRESS**   the **Enter** key twice

5. **TYPE**   the following line followed by two hard returns (press Enter twice).

```
Suggestion:
```

6. **SELECT**   the word **Suggestion:** and the following two blank lines

7. **PRESS**   **Shift/F3**, the **Copy** command

   Note: *F3 may be used to move text; Shift/F3 to copy. The **Copy** command in the **Edit** menu may also be used.*

8. **POSITION**   the cursor on the line following the two blank lines using the **Arrow** keys or mouse

   Note: *It is always important to read the information on the screen and particularly the messages appearing below the status line. Notice that the message is giving instructions on what to do next. In this case they say to select a new location and press **Enter**. If you wanted to cancel this operation, you could press the **ESC** (Escape) key.*

9. **PRESS**   **Enter**

To copy the text again

You can paste the text to a new location again if desired. To do so, the **Shift/F7** key is pressed again when the cursor is in the new location.

COPY THE TEXT AGAIN

1. **POSITION**   the cursor two lines below the last occurrence of **Suggestion:**

2. **PRESS**   **Shift/F7**

The word **Suggestion:** is inserted.

3. **CONTINUE**   to insert the word three more times, leaving blank lines between each one

You can also copy text over selected text. When the **Typing Replaces Selection** command is used from the **Options** menu, the copied text replaces the text that is highlighted. This is much like typing over text when the highlight is on except that you are pasting copied text there instead.

COPYING CHARACTER AND PARAGRAPH FORMATS

Another very useful copy command is the **Copy Special** command also found in the **Edit** menu. This command copies character or paragraph formats only. When using the regular copy command, a block of text that is copied is pasted to a new location. When using the **Copy Special** command, a new block of text can be selected and the formats copied from another paragraph applied to it.

To practice this command, the right indent will be adjusted in the first item in the list of topics in this agenda [those with the bullets (O)]. This will change the format being used for the list. The new format will then be copied to the other paragraphs.

COPY CHARACTER AND PARAGRAPH FORMATS

1. **POSITION** the cursor in the first bulleted paragraph which begins with, **Open house...**

2. **CHOOSE** **Indents & Spacing** from the **Format** menu

3. **TYPE** **1.0** in the **Right indent** box

4. **PRESS** **Enter** or click OK

The right margin is indented 1.0 inch from the right.

With the cursor still in the first bulleted paragraph,

5. **CHOOSE** **Copy Special** from the **Edit** menu

Following the message line instructions at the bottom of the screen,

6. **POSITION** the cursor in the second paragraph

7. **PRESS** **Enter**

A dialog box appears asking if you want to copy the character or paragraph formatting to the selected text. Since the right indent was changed and this is a paragraph format,

8. **CHOOSE** **Paragraph format** (it may be chosen already)

9. **PRESS** **Enter** or click OK

The right margin on the second paragraph is indented.

To copy to multiple paragraphs

You can copy the format from one paragraph to two or more paragraphs. The same procedure is used to copy the text; however, all paragraphs to which the format will be copied are selected after choosing the **Copy Special** command.

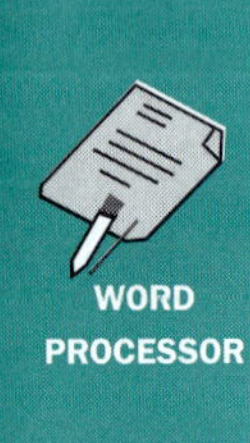

COPY MULTIPLE PARAGRAPHS

With the cursor still in the second paragraph,

1. **CHOOSE**   **Copy Special** from the **Edit** menu
2. **SELECT**   the remaining hanging indent paragraphs
3. **PRESS**   **Enter**
4. **CHOOSE**   **Paragraph format** (it may already be chosen)
5. **PRESS**   **Enter** or click OK

All paragraphs are reformatted.

The **Copy Special** command is a useful one to apply any time a format has been set for a paragraph and needs to be applied to other blocks of text. It could be used when the hanging indent format is applied to a paragraph after the text is typed. It could also be used when paragraphs are written in italics or bold and the same character style is needed in other blocks of text. These commands are timesavers and should be applied whenever formats are being used more than one time throughout a document.

6. **SAVE**   the revised document as **CH7PR1**. **QUIT** or **CONTINUE** to the tutorial.

GUIDED TUTORIAL

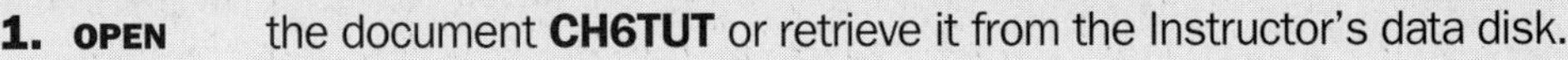

WHAT YOU'LL DO

- Practice undoing a format change.
- Use the function keys to copy and move text.
- Copy special formats.

HOW TO DO IT

INSTRUCTOR'S
DATA DISK

1. **OPEN** the document **CH6TUT** or retrieve it from the Instructor's data disk.
2. **SELECT** all of the first paragraph.
3. **PRESS** the **Delete** key to remove the paragraph.
4. **CHOOSE** **Undo** from the **Edit** menu to replace the paragraph.
5. **POSITION** the cursor under the **I** in If in the third sentence.
6. **PRESS** **Enter** twice to start a new paragraph.
7. **PRESS** **Alt/Backspace** to undo the formatting. Watch the screen!
8. **SELECT** all of the last sentence in the first paragraph, beginning with **If there is...**
9. **CHOOSE** **Move** from the **Edit** menu or press **F3**.
10. **POSITION** the cursor at the end of the last paragraph in the document.
11. **PRESS** the **Enter** key to insert the text.
12. **PRESS** the **Enter** key two more times to create a new paragraph.
13. **SELECT** the last paragraph.
14. **CHOOSE** **Copy** from the **Edit** menu or press **Shift/F3**.
15. **POSITION** the cursor below or at the end of the last paragraph.
16. **PRESS** **Enter** to insert the copied text.
17. **CHOOSE** **Undo** from the **Edit** menu to remove the copy.
18. **SELECT** the first paragraph.
19. **CHOOSE** **Justified** from the **Format** menu.
20. **CHOOSE** **Copy Special** from the **Edit** menu.
21. **SELECT** all of the remaining paragraphs in the document.
22. **PRESS** **Enter**.
23. **CHOOSE** **Paragraph format** from the box that appears (it should be selected).
24. **CHOOSE** **OK** or press Enter.
25. **SAVE** the revised tutorial document as **CH7TUT**.

REVIEW QUESTIONS

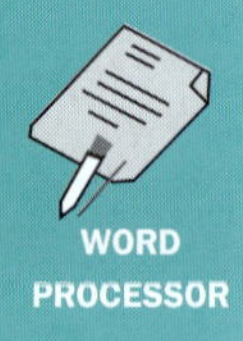

1. The ________________ command from the ______________ menu will remove the last editing change.

2. _____ Any changes made to the current page in a document may be quickly removed using a menu command. (T or F)

3. Which of the following key(s) may be used to move a block of text?

   a. Shift/F3
   b. F1
   c. F3
   d. Shift/F1

4. Which of the following key(s) may be used to copy a block of text?

   a. Shift/F3
   b. F1
   c. F3
   d. Shift/F1

5. The _______________ command from the ____________ menu may be used to move a block of text.

6. Which of the following commands may be used to copy character or paragraph formats?

   a. Insert Special Character
   b. Indents & Spacing
   c. Insert Special
   d. Copy Special

7. Which of the following key(s) may be used to copy text more than one time?

   a. Shift/F3
   b. Shift/F1
   c. Shift/F7
   d. Shift/F8

8. Briefly explain the difference between a copy command and a move command.

HANDS-ON EXERCISES

EXERCISE 1

**INSTRUCTOR'S
DATA DISK**

1. Open the document **CH6HO2** which you created in Chapter 6; or retrieve it from the Instructor's data disk.

2. Move itemized paragraph 1 so that it is the third paragraph. Renumber paragraphs so that they are in sequence again and adjust the spacing as necessary.

3. Copy paragraph 4 to the bottom just below itself, making a new paragraph 5. Replace the words **$25 per meal** with **$30 per hour for services**.

4. Move the bulleted paragraph so that it appears just above the first hanging indent paragraph. Adjust the spacing as necessary.

5. Format the first paragraph for a ragged right margin.

6. Copy the format to all other paragraphs in the document.

7. Renumber the itemized paragraph.

8. Adjust the hanging indents (Hint: use Ctrl/H).

9. Save the revised contract as **CH7HO1**.

10. Run a spell check on the document, save it again, preview it, and print it from the Preview screen.

EXERCISE 2

**INSTRUCTOR'S
DATA DISK**

1. Type the following document or retrieve it from the Instructor's data disk. The name of the document is **CH7HO2A**.

Indent the first line of all paragraphs 0.5 inches. Press the **Enter** key twice after the main heading. This document is a partial section of a moorage agreement contract. Set the text in bold where shown.

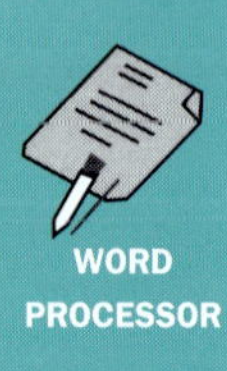

GENERAL TERMS AND CONDITIONS

5.1   Tenant acknowledges that Tenant has examined the Moorage and Tenant accepts the Moorage "as-is" in its present condition without representations or warranties by Landlord.

5.2   Tenant agrees to keep the Moorage neat and clean and in as good as condition as on the date of the commencement of this Agreement, reasonable wear and tear excepted.

5.3   Tenant will not alter, modify, or improve the Moorage, or attach or install any objects or material to walks, ramps, decks, or other properties belonging to the Landlord, without Landlord's prior written consent.

5.4   Landlord and Landlord's agents may inspect the Moorage and the Boat at reasonable times; provided, however, that neither Landlord nor Landlord's agents will board or enter the Boat without reasonable notice to the Tenant except as provided in Paragraph 4 above. The relationship between the parties is simply that of a landlord and a tenant.

2. Set **5.1** in the first paragraph in bold.

3. Justify the first paragraph so that the right margin is even.

4. Using the first paragraph as a format, copy the format to all other paragraphs in the document.

5. Change the positions of paragraphs 5.2 and 5.3. Renumber them after the move.

6. Set **5.2** in the second paragraph in bold. Repeat the character format to 5.3 and **5.4**.

7. Run a spell check on this document.

8. Save the document as **CH7HO2B**. Print a copy.

8 PAGE DESIGN

Objectives

- Change margins.

- Change tab settings.

- Create tables.

- Insert manual page breaks.

- Create headers and footers.

- Review printer setup.

- Create footnotes.

- Use bookmarks.

- Add borders to text.

- Print multipage documents.

PREVIEW »»➡

This chapter focuses on the options available for customizing pages of text. Up to this time, the focus has been on changing the format of text; however, there are many other options available for changing the appearance of a page — margins can be adjusted, tabs set, headers and footers added, page numbers assigned to pages, tables included in text, page breaks determined, borders surrounding blocks of text, and so on. A document with one or more of these added features has the finishing touches of the Works' word processor. With these options, a document takes on a professional appearance that makes it more attractive to the reader, as well as making it easier to read and understand. The appearance of a document is nearly as important as its contents. This chapter covers the remaining commands that give a document the final touches.

ADJUSTING THE MARGINS

One of the most frequently used procedures in page design is that of changing the margin settings. The margin is the blank area between the edge of the paper and the printed text. It is often desirable to change the margins so that text fits better on a page. The left margin of a document may be adjusted to fit into a binder or to be bound in a book. The left or right margin may be widened to hold special notes or comments.

Because setting margins affects the way the page looks when it is printed, the command used to change the margins is found in the **Print** menu. It is the **Page Setup & Margins** command.

ADJUST THE MARGIN

1. **SIGN**   onto the program if necessary

2. **SET**   the directory path and **OPEN** the document **CH7PR1** which you created in Chapter 7. You can also retrieve it from the instructor's data disk.

3. **CHOOSE**   **Page Setup & Margins** from the **Print** menu

The dialog box appears as shown in Figure 8-1.

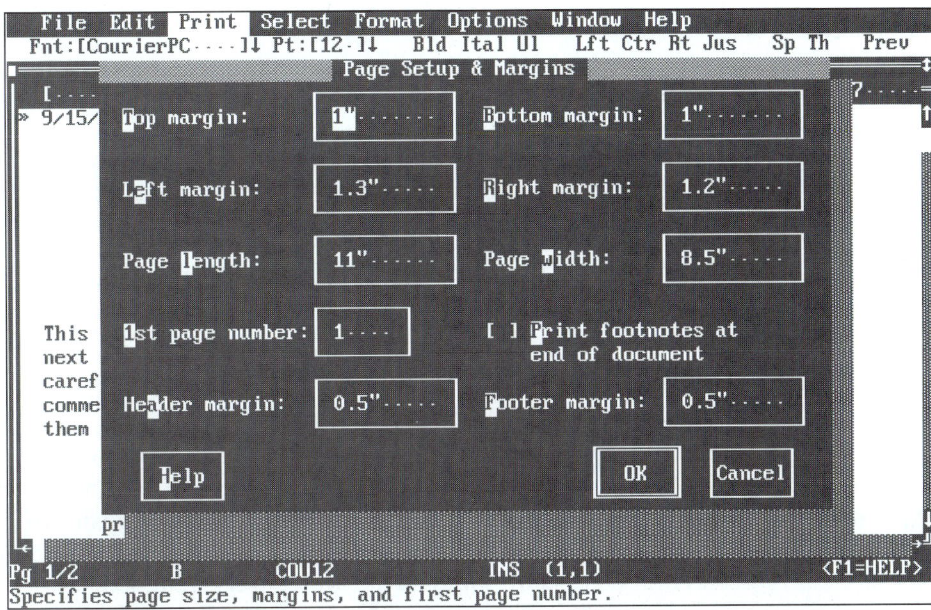

FIGURE 8-1
PAGE SETUP &
MARGINS DIALOG
BOX

The settings shown in this box are the default (or automatic) margin settings. A standard sheet of paper is 8 1/2 by 11 inches wide; therefore, the default page length and width settings are for the standard size. The default top and bottom margins are 1 inch. The left margin is 1.3 inches (from the left edge of the paper); the right 1.2 inches; and the header and footer margins are 0.5 inch. The header and footer will appear within the top and bottom margin area. If the setting is 0.5, they will appear at the half-inch position in the 1-inch margin. Headers and footers will be discussed later in this chapter.

4. TYPE	**2.0** in the **Top margin** box.

Often the top margin of a manuscript, agenda, and other business documents is 2 inches.

5. TYPE	**1.5** in the **Left margin** box
6. PRESS	**Enter** or click OK

The left margin adjustment will not show on the screen. The setting still appears at the zero position on the ruler line; however, when the document is printed, the margin will be slightly wider. The same is true of the top margin setting. The right margin marker, however, did change. This change compensates for the adjustment in the left margin setting. The default right margin shows a bracket (]) at 6.0 on the ruler line. The bracket is now shown just to the left, at 5.8.

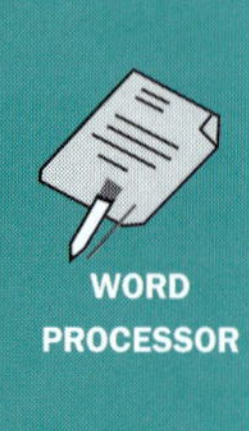

7.	CHOOSE	**Preview** from the **Print** menu
8.	CHOOSE	**Preview** again

The **Print Preview** screen appears. The preview shows the larger top margin setting and a slightly wider left margin setting.

9.	PRESS	**ESC**

CHANGING TAB SETTINGS

In previous exercises, you have pressed the Tab key to move 0.5 inch on the ruler line to a preset tab position. The preset or default tabs are every 0.5 inch along the ruler. You can change the distance between the tab positions or set new positions at specified locations on the ruler line. There are custom tabs as well. They can be set so that text is automatically centered, right-aligned, left-aligned, and decimal-aligned. Other options, such as leaders, are also available in the **Tabs** dialog box accessed through the **Format** menu.

CHANGE TAB SETTINGS

1.	POSITION	the cursor on the line above the last paragraph, beginning with **"The meeting will..."**
2.	PRESS	the **Enter** key **twice** and then the **Up Arrow** key **once** so that the cursor is between the last line of the itemized list and the last paragraph
3.	PRESS	**Ctrl/G** twice to remove the hanging indent format
	Note:	*Watch the ruler line as you do this.*
4.	CHOOSE	**Tabs** from the **Format** menu

The dialog box appears as shown in Figure 8-2.

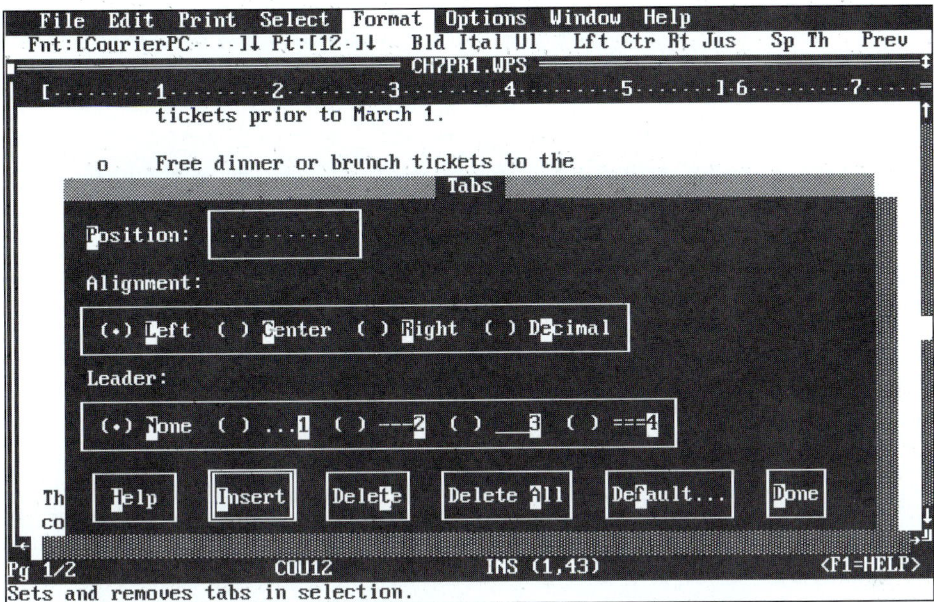

FIGURE 8-2
TABS DIALOG BOX

This dialog box has the following options:

The **Position** box at the top of the dialog box is used to indicate the position of the new tab setting.

The **Alignment** options include a **left-aligned** tab, **centered** tab, **right-aligned** tab, or **decimal** tab setting.

The **Leader** options are **None, dots, dashes, underscore**, or a series of **double line** dashes. A leader is a character that appears from the cursor position to the tab setting.

Option buttons at the bottom of the screen include **Help; Insert**, to insert the new tab; **Delete**, to delete a tab setting; **Delete All** to remove all current tab settings; **Default**, to reset the default tab settings; and **Done** to exit the dialog box.

It is often difficult to guess the exact location on the ruler line for a new tab position. It is also sometimes easier to be able to move across the ruler line as you are making decisions about positions. For that reason, two options are possible when deciding on the tab position: they are typing the number in the **Position** box or pressing **Ctrl/Left Arrow** or **Ctrl/Right Arrow** to move along the ruler line. It is necessary to hold the **Ctrl** key down and press the **Arrow** key for as long as the indicator is moving along the ruler line.

5. PRESS   **Ctrl/Right Arrow**, holding the **Ctrl** key down

While holding the **Ctrl** key,

6. PRESS   the **Right Arrow** key five more times so that the **Position** box in the dialog box reads 0.5 inch

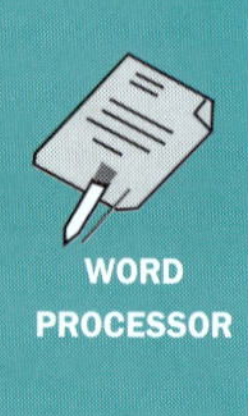

The default settings in the **Alignment** box are **Left** for left-aligned tab and in the **Leader** box, **None**. Leave these settings for this first tab.

  7. PRESS   **Enter** to accept the default selection of **Insert**

      Note: *The **Insert** option is shown at the bottom of the dialog box. Clicking the **Insert** button would work; however, the default in this dialog box is **Insert**. When all options are selected, pressing the **Enter** key will insert the changes.*

An L is placed on the ruler line at the 0.5 inch position.

  8. TYPE   **3.0** in the **Position** box

  9. CHOOSE **Right** in the **Alignment** box

Leave the **Leader** setting at **None**.

  10. PRESS   **Enter** to insert

An **R** is inserted at the 3.0 position on the ruler line. All text at this position will be aligned on the right.

  11. MOVE   to position **4.5** on the ruler line using either the **Ctrl** and **Arrow** keys or by typing the entry in the **Position** box.

  12. CHOOSE **Decimal**

  13. CHOOSE dot leaders **...1**

  14. PRESS   **Enter** insert

  15. CHOOSE **Done**

The ruler should appear similar to that shown in the box below.

```
[....L....1........2........R........4....D....5........].6........7...
```

USING THE NEW TAB SETTINGS

For this exercise, a table will be added to this document showing the persons who made outstanding sales during the past quarter. It will give information on the person's name and the date of the sale.

USE THE NEW TAB SETTINGS

1. PRESS the **Tab** key once

2. TYPE **Gail Sanders**

3. PRESS **Tab**

4. TYPE **9/28/92**

Note: *The date will move to the left as you are typing it so that the last character is the one aligned on the R on the ruler line.*

5. PRESS **Tab**

6. TYPE **10,975.00**

Note: *When the decimal tab is used, numbers line up on the decimal (the period). In this example, the two zeros will be entered to the right of the D on the ruler line. Regardless of the number of figures used, the decimal point will always "catch" the entry and all numbers will be aligned on it.*

7. PRESS **Enter**

8. CONTINUE typing the remaining entries in this table using the following information. Watch the alignment as you do so and use the same procedure as used in steps 1 through 7.

John Stevenson   9/30/92.............9,525.00

Beverly Simms   9/27/92...........13,550.00

Jerry Randall   9/30/92...........11,180.00

9. PRESS the **Enter** key **twice** after the last line

CREATING COLUMN HEADINGS

Tab positions are carried from the point at which they were created through all new paragraph markers until reaching a previously existing paragraph mark (when modifying a document) or until a change is made in the tab settigns. In the table just created, the tab positions were set on the line showing Gail Sanders' name. The line immediately above this line will show the hanging indent settings and none of the tabs used in the table. If you positioned your cursor in the paragraph following the table, the same would be true. It shows only the left and right margin settings and includes the default tabs at every 0.5 inch.

CREATE COLUMN HEADINGS

1. POSITION the cursor in the blank line above **Gail Sanders**

The ruler line now shows the formats of the last hanging indent paragraph.

2. PRESS **Ctrl/G** twice to remove the hanging indent setting

The left margin indicator ([ ) is now at zero on the ruler line.

3. PRESS **Enter** twice

4. PRESS the **Up Arrow** key once

This table needs some column headings to identify the contents of each of the columns. For this step it will be necessary to use the **Tabs** dialog box again to reset the tabs. Since centered tabs are often used in column headings, each of the new positions will be a centered tab.

Before moving into the **Tabs** dialog box, look at the ruler line. With the table showing on the screen and the ruler line at the top of the page, you can locate the approximate center position for each column. By looking at the screen, it appears that 1.3 would be the approximate center for the name column, 2.6 for the date column, and 4.3 for the amount column.

5. CHOOSE **Tabs** from the **Format** menu

6. SET a **Center** tab position at 1.3, 2.6, and 4.3.

Note: Use **Ctrl/Right Arrow** or type the position in the **Position** dialog box. Choose **Center** each time the position is changed. Choose **Insert** after making selections for each position. Watch the ruler line as you are entering the settings.

7. CHOOSE **Done** when finished.

When back in the document working space,

8. PRESS Tab

9. TYPE **Salesperson**

10. PRESS Tab

11. TYPE **Closing**

12. PRESS Tab

13. TYPE **Total**

14. PRESS **Enter**

Since the tab settings are stored in the paragraph marker following the text, pressing the **Enter** key carries the settings down to the next line.

15.	PRESS	the **Tab** key **twice** to position the cursor at the second tab position under **Closing**
16.	TYPE	Date
17.	PRESS	Tab
18.	TYPE	Sales

CHANGING EXISTING TAB POSITIONS

Tab settings can be adjusted by selecting the text containing the tabs and making the changes in the **Tabs** dialog box. Old tab positions are deleted and new positions are inserted.

Looking at the table, the middle column could be moved slightly to the right and dot leaders could be added to the table between the first and second columns. This would give the table a more complete and balanced appearance.

CHANGE EXISTING TAB POSITIONS

1.	SELECT	the four lines of the table containing the salesperson's names
2.	CHOOSE	Tabs from the **Format** menu
3.	PRESS	Ctrl/Right Arrow

While holding the **Ctrl** key down,

4.	PRESS	the **Right Arrow** key to the **3** position on the ruler line so that the **R** is highlighted

With the **Ctrl** key released,

5.	CHOOSE	Delete to remove this tab by pressing **Alt/T** or clicking on the **Delete** option
6.	TYPE	3.2 in the **Position** box or press the **Ctrl/Right Arrow** to the 3.2 position on the ruler line
7.	CHOOSE	Right aligned (it should already be selected)
8.	CHOOSE	dot leaders (...**1**)
9.	CHOOSE	Insert
10.	CHOOSE	Done
11.	SELECT	both lines of the column headings

WORD PROCESSOR

12. MAKE changes in these lines by adjusting the second **Center** tab position to 2.8 on the ruler line. Delete the old tab setting first.

The table appears as shown in the following box.

```
Salesperson            Closing              Total
                       Date                 Sales
Gail Sanders.......9/28/92 .........10,975.00
John Stevenson.....9/30/92 ..........9,525.00
Beverly Simms......9/27/92 .........13,550.00
Jerry Randall......9/30/92 .........11,180.00
```

TO ADD A NEW PARAGRAPH

A paragraph needs to be added above the table to give more information about the contents of the table. When the cursor is positioned on the line above the table, the ruler line will hold the format for the default tab positions and the left and right margin settings.

ADD A NEW PARAGRAPH

1. POSITION the cursor on the blank line above the table column headings

2. TYPE the paragraph shown in the following box. Press the Enter key once at the beginning and **once** at the end of the paragraph to add blank lines.

```
The table below shows the top four salespersons during the
past quarter ending September 30. The Total Sales figure
depicts the total dollar amount of bookings during the
period. This is an outstanding effort. Other members of the
team are to be commended as well.
```

3. USE **Print Preview** to view the document. It has increased in length and has several page formatting commands applied to it. Because the entire document is not visible on the screen, **Print Preview** becomes most useful. Use the **PgDn** key to see the second page of the document. Press **ESC** when finished.

DETERMINING PAGE BREAKS

Page breaks tell the printer where a page is going to stop and where another will begin. When looking at **Print Preview** in the preceding exercise, the document on which you are working was automatically divided into two pages. Works inserts a page break if you have filled up all of the default text lines on a page. The page break is denoted by the appearance of a double greater-than sign (>>) on the left margin. Right now, this sign appears on the same line as the first line of the column headings in the table. **Print Preview** confirms that the second page begins with the column headings.

Page breaks can be manually inserted as well. They can also be removed. Inserting page breaks is done through the **Insert Page Break** command in the **Print** menu. Page breaks are removed by selecting the break and pressing the **Delete** key.

There are other decisions you can make concerning page breaks. They include keeping paragraphs and blocks of text together on pages or keeping a single paragraph from being split between two pages. These decisions are made in the **Indents & Spacing** dialog box in the **Format** menu.

VIEWING PAGE BREAKS

So that this document is extended to more than just two pages, blocks of text will be double spaced.

VIEW PAGE BREAKS

1. **SELECT** the first and second paragraphs of this document

2. **CHOOSE** **Double Space** from the **Format** menu

3. **DOUBLE-SPACE** the following blocks of text.

   The paragraph above the table.

   The paragraph following the table.

4. **INSERT** an extra blank line above the first occurrence of **Suggestion:** at the end of the document.

5. **PRESS** **Ctrl/Home** to position the cursor at the beginning of the document

6. **CHOOSE** **Preview** and **Preview** again from the **Print** menu

   Note: *The first page ends after the third itemized paragraph (do not worry if yours ends in a slightly different location).*

7. **PRESS** **PgDn**

Two more itemized paragraphs appear at the top of the page. Four Suggestions lines appear at the bottom.

8. PRESS   **PgDn** again

The last page contains one *Suggestion*. This is probably not the best final layout for this document. The most obvious format fault lies with the fact that the third page contains only one suggestion. Options in changing the layout could include deleting some lines of text so that the *Suggestion* moved to the second page; however, this might make the material look too squeezed together. Another option that might make more sense would be to insert manual page breaks at different locations from those assigned automatically by Works.

9. PRESS   **ESC** and **Ctrl/Home**

INSERTING MANUAL PAGE BREAKS

The upper left corner of this document shows the beginning of the first page with the page marker (>>).

INSERT MANUAL PAGE BREAKS

1. USING   the **Down Arrow** key, scroll down the screen until you see the second page marker (>>) opposite the fourth itemized paragraph. Continue pressing the **Down Arrow** key until the last page marker is located.

2. PRESS   the **PgUp** key three times

3. PRESS   the **Arrow** keys until the cursor is positioned under the first bulleted paragraph beginning with **Open house...**

4. PRESS   **Ctrl/Enter** or choose **Insert Page Break** from the **Print** menu

A dotted line appears as the manual page break. The page marker (>>) automatically moves to the new page position.

5. PRESS   the **Page Down** key twice

6. POSITION   the cursor on the left margin of the paragraph beginning with The **table below...**

7. INSERT   a manual page break at this location (**Ctrl/Enter**).

8. PRESS   **Ctrl/Home**

9. CHOOSE   **Preview** from the **Print** menu and **Preview** again

The first page appears with the break following the first itemized paragraph.

10. PRESS   PgDn

The second page contains the last three itemized paragraphs.

11. PRESS   PgDn again

The third page now looks much more complete. It contains information pertaining to the **Suggestions** list and looks more filled in. All three pages are much more nicely balanced.

12. PRESS   ESC
13. SAVE   this document under a new name, **CH8PR1**.

CREATING HEADERS AND FOOTERS

Headers are blocks of text that appear at the top of every page, and footers appear at the bottom of every page. These options are commonly used to include things such as chapter headings, text titles, and page numbers. The information at the top of every page in this book was inserted using a header option. Headers and footers are just like any other block of text and they can be formatted just like any other block of text. Bold print, underscoring, and right-aligned tab positions are some of the character or paragraph formats that can be applied to headers and footers — just as in a document.

While you set tab positions within headers and footers, Works includes some preset tab positions that are commonly used, such as a centered tab and a right-aligned tab position. Page numbers are often centered and information is often right-aligned within a header or footer.

With the cursor positioned at the top of the document,

CREATE HEADERS AND FOOTERS

1. CHOOSE   **Headers & Footers** from the **Print** menu

The dialog box shown in Figure 8-3 appears.

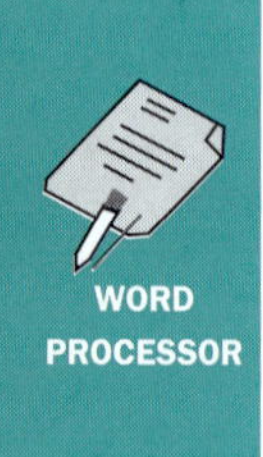

FIGURE 8-3
HEADERS &
FOOTERS DIALOG
BOX

The options found in this dialog box are:

Header and Footer text boxes:

Used for the standard header or footer options rather than creating customized headers and footers.

No header on 1st page: or   No footer on 1st page:

Used so that the header or footer will not appear on the first page. Headers usually do not appear on the first page of a manuscript or other long documents.

Use header and footer paragraphs:

Used for multiple-line headers or footers that are typed in the document space.

Short, one-line headers and footers may be typed in the dialog box. When a header or footer will extend beyond one short line, it is typed in the document window and is considered a custom header or footer. Both of these styles will be used in the following exercises.

CREATING STANDARD FOOTERS OR HEADERS (SINGLE LINE)

Standard header and footer settings are set in the Header: and Footer: text box. This option uses special commands to print the page number or date for example, as well as other text, by using codes to designate what is to be inserted. For example, codes entered into the Footer box as shown below would insert the date and page at the bottom of the page. The footer shown below also includes codes to print the date on the left and the page number on the right.

&l&d - &r&p

The codes that can be used in headers and footers are shown in Table 8-1.

TABLE 8-1
COMMANDS USED
FOR STANDARD
HEADERS AND
FOOTERS

TYPE THIS	TO SHOW THIS WHEN PRINTED
&l or &r	Align the characters on the left or right margin
&c	Center characters that follow between the margins
&p	The page number
&f	The filename
&d	The date
&t	The time
&&	A single ampersand (&)

2. TYPE the following text in the **Footer** text box.

Footer: [&c- &p -............................]

These codes will print the page number in the center of the footer area at the bottom of the page. Each number will include a hyphen mark, a space, the number, a space, and another hyphen in the following format.

- 2 -

Note: The Center code, &c, was used here for practice, although centering is the default. &p would have been centered without the code. The code was included for practice and for showing how multiple codes work together in a header or footer.

3. CHOOSE **No footer on 1st page**

4. CHOOSE **OK**

5. PREVIEW The document using **Preview** from the **Print** menu. Look specifically at pages 2 and 3 to note the footer. Note also that the first page does not contain a footer.

6. PRESS **ESC** when through previewing the document

CREATING A PARAGRAPH HEADER

Most of the time headers and footers will be one line long. The **Headers & Footers** dialog box is used to determine the settings for single-line headers and footers, as well as multi-line ones and the standard ones practiced in the preceding exercise. When a header or footer will contain blocks of typed text customized to your liking, options are selected in the dialog box, and then the header or footer is typed directly in the document space. They are designated by an H or F in the left margin. Although they may appear at the top of the first page in the document, they will print only on pages defined in the dialog box.

CREATE A PARAGRAPH HEADER

1.	CHOOSE	**Headers & Footers** from the **Print** menu
2.	DELETE	the **Footer** setting
3.	LEAVE	the **No footer on 1st page** option on
4.	CHOOSE	**Use header & footer** paragraphs
	Note:	*This command will insert an H for the header and an F for a footer at the top of the page and will allow for either of these blocks of text to be defined separately from other text in the document.*
5.	CHOOSE	**No header on 1st page**
	Note:	*Headers normally do not appear on the first page of a document. This allows for that option.*
6.	PRESS	**Enter** or click **OK**

To type a header paragraph

Text to be used as the header is referred to as a header paragraph. Footers are footer paragraphs. In the document space, an H and an F appear in the upper left corner. Because a footer has already been defined, selecting this option shows the format for the footer.

TYPE A HEADER PARAGRAPH

1.	POSITION	the cursor on the first line of the document next to the **H**

The ruler line shows the automatic settings that are assigned to a header. A center tab is included, as is a right-align tab position on the right margin.

2.	TYPE	the header shown in the following box. Press the **Tab** key twice after typing the word **Agenda** to right align the rest of the text on the right margin.

AGENDA   Puget Sound Charters

To insert special commands

Special commands such as the date, time, or filename may be used in headers and footers. These options are found in the **Insert Special Character** command in the **Edit** menu.

With the cursor immediately after the s in Charters in the header,

INSERT SPECIAL COMMANDS

1. **PRESS** the **Spacebar** to insert a blank space
2. **CHOOSE** **Insert Special Character** from the **Edit** menu
3. **CHOOSE** **Print date** and **OK** or press Enter

The date may wrap to the next line and appear under the word **Agenda**. The **Center** tab position may limit the space that is available on the line.

4. **SELECT** the header line or lines
5. **CHOOSE** **Tabs** from the **Format** menu
6. **PRESS** **Ctrl/Right Arrow**; while holding the **Ctrl** key down use the **Right Arrow** key to move to the C in the ruler line
7. **CHOOSE** **Delete**
8. **CHOOSE** **Done**

If the header appears on two lines delete the tabs preceeding **Puget Sound Charter**

9. **DELETE** the date appearing just below the header and footer markers
10. **PREVIEW** and then save the document as **CH8PR1**.

CREATING A MULTILINE HEADER

Multiline headers are created by inserting an end-of-line mark at the end of the first line of the header. Headers can be as long as you wish. The only requirement is that the header margin be long enough to accommodate the header text (see Setting Margins). An end-of-line marker is a downward arrow ↓. This is achieved by pressing **Shift/Enter** at the end of the line. It may also be inserted by choosing the **Insert Special Character** command in the **Edit** menu and selecting the **End-Of-Line Mark** option in the dialog box.

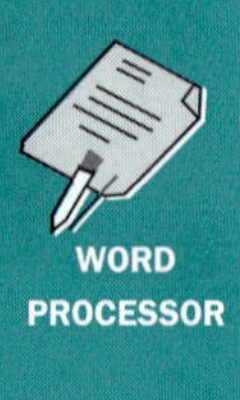

CREATE A MULTILINE HEADER

1. POSITION the cursor immediately after the second asterisk (*) in date (*date*) at the end of the first header line

2. PRESS **Shift/Enter**

Note: *The downward arrow will appear only if the **Show All Characters** option in the Show dialog box is turned on from the **Options** menu.*

3. TAB to the right-align tab position (R)

4. TYPE the following second line for the header

```
                                                      Marketing Department
```

The first page of this document now appears similar to the one shown in the following box. Do not worry if the margins or spacing differ slightly; however, the header and footer lines should be the same.

```
H  AGENDA                              Puget Sound Charters *date*
H                                           Marketing Department
F                          Page - *page*


                         PUGET SOUND CHARTERS
                      AGENDA FOR MARKETING MEETINGS
                         NOVEMBER 20, 1991

This agenda contains a list of items to be discussed at the
next marketing meeting. Please read through each item care-
fully prior to the meeting. If you have any
```

REVIEWING PRINTER SETUP

Works contains commands for changing the type and model of printer in use. The **Printer Setup** dialog box also contains other options for the type of paper in use, the connection being used, and the density of graphics printout. These options may be preset in your computer environment. Unless you are working independently and have set up your own equipment, these options are usually determined by a computer administrator or the instructor. Should you need to make any changes in the current setting, the options available in the **Printer Setup** dialog box will be reviewed briefly.

REVIEW PRINTER SETUP

1. CHOOSE **Printer Setup** from the **Print** menu

The dialog box shown in Figure 8-4 appears.

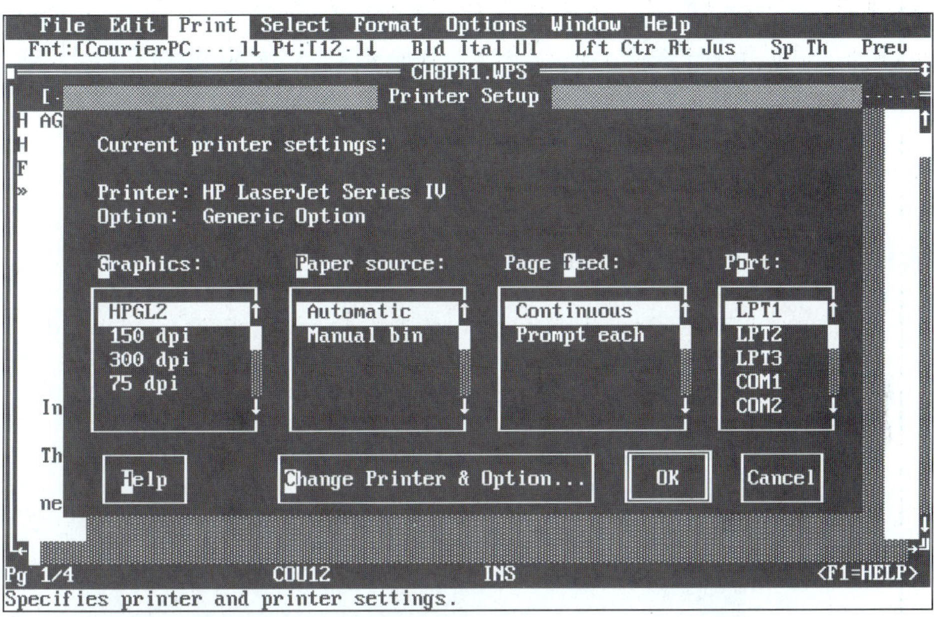

FIGURE 8-4
PRINTER SETUP
DIALOG BOX

The options are summarized in Table 8-2.

USE THIS OPTION	TO CHANGE THIS
Printer:	The name of the printer currently in use.
Option:	Type of fonts in use.
Graphics:	The dots per inch when printing a graphic image. Use of this option will vary with the type of printer you are using. You may have no graph option as shown in the example.
Page feed:	The type of paper in use. The options are continuous (sheets connected in a continuous form) and manual (using individual sheets of paper fed from a paper tray or manually).
Paper Source:	Indicates if paper will be fed automatically, or if you will have to insert paper when printing
Port:	The printer cable connection. Usually the first printer in use is connected to LPT1 (port 1); the second printer to

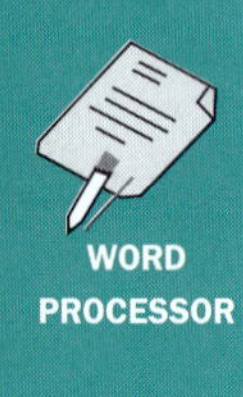

TABLE 8-2
PRINTER SETUP
DIALOG BOX
OPTIONS

	LPT2, and so on. The COM1 and COM2 options are for connecting a mouse or a modem (see Part 5).
Change Printer Option:	Change the type of printer in use when more than one printer file is available.

2. CHOOSE **Cancel** to leave this dialog box

CREATING FOOTNOTES

Footnotes are generally used to cite references used in a document. When a footnote is created, Works inserts a reference number that is superscripted, such as the number 1. Although Works assigns the reference number automatically, you can also specify other characters,such as an asterisk (*), to make the reference. Footnotes are entered in a footnote pane at the bottom of the screen that shows when the **Footnote** command from the **Edit** menu is selected.

CREATE FOOTNOTES

1. POSITION the cursor immediately after the period at the end of the first sentence in the second paragraph **(...meetings.)**

2. CHOOSE **Footnote** from the **Edit** menu

3. CHOOSE **Character mark** for this footnote

4. PRESS the **Down Arrow** key **once**

5. TYPE an asterisk (*)

6. PRESS **Enter** or click **OK**

A footnote pane appears at the bottom half of the screen as shown in Figure 8-5.

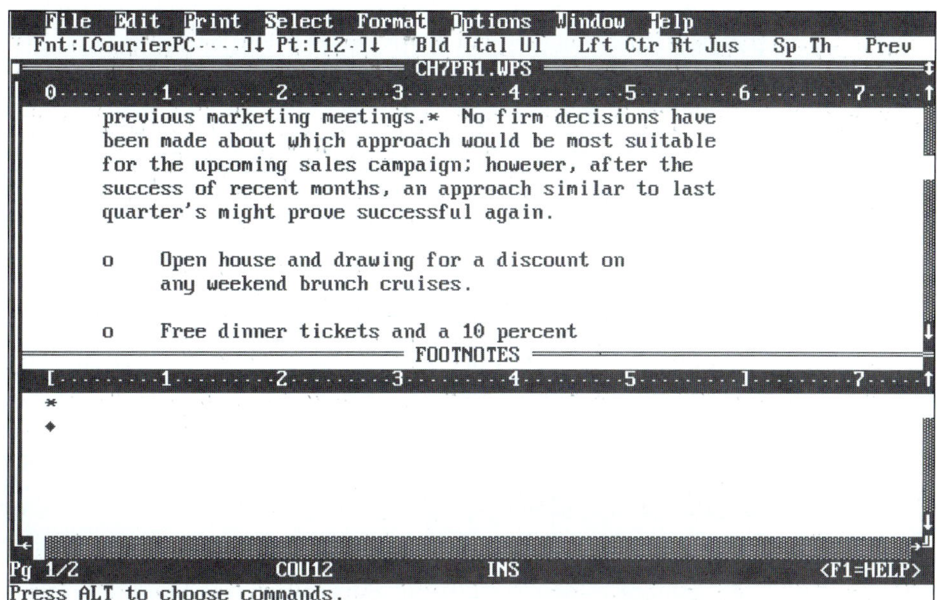

FIGURE 8-5 FOOTNOTE PANE INSERTED INTO A DOCUMENT

Text is then typed into this window as it would be in any other document space.

7. TYPE the text shown in the following box as the footnote.

> See minutes for September 18 and October 15 meetings.

8. PRESS **F6** to return to the document window

All footnotes are entered in the same manner. If you are typing a long document and wish to enter several footnotes while typing text, you can either leave both windows open using the **F6** key to toggle between them or close and open the window.

Closing a footnote pane

You can close the footnote pane without losing the footnote references. Footnotes will appear either at the bottom of the page or at the end of the document when the document is printed or when using **Print Preview** to look at the document.

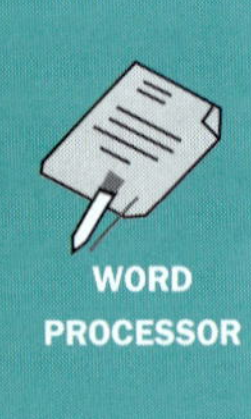

CLOSE A FOOTNOTE PANEL

1. **CHOOSE** **Show** from the **Options** menu
2. **CHOOSE** **Show Footnotes** to turn off the option
3. **PRESS** **Enter** or click **OK**

MOVING A FOOTNOTE REFERENCE MARK

You can move a reference mark using the **Move** command from the **Edit** menu. It is moved as any other block of text.

MOVE A FOOTNOTE REFERENCE MARK

1. **SELECT** the reference mark (*)
2. **CHOOSE** **Move** from the **Edit** menu
3. **POSITION** the cursor immediately after the period at the end of this paragraph
4. **PRESS** **Enter**

INSERTING ADDITIONAL REFERENCE MARKS

The Footnote pane can be opened again using the **Show Footnotes** option in the **Show** dialog box from the **Options** menu. Once the pane is first created and a footnote reference made, it is quickly opened and closed using this command.

INSERT ADDITIONAL REFERENCE MARKS

1. **CHOOSE** **Show** from the **Options** menu
2. **CHOOSE** **Show Footnotes**
3. **PRESS** **Enter** or click **OK**
4. **POSITION** the cursor at the end of the second itemized paragraph ending with **March 1**.
5. **CHOOSE** **Footnote** from the **Edit** menu
6. **CHOOSE** **Character mark**
7. **TYPE** an asterisk (*) in the **Mark** box
8. **PRESS** **Enter** or click **OK**
9. **TYPE** the following footnote

> This offer is limited to no more than 150 tickets.

10. PRESS   **F6** or use the mouse button to move to the document window

11. POSITION the cursor after the word **period** in the paragraph following the itemized listing (second paragraph)

12. CHOOSE   **Footnote** from the **Edit** menu

13. CHOOSE   **Character mark** and type an asterisk in the **Mark** box

14. PRESS   **Enter** or click OK

15. TYPE   the footnote in the following box.

> Based on individual rates.

Note: *You can also scroll through either the document window or the footnote pane as you would any other document space. Doing so at this time would allow you to see all three of the footnotes.*

16. SAVE   the document **CH8PR1** again. (You can save with the pane open.)

17. USE   the scroll bar or the **Arrow** keys to so that all footnotes in the **Footnote** pane are visible (if necessary).

POSITIONING THE CURSOR AT A REFERENCE MARK

The cursor can quickly be positioned at a reference mark point in the document by using the reference numbers or symbols in the Footnote pane. When the cursor is on a particular footnote in the pane and the **F6** key is pressed, the cursor is moved to the same reference mark in the body of the document.

From the Footnote pane and with the cursor on the third footnote,

POSITION THE CURSOR AT A REFERENCE MARK

1. MOVE   to the document window (**F6** or use the mouse button)

The cursor is immediately positioned next to the last footnote entry.

2.	PRESS	F6 again
3.	POSITION	the cursor under the second footnote in the **Footnote** pane
4.	PRESS	F6

The second reference is located in the document.

DELETING A FOOTNOTE

Footnotes are easily removed by deleting the reference mark in the document.

DELETE A FOOTNOTE

1.	PRESS	F6 to return to the **Footnote** pane (if necessary)
2.	POSITION	the cursor under the third footnote (if necessary)
3.	PRESS	F6 to move the cursor to the document window
4.	PRESS	the **Backspace** key to delete the footnote reference mark

The reference mark and the footnote text in the pane are removed.

5.	CHOOSE	**Undo** from the **Edit** menu
6.	CLOSE	the **Footnote** pane (use the **Show** command from the **Options** menu) and save the document again.

USING BOOKMARKS

Bookmarks are used to mark positions in a long document so that you can relocate them quickly. This would be useful, for example, to relocate quickly to any one of several subheadings or sections in a long manuscript. For the exercise in using bookmarks, sub headings will be added to this document. The bookmark will be identified through this subheading.

USE BOOKMARKS

1.	POSITION	the cursor on the line above the first paragraph, **This agenda contains...**
2.	PRESS	the **Enter** key twice
3.	LEFT	align the text if necessary using the Toolbar.
4.	TYPE	the following side heading underlined (use the Toolbar to underline).

Introduction

5. POSITION the cursor on the left margin above the second paragraph, **The following items...**

6. PRESS **Enter** once

Type the following side heading and press **Enter** once.

Marketing Approaches

7. POSITION the cursor under the first word, **the**, in the paragraph following the itemized list

8. PRESS **Enter** once

9. PRESS the **Up Arrow** key once

10. TYPE the following side heading.

Top Sales

11. ADD the following heading on the blank line above the last paragraph beginning with **The meeting will...** Add blank lines as necessary.

Conclusion

12. SAVE the document again.

CREATING A BOOKMARK

CREATE A BOOKMARK

1. **POSITION**   the cursor under the **I** in **Introduction**, the first subheading

2. **CHOOSE**   **Bookmark Name** from the **Edit** menu

The dialog box shown in Figure 8-6 appears.

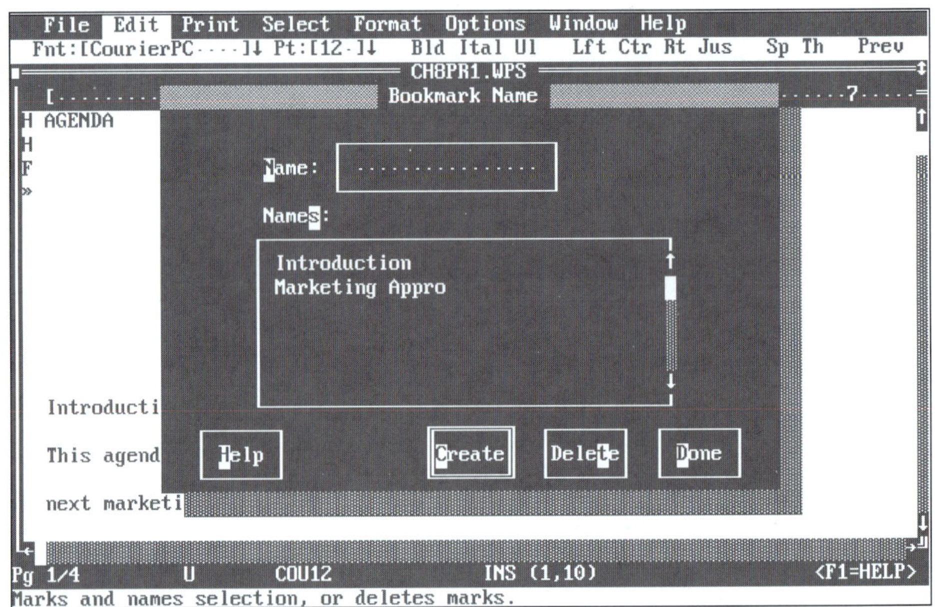

FIGURE 8-6
BOOKMARK NAME
DIALOG BOX

In this dialog box a name is given to the bookmark. As names are created, they will appear in the **Names** list box. When a name is typed, the **Create** option is chosen. **Bookmarks** are deleted using the **Delete** option.

3. **TYPE**   **Introduction** as the name of the first bookmark

   Note: *It is a good idea to use a brief name for the identification and one that you will recognize easily. In the case of these subheadings it is easy to do. When identifying more complex blocks of text, remember to use short titles that tell about the contents of the block of text.*

4. **CHOOSE**   **Create**

5. **POSITION**   the cursor under the second heading, **Marketing Approaches** and press **Enter** once

6. **CHOOSE**   **Bookmark Name** from the **Edit** menu again

7.	TYPE	**Marketing Approaches** as the **Name**
8.	CHOOSE	**Create**
9.	CREATE	bookmarks for the remaining subheadings using the same procedure

GOING TO A BOOKMARK

Now that the bookmarks are created, you can move to them.

GO TO A BOOKMARK

1.	CHOOSE	**Go To** from the **Select** menu

The dialog box with the names of the bookmarks appears.

	Note:	*The name **Marketing Approach** is only partially shown. That is okay. The title can be only as long as the Name text box; however, enough of the title is showing to identify the heading.*
2.	MOVE	to the **Names** list box (use **Alt/N** or the mouse button)
3.	CHOOSE	**Marketing Appro** (for marketing approach)
4.	PRESS	**Enter** or click **OK**

The cursor is positioned at the side heading, **Marketing Approach**.

5.	PRACTICE	moving to other bookmarks on your own

ADDING BORDERS

You can add borders to blocks of text to draw attention to them. Borders are lines that surround the text on one or all sides. They can be shown using a single line, double line, or bold line. Borders are created using the **Borders** command from the **Format** menu.

ADD BORDERS

1.	POSITION	the cursor on the line above the column headings in the sales table in this document
2.	PRESS	**Enter** once to add an extra blank line
3.	SELECT	the entire table, including the blank line above and the blank line below

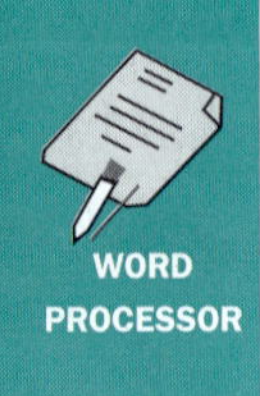

4. CHOOSE   **Borders** from the **Format** menu

The dialog box shown in Figure 8-7 appears.

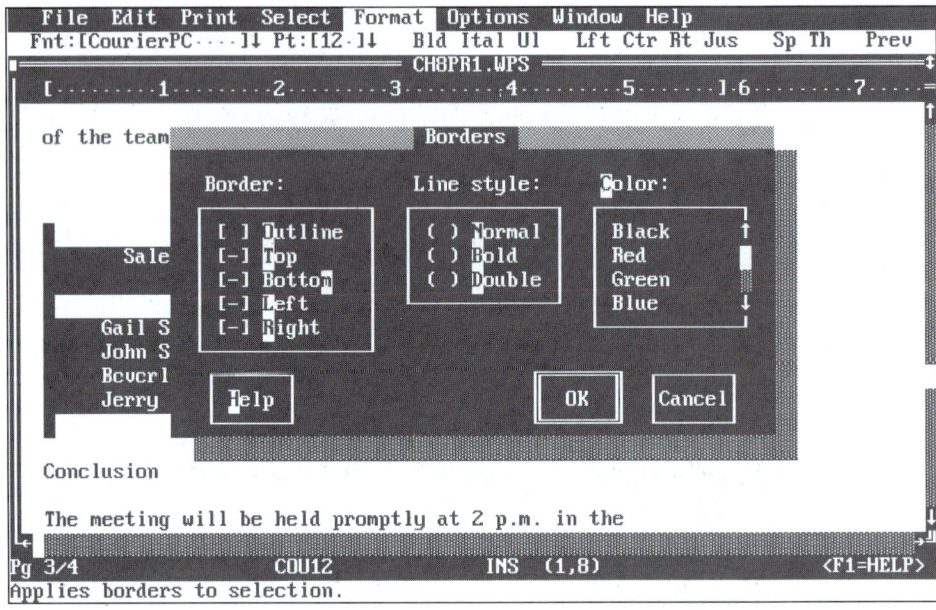

FIGURE 8-7
BORDERS DIALOG
BOX

The **Border** options box shows the following available options.

USE THIS BORDER OPTION	TO DO THIS
Outline	Insert lines on all sides of the text selected.
Top	Insert a line only on the top of the text selected.
Bottom	Insert a line only on the bottom of the text selected.
Left	Insert a line on the left side of text selected.
Right	Insert a line on the right side of text selected.

Options for the line style are shown in the next option box. They include normal, bold, and double style lines. If you have a color monitor and/or printer, you may also change the color of the border in the **Color** list box.

5. CHOOSE   **Outline** from the **Border** box

6. CHOOSE   **Normal** from the **Line Style** box

7. PRESS   **Enter** or click **OK**

A border is added.

Note: *If the last paragraph marker is indented, position the cursor under it and press Ctrl/G twice to left-align.*

MAKING MODIFICATIONS TO BORDERS

To make other modifications, such as changing the line style to double or bold, choose **Border** from the **Format** menu after selecting the entire block of text within the border and make the changes in the dialog box. They will replace the old border settings.

RINTING OPTIONS FOR MULTIPAGE DOCUMENTS

There are several options available from the **Print** dialog box in the **Print** menu. This dialog box was reviewed briefly in Chapter 2 under *Printing a Document*. The options found in this box will be discussed as they relate to printing the current document, **CH8PR1**.

PRINT OPTIONS FOR MULTIPAGE DOCUMENTS

1,   SELECT   **Print** from the **Print** menu.

Table 8-3 gives a description of the options found in this dialog box.

USE THIS OPTION	TO DO THIS
Number of copies: [1. . . .]	Print one or more copies of a document using a single command.
[ ] Print specific pages	Print an individual page or a range of pages from a multipage document using options found in the Print dialog box. Using this document, you could print the entire document, pages 2 and 3 only, page 3 only, and so on.
[ ] Print to file	Create a file containing all commands normally sent to a printer. It can then be sent to another computer, printed using the DOS PRINT command, and so on.
[ ] Draft quality	Print draft quality for all rough draft copies. Choosing this option is usually done using dot matrix printers. Dot matrix printers normally use ink ribbons. If printing letter quality, the print head moves over the surface of the ribbon two or more times. For draft quality, the print head moves over the ribbon surface only once - thus saving the wear and tear on the ribbon. With laser printers, this option would not make a difference.

TABLE 8-3 PRINT DIALOG BOX OPTIONS

PRINTING SPECIFIC PAGES

Leave the setting in the **Number of copies** box at 1.

PRINT SPECIFIC PAGES

1. CHOOSE **Print specific pages**

The **Pages** line appears (it was showing in lighter letters) so that you can specify the pages to print.

2. PRESS the **Down Arrow** key once to move to the **Pages** box (oruse **Alt/G**)

3. TYPE **2-3** to print only pages 2 and 3

When typing a single page, enter the page number by itself, such as 2 or 3. When typing a range of pages, the first and last page numbers are typed separated by either a hyphen (-) as in step 3 or by a colon (:) as in 2:3. Individual pages of a very long document can also be printed: for example, 1,5,8,15,24,48 and so on.

Be sure you are on line to the printer.

4. CHOOSE **Print**

Pages 2 and 3 are printed.

Other options in the **Print** dialog box that will probably be most useful are printing draft-quality or printing multiple copies. Practice both of these at this time if desired.

5. PRINT a copy of the full document (use **Print**, **Print**, and **OK**)

GUIDED TUTORIAL

WHAT YOU'LL DO

- Create paragraph indents.
- Create headers and footers.
- Use bookmarks to move quickly through a long document.
- Set and change tab positions.
- Create footnotes.

HOW TO DO IT

1. TYPE the first part of the manuscript as follows (do not worry about the alignment of the margins) or retrieve it from the instructor's data disk. It is called **CH8TUTA.** Further instructions will follow. Use 12-point Times or a similar font. Bold, center, and justify the text as shown.

PUGET SOUND CHARTERS
NEEDS ANALYSIS
Report Presented to Management
for Computer Equipment Purchases

Introduction

This is a needs analysis requested by the management of Puget Sound Charters. The management team is interested in researching the possibility of purchasing computer equipment for the office to increase productivity.

Justification: The microcomputer has more than proved itself a valuable tool in the office during the past two decades since its inception. In numbers alone, it has shown that people are demanding and using their computers. In 1980, $1 billion worth of microcomputers had been sold; in 1990 that figure reached beyond $50 billion. Microcomputers have consistently increased in speed and efficiency. The storage capacity, processing speed, and power of the microcomputer is the most competitive marketing tactic in use by vendors. Another keen focus of the microcomputer community has been in the development of software programs. Where micros initially were capable of running a single, and somewhat limited, program at a time, they now run very complex and sophisticated programs that do more for the user and perform faster.

The user interface is also important. Users want operating systems and software that are easy to use and takes a minimum of time to learn. This has been provided by both the Macintosh system and the IBM personal computers and compatibles.

WORD PROCESSOR

Programs: Word processing was perhaps the most popular use of micro-computers in the early years of software development; however, other software programs were also heavily used. Among the most popular programs were those for file management and spreadsheet applications. Today, many programs are available. Nearly any need for a particular application can be met. Among some of the popular ones in use today are very sophisticated word processing programs capable of outputting graphic images, using tables, performing calculations, and merging documents, to name a few. Database management programs are not only more sophisticated, but easier to use and capable of handling complex queries on multiple tables. Spreadsheet programs offer worksheets that hold thousands of cells and perform quick calculations. Many programs, such as Microsoft Works, combined these tools into a single application - thus making it easy to move quickly from one application to another and to integrate applications.

2. **SAVE** the document, as **CH8TUTB**.

3. **CHOOSE** **Page Setup & Margins** from the **Print** menu.

4. **TYPE** **2.0** as the Top margin

5. **CHOOSE** **OK** or press Enter to close the dialog box

6. **BE SURE** that the right margin is justified. Use either the **Toolbar** or the **Justified** command from the **Format** menu.

7. **POSITION** the cursor under the **v** of **very** in the fifth sentence of the **Programs** paragraph.

8. **PRESS** the **Enter** key twice to start itemized paragraphs.

9. **TYPE** an asterisk (*) in front of the **V** in **Very** (capitalize the V).

10. **PRESS** the **Tab** key onceafter the *

11. **PRESS** **Ctrl/H** twice to create a hanging indent

12. **POSITION** the cursor under the **D** in **Database** in the next sentence.

13. **PRESS** the **Enter** key twice.

14. **TYPE** *; press **Tab**

The paragraphs should appear similar to the following.

Programs: Word processing was perhaps the most popular use of micro-computers in the early years of software development; however, other software programs were also heavily used. Among the most popular programs were those for file management and spreadsheet applications. Today, many programs are available. Nearly any need for a particular application can be met. Among some of the popular ones in use today are

* Very sophisticated word processing programs capable of outputting graphic images, using tables, performing calculations, and merging documents, to name a few.

* Database management programs are not only more sophisticated, but easier to use and capable of handling complex queries on multiple tables.

Spreadsheet programs offer worksheets that hold thousands of cells and perform quick calculations. Many programs, such as Microsoft Works, combined these tools into a single application - thus making it easy to move quickly from one application to another and to integrate applications.

---

15. INDENT the sentence beginning with **Spreadsheet** the same way.

16. POSITION the cursor under the word **M** in the word **Many** in the sentence following the spreadsheet sentence.

17. PRESS the **Enter** key twice and **Ctrl/g** twice.

The text now appears similar to that shown in the following box.

Programs: Word processing was perhaps the most popular use of micro-computers in the early years of software development; however, other software programs were also heavily used. Among the most popular programs were those for file management and spreadsheet applications. Today, many programs are available. Nearly any need for a particular application can be met. Among some of the popular ones in use today are

* very sophisticated word processing programs capable of outputting graphic images, using tables, performing calculations, and merging documents, to name a few.
* Database management programs are not only more sophisticated, but easier to use and capable of handling complex queries on multiple tables.

> * Spreadsheet programs offer worksheets that hold thousands of cells and perform quick calculations.
>
> Many programs, such as Microsoft Works, combined these tools into a single application - thus making it easy to move quickly from one application to another and to integrate applications.

18. POSITION the cursor on the line following the last paragraph.

19. PRESS the **Enter** key **once**.

20. CHOOSE **Tabs** from the **Format** menu.

21. POSITION **left tab** at **1** on the ruler line.

22. POSITION a **right tab** with dot **leaders** at 5 on the ruler.

23. BE SURE to insert each tab position. Choose **Done** when finished.

24. TYPE Integrated programs may include:

25. PRESS the **Enter** key **twice**.

26. PRESS the **Tab** key **once**.

27. TYPE **Word Processing** and press the **Tab** key.

28. TYPE **A document tool** and press **Enter**.

The first line of the table should appear similar to that shown in the following box.

> Many programs, such as Microsoft Works, combined these tools into a single application - thus making it easy to move quickly from one application to another and to integrate applications.
>
> Integrated programs may include:
>
> Word Processing ....A document tool

29. USE the **Tab** key to complete the table as shown below.

> Spreadsheet... A numbers tool
> Database .... A facts collection tool
> Communications....................... A sending/receiving tool
> Draw... A graphics tool

30. SELECT   all lines of the table, beginning with **Word processing,**

31. CHOOSE   **Tabs** from the **Format** menu.

32. PRESS   **Ctrl/Right Arrow** to **.7** on the ruler and insert a left tab position.

33. MOVE   to position **1** on the ruler and delete this tab position.

34. MOVE   to position **5** and delete it.

35. MOVE   to position **5.5** on the ruler and insert a **right align, dot leader** tab position.

36. CHOOSE   **Done** when finished.

37. POSITION   the cursor on the line below the table and press the **Enter** key **twice.**

38. POSITION   the cursor above the table and press the **Enter** key to add an extra blank line.

39. SELECT   all lines of the table and one blank line above and one below the table.

40. CHOOSE   **Borders** from the **Format** menu.

41. CHOOSE   **Outline** and **Double**. Choose **OK** or press Enter when finished.

42. SAVE   the document with the changes as **CH8TUTB.**

The last paragraph and table should appear similar to the following.

Many programs, such as Microsoft Works, combined these tools into a single application - thus making it easy to move quickly from one application to another and to integrate applications.

Integrated programs may include:

Word Processing	A document tool
Spreadsheet	A numbers tool
Database	A facts collection tool
Communications	A sending/receiving tool
Draw	A graphics tool

---

43. POSITION   the cursor immediately following the word **billion** and the period in the third sentence of the **Justification** paragraph.

44. CHOOSE   **Footnote** from the **Edit** menu.

45. CHOOSE   **OK** or press Enter to accept the **Numbered** format.

46. TYPE   the following footnote in the footnote pane and next to the number **1,**.

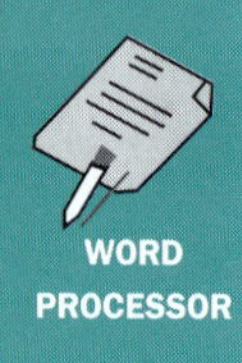

Williams, J. J., "The Rise in Computer Sales", <u>The PC Market</u>, January 1990, Vol. 15, No. 2, pp. 120-125.

47. **INSERT** a second footnote following the word **faster** at the end of the first **Justification** paragraph. The footnote text is:

Johansson, S., "A New Market", <u>Technology Today</u>, March 1989, p. 270.

The footnote window pane should show the following new footnotes.

[1]Williams, J. J., "The Rise in Computer Sales", <u>The PC Market</u>, January 1990, Vol. 15, No. 2, pp. 120-125.

[2]Johansson, S., "A New Market", <u>Technology Today</u>, March 1989, p. 270.

48. **CHOOSE** **Show** and **Show Footnotes** from the **Options** menu to turn off the footnote window.

49. **CHOOSE** **Headers & Footers** from the **Print** menu.

50. **CHOOSE** **Use header & footer paragraphs** and press **Enter** or choose OK.

51. **TYPE** **PUGET SOUND CHARTERS** in the header line at the top of the document and press the **Tab** key twice.

52. **TYPE** **Needs Analysis** on the right **margin**.

53. **POSITION** the cursor immediately to the left of the side heading **Introduction**.

54. **CHOOSE** **Bookmark Name** from the **Edit** menu.

55. **TYPE** **Intro** as the name and choose **Create.**

56. **CREATE** bookmarks for each of the side headings and the table.

57. **RUN** a spell check on the document.

58. **SAVE** the document again as **CH8TUTB**.

59. **PREVIEW** the document and then print a copy.

REVIEW QUESTIONS

1. The _____________________ command from the _________________ menu is used to change the margins in a document.

2. List the margins that may be changed in a document.

3. What are the standard settings for margins in a document?

4. A header is printed in the _____________ margin.

5. A footer is printed in the _____________ margin.

6. The margin is considered the area from the _________________ of the paper to the ____________ text.

7. Which of the following is the standard paper height and width?

    a. 8 1/2 by 11 inches
    b. 11 by 8 1/2 inches
    c. 11 1/2 by 8 inches
    d. 8 by 11 1/2 inches

8. The keystroke combination **Ctrl/G** will remove which of the following?

    a. A hanging indent
    b. A right indent
    c. A left-aligned tab position
    d. Dot leader tab positions

9. Which of the following keystroke combinations may be used to set tab positions when in the **Tabs** dialog box?

    a. Alt/Up Arrow
    b. Ctrl/Up or Down Arrow
    c. Ctrl/Left or Right Arrow
    d. Alt/Left or Right Arrow

10. Describe briefly how you would change existing tab positions in a table.

11. List the four types of tabs available in the **Tabs** dialog box.

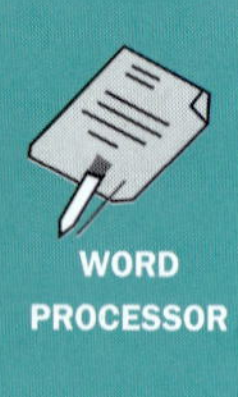

12. What is a tab leader?

13. How is a tab position deleted?

14. Match each of the following phrases to the appropriate keystroke combinations.

______   Moves to the top of the document

______   Inserts a manual page break

______   Moves to a position on the ruler line

______   Moves between a footnote pane and the document pane

______   Used in multiline headers

   a. Ctrl/Right Arrow
   b. Ctrl/Home
   c. Shift/Enter
   d. Ctrl/Enter
   e. F6

15. Which of the following commands is used to open or close a footnote pane?
   a. **Footnotes** from the **Edit** menu
   b. **Show Footnotes** from the **Edit** menu
   c. **Show Footnotes** from the **Options** menu
   d. **Show** from the **Options** menu

16. Briefly describe the function of a bookmark.

17. The _________________ command from the **Select** menu is accessed when using bookmarks.

18. Where may borders be added in a document?

19. How is a border changed?

HANDS-ON EXERCISES 

EXERCISE 1

1. Open the document **CH8TUTB** which you created in Chapter 8; or retrieve it from the instructor's data disk.. If you have not completed the document, it may be retrieved from the instructor's disk. On that disk it is named **CH8HO1A**.

2. Add the following text to the bottom of the document. Leave a single blank line below the table. Tab once to indent the itemized list (*); tab once after the asterisk.

Need: The point at which a company needs to make a decision about the purchase of a microcomputer or other computer equipment can vary. Some of the major factors include:

* Increased volume of paperwork
* Need for additional office personnel
* Difficulty in locating information quickly
* Excessive time spent in organization
* Lack of proper backup of company-related documents

When the efficiency of an office seems to be less than at its peak, it is probably time for an analysis of the situation, as in the case of Puget Sound Charters.

Results: This team has spent the past month monitoring the activities performed on a daily basis at Puget Sound Charters and as a result arrived at the following as an account of the time and money spent on individual activities.

---

3. Run a spell check on the document and proof the content.

4. Double space the main body of the document except the heading, any itemized lists, and the table. Leave one blank line between each paragraph. Leave two blank lines prior to every subheading, such as Programs and Need.

5. Change the margins to a left margin of 2.0 and a right margin of 1.0. The left margin of this document will later be bound in a cover.

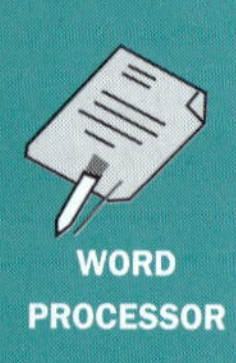

6. Create a third footnote at the end of the **Programs** paragraph. The footnote text is shown below.

Zeigler, B. "Productivity Research Results," Puget Sound Charters, 1991.

7. Create the following footer, centered at the bottom of the first page. Modify the header so that it does not appear on the first page.

Page -1-

8. Add bookmarks for any subheadings added to this document.

9. Save the document as **CH8HO1B**.

EXERCISE 2

1. Open **CH8HO1B** if necessary.

2. Move the **Need** paragraph (including the itemized list) so that it appears just before the **Justification** paragraph.

3. Add the following table at the bottom of the document (on the second line below the last paragraph). Press the Enter key twice after the table. Reset the tabs before typing the column headings (use Center tab settings) and reset them again before typing the main lines in the table (use a left-align in the first column, right-align in the second, and decimal in the third). Start by guessing the tab positions. They may need to be adjusted after the table is completed. Select and underline the column headings.

Activity	Average time	Average overall
Typing	4.5 hours	45.00
Editing & Revisions	3.0 hours	30.00
Photocopying	1.5 hours	35.00
Mailing Activities	1.0 hour	20.00
Printing Services	NA	15.00
Accounting	6.0 hours	120.00
Advertising	4.0 hours	100.00

4. Add the following paragraphs beginning on the second blank line below the table. Format as shown (leaving the double space) and reset tabs where necessary.

Summary: It is the recommendation of this team that time could be saved in all the activities observed during the past month. Time spent making revisions of documents could be lessened through the use of a word processing program. Many observations of completely retyping documents were made.

Photocopies are made of all documents. This is the only method of making multiple copies to send to clients, company personnel, and others. While a photocopy is a good copy, it is not as good as an original and it costs more. It is far less expensive to print multiple copies using a good letter-quality printer or laser printer than to photocopy pages.

Mailing activities included typing original mailing labels. Again, a database file and a word processing program would eliminate the need to retype frequently used mailing labels. The labels can also be used to merge with form letters and a file in a database program to gather information about client needs.

The same observations are true for the printing and accounting expenses and with some of the advertising expenses. Many of the printing services could be eliminated with either a sophisticated word processing program or a desktop publishing program.

Recommendation: It is the recommendation of this team that the following equipment be purchased to increase productivity and decrease costs.

> A personal computer using the DOS operating system.
> A word processing program.
> An accounting or spreadsheet program.
> A database program.
>
> OR
>
> An integrated software program such as Microsoft Works which includes word processing, graphics, spreadsheet, database, and communications capabilities.
>
>
> A letter-quality or laser printer.

Information on cost will be provided early next month.

5. Create bookmarks on any new subheadings.

6. Double-space this part of the document, with the exception of the itemized list in the **Recommendation** paragraph.

7. Create hanging indents of all itemized paragraphs.

8. Run a spell check on the document.

9. Look at the placement of page breaks in **Print Preview.** Make any adjustments. Keep the table with the previous paragraph. The **Recommendation** paragraph should not be separated.

10. Check the document again in Print Preview. When the document looks completed, save it as **CH8HO2**, and print a copy.

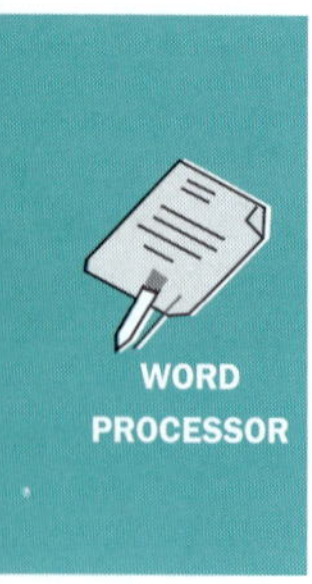
WORD
PROCESSOR

9 WORKS WINDOWS AND OTHER ACCESSORIES

Objectives

- View Works settings.

- Create templates.

- Use templates.

- Edit templates.

- Use windows.

- Use split screens.

- Use the calculator.

- Use the alarm clock.

- Use the WorksWizard.

PREVIEW ➤

In this chapter we wrap up Part 2 by using Works windows and other Works accessories. The Works program includes settings that specialize Works for different environments, a calculator that works like a pocket calculator and may be used for quick calculations, and an alarm clock that will alert you to specific times, dates, and other messages.

We also cover the window options more extensively and review how to move, size, maximize, arrange, and split a window. You will also be introduced to the Works Wizard tool — a quick way to create documents and locate files.

VIEWING WORKS SETTINGS

The **Works Settings** command in the **Options** menu contains many choices for customizing the screens and printouts of Works. Options available include (1) choosing a different country's standard currency format or measurements, (2) adjusting the screen color, (3) connecting modems, (4) modifying the dial tone in communications, and so on. Although you will probably not want to change these options at this time, it is good to know where they are located and how they can be applied. You may wish to make some modifications on your own system, or change some settings later if working with communications. The settings will be reviewed here briefly for your information.

From the opening Works' screen,

VIEW WORKS SETTINGS

1. **CHOOSE**   **Works settings** from the **Options** menu

The dialog box shown in Figure 9-1 appears.

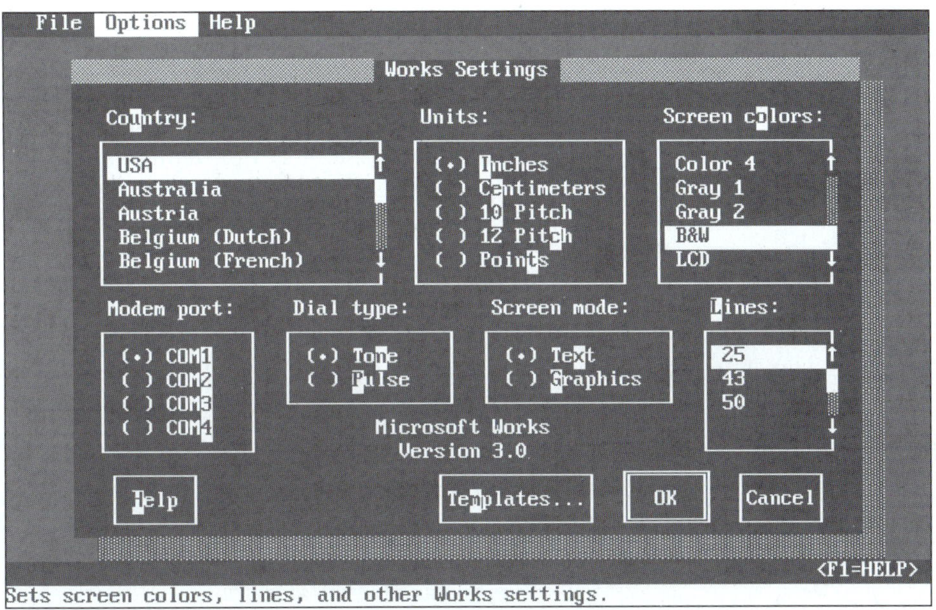

FIGURE 9-1
WORKS SETTINGS
DIALOG BOX

This dialog box includes the options listed in Table 9-1. Some of these are discussed or used in later chapters, such as those dealing with communications.

THIS OPTION	WILL CHANGE THIS
Country	The page length and width, currency symbol, date and time presentation, month name, and other miscellaneous items that Works uses as preset options.
Units	The unit of measure being used for page size and margins. This option also includes mailing labels, tab stops, and paragraph indents.
Screen colors	The color of the screen when using a color monitor or the shade of gray on both color and monochrome monitors.
Modem port	The port to which the communications line is connected.
Dial type	The type of dial tone you want to hear when using a modem.
Screen mode	The display of the text on the screen. Text will display formatted characters in highlighted or colored mode; graphic will display most format options as they will be printed, such as in italics or underlined.
Lines	The number of lines that Works displays on the screen.
Templates	A template containing frequently used formats, such as a word processing document that contains frequently used headers, footers, and margin settings.

TABLE 9-1
WORKS SETTINGS
DIALOG BOX
OPTIONS

CREATING A TEMPLATE

A *template* contains a format for a document space that has with it frequently used settings. *Templates* can be created for any type of file in Works — word processing, spreadsheet, and database. A sample *template* for a word processing document might be one with a standard header, page numbers, and preset margins and tabs. If you are creating many documents that use the same format, designing a *template* saves time in resetting standard formats.

CREATE A TEMPLATE

1. **CHOOSE**   **Cancel** to exit from this dialog box

From the opening Works' screen,

2. **CHOOSE**   **Create New File** from the **File** menu and choose **Word Processor** as the application

Now is the time to set up the exact format that you want to save as a template.

CHANGING THE PAGE LAYOUT

CHANGE THE PAGE LAYOUT

1. **CHOOSE**   **Page Setup & Margins** from the **Print** menu
2. **SET**   the left margin at 1.5; set the right margin at 1.0.
3. **CHOOSE**   **OK** or press Enter
4. **CHOOSE**   **Headers & Footers** from the **Print** menu
5. **CHOOSE**   **No header on 1st page**; **No footer on 1st page**; and **Use header & footer paragraphs**
6. **CHOOSE**   **OK** or press Enter

The default for a centered footer is inserted, and a header line appears (without text inserted).

This is a good format for a template. It contains some format changes in the document. Included are a centered page number at the bottom of the page and a blank space for the header. The cursor appears on the blank line below the footer position in the space where text will begin.

7. **CHOOSE**   **Save As** from the **File** menu

8. **CHOOSE**   **Save As Template**

9. **CHOOSE**   **OK** or press Enter

10. **TYPE**   **logo** as the name of this template

11. **CHOOSE**   **OK** or press Enter

12. **CHOOSE**   **Exit Works** from the **File** menu without saving changes

USING A TEMPLATE

A template may be opened like any other document. Use the **Create New File** command from the **File** menu.

USE A TEMPLATE

1. **CHOOSE**   **Create New File** from the **File** menu

2. **CHOOSE**   **logo** from the **Available Templates** box

3. **CHOOSE**   **OK** or press Enter

The format for the logo is opened.

EDITING A TEMPLATE

You can edit an existing template file by opening it and making changes as you would in any other document.

EDIT A TEMPLATE

1. **PRESS**   the **Tab** key twice to move to the **R** (right-aligned) tab position on the right margin

2. **TYPE**   **Puget Sound Charters** as the heading

3. **CHOOSE**   **Save** from the **File** menu

4. **CHOOSE**   **Save As Template**

5. **CHOOSE**   **OK** or press Enter

6. **TYPE**   **logo** as the name of the template

7. **CHOOSE**   **OK** or press Enter

8. **CHOOSE**   **OK** or press Enter again to replace the existing logo template

9. **CLOSE**   this template without saving the changes.

REMOVING A TEMPLATE

Removing or assigning a template is a selection made in the **Options** menu.

REMOVE A TEMPLATE

1.	CHOOSE	**Works Settings** from the **Options** menu
2.	CHOOSE	**Templates**
3.	CHOOSE	the name of the template from the templates list box (logo)
4.	CHOOSE	**Delete**
5.	CHOOSE	**OK**
6.	CHOOSE	**Done**
7.	CHOOSE	**OK** or press Enter

USING WORKS WINDOWS

In the exercises practiced so far in the book, you have been working primarily with one window — the window containing your document. You can, however, work with up to eight windows at a time and move quickly from one to another. When more than one window is open, the title of the window appears in the upper title bar; and the windows are arranged slightly on top of each other with the titles showing. Essentially, windows are stacked on top of each other much as documents are stacked on a desktop. You can look at one and then the other — all documents are open. Text can also be moved and copied from one document to another.

As you work through this book, you will learn that it is the use of windows that allows you to move text easily from one document to another. One open document may contain a spreadsheet, another a database file, and a third a word processing manuscript. Text can be selected, copied, and pasted from one document (or window) to another, and thus from one application to another. This procedure is what integration is all about.

Figure 9-2 shows three open windows. The window on the top of the stack is the open window. Others are accessed either from the keyboard or by clicking the mouse button.

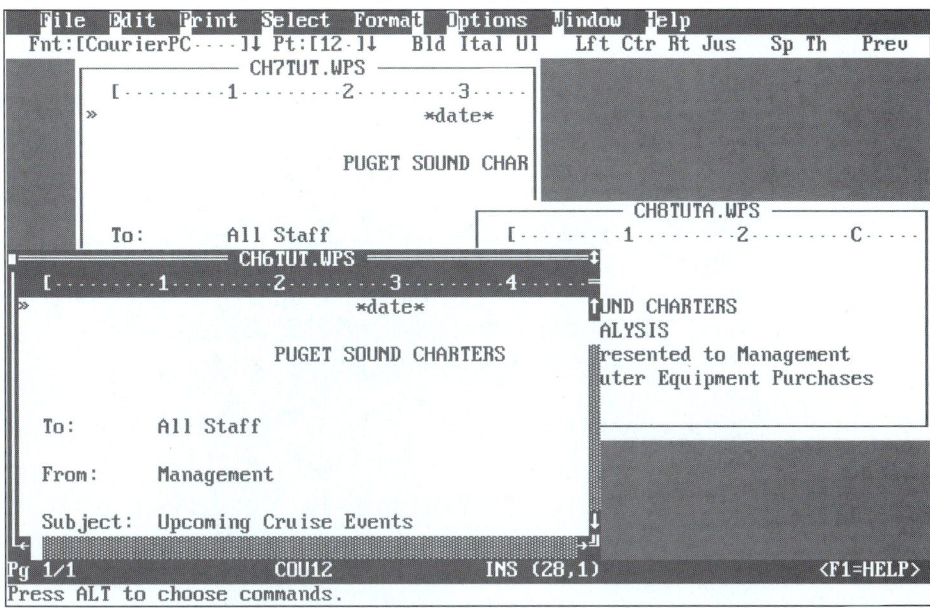

FIGURE 9-2
WORKS WINDOWS

Windows can also be sized, as shown in Figure 9-2, so that more than a single window's contents may be seen at a time.

OPENING MULTIPLE WINDOWS

Showing multiple windows on the screen at one time is simply a matter of opening multiple documents. As you open them, they will appear in the standard document size on the screen. You will practice reducing the size of the windows and moving from one window to another in the following exercise.

OPEN MULTIPLE WINDOWS

INSTRUCTOR'S DATA DISK

1. OPEN   the following three documents which you created in earlier chapters or retrieve them from the instructor's data disk

CH6TUT

CH7TUT

CH8TUTA

They are now shown on the screen layered on top of each other like sheets of paper on a desktop. You can see the names of all three documents stacked on top of one another.

You could continue to open up to eight windows. For now, practice with three. Later, open additional windows and practice moving between them, resizing them, and so on.

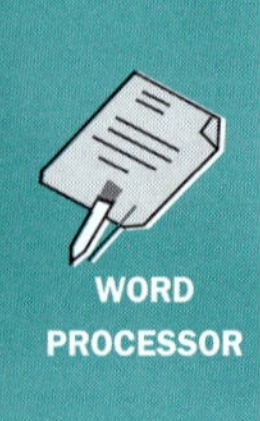

MOVING BETWEEN WINDOWS

MOVE BETWEEN WINDOWS

1. CLICK   on the **CH6TUT** document title

The active window, **CH6TUT,** is the document on which you can work. If you desired, however, you could switch quickly to **CH7TUT** or **CH8TUTA** and work on it. When ready, you could switch back again. This can be done using either the keyboard or the mouse as with other Works' commands.

2. PRESS   **Ctrl/F6**

The first document **CH7TUT** is now active. Works refers to the document under the *active* one as the previous document. The document that you cannot see at this time, but which is still open, **CH8TUTA,** is called the next window.

3. PRESS   **Ctrl/F6** to see the next window

USING MENUS TO MOVE FROM WINDOW TO WINDOW

You can also use the **Window** menu to move from one open window to another. A list of all open documents is shown in the **Window** menu. Selecting any one of them will make that one the active window.

USE MENU TO MOVE FROM WINDOW TO WINDOW

1. CHOOSE   the **Window** menu

The three open documents are shown at the bottom of the **Window** menu.

2. CHOOSE   **CH6TUT** to make it the active window

All documents are still open, and **CH6TUT** is the active window.

REDUCING THE SIZE OF A WINDOW

It is useful to change the size of windows so that more of the contents of each open window are visible. Use either the keyboard and menu options or the mouse button to size the window. Since these instructions are quite different, the two options will be listed separately.

REDUCE THE SIZE OF A WINDOW (KEYBOARD)

1. CHOOSE   **Size** from the **Window** menu

A black border appears around the document. This is the window frame and allows for reducing the window's size using the **Arrow** keys.

2. PRESS   the **Left Arrow** key 15 times

3. PRESS   the **Up Arrow** key 6 times

4. PRESS   **Enter** to confirm the size

REDUCE THE SIZE OF A WINDOW (MOUSE)

1. POSITION   the mouse button in the size box in the lower right corner of the screen (it looks like two backward Ls)

2. HOLD   the left mouse button down and drag the window so that it moves to the left and upward so that it looks approximately the size shown in Figure 9-3

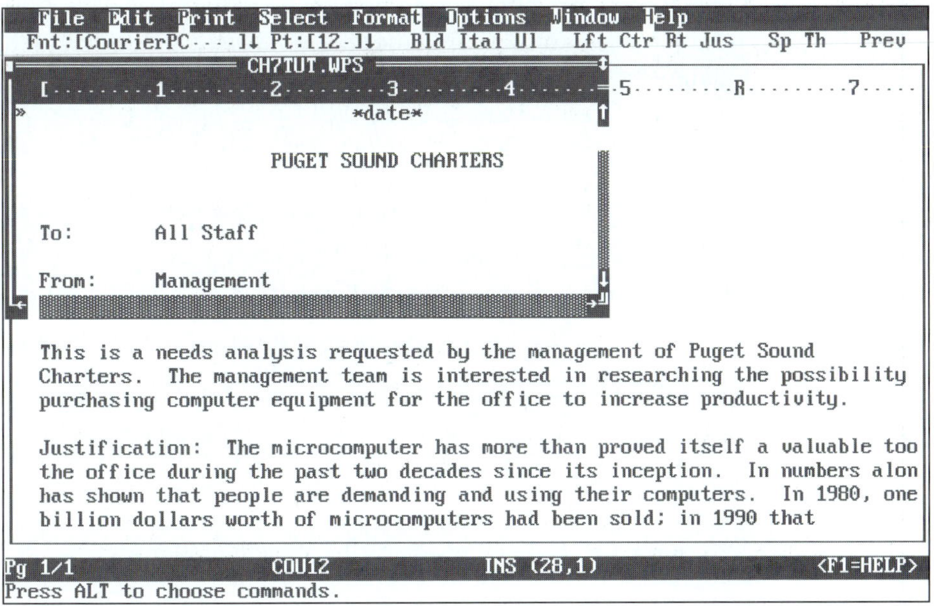

FIGURE 9-3
REDUCED WINDOW

REDUCING OTHER OPEN WINDOWS

Make the background window active:

REDUCE OTHER OPEN WINDOWS

1. **PRESS** **Ctrl/F6** or click the mouse button anywhere on the document
2. **REDUCE** the size of this window so that it is approximately the same size as the document you just sized

Note: *Use one of the options discussed — the mouse or the **Size** command from the **Window** menu and **Arrow** keys.*

ARRANGING THE WINDOWS

The way in which the windows appear on the screen now is not much more useful than they were when larger — in fact, probably less so. Windows are most useful when they are reduced and arranged in such a way that information in each is partially visible.

ARRANGE THE WINDOWS (KEYBOARD)

1. **CHOOSE** **Arrange All** from the **Window** menu

All windows are shown side by side with text partially visible in each. This is a much more useful arrangement. The active window is still highlighted. You can still move from window to window using **Ctrl/F6** or clicking the mouse button.

ARRANGE THE WINDOWS (MOUSE)

1. **POSITION** the mouse button anywhere in the left border of the active window
2. **HOLD** the left mouse button down and drag the window to the lower right corner of the screen

The windows are now partially visible. Move back and forth between the windows by clicking the mouse button once on the desired window.

3. **MOVE** the window back to its original location

EXPANDING THE SIZE OF A WINDOW

EXPAND THE SIZE OF A WINDOW (KEYBOARD)

With the **CH7TUT** window active,

1. CHOOSE   **Maximize** from the **Window** menu

EXPAND THE SIZE OF A WINDOW (MOUSE)

With the **CH7TUT** window active,

1. CLICK   **twice** in the double-headed arrow in the upper right corner of the window

SPLITTING A WINDOW

It is also useful to be able to split a large window into two halves. When windows are split, you can work in either half of the window just as you would in the full document space. As you scroll through one half, the other half remains stationary and thus visible on the screen. This is often used when it is convenient to see part of the document while working in another section of the text. For example, in the **CH8TUTA,** you could work on the table while viewing other paragraphs in the document that may contain information needed for the table.

With the **CH7TUT** window active,

SPLIT A WINDOW (KEYBOARD)

1. CHOOSE   **Split** from the **Window** menu
2. PRESS   the **Down Arrow** so that the bar is just below the centered heading
3. PRESS   **Enter** to confirm

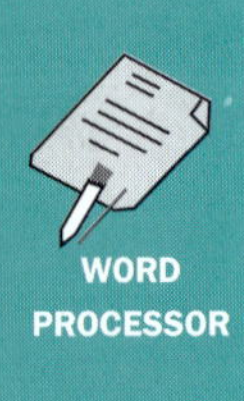

SPLIT A WINDOW (MOUSE)

1. POSITION the cursor on the split bar in the upper right corner of the active window

2. DRAG the left mouse button so that the bar is positioned just below the the centered heading

MOVING BETWEEN TWO WINDOW PANES

The screen is split in two parts. These two halves are called window panes. You can work in one pane or the other and move quickly between them.

MOVE BETWEEN TWO WINDOWS

1. PRESS **1F6** to move to the next pane or click the mouse button once in the desired pane

Practice moving from pane to pane. Also practice scrolling and using the cursor movements just as you would in any document space.

REMOVING THE SPLIT WINDOW

REMOVE THE SPLIT WINDOW (KEYBOARD)

1. CHOOSE **Split** from the **Window** menu

2. PRESS the **Up Arrow** key until the bar is at the top of the document (as far as it will go)

3. PRESS **Enter**

4. CLOSE all windows using the close box in the upper left corner of each window

REMOVE THE SPLIT WINDOW (MOUSE)

1. **POSITION** the cursor on the split lines (=)
2. **HOLD** down the mouse button and drag the bar all the way to the top of the screen
3. **RELEASE** the mouse button
4. **CLOSE** all windows

USING WORKS OTHER ACCESSORIES

Among the other accessories included in Works are a calculator and an alarm clock. While you may not have a great deal of use for these at this time, they may become useful as you continue using Works and as you discover needs for each of its tools.

USING THE CALCULATOR

The Works' calculator operates just like any other pocket calculator. Selections are made by pressing the numbers on the keyboard or by clicking on a number using the mouse.

USE THE CALCULATOR

1. **CHOOSE** **Calculator** from the **Options** menu

Note: *The calculator may be accessed in this opening screen or in a document space using the same menu.*

The following calculator appears as shown in Figure 9-4.

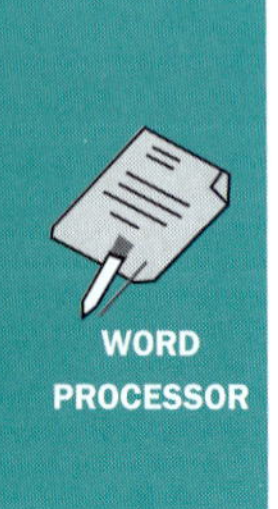

WORD PROCESSOR

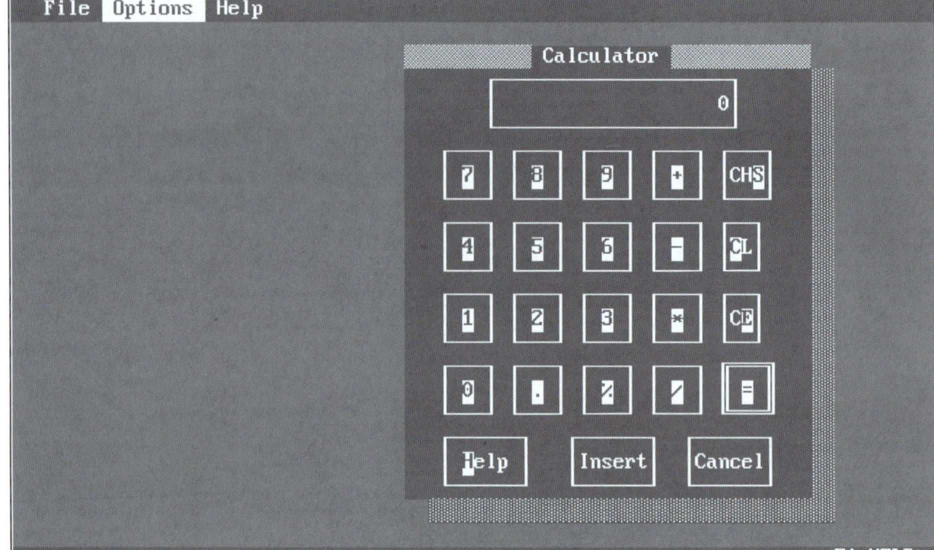

FIGURE 9-4
WORKS
CALCULATOR

Use the numbers across the top of the keyboard unless a numeric keypad is available. If you have a numeric keypad on the right of your keyboard, use it for the following exercises.

To change the sign of a number <CHS>

CHANGE THE SIGN OF A NUMBER

1. MAKE the numeric keypad active by pressing the **Num Lock** key, or use the keys at the top of the keyboard if the numeric keypad is not available

2. TYPE **33** or click on 3 twice with the mouse button

33 is entered in the calculator window.

3. PRESS **Alt/S** to change the number to a negative number or click on the **<CHS>** with the mouse button

4. PRESS **Alt/S** again to make the number positive or click on **<CHS>** with the mouse button

ADD TWO OR MORE NUMBERS

1. **PRESS**   the **plus** (+) key or click on **<+>** in the calculator window
2. **ENTER**   43
3. **PRESS**   the **equals** key (=) or click on **<=>**

The total of the two numbers appears in the window.

CLEAR ALL NUMBERS

1. **CHOOSE**   **<CL>** to clear everything

CLEAR THE LAST ENTRY

1. **ENTER**   44
2. **PRESS**   the **plus** key or click on **<+>**
3. **ENTER**   44
4. **PRESS**   the **plus** key or click on **<+>**
5. **ENTER**   10
6. **CHOOSE**   **<CE>** to clear the last entry
7. **PRESS**   the **equals** key (=) or click on **<=>**

The total, **88**, appears. The last entry of 10 was ignored.

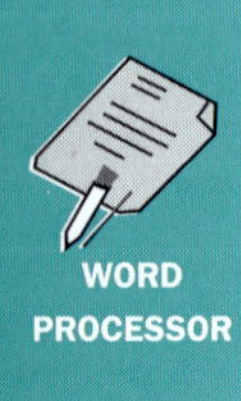

SUBTRACT A NUMBER

1. **CHOOSE**   **<CL>** to clear all entries
2. **ENTER**   **50**
3. **PRESS**   the **minus** (-) key or click on **<->**
4. **ENTER**   **20**
5. **PRESS**   the **equals** key (=) or click on **<=>**

The total, **30**, appears.

6. **CHOOSE**   **<CL>** to clear all entries

Performing any calculations works in the same way. It is the same as using any pocket calculator. Use other keys on the calculator, such as the multiplication key (*), division key (/), or percentage key (%), for the corresponding function.

7. **CHOOSE**   **Cancel** to close the calculator

To insert an answer into a document

Answers to calculations can be inserted into a document. To do so, position the cursor where the number will be inserted and call up the calculator using the **Calculator** command from the **Options** menu. **Perform** the calculation and choose **<Insert>** on the calculator. The number will be inserted at the cursor position in the document.

USING THE ALARM CLOCK

Works contains an alarm clock as part of its accessories. The alarm clock command is found in the **Options** menu.

USE THE ALARM CLOCK

1. **CHOOSE**   **Alarm Clock** from the **Options** menu

The dialog box shown in Figure 9-5 appears.

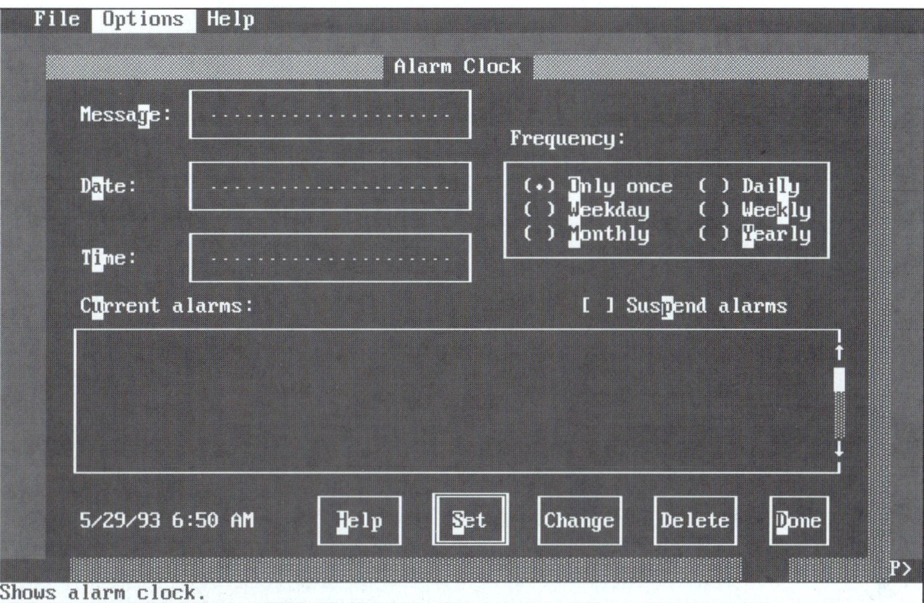

The alarm clock dialog box contains the options listed in Table 9-2 for working with an alarm clock.

THIS COMMAND	IS USED FOR THIS
Message:	To write text about the purpose of the alarm. For example, if you are taking an exam next Friday, this message could tell you about times to study and for which exam. You can use up to 60 characters in this box.
Date:	To set the date the alarm will sound.
Time:	To set the time the alarm will sound.
Frequency:	To set how often the alarm will sound.
Current alarms:	To show the date, time, and message for all alarms currently set. Snoozed alarms are those that are set to go off more than once. They will appear with an S next to them.
Suspend alarms:	To prevent an alarm from going off without deleting it.
Set:	To add a new alarm to the stored list.
Change:	To change an alarm setting.
Delete:	To delete an alarm when it is selected in the list.

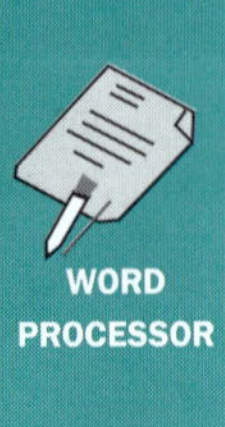

2. POSITION   the cursor in the **Message** text box (if necessary)

3. TYPE   **Read Chapters 2 and 3 for calculus exam on Tuesday**

4. PRESS   the **Down Arrow** key once

5. TYPE   today's date, such as **2/15/93**

6. PRESS   the **Down Arrow** key once

7. TYPE   the time 5 minutes from now, such as **11:24**

8. LEAVE   the setting at **Only once** in the **Frequency** box

9. CHOOSE   **Set**

The date, time, and message are inserted into the **Current alarms** list box.

10. CHOOSE   **Done**

Wait for the alarm to go off. When it goes off, Works displays the **Alarm clock** dialog box, showing the date, time, and message. You can shut the alarm off by choosing **OK**, reset the alarm by choosing **Reset** and adjusting the settings or have the alarm go off in 10 minutes by choosing **Snooze**.

11. CHOOSE   **OK** in the dialog box after the alarm has sounded

REMOVING AN ALARM SETTING

If an alarm has not played, it may be removed using the following steps.

REMOVE THE ALARM SETTING

1. CHOOSE   **Alarm clock** from the **Options** menu

2. SELECT   the setting in the **Current alarms** list box using the mouse or **F8**

3. CHOOSE   **Delete**

4. CHOOSE   **Done**

USING WORKSWIZARD

The **Wizard** command is found in the **File** menu. It is used to access shortcuts, such as instant templates or quick file finder assistance. We discuss some of the Wizard tools later in this book; however, for now, you may find the **File Finder** useful. It is a tool used to locate files quickly when you are unsure of the directory or file name.

USE WORKSWIZARD

1. **CHOOSE** **WorksWizards** from the **File** menu

The dialog box shown in Figure 9-6 appears.

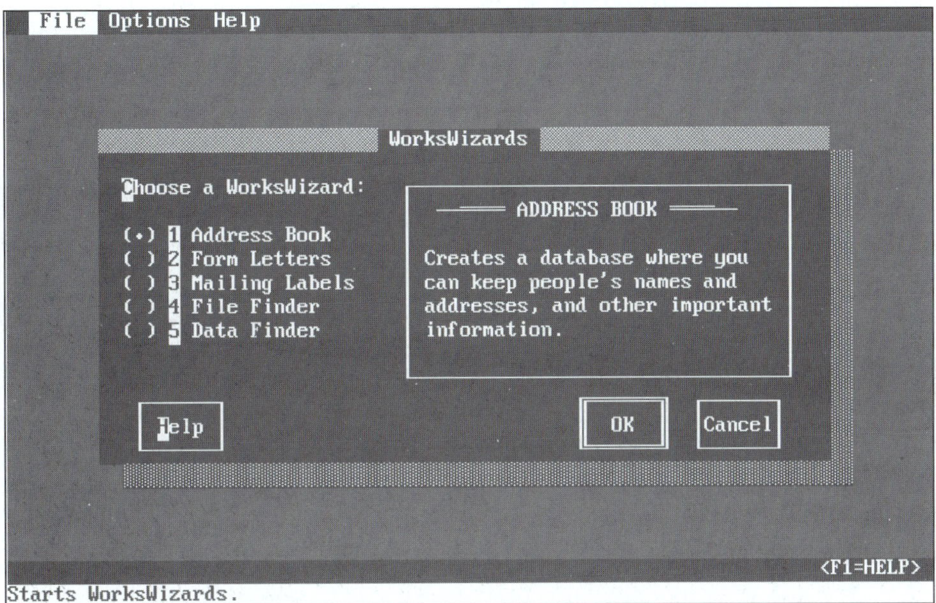

FIGURE 9-6
WORKSWIZARDS
DIALOG BOX

As each option in the **Choose a WorksWizard** list is selected, a description of its function is given in the box to the right. You can access help on using the Wizard through the **Help** button.

2. **CHOOSE** **File Finder** by pressing the number 4 or clicking on the option

3. **CHOOSE** **OK** or press Enter

Instructions are given on the screen for locating files. If there is a file you wish to find, choose **PgDn** by pressing the **PgDn** key or clicking on the **PgDn** button. Further instructions await you when you do so. **WorksWizard** will ask you for information about the file, and based on what you remember, will locate it.

4. **CHOOSE** **Cancel** to leave the **Wizard** at this time

5. **QUIT** or **CONTINUE** to the Tutorial

GUIDED TUTORIAL

WORD PROCESSOR

WHAT YOU'LL DO

- Create and save a template.
- Resize windows.
- Use multiple windows.
- Move between two or more windows.

HOW TO DO IT

1. CREATE the following logo. Make it as close to the one shown as possible. Determine the margins and tab settings on your own. Also determine the font styles and sizes.

PUGET SOUND CHARTERS

The Northwest Charter Company

————————————————————

2. SAVE this logo as a template.

3. CLOSE the document window.

4. OPEN a new document showing the logo.

5. TYPE the following letter (your choice).

Today's date

Ms. Sandra Collins
12345 N.E. 148th
Bellevue, WA 98007

Dear Ms. Collins:

It has been brought to my attention that you recently inquired about deckhand positions with Puget Sound Charters.

We are always interested in receiving resumes from interested persons. The deckhand positions require previous experience on 60- to 100-foot vessels. In addition to manning the lines, job responsibilities include helping customers to board the ship, assisting in cleanup, and following the orders of the captain at all times.

If you have had past experience as a deckhand, we would be interested in receiving a copy of your resume. Please send it to our Lake Union offices.

Thank you for your interest in Puget Sound Charters.

Sincerely,

J. P. MacRannall
President

---

6. RUN a spell check on the letter.

7. PRINT a copy.

8. SAVE the letter as **CH9TUT**.

9. OPEN two other documents (your choice).

10. ADJUST the size of each document window so that all three are visible on the screen.

11. MOVE from one document to another.

12. MAXIMIZE the size of the active window.

13. SPLIT the window into approximately two halves.

14. MOVE from one window pane to another.

15. CLOSE the window panes.

16. CLOSE all windows.

REVIEW QUESTIONS

1. List at least three options found in the **Works Settings** dialog box.

2. Briefly describe a template.

3. The _______________ command from the ____________ menu is used to open an existing template.

4. A template is best used for which of the following?

    a. Changing existing document formats
    b. Creating letters
    c. Creating standard formats
    d. Editing standard formats

5. Match each of the following phrases to the appropriate command or action.

    ____ Adjusting the height and width of a window
    ____ Changing the layout of multiple windows
    ____ Dividing a window into two parts
    ____ Moving from one window pane to another
    ____ Making a window active

    a. Shift/F6
    b. Ctrl/F6
    c. Split
    d. Size
    e. Arrange All

6. _____ The calculator feature in Works acts much like a pocket calculator.

7. _____ CE on the calculator will clear all entries.

8. _____ The alarm clock may be used to remind you of important meetings or dates.

HANDS-ON EXERCISES 

EXERCISE 1

Note: *Some of the following documents contain review features, in addition to those features found in Chapter 9. Refer to the index and to other chapter summaries for reference if needed.*

1. Create the following logo as a template. Decide on an appropriate name. Use bold print and Helvetica font: size 14. (**Note**: Use another if this is not available.) Enclose the logo in a double-line border on the top and bottom.

   Hint: Type the logo first, center it, and then choose the font style. Insert a hard return above the first line of the heading; insert two hard returns (press Enter twice) after the last line of the heading. When adding the border, position the cursor under the paragraph marker or on the blank line above the company name (or select all lines of the heading). Apply the border to the top and bottom of the text. Leave at least one unformatted paragraph marker below the borders. This will be used later to insert text.

PUGET SOUND CHARTERS
West Lake Union Way
Seattle, WA 98108
(206)555-9200

EXERCISE 2

1. Edit the template created in Exercise 1. Change it to the following format.

   a. A left margin setting of 1.5 and a right margin of 1.0.
   b. A print date marker inserted for the current date (use Insert Special Character from the Edit menu).
   c. Paragraph markers below the date formatted for a right justified margin.

2. Save the template again and close it.

3. Create a new document using the template.

4. Type the following letter. Use appropriate tab settings for the table. Save the document as **CH9HO2**.

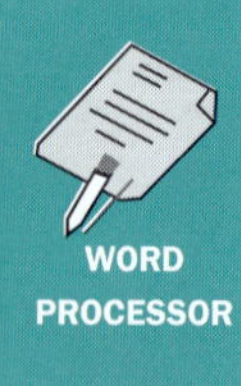

PUGET SOUND CHARTERS
West Lake Union Way
Seattle, WA 98108
(206)555-9200

(current date inserted)

Cheryl Chow, Owner
Lake Union Caterers
22525 Center Blvd.
Seattle, WA 98110

Dear Cheryl:

During the last quarter, sales increased dramatically at Puget Sound Charters. We believe that this is due in part to increased emphasis on new marketing strategies. It is, however, important to bring to your attention that this could not have happened without the excellent service and attention your company has given to us.

As you know, prior to signing Lake Union Caterers on as our primary caterer late last year, we had been experiencing some difficulty finding responsible, competitive, and friendly catering services. We had experimented with several catering companies prior to our first experience with yours. That first experience was a memorable one and led to many others, and finally,to a full-time, permanent contract.

Below is a summary of our earnings through the second quarter last year and those through the second quarter this year. I think they are outstanding, and I think you will agree. Feel free to use these figures as promotion for your services. You may also use the name of Puget Sound Charters as a very pleased customer.

TOTAL SALES
FIRST AND SECOND QUARTER
PUGET SOUND CHARTERS

Boat Name	Sales Las Location	Sales Year	This Year
Delano	Kirkland	36,890.00	42,520.00
The Spirit	Lake Union	35,550.00	41,236.00
Sea Wolf	Seward Park	38,950.00	45,780.00
Irish Sea	Shilshoe	40,150.00	58,695.00

Needless to say, we are delighted with the increase in our business and our increased popularity in the Puget Sound area as one of the outstanding charter boat companies. We believe that we offer excellent service, fine dining, an outstanding staff, and scenic cruises.

A successful charter business cannot be that without the effort of many persons from many different directions. Timeliness is one of the most critical factors, and you have always been there on time and ready to go.

Thank you for your efforts and your part in making Puget Sound Charters so successful. We look forward to many more years of business with your company.

Sincerely,

P. J. MacRannall
President

5. Run a spell check on the document.

6. Add an appropriate header for the second page of the letter; Include the company name and page number.

7. Change the company name to italics whenever it appears in the body of the letter (use Search and Replace).

8. Use the calculator to add a total amount for sales from last year and this year. Insert an extra blank line below the table for the total amount.

9. Save the final version of this document, **CH9HO2,** and print a copy.

WORD PROCESSOR

EXERCISE 3

1. Create the following newsletter. Use fonts similar to those shown (bold text is Helvetica) or others available with your system. Add borders as shown or in a similar format. Create the document using the Puget Sound Charters logo.

PUGET SOUND CHARTERS
West Lake Union Way
Seattle, WA 98108
(206)555-9200

***************STAFF MEETING**************

The monthly staff meeting will be held on board the Delano next Friday at 2 p.m. Topics to be covered include:

* Annual pay raises
* Increase in deckhand salary
* Increase in overtime by captains
* Training for deckhands
* Schedules for next month
* Review of emergency policies

If you have any other topics you would like to bring up at the meeting, please let the administration know by the end of the working day next Wednesday.

Increase in vacation benefits

The board of administrators met recently to discuss increased vacation time for employees. Beginning next month, all employees who have been with Puget Sound Charters for one year or more will receive an extra five days' paid vacation time per year. This will increase the maximum annual paid vacation for all staff and deckhands to three weeks and the maximum annual paid vacation for captains to four and one-half weeks.

Summary reports

Summary reports will be required of all captains at the end of each week. These reports will include important information about each cruise. A standard report will be developed at a later date. The temporary report will include:

* List of the names of staff reporting to work
* List of the names of staff reporting more than 20 minutes late to work
* Name of the chartering company
* Weather conditions
* Any outstanding conditions in the vessel, weather, or general circumstances of the trip
* Any obstacles or difficulties arising during the cruise

    *   Total time of the cruise
    *   Total cleanup and closing time

    This information will assist management in better understanding difficulties that may arise during cruises. A better understanding of these will result in better service to our employees and customers.

____

2. Move the **Staff Meeting** paragraphs to the bottom of the newsletter.

3. Run a spell check on the document and then save it as **CH9HO3**.

4. Change the alignment of the itemized lists in the newsletter (*) so that the indent begins 1.5 inches from the left margin.

5. Justify the right margin.

6. Underscore all headings appearing at the left margin, such as **Increase in vacation benefits**.

7. Change the newsletter in any other way so that it looks attractive and draws attention. This could include adding double borders around some of the text or changing the font on certain words. Use your imagination to alter the format.

8. Save the revised copy of the newsletter and print a copy.

EXERCISE 4

1. Write a short memo to all staff members. Include a memo heading as shown below:

    TO: All Employees

    FROM: P. J. MacRannall, President

    SUBJECT: Further explanation of Staff Meeting topics as listed in this week's newsletter

2. Open the newsletter document **CH9HO3** which you credated in Chapter 19. You can also retrieve it from the instructor's data disk. Leave the memo window open as well. Reduce the size of both windows so that the items in the newsletter under **Staff Meeting** are showing and so that you have room in the current window to write the memo.

3. Write an introductory paragraph explaining that this memo will clarify the following items:

    Annual pay raises

    Increase in deckhand salary

    Training for deckhands

4. Create subheadings for each of these items. Underline the subheadings and then write a short paragraph that includes the following information for each.

    Annual pay raises
    Suggested by management — 6.8 percent with increased vacation time.

    Increase in deckhand salary
    Suggested by management — from $5.00 per hour to $5.50 per hour with overtime.

    Training for deckhands
    To be given by the Coast Guard. Will start on the first Monday of next month and run for two months. Classes will meet every Monday from 7 p.m. to 9 p.m. Will include safety, emergency landings, and information on the Coast Guard exam.

    Include an appropriate closing paragraph.

5. Save this document as **CH9HO4**.

6. Expand the active window. Run a spell check. Make any changes necessary to the contents. Print a copy of the memo.

10 CREATING A SPREADSHEET

Objectives

- Create a spreadsheet.

- Move through a spreadsheet.

- Enter text and values.

- Change column width.

- Edit cells.

- Save a spreadsheet.

PREVIEW ▶▶▶

Spreadsheets are the second powerful Works tool covered in this book. A spreadsheet is much like an accountant's worksheet. In fact, the area in which you work in a spreadsheet program is often called a *worksheet*. It can be used for creating income statements, budget projections, financial planning, and other financial recordkeeping documents. Spreadsheets allow for the extensive use of computations through formulas entered into sections of the worksheet. Values entered into the worksheet are recalculated automatically using the formulas.

**SPREAD-
SHEET**

CREATING A SPREADSHEET

Beginning a new spreadsheet is like starting other documents in Works — through the **Create New File** command in the **File** menu at the opening screen.

CREATE A SPREADSHEET

1. **CHOOSE** **Create New File** from the **File** menu at the opening Works screen or from the "quick start" box

2. **CHOOSE** **Spreadsheet**

3. **CHOOSE** **OK** or press Enter

The spreadsheet window shown in Figure 10-1 appears.

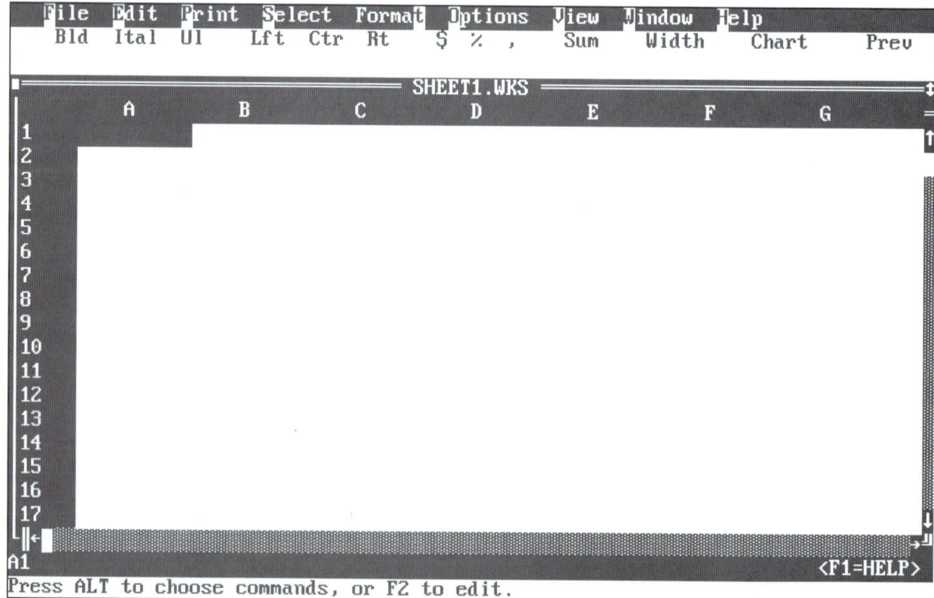

**FIGURE 10-1
NEW SPREADSHEET
DOCUMENT**

192

The parts of the screen are described in Table 10-1.

Menus	The menus are very similar to those used in word processing. An additional menu, View, is added.
Toolbar	Shows tools used for quick access to commands and functions.
Title bar	Shows the current title of the spreadsheet. This is changed using the Save or Save As commands in the File menu.
Columns	The columns appear across the top of all spreadsheets. They are identified as A, B, C, and so on. Columns are set at 10 spaces unless the width is changed.
Rows	Rows are numbered down the left side of the spreadsheet: 1, 2, 3, and so on.
Active Cell	The active or current cell is the one that is highlighted. This is like a cursor position except that it fills up the entire width of the cell. A cell is the intersection of a row and a column.
Split Bar	Splits the current window into two halves by dragging the mouse button on it. Menu options are used when splitting the window from the keyboard.
Scroll Bar	Functions the same as in word processing or other Works' windows. Dragging the mouse button on this bar will scroll through the document space. Menu options or keystrokes are used when scrolling from the keyboard.
Size Box	The size box adjusts the size of the window when using a mouse. It is located in the lower left corner of the window. Menu options are used when using the keyboard.
Status Line	Shows address of active or Highlighted cell(s) and indicates toggle ON of F8 (EXT), Caps Lock (CL), or Num Lock (NL).
Message Line	Shows actions to take next or keys that can be pressed during the current action.

<u>Other comments about the screen:</u>

The lower left corner of the screen also contains the horizontal scroll bar used when working with a mouse. Below the scroll bar are the characters A1. The A1 designates the active cell. As you move through the spreadsheet, the A1 will change to show the active cell position. The F1 key for help is also shown in the lower right corner of the screen.

TABLE 10-1
DESCRIPTION OF A NEW SPREADSHEET SPACE

MOVING THROUGH A SPREADSHEET

When a cell is selected, it is referred to as being *highlighted*. Sometimes a range of cells is highlighted, much like a block of text in word processing, so that special formats can be applied to it or so that it can be printed, and so on. Highlighted blocks of cells will be used in exercises in this chapter. For now, you will practice moving the highlighted cell to other positions in the worksheet. This can be done by using the keyboard, pressing the mouse button, or choosing menu commands.

To use the keyboard for scrolling

The use of the keyboard for scrolling is the most frequently used method. Most of the time you will use the keyboard to move from cell to cell or across the width of the spreadsheet. When using a mouse, some of the same movements are done by clicking the mouse button or by using the scroll bars on the right and bottom of the screen. Table 10-2 shows ways of moving the highlight or position of the current or active cell.

PRESS THE FOLLOWING KEY(S)	OR THE MOUSE BUTTON	TO MOVE TO THIS POSITION
Left or Right Arrow	Click in the cell	Left or right one cell position
Down or Up Arrow	Click in the cell	Up or down one cell position
Home	Click in the cell	To the first cell in the row
End	Click in the cell	To the last non-empty cell in the row
Page Down	Click once in the lower right of the scroll bar (above the arrow)	To move down one screen
Page Up	Click once in the upper right of the scroll bar (below the arrow)	To move up one screen
Ctrl/Page Down	Click once in the right corner of the bottom scroll bar (left of the arrow)	To move right one screen
Ctrl/Page Up	Click once in the left corner of the bottom scroll bar (right of the arrow)	To move left one screen
Ctrl/Home	Drag the scroll bar(s) and click in the cell	To move to the upper left cell of a spreadsheet, usually cell A1

SPREAD-SHEET

Ctrl/End	Drag the scroll bar(s) and click in the cell	To move to the lower right corner of the spreadsheet; the last cell in a column and row in the spreadsheet
F5 (the GoTo key)		To move to a specific cell
Ctrl/Arrow Keys		To move the cursor to outermost cell as follows:
Ctrl/Right Arrow		to column IV (last column)
Ctrl/Left Arrow		to column A
Ctrl/Down Arrow		to row 16384 (last row)
Ctrl/Up Arrow		to row 1

TABLE 10-2
SELECTION OF
MOVEMENTS IN A
SPREADSHEET

USE THE KEYBOARD FOR SCROLLING

1. **PRACTICE** moving through the empty spreadsheet on the screen. The **End** commands will not work at this time since values and labels are not yet entered on the spreadsheet. Practice other movements, however, so that you can see how the highlight moves from one location to another.

The size of the spreadsheet

The area of the spreadsheet now visible is only a small portion of the entire worksheet area. Column letters repeat themselves and rows extend into the thousands. The last column and row is number IV16384. This is column IV and row 16384. The spreadsheet is, therefore, extremely large, and what you now see on your screen is only a small representation of the entire spreadsheet. Figure 10-2 graphically represents the size of the screen in relation to the entire worksheet. The small box in the upper left corner is the visible worksheet on the screen, and the remaining area is all of the spreadsheet space available.

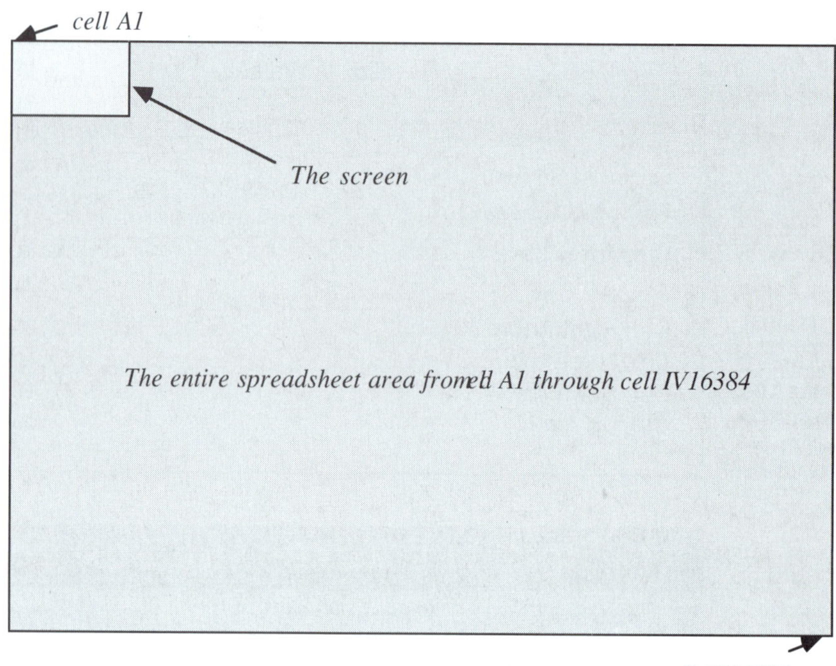

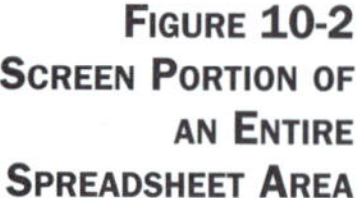

SPREAD-SHEET

FIGURE 10-2
SCREEN PORTION OF AN ENTIRE SPREADSHEET AREA

SIZE THE SPREADSHEET

1. POSITION the highlight in cell **A1** by pressing **Ctrl/Home** or by dragging the scroll bars with the mouse button

2. MOVE the highlight across the spreadsheet to cell **AA1** by pressing the **Right Arrow** key or by dragging the bottom scroll bar with the mouse button

Note: *Watch the lower left corner of the status bar as the cell position indicator changes from A1 to AA1. Whichever cell is showing in the lower left corner is often referred to as the current cell.*

As the cell location moves right, the column letters change. They increase from A through Z and then begin repeating themselves. The first repeat begins by inserting an A in front of each column, such as AA, AB, AC, and so on. If you continue moving to the right, the letters (columns) will adjust again to BA, BB, BC, and so on, until the final columns increase through the Is and become IA, IB, IC through IV as shown in Figure 10-2. The rows in the spreadsheet increase as well, through approximately 16384. This illustrates how large the spreadsheet area is.

ENTERING TEXT AND VALUES

Text and *values* are entered into the cells in a worksheet. A *value* is a number, such as **175.42** or **10**. *Text* is any label, such as **First Quarter** or **Balance Sheet**. When text is entered into a cell in which there is no text or value in the cell to the right, it will overlap automatically into the next cell or cells. This is the procedure normally used to enter a long heading at the top of a spreadsheet. Other cells in the spreadsheet that contain text and where values or text appear in the cells to the right usually have the width of the column adjusted so that the contents of the cell fit within the cell boundaries. To begin this spreadsheet, you will start by entering a heading at the top and then entering text and values in the spreadsheet body. As the spreadsheet is modified, it will be necessary to adjust the width of the columns, insert rows, add formulas, and apply other keyboard and menu commands.

ENTER TEXT AND VALUES

1. **POSITION** the highlight in cell **A1** by pressing **Ctrl/Home** or by using the scroll bar and mouse

2. **MOVE** to cell **C1** by pressing the **Right Arrow** or by clicking once in the cell with the mouse button

   Note: *The cell address, C1, appears in the lower left corner of the window.*

3. **TYPE** **PUGET SOUND CHARTERS**

   Note: *As you are typing, watch the upper left corner of the screen. The text you are typing appears in the **Formula** bar. You can view the contents you are typing either in the **Formula** bar or in the cell. This is helpful for checking for accuracy prior to pressing the **Enter** key to confirm. Use the **Backspace** key or the **Delete** key to make corrections if necessary.*

When the title appears correct,

4. **PRESS** **Enter**

When **Enter** is pressed, the entire title appears in cell C1 and overlaps to cell D1. Because you entered this heading in cell C1, you will always need to be in the same cell to make changes to its contents. The entire heading is contained in cell C1, even though it overlaps into another cell.

Look in the upper left corner of the screen where the title appears. This corner shows the title as it is entered into the cell.

5. PRESS   the **Right Arrow** key once or click the mouse button in cell D1

Notice that this cell does not show any contents in the upper left corner of the screen. The cell is recognized as empty. If you entered a value or other text into it, it would replace the text overlapping into the cell — in this case the **D CHARTERS**; however, it would not affect the contents of the cell. Even though the text would replace the "visible" contents in the cell, the **Formula** bar would show that the entire contents was still contained in the cell.

6. POSITION   the highlight in cell **C1** again

The text appears as follows.

> "PUGET SOUND CHARTERS

The double quotation mark identifies the heading as text and not as values that could be used in calculations. The double quote is inserted in front of text automatically. If labels such as column headings begin with values such as 1992, a double quote must be typed prior to typing the heading.

7. POSITION the highlight in cell **B3** (watch the lower left corner as the address changes)

8. TYPE   "**1989** (including the double quote)

9. PRESS   **Enter** or click the left mouse button once in the cell

The column heading, 1989, is entered into the cell as text because of the double quotes prior to the numbers. Notice that this text is also aligned on the left side of the cell. If it had been entered as a value, it would align on the right side of the cell. Pressing **Enter** or clicking the mouse button once in the same cell inserts the text into the cell and leaves it highlighted.

10. POSITION the highlight in cell **C3**

11. TYPE   "**1990**

12. PRESS   the **Right Arrow** key once or click the mouse button in the cell to the right, **D3**

The text is entered into the cell and the highlight moves one cell position to the right. Steps 9 and 12 are two ways of inserting text or values into cells. The first leaves the highlight in the current cell; the second moves the highlight to the cell in the direction of the **Arrow** key or the cell in which the mouse button is clicked once. Any of the **Arrow** keys will insert the text and move to the next cell in the direction of the **Arrow** key used. The mouse button works the same way. When text or values are typed, clicking the mouse button in any other cell will insert the text into the highlighted cell and move the highlight to the new cell.

Use either of the methods in the paragraph above to enter the following column headings.

13. POSITION the highlight in cell **D3** (if necessary)

14. TYPE   **1991** as text (with the double quote, ")

15. TYPE   **1992** in cell **E3** as text

16. POSITION the highlight in cell **A4** and type the following text labels down the column in **A5, A6,** and so on, as indicated (do not worry if they overlap into other cells)

A4	Gross Sales
A5	Cost of Goods Sold
A6	Net Sales
A7	(make no entry)
A8	Expenses
A9	Catering
A10	Salaries
A11	Operations
A12	Miscellaneous
A13	Total Expenses
A14	(make no entry)
A15	Net Earnings

CHANGING COLUMN WIDTH

The text entered into column A in this spreadsheet overlaps into column B. **Cost of Goods Sold**, for example, extends under the column heading 1989. Labels are often wider than the column width. For that reason, one of the commands used most often is that for making the column wider. This is done through the **Column Width** command in the **Format** menu.

CHANGE THE WIDTH OF COLUMNS

1. POSITION the highlight anywhere in column **A**

2. CHOOSE **Column Width** from the **Format** menu

The default width of 10 characters is showing. Since **Cost of Goods Sold** is the widest block of text, the column width should be slightly wider than this label, which is 18 characters wide. Make the column width 20.

3. TYPE **20** in the **Width** text box

　　Note: *As soon as 20 is typed, the 10 will be removed automatically.*

4. CHOOSE **OK** or press Enter

SPREAD-SHEET

Note: *If you have any questions about how to make dialog box or menu selections, read through Chapter 5. It explains these selections in more detail. This part on the Spreadsheet tool assumes that you have completed the Word Processing part and are experienced with making menu and dialog box selections.*

The column width is adjusted and the labels no longer overlap into column B.

ENTERING VALUES INTO CELLS

Values are typed directly into a cell without inserting special characters (such as double quotes) prior to the numbers.

ENTER VALUES INTO CELLS

1. POSITION the highlight in cell **B4**

2. TYPE 110950

3. PRESS the **Right Arrow** once or click the mouse button in cell **C4**

4. TYPE 116300 in cell **C4**

5. PRESS the **Right Arrow** once or click the mouse button in cell **D4**

6. TYPE 151540 in cell **D4**

7. PRESS the **Right Arrow** once or click the mouse button in cell **E4**

8. TYPE 188231 in cell **E4**

9. PRESS the **Down Arrow** key once and then the **Left Arrow** three times so that the highlight is in cell **B5** or click the mouse button in cell **B5**

10. TYPE the remaining values as follows

Note: *All values are aligning on the right side of the cell. Do not worry at this time that the column headings are to the far left of the column and the values to the far right. Spreadsheets often align in this manner until other special formatting commands are given. These are covered later in this chapter.*

	A	B	C	D	E
1		PUGET SOUND CHARTERS			
2					
3		1989	1990	1991	1992
4	Gross Sales	110950	116300	151540	188231
5	Cost of Goods Sold	8540	9430	10500	18900
6	Net Sales				
7					
8	Expenses				
9	Catering	8800	9250	12325	15800
10	Salaries	15000	22500	60500	60800
11	Operations	5500	3000	5500	7530
12	Miscellaneous	4000	6500	8000	2500
13	Total Expenses				
14					
15	Net Earnings				
16					
17					
18					

EDITING CELLS

Cells can be edited in a number of ways. If you have made an error in one of the cells entries, you could use any of the following methods to correct the error(s).

Position the cursor in the cell with the error, and

- Type the cell contents again. When an **Arrow** key or the **Enter** key is pressed, the new contents will replace the old.

- Enter a blank space into the cell by pressing the spacebar once and then pressing **Enter**.

- Press the **F2** key and edit the cell contents in the **Edit** bar in the upper left corner of the screen. The editing changes may also be viewed in the cell as changes are made. When the **Enter** key is pressed, the edit is complete.

- Choose the **Clear** command from the **Edit** menu.

These options will be used on the current worksheet.

REPLACE CELL CONTENTS

1. **HIGHLIGHT**   cell **A4**

    Note: *From now on the instructions will use Select when referring to relocating to a particular cell on the spreadsheet.*

2. **TYPE**   **GROSS SALES** in all CAPS

3. **PRESS**   **Enter**

The capital letters replaced the old cell contents.

4. **HIGHLIGHT**   cell **A6**

5. **TYPE**   **NET SALES** in all CAPS and press **Enter**

EDIT WITH F2 KEY

1. **HIGHLIGHT**   cell **A8**

2. **PRESS**   **F2**

The cursor moves to the **Edit** bar at the top left of the screen.

3. **PRESS**   the **Backspace** key to remove all lowercase letters

4. **TYPE**   **EXPENSES** (the E is already in place)

5. **PRESS**   **Enter**

    Note: *You can edit the contents of cells at any time using the **F2** key. The advantage of this option is that you do not have to retype the entire contents.*

CLEARING AND DELETING CELL CONTENTS

Cell contents can be cleared using the **Clear** command in the **Edit** menu. This command erases the contents of one or more highlighted cells.

WHAT YOU'LL DO

- Enter values and labels into the spreadsheet.
- Edit cell contents and adjust the column width.

HOW TO DO IT

1. CREATE the following partial spreadsheet. Enter the values and labels in the cells shown. Do not worry about the alignment of values or labels in the cells.

	A	B	C	D	E	F
1			PAYROLL			
2						
3	Employee	Hours	Rate	Total	Tax	Net
4	Eiler	40	10			
5	Kennedy	40	8			
6	MacRannall	42	12			
7	Shepard	41	10			
8						
9						
10						
11						
12						
13						
14						

2. PRESS F5, the GoTo key.

3. TYPE A9 as the cell to go to.

4. CHOOSE OK or press Enter.

5. TYPE Total and press **Enter.**

6. HIGHLIGHT cell **C4.**

7. PRESS F2, the edit key.

8. CHANGE the value to **12**, the new rate for Eiler.

9. **CAPITALIZE** the label, **Employee**, in cell **A3** by typing the new text over the old.

10. **SELECT** any cell in column **A**.

11. **CHOOSE** **Column Width** from the **Format** menu.

12. **TYPE** **15** as the new width.

13. **CHOOSE** **OK** or press Enter.

14. **CHOOSE** **Save As** from the **File** menu.

15. **TYPE** **CH10TUT** as the name of this document.

SPREAD-SHEET

REVIEW QUESTIONS

1. List two ways to start a new spreadsheet.

2. The _________________ at the lower left corner of the screen shows the current cell position.

3. The _________________ may be used to divide the screen into two parts.

4. _____________ appear horizontally on a spreadsheet.

5. _____________ appear vertically on a spreadsheet.

6. Match each of the functions to the appropriate keystroke or action.

    _______ Moves down a screen at a time
    _______ Moves left one screen
    _______ Moves to a specific cell
    _______ Moves to the last nonempty cell
    _______ Moves to the first cell in a row

    a. F5
    b. Page Down
    c. Ctrl/Page Up
    d. End
    e. Home

7. _______ Cell A1 is always considered the **active** cell.

8. _______ Ctrl/Home will position the highlight in cell A1.

9. _______ The Spacebar may be used to erase cell contents quickly.

10. _______ The entire column must be highlighted when changing column width.

HANDS-ON EXERCISES

SPREAD-SHEET

EXERCISE 1

1. Type the following partial spreadsheet. Do not worry about the alignment of values and labels at this time.

2. Determine the correct column and row placement.

3. Remember to enter 1990 and 1991 as labels (").

SALES BY BOAT

Boat Name	1990	1991	Change	% of Change
Delano	36890	42520		
The Spirit	35550	41236		
Sea Wolf	38950	45780		
Irish Sea	40150	58695		
Total				
Average				
Minimum				

4. Proof the spreadsheet.

5. Save the spreadsheet as **CH10HO1.**

6. Change the headings:

> Boat Name
> Total
> Average
> and Minimum

to all CAPS

7. Change 1990 to 1991, and 1991 to 1992 using the F2 key.

8. Save the spreadsheet again.

9. Practice the following movements through the spreadsheet. Use both the mouse and keyboard movements.

   a. To the first cell in a row
   b. To the last cell in a row
   c. To the last cell in the spreadsheet
   d. To the first cell in the spreadsheet
   e. To cell E12
   f. Down one screen
   g. Up one screen

10. Exit Works saving any changes.

EXERCISE 2

1. Sign onto Works.

2. Open the spreadsheet **CH10HO1** which you created in Exercise 1; or retrieve it from the instructor's data disk.

INSTRUCTOR'S DATA DISK

3. Change the columns headings **Change** and **% of Change** to all CAPS.

4. Change the following values:

   > Delano, 1991 to 37890
   > SeaWolf, 1992 to 45800
   > Irish Sea, 1991 to 41250

5. Change the width of column A to 20.

6. Save the changes to the spreadsheet as **CH10HO2**.

7. Exit Works.

SPREAD-
SHEET

11 FORMULAS

Objectives

- Use formulas.

- Retrieve a file.

- Sum a range of values.

- Select cells in formulas.

- Search for true/false conditions.

- Understand function hierarchy.

- View formulas.

PREVIEW »»➡

Formulas create new values by performing calculations on cells. Formulas are used for all spreadsheet calculations, regardless of how minor they might be. For example, they are used to add two values together or to subtract one value from another. They are also used to perform more complex calculations involving multiplication, division, addition, and/or subtraction in a single formula. They can be used to perform searches as well as using IF-THEN-ELSE structures.

USING FORMULAS

The primary advantage of using formulas is that values are computed quickly and accuracy is assured as long as the formula is correct. A second advantage is that any time values used as part of the equation are changed, the values calculated by the formula are recalculated automatically.

Formulas can include any of the figures and text shown in Table 11-1.

Formulas may include functions, operands, and operators as shown in this table.

Operators:
Addition   +
Subtraction   -
Multiplication   *
Division   /

Operands:
Constant values:
any number,
such as: 10, 20, -25, 56.25, and so on

Cell and range
references, such as: A1, B3, D25, B2:B25, and so on

Range names, such as: Net Earnings and Total Expenses

Functions:
Functions that come with
Works, such as: SQRT (Square Root), SUM (Addition), and
                        IF (IF-THEN-ELSE) (See the User's Guide
                        for a complete list of functions)

TABLE 11-1
TEXT AND FIGURES
USED IN FORMULAS

RETRIEVING A FILE

Retrieving a spreadsheet file is done in the same way as retrieving a word processing file. In fact, as you proceed through this part and continue through the book, most of the commands are performed the same way from one application to another. This is the advantage of an integrated program such as Works; it makes using each application and moving from one application to another a painless process.

RETRIEVE A FILE

1. SIGN   onto Works if necessary

2. CHOOSE   **Open Existing File** from the **File** menu or open an existing file from the "quick start" box

3. CHANGE   the directory in the **Directories** list box if necessary to that of your data disk

4. SCROLL   through the list box containing the document names by using the **Arrow** keys or the mouse

    Note: *As you are scrolling, subheadings appear in this list box. They are those for each of the applications in Works, and they include Word processing, Spreadsheet, Database, and Other Files. Look at the Spreadsheet files for all retrievals in this part.*

5. CHOOSE   **CH10PR1.WKS** from the **Spreadsheet** list by selecting the name and choosing **OK** or by clicking on the name with the mouse button

    Note: ***CH10PR1.WKS** can also be **retreived** from the instructors data disk*

The spreadsheet appears on the screen.

INSTRUCTOR'S DATA DISK

SUBTRACTING ONE VALUE FROM ANOTHER

All formulas begin with an equals sign (=). The cell into which the answer to the formula should appear is first highlighted, then the formula is typed and entered into the cell. When it is entered into the cell, the answer to the formula will appear in the cell and the formula will appear in the upper left corner of the spreadsheet (the **Formula** bar).

SUBTRACT ONE VALUE FROM ANOTHER

1. HIGHLIGHT   cell **B6**

2. TYPE   **=B4-B5** (in uppercase or lowercase)

This formula will subtract the value found in cell B5 from that in B4. You can use either uppercase or lowercase when typing the location of the cell. The cell in a formula is often referred to as the *address*. B4 and B5 are the cell addresses in the formula above.

---

3. **PRESS**   **Enter** or click the mouse button once

The **Net Sales** amount appears in cell B6.

SUMMING A RANGE OF VALUES

A range of values can be summed by typing each of the cells in a string, such as the values found in cells B9 through B12. These values could be added together using a string of cell addresses, such as =B9+B10+B11+B12. This could, however, become long and tedious when summing many cells. For this reason, Works uses ranges to identify a group of cells from one point to another. The group of cells used in the formula above could be abbreviated to read B9:B12, which is much more compact. When a range is used, the SUM function is also used. SUM is one of Works' built-in functions used to identify the type of calculation being done. Examples of a few of Works functions are given in Table 11-1. For a a more complete list see the User's Guide for Micrsoft Works. Sum is used when performing addition, subtraction, multiplication, division, and other mathematical functions on a group or range of cells.

In the following exercise, you will sum the values in B9, B10, B11, and B12.

SUM A RANGE OF VALUES

1. **HIGHLIGHT** cell **B13**

2. **TYPE**   **=SUM(B9:B12)** (in uppercase or lowercase)

3. **PRESS**   **Enter** or click the mouse button in the cell

The total of all values in B9, B10, B11, and B12 is inserted into B13.

SELECTING CELLS FOR FORMULAS

The **Arrow** keys or the mouse pointer can be used to highlight cells to be used in formulas. Selection of cells is used in place of typing the cell address from the keyboard. Either option may be used. Sometimes it is convenient to use the **Arrow** keys or the mouse pointer when spreadsheets are extremely large and the location of cells is not visible on the screen. After making the following selections, use whichever method is easiest for you when entering cell addresses into formulas.

SELECT CELLS FOR FORMULAS

1. **HIGHLIGHT**   cell **B15**

2. **TYPE**   =

3. **PRESS**   the **Up Arrow** key until cell **B6** is highlighted or click the mouse button in cell **B6**

4. **TYPE**   - to subtract the next value (the highlight returns to the formula cell, **B15**)

5. **PRESS**   the **Up Arrow** key until cell **B13** is highlighted or click the mouse button in cell **B13**

The formula is complete.

6. **PRESS**   **Enter** or click the mouse button in cell **B15**

A positive Net Earnings of 69110 is entered into the cell.

COMPUTING AVERAGES

Averages are computed using the built-in function, AVG, for average. The function is written in the same way as a SUM function and uses a range of values to compute the answer. To enter the average of cells B9, C9, D9, and E9 in cell F9, you would do the following.

COMPUTE AVERAGES

1. **HIGHLIGHT**   cell **F3**

2. **TYPE**   **Average** to label the column and press **Enter**

3. **HIGHLIGHT**   cell **F9**

4. **TYPE**   =AVG(B9:E9)

This function will compute the average of all catering expenses over the four-year period. Enter the range by either typing it in or by using the **Arrow** keys or mouse button to point to the range.

5. **PRESS**   **Enter** or click the mouse button once in cell **F9**

SEARCHING FOR TRUE OR FALSE CONDITIONS

The IF-THEN-ELSE function is used to search for existing conditions. If the function locates a true condition, it will perform one command; if a false condition, it will perform another command. In other words, IF it locates a true condition, THEN it performs one command, ELSE it performs another. The formula used for this type of search uses the built-in Works function, IF.

SEARCH FOR TRUE OR FALSE CONDITIONS

1. **HIGHLIGHT**   cell **A17**
2. **TYPE**   **PROFIT** to label the column
3. **HIGHLIGHT**   cell **A18** and type **Yes (1)**
4. **HIGHLIGHT**   cell **A19** and type **No (0)**
5. **HIGHLIGHT**   cell **B17**
6. **TYPE**   **=IF(B15<=0,0,1)** and press **Enter**

This function looks in the cell B15. If it locates a value less than or equal to zero (0), THEN it inserts a zero for No (also a TRUE condition), ELSE it inserts a 1 for Yes (a FALSE condition), meaning that it located a value greater than zero (0).

This type of function can be used to perform calculations if certain values are located. For example, if a certain amount is located in a cell, that amount could be multiplied by a given percentage. Suppose that you had a spreadsheet that contained sales amounts and that any amount greater than $10 should be taxed 0.08 percent. The IF function to search for those values and then compute the tax would be written as follows:

=IF(B9>10,B9*.08,B9)

The function looks in cell B9 for a value greater than 10. IF that value is located (a TRUE condition), it multiplies the value by 0.08 percent; ELSE if it is not located (a FALSE condition), it inserts the value of B9 in the current cell. The answer to this function would be either the computed percentage or the value in B9.

You could also write the function to add the computed tax to the value in B9 as shown below.

=IF(B9>10,B9*.08 + B9, B9)

COMPUTING A PERCENTAGE

This spreadsheet could give further information about the way the total Net Earnings has changed over the years. One way would be to compute the percentage of Net Earnings to Net Sales. This is computed by dividing one value into another or one cell's value into another cell's value.

COMPUTE A PERCENTAGE

1. **HIGHLIGHT** cell **A21**
2. **TYPE** **% of Net Sales** as the label
3. **HIGHLIGHT** cell **B21**
4. **TYPE** **=B15/B6**

   Note: *B15 contains the value for net earnings for 1989; B6 contains the value for net sales. By dividing the net sales into the net earnings, the percentage is computed.*

5. **PRESS** **Enter**

FUNCTION HIERARCHY

Works evaluates expressions/formulas based on the hierarchy shown in Table 11-2. It follows the standard algebraic rules when evaluating and includes:

- Evaluation of the contents of parentheses () first, with the innermost parenthesis having priority, for example:

  =(F6*3(G6*(H5-H4)))

- Evaluation of operators as shown in the following table.

- Evaluation of two or more operators, which are the same from left to right.

THIS OPERATOR	IS EVALUATED
^ exponential	first
- negative; + positive	second
* multiplication; / division	third
+ addition; - subtraction	fourth
= equal to; <> not equal to	fifth
< less than; > greater than	
<= less than or equal to	
>= greater than or equal to	
~ NOT	sixth
I OR, & AND	seventh

TABLE 11-2 HIERARCHY OF OPERATORS IN FORMULAS

VIEWING FORMULAS

The formulas can be viewed on the spreadsheet using the **Show Formulas** command in the **Options** menu. You can also see the formulas used by highlighting the cell containing the computed value and looking in the upper left corner of the spreadsheet (the Formula bar).

VIEW FORMULAS

1. **HIGHLIGHT** cell **F9**

The AVG formula appears in the **Formula** bar in the upper left corner of the screen.

2. **CHOOSE** **Show Formulas** from the **Options** menu

When this command is chosen, the columns in the spreadsheet become much wider, to accommodate the width of the formula. Often, the columns become even wider than the formula, so the worksheet is spread out over a large area. To see all of the formulas used, scroll around the worksheet. The formulas are shown in each cell in which formulas appear on the spreadsheet.

3. **CHOOSE** **Show Formulas** from the **Options** menu to turn off the formula command

4. **SAVE** this document again as **CH11PR1**

5. **QUIT** or **CONTINUE** to the tutorial

GUIDED TUTORIAL

WHAT YOU'LL DO

■ Use formulas and functions to calculate values.

HOW TO DO IT

INSTRUCTOR'S DATA DISK

1. OPEN the spreadsheet **CH10TUT** which you created in Chapter 10; or retrieve it from the instructor's data disk.

2. POSITION the highlight in cell **D4**.

3. TYPE =**B4*C4** and press **Enter**.

4. POSITION the highlight in cell **E4**.

5. TYPE =**D4*.08** to compute the tax and **PRESS Enter** or the **Right Arrow** key once.

6. With the highlight in cell **F4**, type =**D4-E4** and **PRESS Enter** to compute the net pay.

7. POSITION the highlight in cell **B9**.

8. TYPE =**SUM(B4:B7)** and press **Enter** to compute the total hours.

9. Do not compute other values at this time.

10. PROOF and save the spreadsheet under the new name **CH11TUT**.

REVIEW QUESTIONS

1. A _______________ shows a group of cells in a formula.

2. _________________ are built-in mathematical spreadsheet tools that perform specific calculations.

3. A cell address consists of the _______________ and ___________ intersection in a spreadsheet.

4. Write the correct syntax (format) that will add a string of values in a group of cells.

5. Write the correct syntax (format) that will search for a true/false condition and, if located, will perform specific actions.

6. Number each of the following to show the correct mathematical hierarchy used to compute values in a spreadsheet. Use number 1 as low; number 5 as high.

    _______   negative (-); positive (+)
    _______   exponential (^)
    _______   addition (+); subtraction)-
    _______   multiplication (*); division (/)
    _______   values within parentheses

HANDS-ON EXERCISES

EXERCISE 1

INSTRUCTOR'S DATA DISK

1. Open the file **CH10HO2** which you created in Chapter 10; or retrieve it from the instructor's data disk.

2. Compute the **Change** in sales from 1991 to 1992 by subtracting the 1991 value from the 1992 value. Insert the answer into the Delano change cell.

3. Compute an answer for the Delano **% of Change** value by dividing the **1992** value into the **Change** value.

4. Compute the **Total** for all **1991** sales and insert the answer into the **1991 Total** cell in column B.

5. Compute the **Average** for **1991** and insert it into the cell below the **Total** amount.

6. Compute the **Minimum** value (**=MIN**) and insert that answer into the cell below **Average**.

7. Save this spreadsheet under the new name **CH11HO1**.

EXERCISE 2

1. Create the following partial spreadsheet.

PUGET SOUND CHARTERS

	Current Year	Next Year	Five-year Projection	Ten-year Projection	Percentage of Increase
Delano	37890				
The Spirit	35550				
Sea Wolf	38950				
Irish Sea	41250				

SPREAD-SHEET

2. Save the spreadsheet as **CH11HO2**.

3. Compute the **Next Year** projected sales by multiplying the **Current Year** sales by **1.10** percent (110%, an increase of 10 percent over this year). Compute for the **Delano** only.

4. Compute **Delano's Five-year Projection** amount by multiplying **Next Year's** projected sales by **1.10** percent.

5. Compute the **Ten-year Projection** by multiplying the **Five-year Projection** by **1.30** percent. Compute for the **Delano** only.

6. Compute the **Percentage of Increase** value for the **Delano** by dividing the **Ten-year Projection** amount into the **Current Year** amount.

7. Proof for typographical errors and save the worksheet again.

Objectives

- Understand relative and absolute cell addresses.

- Copy to adjacent and nonadjacent cells.

- Insert and delete rows and columns.

- Move a range of cells.

- Select cells.

- Remove a range of cells.

PREVIEW »»➡

Modifications can be made to a spreadsheet, such as inserting or deleting rows and columns. Entire blocks of text or values can also be moved from one section of the worksheet to another, and formulas can be copied from one cell to a single cell or a range of cells. Some editing commands were discussed in Chapter 10. They included the use of the **F2** key for editing, using the **Clear** command in the **Edit** menu, as well as replacing the contents of a cell by typing a new entry. Other editing commands include copying and moving cell contents and clearing ranges of cells. These and other editing commands will be reviewed in this chapter.

SPREAD-
SHEET

USING RELATIVE CELL ADDRESSES

One method of editing is copying cells. You can copy the cell contents from one cell to another single cell or to a range of cells. If the cell contains a formula, the formula is copied. Any cell addresses in the formula are automatically adjusted to apply to the row and column to which they are copied. For example, copying a formula in cell B6 containing the cell address C6 to columns D through E in row 7 would change the address, C6, to E7 and F7. The address C6 is copied two columns to the right and down one row (column E and column F in row 7). Automatic changes in the cell address, as in this example, is called *relative* cell addressing. The address in a formula changes *relative* to the new location.

COPYING TO ADJACENT CELLS

Copying to adjacent cells in a spreadsheet means that values and text from one cell will be copied to the cells immediately around them, such as across the same row or down the same column.

COPY TO ADJACENT CELL

INSTRUCTOR'S
DATA DISK

1. SIGN onto Works and **OPEN** the spreadsheet **CH11PR1.WKS** which you created in Chapter 11; you can also retrieve it from the instructors data disk.

To copy a formula
The following steps will copy a formula in cell B6 to adjacent cells in C6 through E6. To do so, all cells in the range, from the one containing the correct formula through the last cell, are highlighted.

COPY A FORMULA

1. HIGHLIGHT cells **B6, C6, D6,** and **E6** by pressing the **F8** key and the **Right Arrow** or by dragging the mouse button

Cell B6 contains a value (the NET SALES amount) and the formula shown in the upper left corner of the screen. All cells to which B6 will be copied are also highlighted at this time.

2. **CHOOSE** **Fill Right** from the **Edit** menu

3. **LOOK** at the formula in the cell **B6** shown in the **Formula** bar at the top left of the screen.

4. **PRESS** the **Right Arrow** key once or click in cell **C6**

This cell shows the NET SALES for column C and the formula is relative to the column to which it was copied.

5. **PRESS** the **Right Arrow** two more times and look at the formula in each of the cells

To copy additional cells

The following steps will copy the formula contained in cell F9 to the adjacent cells through F13.

COPY ADDITIONAL CELLS

1. **HIGHLIGHT** cells **F9** through **F13**

2. **CHOOSE** **Fill Down** from the **Edit** menu

In step 3, the formula in cell B13 will be copied through cell E13.

3. **HIGHLIGHT** cells **B13** through **E13**

4. **CHOOSE** **Fill Right** from the **Edit** menu

5. **HIGHLIGHT** and copy to the following cell ranges. They are:

   Cells B15 through E15

   Cells B17 through E17

   Cells B21 through E21

When finished, the spreadsheet should appear similar to the one shown in Figure **12-1**.

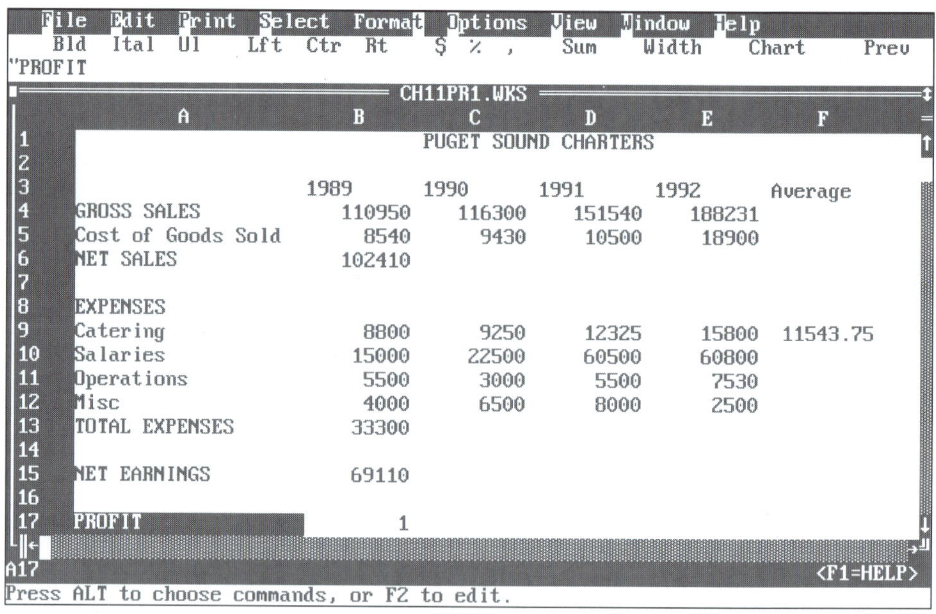

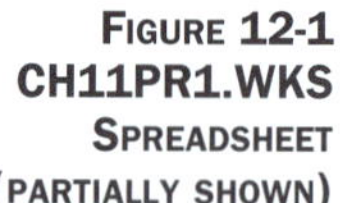

SPREAD-SHEET

FIGURE 12-1
CH11PR1.WKS
SPREADSHEET
(PARTIALLY SHOWN)

COPYING TO NONADJACENT CELLS

Copying to nonadjacent cells involves copying one or more cells to other areas of the worksheet not directly adjacent to the current cell(s). When this is the case, the cells to which you are copying cannot be highlighted at the same time as the cell from which you are copying. When this is the case, the **Copy** command in the **Edit** menu or the **Shift/F3** key combination is used in place of the **Fill** command.

COPY TO NONADJACENT CELLS

1. **HIGHLIGHT** cells **A21** through **E21** using either the **F8** key and the **Right arrow** key or dragging the mouse button

2. **PRESS** **Shift/F3** or use **Copy** from the **Edit** menu

3. **HIGHLIGHT** cell **A16**

4. **PRESS** **Enter**

Note: *Relative cell addressing is in effect with the cell addresses used in the formulas in this row. For that reason, the addresses in the formula changed relative to the cells to which it was copied. Because the new cell addresses in the formulas do not contain the correct values, an **ERR** message may appear.*

226

USING ABSOLUTE CELL ADDRESSES

Absolute cell addresses in a formula are those that will not change *relative* to the new location when copied. Cell addresses that are absolute are "locked" into position so that they will always read the same cell address regardless of where they are copied in the spreadsheet. A dollar sign ($) appearing in the cell address locks either the column, row, or both the column and the row.

USE ABSOLUTE CELL ADDRESSES

1. **HIGHLIGHT**   cell **B21**

2. **PRESS**   **F2** to **Edit** the cell

3. **INSERT**   dollar signs **($)** into the formula in the **Edit** bar as shown in the following example.

   =B$15/B$6

   Note: *You do not need to delete and retype the formula. Position the cursor prior to the 15 and prior to the 6 and type the dollar sign. Text will move right automatically.*

This formula, =B$15/B$6, locks the row addresses so that they will not change when copied (as they did previously). Wherever the formula is copied in the worksheet, the rows will remain the same. In cell B16, the formula that was copied changed to rows 10 and 1 and the formula could no longer work. The columns, however, remained the same, B, since the formula was copied directly up the same column in the spreadsheet.

Locking both columns and rows

It is possible to lock both columns and rows in a formula, and thus have a formula that is totally absolute when it is copied. This formula would read

    =$B$15/$B$6

in which case column B is locked and rows 15 and 6 are locked. Wherever this formula is copied, such as to cell F25, it will always divide the contents of cells B15 and B6.

Locking only the columns

To lock only the columns in a formula, insert the dollar sign ($) in front of the columns in the formula as shown in the following example.

    =$B15/$B6

Rows 15 and 6 will change relative to the new row location; column B will always read column B.

4. **PRESS**   **Enter** when the formula is correct

To copy the new formula

The following steps will copy the formula in B21 to cells C21 through E21.

COPY THE NEW FORMULA

1. **HIGHLIGHT** cells **B21** through **E21**
2. **CHOOSE** **Fill Right** from the **Edit** menu

This will copy the new formula to the cells in columns C through E.

SPREAD-SHEET

MOVING A RANGE OF CELLS

When the data in row 21 was copied previously, it remained in its original location and was also inserted into row 16. This time, with the formula corrected, this row will be moved rather than copied. It will be deleted from its old location, row 21, and inserted into its new location, row 16. When it is inserted into row 16, the contents of that row will be replaced automatically.

MOVE A RANGE OF CELLS

1. **HIGHLIGHT** cells **A21** through **E21**
2. **PRESS** **F3** or choose **Move** from the **Edit** menu
3. **HIGHLIGHT** cell **A16**
4. **PRESS** **Enter**

The data in row 21 is removed and is now inserted into row 16. It also shows the correct percentages.

VIEWING CELL ADDRESSES

To understand further how absolute cell addresses change (or do not change) when they are moved or copied to a new location, you can position the highlight in any cell into which an absolute formula is copied.

VIEW CELL ADDRESSES

1. **HIGHLIGHT** cell **B16**

The formula still reads rows 15 and 6. When it was copied the first time, without the dollar signs inserted, the rows were adjusted accordingly to 10 and 1. Since the formula was copied five rows up in the spreadsheet, 5 rows were subtracted from 15 and 6, respectively; therefore, the addresses became relative to their new location in the spreadsheet. With the rows locked, 15 and 6 remained stationary.

2. **MOVE**   through cells **C16**, **D16**, and **E16** and note the same absolute row addressing.

USING THE COPY SPECIAL COMMAND

The **Copy Special** command in the **Edit** menu is used for occasional copy operations where special conditions must be met. This command will not be applied in the spreadsheet on the screen; however, you should know about the options available with the **Copy Special** command for possible future use.

The command works in two ways:

- To copy values and formatting in a cell or range without copying the formulas used.

- To copy values in a cell or range and add to or subtract from the values in another cell or range.

The first option is used any time it is desirable to have the values in the cells moved or copied to another location in the spreadsheet; yet, it is not necessary to use the formulas in the new location. On some occasions, all computations are performed in one location of the spreadsheet and results are posted in another.

The second option is used when it is necessary to see only the results of a computation (addition or subtraction) and not the original values. For example, you could subtract one set of values from another by copying the results into a single column or row that also contains the values you are using in the formula. The result would be that only the answer is visible.

INSERTING AND DELETING ROWS OR COLUMNS

Rows or columns can be inserted and deleted in a spreadsheet. When a row is inserted, highlight the row below where the new row will appear. A column is inserted to the left of the highlighted column. It is also possible to insert several rows or columns in a single command. Inserting rows and columns is done through the **Insert Row/Column** command in the **Edit** menu. Deleting them is done through the **Delete Row/Column** command in the **Edit** menu.

INSERTING A SINGLE ROW OR COLUMN

INSERT A SINGLE ROW OR COLUMN

1. HIGHLIGHT   cell **A17**

> *Note:*   *It is not necessary to highlight the entire row. When the command is given to insert a row, Works knows to insert all the way across the worksheet. The same is true when inserting or deleting columns.*

2. CHOOSE   **Insert Row/Column** from the **Edit** menu

3. CHOOSE   **Row** (it should be selected)

4. CHOOSE   **OK** or press Enter

Row 17 is now the new row and the remaining rows are moved down.

> *Note:*   *When rows or columns are inserted, formulas may change. This spreadsheet is okay. The formula in cells B18 through E18 refer to the contents of row 15, which has not been moved. Sometimes it is necessary to change formulas to absolute or partial absolute formulas so that the values remain the same when columns and rows are inserted.*

SELECTING CELLS IN A SPREADSHEET

Works' spreadsheet tool contains the same extension mode for highlighting large blocks of cells as that used to select large blocks of text in word processing - the **F8** key. When the **F8** key is pressed, the **EXT** mode is turned on and blocks of cells can be highlighted using a few quick keystrokes. If you are familiar with using the mouse for highlighting, you may prefer that method. The **F8** key is useful for those more comfortable with using the keyboard or where that is the only option.

SELECT CELLS IN A SPREADSHEET

1. HIGHLIGHT   cells **A3** through **F4** by dragging the mouse button

> *Note:*   *You could also have pressed **F8** first to turn on the **EXT** mode and then used the **Right** and **Down Arrow** keys to extend the highlight.*

MAKING SPREADSHEET SELECTIONS

Table 12-1 shows ways in which other selections can be made in the spreadsheet tool. Read through them and practice each on the current worksheet. If using a mouse, you may be more comfortable with clicking and dragging the mouse button.

TO HIGHLIGHT THIS	DO THIS
A single cell	Press the Arrow keys or click the mouse button.
A row	Press Ctrl/F8; choose Row from the Select menu; or click the mouse button on the row number.
A column	Press Shift/F8; choose Column from the Select menu; or click the mouse button on the column letter.
A range	Select the upper left cell in the range; press F8 or choose Cells in the Select menu; press the Arrow keys to highlight or drag the mouse button.
The entire spreadsheet	Press Ctrl/Shift/F8, choose All from the Select menu, or click the mouse button in the corner of the window to the left of column A and above row 1. This command selects the entire spreadsheet, from A1 through IV16384.

TABLE 12-1
MAKING SELECTIONS ON A SPREADSHEET

INSERTING MULTIPLE ROWS OR COLUMNS

Inserting multiple rows or columns is a matter of highlighting the area into which they will be inserted (as done in Selecting cells in a spreadsheet) and then using the **Insert Row/Column** command from the **Edit** menu.

INSERT MULTIPLE ROWS OR COLUMNS

With rows 3 and 4 highlighted,

1. CHOOSE   **Insert Row/Column** from the **Edit** menu
2. CHOOSE   **Row**
3. CHOOSE   **OK** or press Enter

All rows are pushed down on the spreadsheet and two new rows are inserted.

TYPE A SUBHEADING

1. HIGHLIGHT   cell **C2**
2. TYPE   **Comparison of Earnings**
3. PRESS   **Enter** or click in the cell

DELETING ROWS OR COLUMNS

Deleting rows or columns is the same as inserting rows or columns. The command is located in the **Edit** menu and the row or column is highlighted prior to using the command.

**SPREAD-
SHEET**

DELETE ROWS OR COLUMNS

1.	HIGHLIGHT	cell **A4**
	Note:	*You could use any cell in row 4 if this is the row to be deleted.*
2.	CHOOSE	**Delete Row/Column** from the **Edit** menu
3.	CHOOSE	**Row** (if necessary)
4.	CHOOSE	**OK** or press Enter

All rows are moved upward and row 3 is the only blank row between the main heading and the column headings.

INSERT AN ADDITIONAL ROW

1.	HIGHLIGHT	cell **A5**
2.	INSERT	a new row at this position
3.	CHOOSE	**Save As** from the **File** menu and save this file as **CH12PR1**
4.	EXIT	Works or **CONTINUE** to the tutorial

CLEARING A RANGE OF CELLS

Sometimes it is desirable to clear an entire range of cells. To do so, use one of the highlight methods listed in Table 12-1 to highlight all of the cells to be deleted, and choose **Clear** from the **Edit** menu. Since this spreadsheet is complete, it is not necessary to delete any large blocks of cells at this time; however, if you have made errors, or if you need to make corrections when doing practice documents, you may decide to use the **Clear** command. It is the fastest way to remove text and values in large ranges of cells.

GUIDED TUTORIAL

WHAT YOU'LL DO

- Copy cell contents.
- Create formulas containing cell addresses.
- Insert columns and rows.

HOW TO DO IT

INSTRUCTOR'S DATA DISK

1. **OPEN** the spreadsheet **CH11TUT** which you created on Chapter 11; or retrieve it from the instructor's data disk.

2. **HIGHLIGHT** cells D4 through D7, the Total range for all employees.

3. **CHOOSE** **Fill Down** from the **Edit** menu.

4. **HIGHLIGHT** cells E4 through E7, the Tax range for all employees.

5. **CHOOSE** **Fill Down** from the **Edit** menu.

6. **FILL IN** the Net values for all employees using the same techniques as steps 4 and 5.

7. **POSITION** the highlight in cell B9 and select all total cells across the row through Net.

8. **CHOOSE** **Fill Right** from the **Edit** menu.

The spreadsheet should appear similar to the following.

PAYROLL

EMPLOYEE	Hours	Rate	Total	Tax	Net
Eiler	40	12	480	38.4	441.6
Kennedy	40	8	320	25.6	294.4
MacRannall	42	12	504	40.32	463.68
Shepard	41	10	410	32.8	377.2
Total	163	42	1714	137.12	1576.88

9. POSITION the highlight in cell A1. (Use F5 to go to the cell or press Ctrl/Home.)

10. TYPE **0.07** into the cell. This value is the amount of expected pay increase over the next year.

11. POSITION the highlight in cell A11.

12. TYPE **Payroll Increase**.

13. ADJUST the column width if necessary by choosing **Column Width** from the **Format** menu or by clicking **Width** on the **Toolbar**.

14. MOVE the highlight to cell B11.

15. TYPE **=D4*$A$1+D4**.

SPREAD-SHEET

This formula will multiply Eiler's Total pay times the percentage rate found in cell A1 and add that increase to the Total pay — showing the increase above the present total. The dollar signs ($) are included to show an absolute cell address, which is one that will not change when copied to other cells in the spreadsheet.

16. SELECT cells B11 through B14.

17. CHOOSE **Fill Down** from the **Edit** menu.

Because D4 is used in the formula and does not contain dollar signs, it is a relative cell address. Therefore, it will increase in value as it is copied down. When D4 is copied down one cell address lower, it will change to D5 (Kennedy's Total amount), then to D6 (MacRannall's Total), and so on.

18. SAVE the spreadsheet as **CH12TUT**.

19. HIGHLIGHT cell **A4**.

20. CHOOSE **Insert Row/Column** from the **Edit** menu.

21. CHOOSE **Row** (it should be selected).

22. CHOOSE **OK** or press Enter.

23. HIGHLIGHT **B12** through **B15**.

24. CHOOSE **Move** from the **Edit** menu.

25. HIGHLIGHT **B13** and press **Enter**.

26. HIGHLIGHT **A5** through **A8**.

27. CHOOSE **Copy** from the **Edit** menu.

28. HIGHLIGHT **A13** and press **Enter**.

The spreadsheet should appear similar to the following.

```
0.07                              PAYROLL

EMPLOYEE    Hours       Rate        Total         Tax          Net

Eiler         40         12          480          38.4         441.6
Kennedy       40          8          320          25.6         294.4
MacRannall    42         12          504          40.32        463.68
Shepard       41         10          410          32.8         377.2

Total        163         42         1714         137.12       1576.88

Payroll Increase
Eiler       513.6
Kennedy     342.4
MacRannall  539.28
Shepard     438.7
```

29. **SAVE**   again under the same name.

REVIEW QUESTIONS 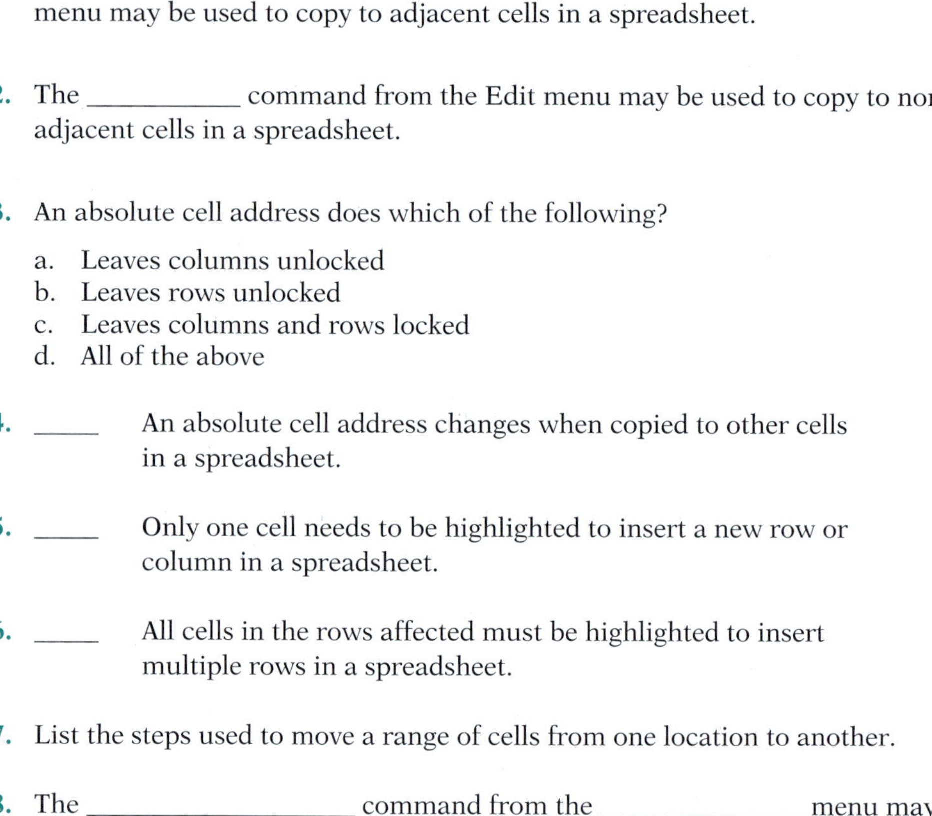

SPREAD-SHEET

1. The ________________ or the ________________ command from the **Edit** menu may be used to copy to adjacent cells in a spreadsheet.

2. The ____________ command from the Edit menu may be used to copy to non-adjacent cells in a spreadsheet.

3. An absolute cell address does which of the following?

   a. Leaves columns unlocked
   b. Leaves rows unlocked
   c. Leaves columns and rows locked
   d. All of the above

4. _____   An absolute cell address changes when copied to other cells in a spreadsheet.

5. _____   Only one cell needs to be highlighted to insert a new row or column in a spreadsheet.

6. _____   All cells in the rows affected must be highlighted to insert multiple rows in a spreadsheet.

7. List the steps used to move a range of cells from one location to another.

8. The ________________ command from the ________________ menu may be used to remove cell contents.

HANDS-ON EXERCISES

EXERCISE 1

1. Open the spreadsheet **CH11HO1** which you created in Chapter 11; or retrieve it form the instructor's data disk.

2. Copy the **Change** formula for the **Delano** to pertinent cells for each of the boats in the spreadsheet.

3. Copy the **% of Change** formula for **Delano** to other pertinent cells in the spreadsheet.

4. Copy the **Total** formula for **1991** sales to the **1992** column.

5. Copy the **Average** formula to other cells in the **1992** column.

6. Copy the **Minimum** formula to other cells in the **1992** column.

7. Insert a blank row between **Total** and **Average**.

8. Save the spreadsheet again as **CH12HO1**.

EXERCISE 2

1. Open the spreadsheet **CH11HO2** which you created in Chapter 11; or retrieve it from the instructor's data disk.

2. Copy the formulas for **Next Year**, **Five-Year Projection**, **Ten-Year Projection**, and **Percentage of Increase** to other pertinent cells in the column for each of the boats.

3. Position the highlight two cells below **Irish Sea** in column **A**.

4. Type **Total**.

5. Compute the total for the **Current Year** and copy to compute totals for each column **except** Percentage of Increase.

6. Save the spreadsheet under the new name **CH12HO2**.

7. Insert three new rows after the one-line main heading.

8. Move the **Total** line so that it appears two blank lines below the main heading.

9. Edit the **Total** cell and change it to **Grand Totals**.

10. Adjust the width of the columns to **15** each.

11. Save the spreadsheet again.

13 FORMATTING

Objectives

- Change character formats.

- Format values.

- Create headers and footers.

- Preview the spreadsheet.

- Insert page breaks.

- Change margins.

- Print the spreadsheet.

Formatting a spreadsheet includes using commands from the **Format** menu that will change the appearance of the values and text in the spreadsheet. From this menu, it is possible to add the missing commas and decimal points to the values and to enhance the appearance of headings by using different fonts or character styles such as bold and underline.

As with editing commands, ranges of cells are highlighted and the formatting commands applied. Formatting decisions can be changed by highlighting the cells and choosing menu commands again.

SPREAD-SHEET

CHANGING THE CHARACTER FORMATS

Character formats include anything that affects the appearance of the individual characters in the spreadsheet. Options may include changing the text to bold print, underline, or italics. It also includes changing the type of font. These options were applied to text in word processing as well. You will recognize some of the dialog boxes and menu commands when applying character formatting in the following exercise.

CHANGING THE FONT

A spreadsheet can contain only one font. You may recall that in word processing, the font could change for a character, word, or line of text, and so on. In a spreadsheet document, the font selected affects the entire spreadsheet.

CHANGE THE FONT

INSTRUCTOR'S DATA DISK

1. OPEN the spreadsheet **CH12PR1** which you created in Chapter 12; or retrieve it from the instructor's data disk

With the highlight in any cell in the worksheet,

2. CHOOSE **Font** from the **Format** menu

A dialog box similar to the one shown in Figure 13-1 appears.

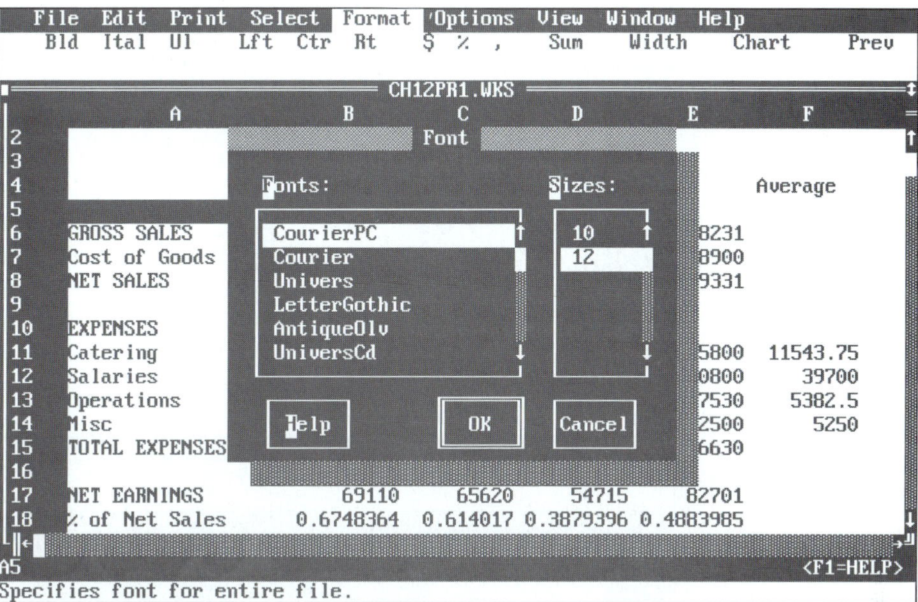

FIGURE 13-1
FONTS DIALOG BOX

This figure is similar to the **Fonts** list box in word processing. The image may appear different from that shown in the figure, depending on your system and the fonts in use, and upon the fonts available with your printer.

3. SCROLL   through the list of fonts available. Notice that the point size changes as different fonts are selected. With some fonts, more than one point size may be available.

4. CHOOSE   **Prestige[D/H/J/M]** in the **Fonts** list box or another font different from the one in use

5. CHOOSE   **10** in the **Sizes** list box

6. CHOOSE   **OK** or press Enter

Note: *The change will not be apparent on the screen. Later, when you print the spreadsheet, you will notice the difference in appearance from the default Courier 12 point.*

CHANGING THE STYLE

Changing the style includes altering the appearance of individual characters in the spreadsheet, such as bold, underline, and italics. It also includes the placement of text or values within the cell boundaries. For the most part, changing the appearance of characters involves changing the column headings, side headings, and main headings of a spreadsheet. Menu commands are discussed in the following steps; however, you may also use the Toolbar as a shortcut to formatting text and values.

CHANGE THE STYLE

1. **HIGHLIGHT** cell **C1**

   Note: *Since all of the main heading is contained in the cell, it is not necessary to highlight any of the text overlapping into the next cell.*

2. **CHOOSE** **Style** from the **Format** menu

The dialog box shown in Figure 13-2 appears.

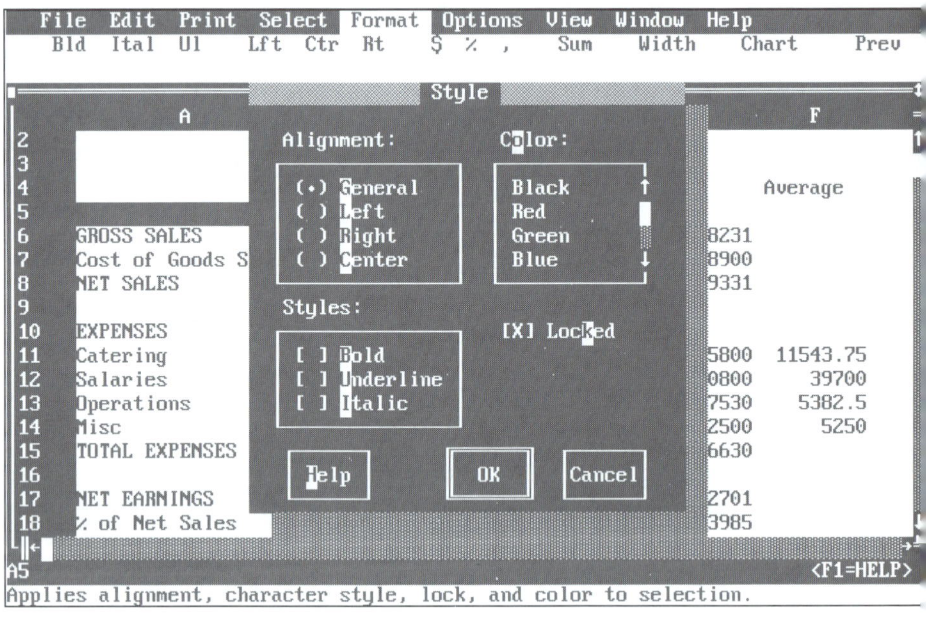

FIGURE 13-2
STYLE DIALOG BOX

Selections from this dialog box are shown in Table 13-1.

<u>Alignment</u>

	General:	The default alignment in the cell as the program inserts it when you type
	Left:	Alignment on the left side of the cell
	Right:	Alignment on the right side of the cell
	Center:	Alignment in the center of the cell between the cell margins

<u>Color</u>

Black

Red

Green

Blue. . .   Change the color of text on the screen and in print if using a color printer

<u>Styles</u>

Bold: Bolded text or values

Underline: Underlined text or values

Italic: Italicized text or values

<u>Locked</u>   To unlock or lock a cell or range of cells. This option is used to protect the contents of cells.

TABLE 13-1
OPTIONS IN THE
STYLE DIALOG BOX

---

3. **CHOOSE** **Bold**

4. **CHOOSE** **OK**

The heading appears in a different shade or color, indicating that the bold format has been applied.

---

5. **HIGHLIGHT** **all column headings** in row 4

6. **CHOOSE** **Style** from the **Format** menu

7. **CHOOSE** **Center** in the **Alignment** box

8. **CHOOSE** **Underline** and **Bold** in the **Styles** box

9. **CHOOSE** **OK** or press Enter

The column headings appear shaded or in a different color print. When printed, the spreadsheet will show the headings centered between the cell borders and underlined and bolded.

> **10.** HIGHLIGHT **all of the headings** in column A
>
> **11.** CHOOSE   **Bold** from the Toolbar, **Bld**

While it is important to know where to locate format commands in the menus, practice using the Toolbar as often as possible. The toolbar options include bold (Bld), italic (Ital), underline (Ul), left (Lft), center (Ctr), right (Rt), currency ($), percentage (%), and comma (,) formats. You may also use the Sum tool to automatically insert the sum function format, width to change the width, and preview to preview the document. These and other toolbar options will be discussed throughout the spreadsheet instructions.

FORMATTING VALUES

SPREAD-SHEET

Commands for changing the appearance of values in a spreadsheet are shown in the **Format** menu along with the character formats. When dollar signs and commas are typed in with the numbers, Works accepts the contents as whole numbers. However, it is easier to type in the numbers plain, and format the cells later. Essentially, Works waits until a format command is given before changing the appearance of values in the spreadsheet.

FORMAT VALUES

1. HIGHLIGHT   cells **B6 through E8** (turn on the **EXT** mode, **F8**, or use the mouse button)

2. CHOOSE   **Currency** from the **Format** menu

3. ACCEPT   the setting of two decimal places when the dialog box appears by pressing **Enter**

Some values appear showing the dollar sign ($); however, most cells show a series of number signs (#########) running from cell to cell. This occurs when the column is not wide enough to hold the values entered into it, such as a very wide formatted currency value.

Changing the column width

Whenever number signs (###########) appear, change the column width. Once it is changed, the numbers will show in the cells.

With all of the value cells in rows 6 through 8 still selected,

CHANGE THE COLUMN WIDTH

1. **CHOOSE**   **Column Width** from the **Format** menu

2. **TYPE**   **15** as the new column width

    Note: *It is necessary to guess how wide the cells need to be. Since the default is 10, and 10 was too narrow, adding five spaces should accommodate the larger, formatted figures.*

3. **PRESS**   **Enter** or choose OK

The values appear.

FORMAT FROM THE TOOLBAR (MOUSE)

1. **HIGHLIGHT**   cells **B11 through E15**

2. **CHOOSE**   **$** from the **Toolbar**

The values appear in currency format with two zeros to the right of the decimal, which is the default setting when using the toolbar.

3. **FORMAT**   the values in **row 17 as currency**

4. **FORMAT**   the values in **row 18 as percent** with two places to the right of the decimal point by using the Toolbar (the default is 2)

5. **FORMAT**   the values in **column F, rows 11 through 14** as **currency.** Leave two places to the right of the decimal.

6. **CLICK**   on **Width** in the Toolbar

7. **TYPE**   **15** and press **Enter**

8. **SAVE**   again as **CH13PR1**

Other formatting commands

There are several format commands listed in the **Format** menu. As you work with spreadsheets, you will find more uses for these. A summary of each option is given in Table 13-2.

USE THIS FORMAT COMMAND:	TO DISPLAY THIS:
General	Values displayed as integers (123), decimals 123.23, or exponential notations (1.23E+25) when the number is too large to fit into the cell. General formats also display negative numbers with the minus sign (-). General is the format for cells prior to any other format given by the user.
Fixed	Values showing a specified number of digits to the right of the decimal point. Also showing negative numbers with a minus sign (-).
Currency	Values displaying commas every three places, currency signs ($), and a designated number of digits to the right of the decimal. Typing a dollar sign ($) prior to entering a value also displays the currency format, although this method is usually not as fast as formatting ranges of cells. Shows negative numbers in parentheses.
Comma	Values displayed with commas every three places. Displays negative values in red when the box is checked.
Percent	Values displayed as percentages, such as 43.00%. With the general format, they would be displayed as 0.43. Negative numbers are shown with the minus sign (-).
Exponential	Values displayed in scientific notation. 1234567 becomes 1.23E+06 if formatted as exponential with two decimal places. Negative numbers appear with the minus sign (-).
True/False	Values are displayed as 1 or 0. Zero values are false; nonzero values are true.

TABLE 13-2
VALUE FORMATS
FROM THE FORMAT
MENU

CREATING HEADERS AND FOOTERS

Spreadsheets can contain headers and footers like those created in word processing. A header appears at the top of every page (the first page is optional); a footer appears at the bottom of every page (the first page is optional). As in the word processor, the header or footer does not appear on the screen. It does appear when the spreadsheet is printed, and is therefore a command found in the **Print** menu. Because adding headers and footers to a spreadsheet enhances the overall formatting of it, it is included in this formatting chapter. If more information is desired, see the word processing section of this book.

CREATE HEADERS & FOOTERS

1. CHOOSE   **Headers & Footers** from the **Print** menu

2. TYPE   **Payroll Report, Puget Sound Charters** in the **Header** box

3. CHOOSE   **OK** or press Enter

    Note: *Since headers and footers do not appear on the spreadsheet, the **Use header & footer paragraphs** option is not available. For further information on the symbols that can be used in the **Header and Footer** text box, see Part 2.*

PREVIEWING THE SPREADSHEET

A spreadsheet can be viewed in **Print Preview**, as can any other document created using Works. Since the header does not appear on the spreadsheet and since all columns are not visible on the screen, this option will assist in viewing the appearance of the entire spreadsheet as it will print.

PREVIEW THE SPREADSHEET

1. CHOOSE   **Preview** from the **Print** menu

2. CHOOSE   **Preview** again

The first page of the spreadsheet appears on the screen as it will print. When the columns of a spreadsheet extend far to the right side of the screen and will not fit on an 8 1/2- x 11-inch sheet of standard paper, the columns to the right become the second page.

3. PRESS   the **PgDn** key to see the second page of the spreadsheet

Notice that the header appears on both pages.

4. PRESS   **PgUp** again and then **ESC** to return to the spreadsheet working space

---

INSERTING PAGE BREAKS

The text in column A and the values in columns B through D appear on the first page. Works automatically determines where pages will break unless you specify otherwise. To change the location of the page break, the **Insert Page Break** command is used in the **Print** menu.

<table>
<tr><td colspan="2" align="center">INSERT PAGE BREAKS</td></tr>
<tr><td>1. HIGHLIGHT</td><td>any cell in column D</td></tr>
<tr><td>2. CHOOSE</td><td>Insert Page Break from the Print menu</td></tr>
<tr><td>3. CHOOSE</td><td>Column</td></tr>
<tr><td>4. CHOOSE</td><td>OK or press Enter</td></tr>
</table>

A double arrow (>>) called a break mark appears between columns C and D at the top of the screen.

5. CLICK   **PREV** from the Toolbar to preview the spreadsheet

Three columns now appear evenly on each page. Notice, however, that the main and subheadings are divided — half appearing on one page and half on the second page. The two heading lines should be moved to column B.

6. PRESS   **ESC**

SPREAD-
SHEET

DELETING PAGE BREAKS

To delete a page break, highlight any cell in the column containing the page break and choose **Delete Page Break** from the **Print** menu.

To move the heading:
When in the spreadsheet space, notice the page break marker (>>) just above the main and subheadings, indicating that the headings will be split when the page is divided.

<table>
<tr><td colspan="2" align="center">MOVE THE HEADING</td></tr>
<tr><td>1. HIGHLIGHT</td><td>cells C1 and C2</td></tr>
<tr><td>2. PRESS</td><td>F3 to move</td></tr>
<tr><td>3. HIGHLIGHT</td><td>cell B1</td></tr>
<tr><td>4. PRESS</td><td>Enter or click the mouse button in the cell</td></tr>
</table>

The headings are now to the left of the page break marker and will appear on the first page only.

CHANGING THE MARGINS

CHANGE THE MARGINS

1. **PREVIEW** — the spreadsheet again using the **PREV** command on the Toolbar

The spreadsheet pages are looking more balanced, but still not quite perfect. The right margin is much larger than the left. The margins can be adjusted so that the columns are better placed on the page. In this spreadsheet, the best adjustment would be to increase the size of the left margin.

2. **PRESS** — **ESC** when finished
3. **CHOOSE** — **Page Setup & Margins** from the **Print** menu
   Note: *For a full explanation of the **Page Setup & Margins** dialog box, see Part 2.*
4. **TYPE** — **2** in the **Left margin** box
5. **CHOOSE** — **OK** or press Enter
6. **USE** — **Print Preview** to see the margin adjustment
7. **PRESS** — **ESC** when finished

PRINTING THE SPREADSHEET

The print options in the **Print** dialog box are the same as for word processing. If you have further questions concerning these options, see the full explanation in Part 2.

PRINT THE SPREADSHEET

1. **SAVE** — the spreadsheet again under the same name, **CH13PR1**
2. **CHOOSE** — **Print** from the **Print** menu

The one additional option in this dialog box that differs from word processing is the **Print row and column labels** option. This option allows for printing the row and column labels with the spreadsheet. For this exercise, print the entire worksheet without the row and column labels.

3. **CHOOSE** — **Print**

PRINTING SELECTED CELLS

A block of selected cells can be printed using the **Set Print Area** command in the **Print** menu. This command allows for specific areas of a spreadsheet to be printed rather than the entire spreadsheet.

PRINT SELECTED CELLS

1. HIGHLIGHT   **all cells** in **rows 4 through 8**
2. CHOOSE   **Set Print Area** from the **Print** menu
3. CHOOSE   **OK** or press **Enter** to the box that appears
4. USE   **Print Preview** to see how this block of the spreadsheet would look if printed. CHOOSE **Esc** to not print.
5. HIGHLIGHT   the entire spreadsheet and choose **Set Print Area** again
6. QUIT   or **continue** to the tutorial

GUIDED TUTORIAL

WHAT YOU'LL DO

- Change font and point size.
- Apply character and page formats.
- Print selected blocks of the spreadsheet.
- Print the entire spreadsheet.

HOW TO DO IT

INSTRUCTOR'S
DATA DISK

1. **OPEN** — **CH12TUT** which you created in Chapter 12; or retrieve it from the instructor's data disk.
2. **HIGHLIGHT** the main heading, **PAYROLL**.
3. **CHOOSE** **Font** from the **Format** menu.
4. **CHOOSE** a font different from the one you are using.
5. **CHOOSE** **12** from the **Size** list or another size font.
6. **CHOOSE** **OK** or press Enter.
7. **HIGHLIGHT** the entire row containing the column headings **Employee** through **Net**.
8. **CLICK** **Bld** on the Toolbar.
9. **CLICK** **UI** on the Toolbar to underline.
10. **CLICK** **Ctr** on the Toolbar to center the text.
11. **HIGHLIGHT** all values for all employees in the **Rate** column.
12. **CHOOSE** **Currency** from the **Format** menu.
13. **ACCEPT** the default setting of two decimal places when the box appears by pressing **Enter**.
14. **ADJUST** the column width if necessary.
15. **HIGHLIGHT** all other currency values in the **Total** through **Net** columns.
16. **CLICK** **once** on the dollar sign ($) on the Toolbar.
17. **FORMAT** all other dollar values as currency with two places to the right of the decimal.
18. **CHOOSE** **Headers & Footers** from the **Print** menu.
19. **TYPE** **PAYROLL REPORT, March** in the Header box.
20. **CHOOSE** **OK** or press Enter.
21. **PREVIEW** the spreadsheet using the **PREV** command from the Toolbar.
22. **PRESS** **ESC** when finished.

The spreadsheet should appear similar to the following.

PAYROLL

EMPLOYEE	Hours	Rate	Total	Tax	Net
Eiler	40	$12.00	$480.00	$38.40	$441.60
Kennedy	40	$8.00	$320.00	$25.60	$294.40
MacRannall	42	$12.00	$504.00	$40.32	$463.68
Shepard	41	$10.00	$410.00	$32.80	$377.20
Total	163	$42.00	$1,714.00	$137.12	$1,576.88

Payroll Increase

Eiler	$513.60
Kennedy	$342.40
MacRannall	$539.28
Shepard	$438.70

23 POSITION	the highlight anywhere in column D.
24. CHOOSE	**Insert Page Break** from the **Print** menu.
25. CHOOSE	**Column**.
26. choose	**OK** or press Enter.
27. CHANGE	the left, top, and right margins to 2.
28. PREVIEW	the spreadsheet again to note the change.
29. SAVE	the spreadsheet as **CH13TUT**.
30. PRINT	a copy of the spreadsheet.
31. PRINT	a copy of the employee, hours, and rate columns only on the spreadsheet.

REVIEW QUESTIONS

1. The ___________ command from the ___________ menu is used to change the type and size of print on the spreadsheet.

2. The alignment and style of print displayed may be changed in the ___________ dialog box.

3. List two ways to format values as currency.

4. The _______________ command from the **Format** menu is used to adjust the width of the column.

5. The _______________ may be used to change column width and change the format of values.

6. Briefly explain what the **Headers & Footers** command is used for.

7. The _________________ command from the ______________ menu is used to change the margins in a spreadsheet.

8. What is the only way to see the changes made to a spreadsheet without printing it?

9. What command is used to print only selected cells of a spreadsheet?

10. What command is used to change the alignment of text or values?

11. _____ Page breaks are inserted to the left of the highlight position when the Insert Page Break command is chosen.

12. _____ The entire column must be highlighted when inserting a page break.

HANDS-ON EXERCISES

EXERCISE 1

1. Create the following partial spreadsheet as shown. Enter the values and labels in the columns and rows shown. Adjust the column widths as necessary. Do not worry about the alignment at this time.

SPREAD-
SHEET

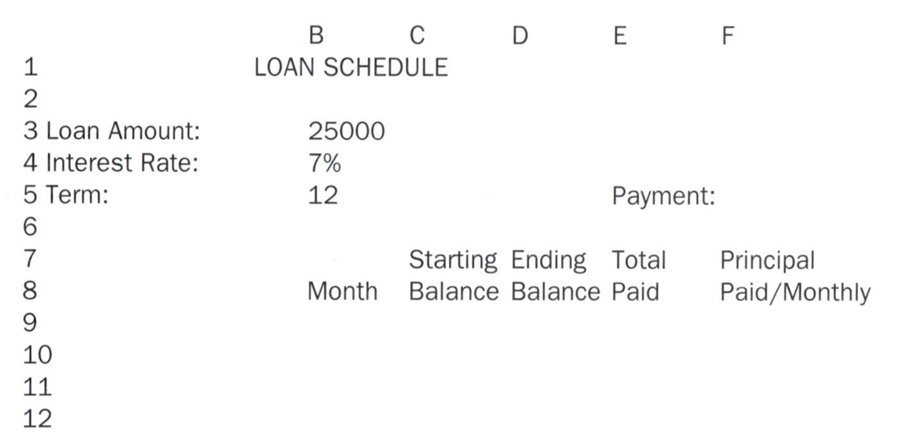

	B	C	D	E	F
1	LOAN SCHEDULE				
2					
3 Loan Amount:	25000				
4 Interest Rate:	7%				
5 Term:	12			Payment:	
6					
7		Starting	Ending	Total	Principal
8	Month	Balance	Balance	Paid	Paid/Monthly
9					
10					
11					
12					

2. For the Payment (F5), use a function called PMT which computes the amount of payments to be made based on the term, loan amount, and interest rate. The formula is written as follows:

    =PMT(Loan Amount, Interest rate/12, Term)

    Substitute the correct cell addresses for each of the values (loan amount, interest rate, and term). Be sure to use the parentheses as shown, as well as the commas and division mark.

3. In cell B9 enter the number **12**. In cell B10 enter the formula **=B9-1**. Copy this formula through cell B20. This spreadsheet will show the accumulation of an investment through the next 12 months.

4. In cell C9 insert the value for loan amount by typing **=B3**.

5. In cell C10 insert the value for the Ending Balance, **=D9**. (The values will fill in as the rest of the spreadsheet is completed.)

6.   Copy the formula in C10 down the column through cell C20. (The values will fill in later.)

7.   In cell D9 enter a formula to compute the Ending Balance. Use the following formula:

=C9+(C9*$B$4/12)-$F$5

8.   Copy the formula in D9 down the column through cell D20.

9.   In cell E9, enter the value for payments made, **=F5**.

10. In cell E10, enter a formula to add the **absolute cell address** value in F5 (**$F$5**) to the value in E9. The dollar signs in this absolute address will lock both the column and row so that it remains the same wherever it is copied. Copy this formula to other cells in the column.

11. In cell F9 insert the formula to compute the principal, **=C9-D9**, and copy down the column.

12. Save the worksheet as **CH13HO1**.

13. Format the main heading in bold.

14. Change the font of the spreadsheet to Helvetica 10 point or another font style.

15. Bold all headings in column A.

16. Bold and center the column headings. Underline the second line in the heading.

17. Bold the heading **Payment** in E5.

18. Center all values.

19. Format all dollar values as currency with no decimal places.

20. Proof and save the spreadsheet.

21. Preview and print a copy.

EXERCISE 2

1. Open the following documents which you created in Chapter 12.

    CH12HO1and **CH12HO2** or retreive them from the instructor's data disk.

2. Center and bold all main and column headings.

3. Bold any headings in column A.

4. Format all dollar values as currency with two places to the right of the decimal. Format all percentages as whole numbers without decimals.

5. Insert a page break on any spreadsheet that goes beyond column D. The second page should start with column E.

6. Change the top margins to 2.0. Change the left margin to 1 and the right margin to 1.

7. Adjust the column width as necessary.

8. Add appropriate headers (use your name and the page number) to both spreadsheets.

9. Save both spreadsheets again under the following new names:

    CH12HO1   as   **CH13HO2A**

    CH12HO2   as   **CH13HO2B**

10. Print copies of both spreadsheets.

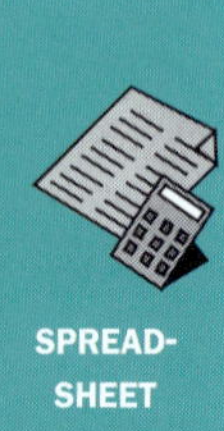

14 INCREASED SPREADSHEET POWER

Objectives

- Calculate with dates and times.

- Enter a series of values.

- Use range names.

- Sort contents of cells.

PREVIEW 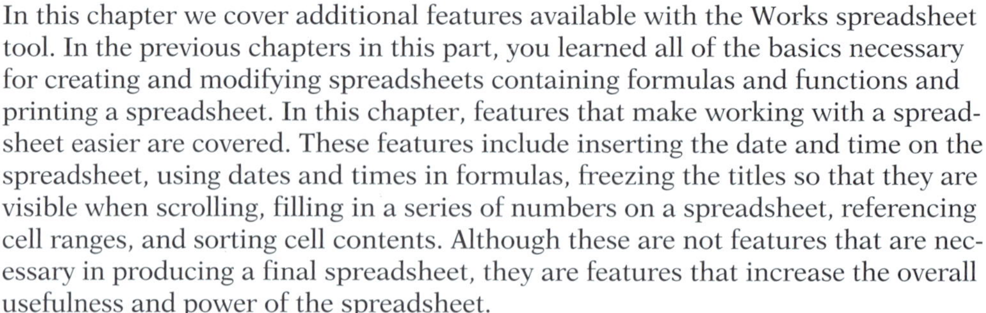

In this chapter we cover additional features available with the Works spreadsheet tool. In the previous chapters in this part, you learned all of the basics necessary for creating and modifying spreadsheets containing formulas and functions and printing a spreadsheet. In this chapter, features that make working with a spreadsheet easier are covered. These features include inserting the date and time on the spreadsheet, using dates and times in formulas, freezing the titles so that they are visible when scrolling, filling in a series of numbers on a spreadsheet, referencing cell ranges, and sorting cell contents. Although these are not features that are necessary in producing a final spreadsheet, they are features that increase the overall usefulness and power of the spreadsheet.

SPREAD-SHEET

INSERTING DATE AND TIME

The date or time may be inserted on a spreadsheet and used in a number of ways. When either is used in a spreadsheet, it can then be used as part of a formula. For example, if Puget Sound Charters wanted to keep track of scheduled cruises, the date and time of the cruises could be kept in a sort of spreadsheet log. Once dates and times are logged, they can be subtracted or added to each other to count the total hours and minutes or the total number of days.

Ways in which dates and times may be entered are shown in Table 14-1.

TYPE THIS	TO DISPLAY THIS
Nov 1, 1991	Month, day, year
Nov, 1991	Month, year
Nov 30	Month, day
Nov	Month only
11/1/91	Month, day, year
11/91	Month, year
11/30	Month, day
24-HOUR TIME	
15:30:00	Hour, minute, second
15:30	Hour, minute
12-HOUR TIME	
3:30:00 PM	Hour, minute, second
3:30 PM	Hour, minute
3 PM	Hour only

TABLE 14-1
FORMAT FOR TYPING DATES AND TIMES

TYPING THE DATE AND TIME

Dates can be entered into a cell in a long or short format. Long and short formats are shown in Table 14-1. Works recognizes these formats as those that can be used in calculations. It is necessary when typing the time to include AM or PM after the time if this information is important. In the case of the Puget Sound Charters time schedule, knowing whether a cruise is in the morning or evening is important, so a PM has been entered to designate the time of the cruise.

TYPE THE DATE AND TIME

1. CREATE the following worksheet. **Insert** text and values as shown. **Underline** and **Center** the column headings. Column headings appear in columns B, D, and E; dates appear in B and C. Adjust the column width as necessary. Do not worry about the alignment of dates and values or text at this time.

	A	B	C	D	E
1		CHARTER TIME SCHEDULE			
2					
3		Dates Scheduled		Total	
4		this month		Days	
5					
6	Delano	11/1/92	11/26/92		
7	The Spirit	11/2/92	11/29/92		
8	Sea Wolf	11/1/92	11/30/92		
9	Irish Sea	11/5/92	11/25/92		
10					
11	Next scheduled cruise:				
12					
13		Date	Start	End	Total Hours
14					
15	Delano	12/2/92	12:00 PM	4:00 PM	
16	The Spirit	12/4/92	1:00 PM	5:00 PM	
17	Sea Wolf	12/1/92	4:30 PM	10:30 PM	
18	Irish Sea	12/2/92	4:00 PM	9:00 PM	

FREEZING TITLES

Titles on a spreadsheet can be frozen so that text above and to the left of the selected cell always appears on the screen. This is useful when the spreadsheet is longer or wider than the screen. By scrolling to the right, for example, the titles telling about the contents of rows are always visible. This aids in inserting information accurately on a spreadsheet.

> ### FREEZING TITLES
>
> **1.** HIGHLIGHT cell **B5**
>
> **2.** CHOOSE **Freeze Titles** from the **Options** menu
>
> **3.** SCROLL around the worksheet. Try scrolling up into the titles or to the left. The titles remain frozen.

Titles can be unfrozen by making the same selection from the Options menu.

CHANGING THE TIME FORMAT

The format for the start and end time for the next scheduled cruises needs to be changed so that the total hours for the cruises can be computed. The 24-hour format is necessary to calculate the amount of elapsed time. Since it is often easier to enter the more familiar 12-hour format, the times were entered in that format. Now, they can be adjusted quickly using the **Time/Date** command in the **Format** menu.

> ### CHANGE THE TIME FORMAT
>
> **1.** HIGHLIGHT cells **C15** through **E18**
>
> *Note:* *It is necessary to select the **Total Hours** column as well so that the correct number will show when the hours are calculated. Works needs to know that the total column is formatted for a 24-hour time format as well.*
>
> **2.** CHOOSE **Time/Date** from the **Format** menu

The dialog box shown in Figure 14-1 appears.

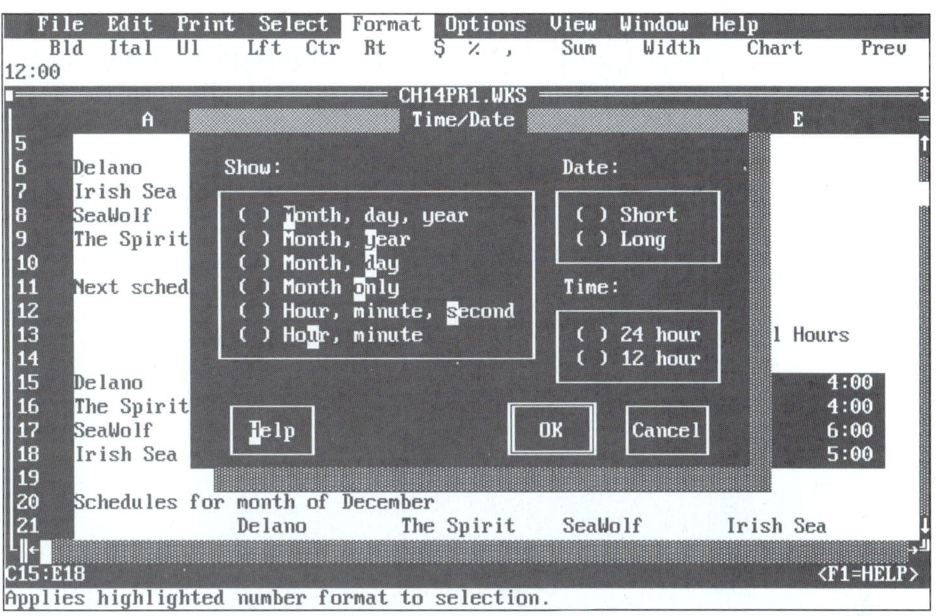

Using this dialog box, changes can be made to cells or to dates and times already in cells. With the cells currently selected, the format can be changed to read the hour and minute in a 24-hour format. Any other changes could be made in the spreadsheet, such as changing the format of the month, date, and year. Whatever format is originally entered can be selected and changed from this dialog box.

3.	CHOOSE	**Hour, minute** in the **Show** box
4.	CHOOSE	**24 hour** in the **Time** box
5.	CHOOSE	**OK** or press Enter

Because the times were entered using PM, Works knows to change the hours according to the 24-hour format.

CALCULATING THE DATES OR TIMES

As noted, when calculating the times, 24-hour formats must be used. Times can be entered in any format and then changed to the 24-hour format if calculations are to be performed. When calculating dates, any long or short format may be used.

CALCULATE THE DATES OR TIMES

1.	HIGHLIGHT	cell **D6**

Puget Sound Charters would like to know how many total days each boat was scheduled during the past month. This is done as any other calculation would be done, by subtracting one cell from another. In this case, the beginning date should be subtracted from the ending date to calculate the total days.

> **2.** TYPE   **=C6-B6**
>
> **3.** COPY   this formula through cell **D9**
>
> The total days for each vessel is computed.
>
> **4.** HIGHLIGHT   cell **E15**
>
> To compute the total time of each upcoming cruise, subtract the ending time from the starting time.
>
> **5.** TYPE   **=D15-C15**
>
> **6.** PRESS   **Enter**

A **4:00** appears in cell **E15**. This format must be read differently from the time format in columns C and D. In this case, it is read as the total hours and the number of minutes of the cruise.

> **7.** COPY   the formula in **E15** down the column through cell **E18**
>
> The total hours are **4, 4, 6,** and **5** (shown as 4:00, 4:00, 6:00, and 5:00).
>
> **8.** SAVE   the spreadsheet as **CH14PR1**
>
> **9.** PRINT   a copy of the spreadsheet

ENTERING A SERIES

In the last practice exercise at the end of Chapter 13, a spreadsheet was created using a series of numbers indicating the total years for the term of an investment. The spreadsheet used a formula to accumulate the total years by adding one to the value in the previous cell. There is another way to build a series of values or dates on a spreadsheet. It is the **Fill Series** command found in the **Edit** menu.

Suppose that you wanted to keep a log of the boats going out on particular days through the month of December on the current spreadsheet. If you wanted to indicate every day of the month down a column, you could use the **Fill Series** command.

ENTER A SERIES

1. **CHOOSE**   **Freeze Titles** from the **Options** menu to turn the option off

2. **HIGHLIGHT**   cell **A20**

3. **TYPE**   **Schedules for month of December** (let it overlap into the cells to the right)

4. **HIGHLIGHT**   cell **A22**

5. **TYPE**   **1**

6. **PRESS**   **Enter**

7. **HIGHLIGHT**   cells **A22** through **A32** (assume that the remainder of the month will be added later)

8. **CHOOSE**   **Fill Series** from the **Edit** menu

The dialog box shown in Figure 14-2 appears.

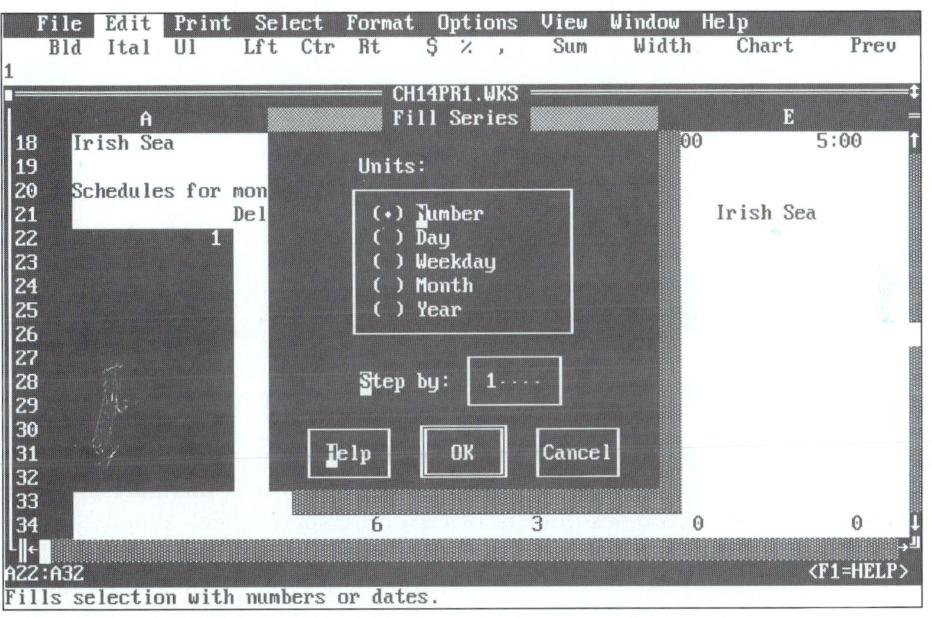

Depending upon the format entered in the selected cell(s) in the spreadsheet, a selection will be made in the **Units** list box. If dates were used and were to be incremented, they would be selected in the box. The **Step by** option is used to increment by any number such as 1 (the default) or 5, 10, and so on.

9. LEAVE the settings as they are shown

You are incrementing by one for the days of the month.

10. CHOOSE **OK** or press Enter

Numbers 1 through 11 are inserted into the selected cells.

11. COMPLETE the worksheet as follows:

20	Schedules for the month of December				
21		Delano	The Spirit	Sea Wolf	Irish Sea
22	1		4:30 PM		
23	2	12:00 PM			4:00 PM
24	3				
25	4		1:00 PM		
26	5	12:00 PM		6:30 PM	
27	6		6:00 PM		11:00 AM
28	7	3:00 PM			
29	8	12:00 PM	6:00 PM		3:00 PM
30	9	6:00 PM		7:00 PM	6:00 PM
31	10			8:00 PM	
32	11	4:30 PM			

USING RANGE NAMES

Ranges have been used in various formulas throughout this section of the book. A range is any area of a spreadsheet, that may include a single cell, a row or column, a block of cells, or the entire spreadsheet. When a range is more than one cell it is considered the area from the upper left cell to the lower right cell, such as A1 through G37. You can give names to cell ranges and then use the range name in a formula. This saves time in rewriting formulas or in identifying frequently used ranges in a spreadsheet.

In the current spreadsheet, Puget Sound Charters would like to know how many days each of the vessels is committed at any given time in the month. Right now the spreadsheet shows days 1 through 11 for the month of December. Additional rows will be added later as more bookings come in. To complete the calculations on this spreadsheet, an additional row will be added below the last day shown thus far, the 11th. It will use a formula to count the total number of days that each vessel is booked. The range used in the individual totals will be named. The formula using the named range will be copied to other areas of the spreadsheet just like any other formula.

CREATING A RANGE

CREATE A RANGE

1. **HIGHLIGHT** cells **B22** through **B32** as the range to name
2. **CHOOSE** **Range Name** from the **Edit** menu

The following dialog box appears as shown in Figure 14-3.

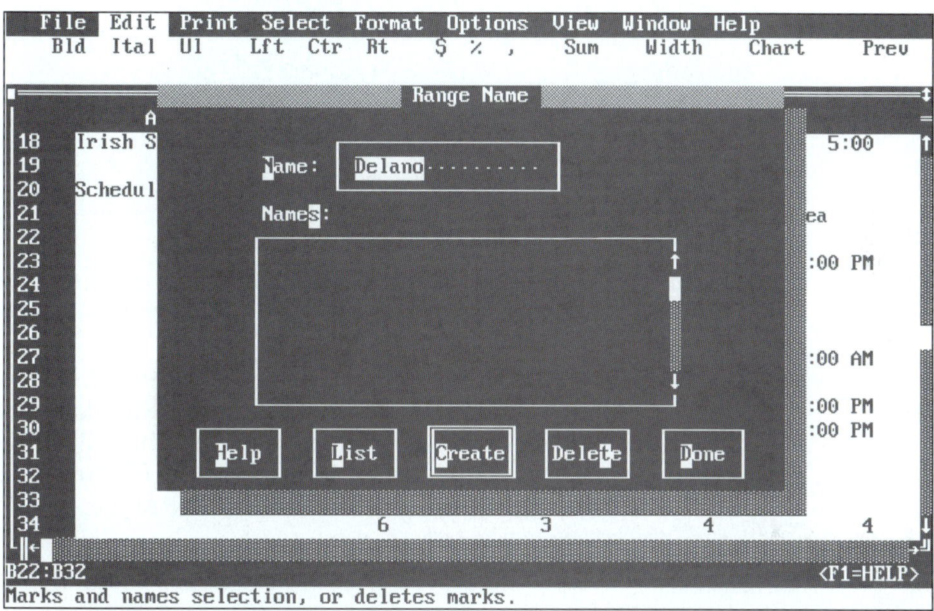

**FIGURE 14-3
RANGE NAME
DIALOG BOX**

The name Delano is suggested because the range is within this column heading. As range names are given, the list of names will appear in the **Names** box. You can **List**, **Create**, **Delete**, exit (**Done**), or reach **Help** from the dialog box.

Delano would be an acceptable name; however, it does not tell the user too much about what the range does. A more detailed description of this range's function might be **total days**.

3. **TYPE** **total days** in the **Name** text box
4. **CHOOSE** **Create**

A new range has been created called **total days**.

USING A RANGE

This range name can now be applied in a formula in place of the cell addresses. First, it will be necessary to format the range of cells correctly, in order to hold the total days.

USE A RANGE

1. HIGHLIGHT   cell **B34**

2. TYPE   **=COUNT(total days)**

This formula will count the number of cells containing entries in the designated range.

3. PRESS   **Enter**

The number 6 appears. The Delano is booked for six days so far this month.

4. COPY   this formula through cell **E34** in the same row

The total days, 6, 4, 3, and 4 appear in the totals row. When changes are made such as deletions or additions in the bookings, the total days will be recalculated automatically, just as with a formula containing the cell addresses. When the formula in cell B34 was copied, the formulas in the cells to which it was copied contain the cell addresses instead of the name of the range.

SORTING CONTENTS OF CELLS

Text, dates, or values can be sorted in a worksheet. Sorting rearranges the cell contents alphabetically or numerically in ascending order (from A to Z or from 1 through the highest number). Works can also sort the contents in descending order. Sorts can be performed on one column, such as on the boat names in this spreadsheet, or a sort can be performed within a sort, such as dates for each vessel. The most useful sort in the current spreadsheet would be on just one column, such as the boat's name or on a date. When the column list to be sorted is selected, all values to the right of the column, which pertain to the column items, will also be sorted. All dates to the right of the boat name, for example, would be adjusted when the boat name is sorted in ascending or descending order.

SORTING ON SELECTED CELLS

SORT ON SELECTED CELLS

1. **HIGHLIGHT** Cells **A6** through **A9**
2. **CHOOSE** **Sort Rows** from the **Select** menu

The dialog box shown in Figure 14-4 appears.

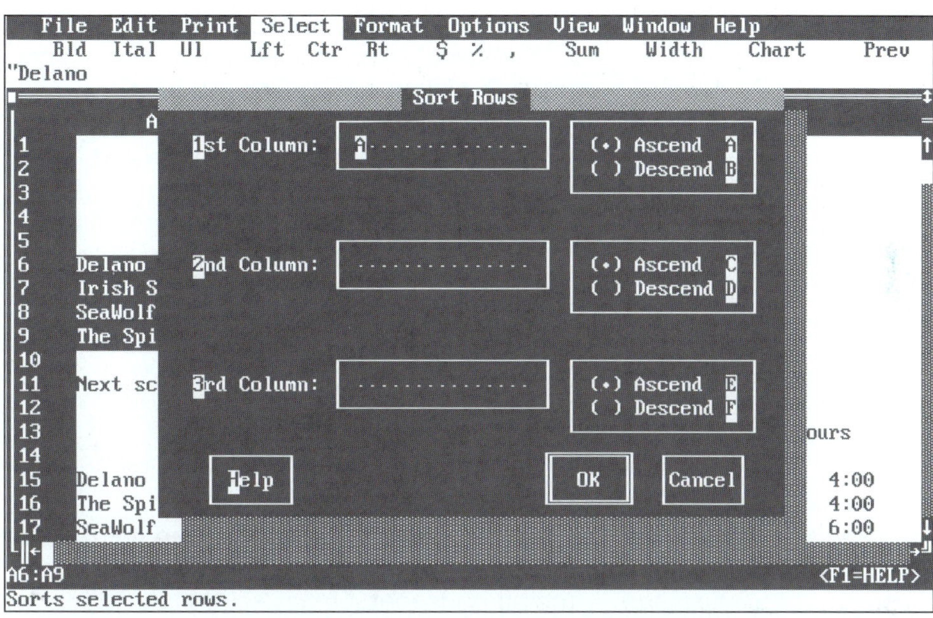

FIGURE 14-4
SORT ROWS DIALOG BOX

This dialog box shows text boxes for the **1st Column**, **2nd Column**, and **3rd Column** sorts. When you want to do a sort within a sort, the first and second columns being used in the sort would be selected. In this case, only the boat names from column **A** were selected, so the **1st Column** text box shows the letter **A**. Within each sort, the order of the sort can be decided. The order options are ascending or descending, with the **Ascend** option selected as the default choice.

All options selected in the dialog box at this time are correct for this sort.

3. **CHOOSE** **OK** or **PRESS** Enter

The order of the vessels now appears in ascending order from Delano through The Spirit and all values to the right of the names are also rearranged.

4. **SAVE** the spreadsheet again and **PRINT** a copy
5. **QUIT** or **CONTINUE** to the tutorial

GUIDED TUTORIAL

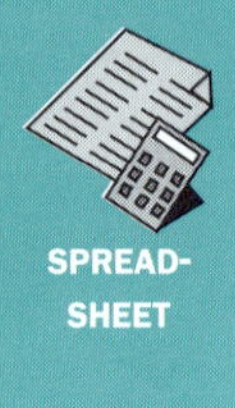

SPREAD-SHEET

WHAT YOU'LL DO

- Compute time and date values.
- Format fills for time and date.

HOW TO DO IT

1. CREATE a spreadsheet that shows your class schedule. In it include the title of each of the classes and the start/end time as shown in the following example.

	Start time	End time
Class 1	9:00 AM	9:50 AM
Class 2	11:00 AM	11:50 AM
Class 3	1:10 PM	2:00 PM
Class 4	2:10 PM	3:00 PM

2. CREATE an appropriate main heading for the spreadsheet.

3. CREATE a column heading called **TOTAL TIME** in a column to the right.

4. FORMAT each of the times in the 24-hour format using the **Time/Date** command from the **Format** menu.

5. SUBTRACT the **End** time from the **Start** time and insert the results into the **TOTAL TIME** column.

6. CREATE columns below this section of the spreadsheet for dates. Copy the class names to column A in this section at the bottom of the spreadsheet.

7. ACROSS from the names of the class, enter column headings and dates as shown in the following partial example.

	Today's date	Last day of quarter/semester	Days remaining
Class 1	03/05/93	03/28/93	

8. BE SURE that the date cells are formatted as dates in the short format. Use the **Date/Time** command from the **Format** menu.

9. SUBTRACT **the last day from today's date** to compute the total days remaining in the quarter or semester.

10. SAVE the spreadsheet as **CH14TUT**.

REVIEW QUESTIONS 

1. List two or more formats that are available for time and date in a spreadsheet.

2. The _______________ command from the _____________ menu is used to lock columns to the left and above the highlight position.

3. The ______ __________ command from the _____________ menu is used to set the format for dates and times.

4. Explain briefly how you would calculate dates and times.

5. What is the function of the **Fill Series** command from the **Edit** menu?

6. ________ range name may be used in place of cell addresses in a function.

7. ________ sorts may be performed one within another.

8. ______ A sort changes the order of data in all columns.

HANDS-ON EXERCISES

The following exercises focus primarily on completing practice documents; however, they will also introduce integration — the most powerful feature of using Works. The documents will include spreadsheet functions, a review of word processing, and document integration. The documents that are integrated include commands used to move a document from one Works' tool to another, such as from a spreadsheet to a word processing document. This is an easy and useful process and is included throughout the remainder of the book in various practice exercises.

COPYING A SPREADSHEET

A spreadsheet can be copied to a word processing document or to a database file. Spreadsheets (or any other document produced with Works) can also be sent to another computer. That feature is covered in Part 6.

When a spreadsheet is copied to a word processing document, it is done as a table. All cells in the spreadsheet become separated by tabs rather than individual cells. In the following exercise, you will take one of the spreadsheet files already created and copy it to a word processing document space. You will then create a short report explaining the table in more detail. This exercise will give you additional practice not only in moving blocks of data from one tool to another, but also in experiencing the small changes that take place in the format of the data.

EXERCISE 1

1. Open the spreadsheet **CH13PR1.WKS**.which you created in Chapter 13; or retrieve it from the instructor's data disk

2. Highlight cells **A1** through **F22**.

   Note: Do not select the entire spreadsheet (including all other blank rows and columns). Doing so will copy all cells on the entire spreadsheet, not just those containing values or text.

3. Choose **Copy** from the **Edit** menu.

   *Note: In the next step, you will create a new word processing document. After choosing copy when the spreadsheet file is selected, pressing **Enter** is all that is necessary to insert the spreadsheet information into the word processing document. Be careful not to press **Enter** until you are in position.*

Creating a new document

1. Choose **Create New File** from the **File** menu.

2. Choose **Word Processor.**

3. Choose **OK** or press Enter.

4. Press **Enter** in the new word processing document.

WAIT as the document is copied into this new word processing document. It will take a few seconds. As you are waiting, percentages show in the lower left corner indicating what percentage of the document is copied thus far. Finally it will reach 100% and the spreadsheet will appear. It will appear different in appearance and format from the layout in the spreadsheet tool. It now appears in word processing format and must be aligned through the use of tab settings.

Adjusting tab positions

Scroll down the screen. You can see that Works has inserted tabs in place of cell positions. This does not mean that the tabs line up. In fact, they usually do not. Using Works' word processing **Tabs** command in the **Format** menu with selected lines, however, makes realigning the positions relatively quick and easy. Keep in mind when resetting tab positions that column headings, side headings, and so on may need different tab settings. When creating tables in the table exercises in word processing, different tab settings were used for main headings, column headings, and changes in the number of columns throughout the table. The same changes must take place when a spreadsheet is copied into a word processing document. Keeping a copy of the printed spreadsheet nearby may be useful as well.

1. Select the years **1989** through **Average** as follows:

1989	1990	1991
1992	Average	

2. Choose **Tabs** from the **Format** menu.

3. Delete all existing tab settings with **Delete all.**

4. Press **Ctrl/Right Arrow** to move the cursor into the ruler line.

   Note: *When doing this on your own, remember that it is often a guessing game deciding where the tabs should be changed. It may take a couple of tries to get the settings exactly right.*

5. Reset tab positions at the following locations on the ruler line. Either type the position in the **Position** box and then choose **Insert** (by pressing **Enter**) or hold the **Ctrl** key down and press the **Left** and **Right Arrow** keys to the position and then choose **Insert** in the dialog box by pressing **Enter**, or click on the position on the ruler line and click on **Insert**.

Left tab at:	0.2
Center tabs at:	2.0
	3.5
	5.0
	6.3
	7.8

This will set the tab positions correctly for centered headings above each column.

6. Choose **Done** when finished.

7. Choose **Page Setup & Margins** from the **Print** menu.

8. Change the settings as follows:

Left margin:	0.5
Right margin:	0.25
Page length:	8.5
Page width:	11

9. Choose **OK** or press Enter.

10. Highlight all remaining lines in the spreadsheet.

11. Choose **Tabs** from the **Format** menu.

12. Delete all existing tab positions.

13. Reset **Decimal** tab positions at the following locations:

2.2

3.8

5.2

6.5

7.7

14. Reset left tab position at 0.2.

15. Choose **Done** when finished.

Making final adjustments

1. Position the cursor under the **G** in **Goods Sold** in the subheading **Cost of Goods Sold**.

2. Press the **Enter** key once and the **Tab** key once so that this line becomes a two-line heading.

3. Position the cursor under the **E** in **TOTAL EXPENSES** and press **Enter** once and the **Tab** key once to make this one a two-line heading.

4. Type the logo at the top of the document as follows (use the company name and press Enter to add blank lines before and after the name as necessary. Delete all tab settings and then center the name and address. Use a double-line border above and below the heading. Use the **Border** command from the **Format** menu and include the border at the top and bottom of the heading lines selected. Choose the **Double** line option in the dialog box.

   Press **Enter** on the first line of the document to add blank space at the top.

PUGET SOUND CHARTERS

West Lake Union Way
Seattle, WA 98108
(206)555-9200

---

5. Choose **Preview** from the **Print** menu or the Toolbar to look at the spreadsheet in its word processing format. Make any necessary adjustments in alignment using margin and/or tab settings.

Note: *This will print in landscape mode* **only** *if using a laser printer. Whether or not you have a laser printer, save this document as an example of setting up for "landscape" (horizontal) printing.*

6. Save the document as **CH14HO1.WPS**.

7. Print a copy of the document.

Adding text to the document

1. Type the text in the following box in a new word processor document space.

```
                        EARNINGS REPORT

INTRODUCTION
The attached spreadsheet gives a summary of the earnings
over the past four years. It is broken down into the fol-
lowing categories:


     1.                 GROSS SALES
     2.                 Cost of Goods Sold
     3.                 NET SALES

     4.                 EXPENSES
                        Catering
                        Salaries
                        Operations
                        Miscellaneous
                        TOTAL EXPENSES

     5.                 NET EARNINGS
     6.                 % of Net Sales

SUMMARY
Over the past four years net sales have steadily increased
from $102,410.00 to $169,331.00. Expenses have increased
moderately as well. It is to our credit that the expenses
have increased in proportion to the Net Sales from
$33,300.00 to $86,630.00.
Business has increased steadily. The only decline is shown
in the percentage of net sales, which has declined from
67.48 percent in 1988 to 48.84 percent in 1991. This per-
centage is expected to decrease as the total net sales
increases and as expenses are stabilized.

CONCLUSION
Close study of the summary of earnings on the attached
spreadsheet will show that expenses have increased propor-
tionally with the increase in business. This is naturally a
necessary incline and should stabilize as the business
becomes better and as charters for each vessel steadily
increase.
```

2. Save the document as **CH14HO1B.**

3. Run a spell check on the document, justify the right margin, double space the body with the exception of the itemized list following the first paragraph, and change the top margin to 2.0 inches.

4. Create the following header to appear on all but the first page. Use header/footer paragraphs to create the header.

<u>EARNINGS REPORT</u>, Puget Sound Charters   <u>1992</u>

5. Save the document again and print a copy.

To create a cover page

1. Create a cover page similar to the following. Use the **Borders** command in the **Format** menu to add the border around the text.

PUGET SOUND CHARTERS
EXPENSE SUMMARY REPORT

1989 through 1992

2. Save the cover as **CH14HO.COV.**

3. **Print** a copy of the cover.

4. Put the **cover**, **report**, and **spreadsheet** together as the final document.

5. **Quit** or **continue** to the next exercise.

EXERCISE 2

This worksheet shows the six-month expenditures of CTech Corporation, a small consulting firm. They would like you to print several copies of the worksheet, first in its original format, and then considering the following possibility:

What if expenditures increased in all categories by 10 percent and income remained the same?

CTech would like a hard copy (printed copy) of both spreadsheets.

1. The input document is shown below. Enter the values and labels approximately as shown.

	A	B	C	D	E	F	G	H
1			CTech Corporation					
2			Six-month Expenditures					
3								
4		January	February	March	April	May	June	TOTAL
5								
6	EXPENDITURES							
7	Insurance	450	450	450	450	450	450	
8	Supplies	200	500	250	600	400	250	
9	Salary	10000	10000	10000	10000	10000	10000	
10	Equipment	2000	0	0	0	500	1500	
11	Manuals/Production	4000	4000	5000	3500	4000	5000	
12	Consulting Fees	500	250	550	600	500	500	
13	Copy Machine	500	450	400	550	600	500	
14	Distribution	200	250	200	250	300	250	
15	TOTAL							
16								
17	INCOME							
18	Training	12000	10000	12000	16200	13500	17500	
19	Manuals	3000	4000	6000	7000	8000	9000	
20	Consulting	7000	4000	8000	12000	8000	8500	
21	TOTAL							
22								
23								
24								
25	Profit/Loss:							
26								

2. Adjust the column width as necessary.

3. Create formulas to compute the TOTAL in H7, TOTAL in B15, TOTAL in B21, and Profit/Loss in B25. Copy these formulas to appropriate cells. Save the worksheet as **CH14HO2.**

4. Copy all side headings in column A to A27. Beginning in cell B28 (Insurance for January), create a formula to increase the original January insurance value by 10 percent (B7 *1.10). Copy this formula to other cells in the Expenditures category (through Distribution). Use **Fill Down** and **Fill Right** to copy. Copy a column first and fill right. You can select all cells in the column and all cells in all columns to which you are copying prior to using the **Fill Right** command. **Fill Down** works in the same way. As you do so, it may assist you to split the screen so that both halves are visible.

5. Format all values as currency with two places to the right of the decimal. You may select all values in the spreadsheet and then click on the dollar sign ($) in the Toolbar to format the values quickly.

6. Adjust the column width as necessary.

7. Use Preview to look at the worksheet prior to printing.

8. Print the entire worksheet to reflect predictions.

9. Save the final copy under the same name.

EXERCISE 3

A small department store would like a worksheet printed showing the change in their sales over last year. A partial worksheet is shown below in the input document. They would also like to have:

a. The percentage of change over the year

b. The store totals for each year, the change column, and the total percentage of change

The input document follows.

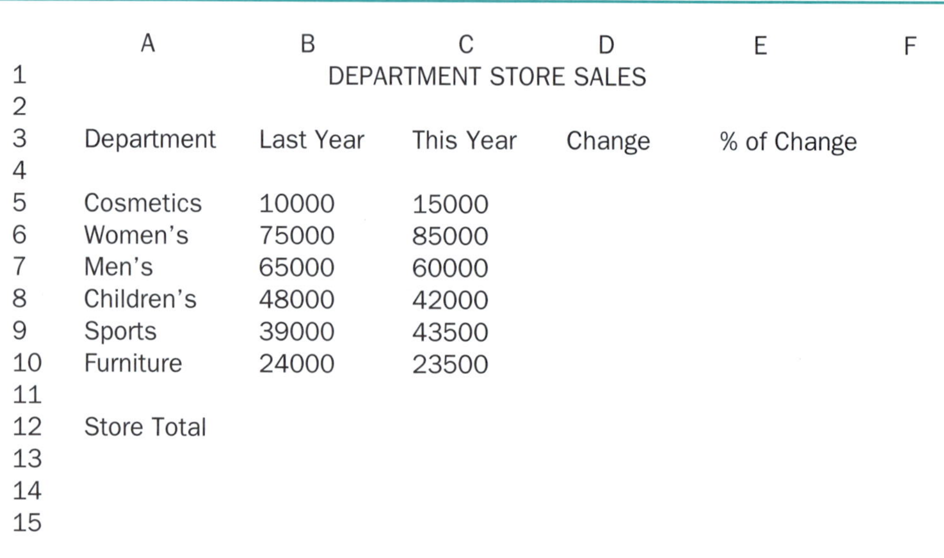

	A	B	C	D	E	F
1		DEPARTMENT STORE SALES				
2						
3	Department	Last Year	This Year	Change	% of Change	
4						
5	Cosmetics	10000	15000			
6	Women's	75000	85000			
7	Men's	65000	60000			
8	Children's	48000	42000			
9	Sports	39000	43500			
10	Furniture	24000	23500			
11						
12	Store Total					
13						
14						
15						

1. Enter the values and labels as shown.

2. Center all column headings and center the main heading over the entire worksheet.

3. Adjust the column width for each column to 15.

4. Create a formula for the Store Totals, Change (this year less last year), and % of Change (this year divided into the change), and copy the formulas to all pertinent cells.

5. Underline the column headings.

6. Format all dollar amounts as currency with two places to the right of the decimal and all percentages three places to the right of the decimal.

7. Save the worksheet as **CH14HO3**.

8. Type the short word processing memo below describing this spreadsheet. Save this memo as **CH14HO3.** It will save as a word processing document with the WPS extension, thus giving it a different name.

```
The following worksheet shows the change in sales over the
last two years. It also summarizes the percentage of change
(negative or positive).

We are putting together an active sales campaign this month
which will go into effect in January of next year. It is
hoped that the negative numbers in sales will be eliminated
over the next two years and that the sales will begin a
steady growth over the next 10 years.

Input from all employees is appreciated.
```

9. Copy **CH14HO3.WKS** to the bottom of **CH14HO3.WPS**, the word processing document, and adjust the settings as needed. As you do so, select all values and change the margins first. This will make the process of changing tab positions easier.

10. Perform a spell check, preview the document, and print a copy.

11. Save the document again. Quit or continue to the next exercise.

EXERCISE 4

Background
The following input document shows a set of three numbers. Your statistics teacher has asked you to find the following values for each of the groups:

Average
Count
Maximum
Minimum
Sum
Standard Deviation

The input worksheet follows. Enter the worksheet as shown.

	A	B	C	D	E
1		Statistical Characteristics of 3 Sets of Numbers			
2					
3		Set 1	Set 2	Set 3	
4					
5		10	8	3	
6		8	5	4	
7		6	7	2	
8		9	12	10	
9		25	45	8	
10		18	7	45	
11		12	32	68	
12		4	3	12	
13		8		77	
14		9		67	
15		5			
16					
17	Average:				
18	Count:				
19	Maximum:				
20	Minimum:				
21	Sum:				
22	Stand. Dev.:				
23					
24					

1. Center the main heading.

2. Add an extra row at row 2 and create a subheading that reads:

   Prepared by (your name).

3. Underline the column headings.

4. Center each of the column headings.

5. Compute each of the values asked for in the background information. Copy all functions to appropriate cells. The correct format for the functions is

   =Avg
   =Count
   =Max
   =Min
   =Sum
   =Std

Write these functions as you would the SUM function. Use ranges in the format. Format to two decimal places, fixed.

6. Widen columns as necessary.

7. Save the spreadsheet as **CH14HO4**.

8. Print the spreadsheet.

EXERCISE 5

1. Create a new word processing document and type the following text.

```
                    SALES PROJECTIONS

Below is a summary of the sales projections as submitted
recently by the marketing department. They show an increase
in the next year of 10 percent, five years of 10 percent
over next year's projection, and 10 years of 30 percent over
the five-year projection. These summaries are based on past
earnings as stated in the recent profit report and on future
predictions and expectations of marketing strategies.
```

2. Save this document as **CH14HO5**.

3. Open the spreadsheet document called **CH13HO2B** (if necessary) or move to it using the **Window** menu. You can also retrieve it from the instructor's data disk.

4. Select all cells in the spreadsheet.

5. Copy the cells.

6. Move to the word processing document called **CH14HO5** using the **Window** menu.

7. Position the cursor two lines below the paragraph in the document.

8. Press **Enter** to insert the spreadsheet.

9. Adjust the tab settings as necessary; however, keep the columns within the margin settings.

10. Add the following paragraph at the end of the document.

```
We expect the projections to be accurate and look forward to
continued success and growth in the future. The Puget Sound
area is growing rapidly due to increases in high-tech indus-
try as well as in the airline and shipping industries. With
this continued optimistic outlook on the future of the geo-
graphic area, the chartering business looks bright as well.
```

11. Run a spell check on the document.

12. Double-space the paragraphs.

13. Add a footer to include the page number at the bottom center of the page.

14. Preview the document.

15. Print a copy of the report and save it again.

**SPREAD-
SHEET**

15 CHARTS

Objectives

- Create charts.

- Make modifications to charts.

- Create legends.

- Name charts.

- Copy charts.

- Change data format.

- Print charts.

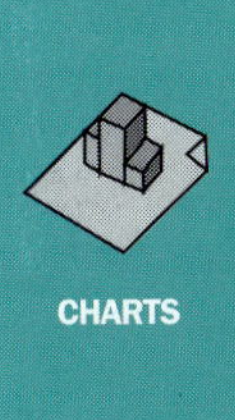

Charts allow you to represent spreadsheet information in graphic format. They aid in the interpretation of data values otherwise shown in rows and columns. It can be easier for those looking at spreadsheet information to see also a representation of the information in chart form. A chart can show values as various size bars in a bar chart, as sections of a pie chart, by making comparisons in line charts, and in other formats.

Works contains eight different chart formats. You can create and save up to eight charts with each spreadsheet created. Some of the most frequently used and common charts are shown below. Others are described.

The bar chart

A bar chart explains the differences between categories of values on a spreadsheet. Values are selected on the spreadsheet. Those belonging to different groups are shown in different shades or patterns. Usually, the Y-axis (the left side of the chart) contains values increasing in order up the chart (Figure 15-1). The X-axis (the bottom of the chart) shows the categories. For example, if you created a bar chart on one of the spreadsheets created in previous lessons in this book, the Y-axis might show the total sales values and the X-axis the names of the boats.

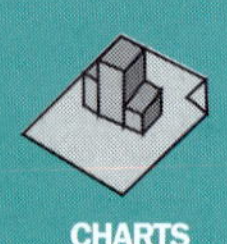

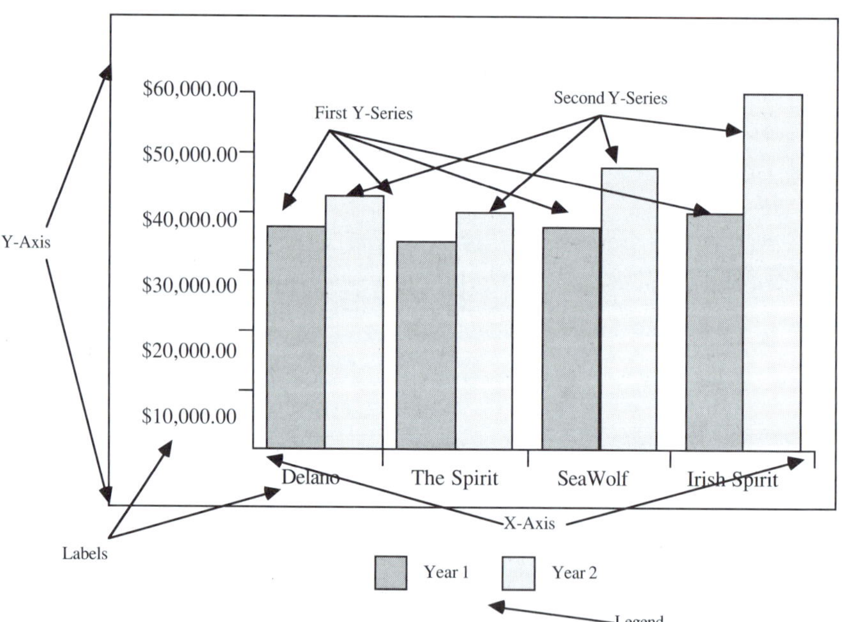

FIGURE 15-1
BAR CHART

The stacked bar chart

The stacked bar chart shows bars with totals stacked on top of each other (Figure 15-2). Each bar represents a selected row or column in the spreadsheet.

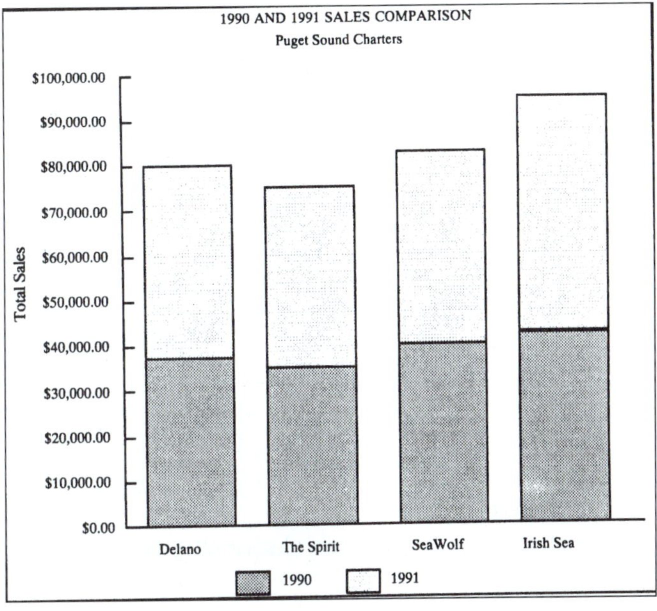

**FIGURE 15-2
STACKED BAR
CHART**

100% bar chart

Each selected column or row value in this type of chart is shown as a percentage of a total bar. One bar equals 100% and various sections of the bar are shaded to represent a percentage.

Line chart

A line chart represents data in lines across the chart. Three or four groups of data, such as sales over a period of time, may be represented. Line charts are commonly used to show comparisons and trends, such as increases and decreases over a period of time.

Stacked line chart

An area line chart stacks or combines values to show the total amount in a given category. For example, each line's values are added to the previous line's values. If making a comparison of sales over a period of time, sales of the Delano might be added to sales of The Spirit, and so on.

Hi-Lo-Close chart

This chart shows the range between high and low values within a single category. For example, this type of chart could be used to show the high and low sales by boat over a period of weeks, months, years, and so on.

Pie chart

A pie chart shows the percentages of a group of selected values as they relate to the whole (Figure 15-3). A pie chart represents one column or row in a spreadsheet.

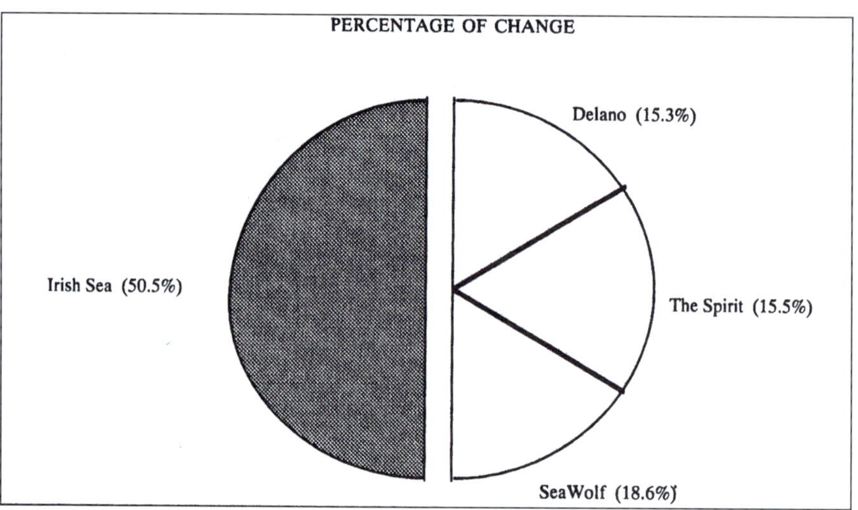

FIGURE 15-3
PIE CHART

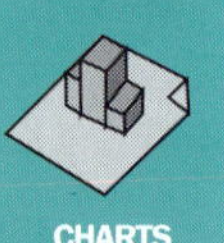

CHARTS

X-Y chart

The X-Y chart shows the relationship between X and Y values in the form of a scatterplot.

CREATING CHARTS

Every chart created is based on the text and values found in a spreadsheet. The values are selected to represent bars, lines, scatterplots, or sections of a pie chart. The chart that is created uses the values in the current spreadsheet and is attached to that spreadsheet. If the values are changed, the chart is updated automatically.

Up to as many as six rows and columns may be used in a single chart. Usually, charts are easier to read and interpret when they represent a limited number of comparisons.

In most spreadsheets, text appears in the first row or the first column of a spreadsheet. That text automatically becomes the X-axis labels. The selected numbers in a row or column become the Y-series. Once a chart is created, there are many options available to change the appearance of the chart, such as adding legends or X- and Y- titles and main and subheadings.

CREATING A BAR CHART

The first step in creating a chart is to open the spreadsheet file containing the values you want to display graphically. The text and values are then selected (up to six adjacent rows or columns). The **New Chart** command from the **View** menu is then used and the graph appears on the screen. These steps are the basic ones used to create an instant chart with Works. After the initial chart selections are made, modifications can be made to it.

CREATE A BAR CHART

1. **SIGN** onto Works (if necessary)

2. **OPEN** the file **CH13HO2A.WKS** which you created in Chapter 13; or retrieve it from the instructor's data disk

3. **SELECT** the first four rows and columns **A**, **B**, and **C** of the spreadsheet starting with the column headings as shown below:

Delano	$37,890.00	$42,520.00
The Spirit	$35,550.00	$41,236.00
Sea Wolf	$38,950.00	$45,800.00
Irish Sea	$41,250.00	$58,695.00

4. **CHOOSE** View

5. **CHOOSE** New Chart

A bar chart similar to the one shown in Figure 15-4 appears.

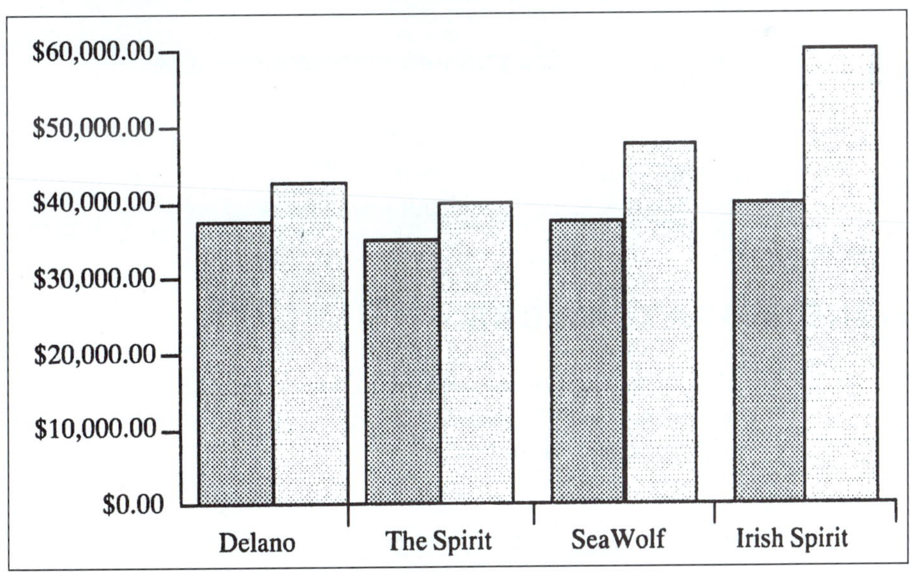

**FIGURE 15-4
A BAR CHART**

The X-axis shows the name of each of the boats. Each boat contains two bars for the years 1990 and 1991. The Y-axis shows the dollar values in sales for the two years. The Y-axis scale is automatically set to contain the values necessary for the rows selected.

6. PRESS   **ESC** when finished

Note: *The **View** menu now shows a chart created with this spreadsheet called **Chart1**. Look at this list. If you wanted to see the same chart again, you could choose **Chart1** from the **View** menu. The **New Chart** command is used only when a new range of text and values is being used to create a new chart.*

SWITCHING BETWEEN CHART AND SPREADSHEET MODE

The status line at the bottom of the screen shows the word **CHART**. When you press **ESC** to return to the spreadsheet, you are still in **CHART** mode. It is necessary to leave this mode to create new charts or to continue working with the spreadsheet. Pressing F10 to leave **CHART** mode changes the menu options and the Toolbar from those functions applying to charts to those applying to spreadsheets.

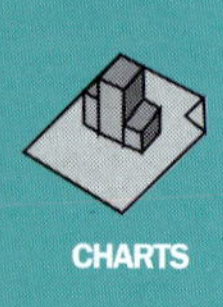

SWITCH BETWEEN CHART AND SPREADSHEET

1. PRESS   **F10** to return to spreadsheet view or choose **Spreadsheet** from the **View** menu

2. PRESS   **Shift/F10** to return to the graph or choose **Chart1** from the **View** menu

3. PRESS   **Esc** to return to the spreadsheet

Use the **F10** and **Shift/F10** keys to move any time from the current graph to the spreadsheet mode or press **F10** alone to move from Chart mode to Spreadsheet mode without viewing the graph.

MAKING MODIFICATIONS

The current chart could be modified in a number of ways. Among those that would enhance the readability and appearance of the chart are adding legends and titles, and even data labels.

CREATING A LEGEND

A legend gives additional information about each of the bars in a bar chart or about each of the sections of a stacked-bar chart, the lines in a line chart, and so on. In the current chart, a legend would assist the reader in identifying what each of the bars represents. This information is not known by looking at the current chart. **Options** for adding or removing legends on a chart are found in the **Legends** command in the **Data** menu.

CREATE A LEGEND

1. PRESS   **F10** to return to **CHART** mode

2. CHOOSE   **Legends** from the **Data** menu

The dialog box shown in Figure 15-5 appears.

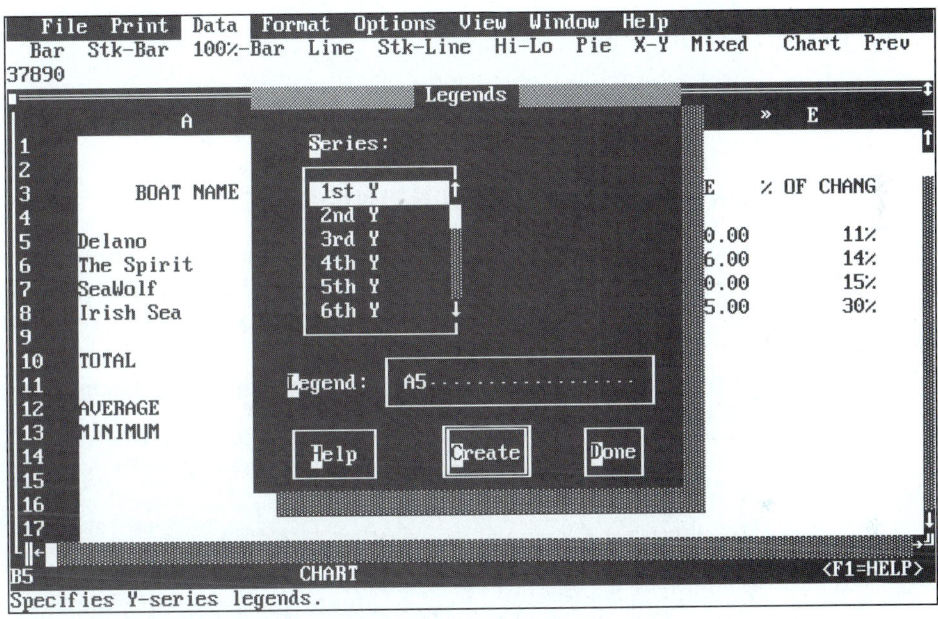

FIGURE 15-5
LEGEND DIALOG BOX

This box includes options for up to six groups of values. The current chart uses only two groups of Y-axis values: the sales for 1990 and 1991. The **Legend** text box at the bottom of the dialog box is used to type the text used to describe each of the series of values. In this chart, the **1st Y** will be used to describe 1990 and the **2nd Y** to describe 1991.

With the selection on **1st Y**,

3. CHOOSE   **Legend** by clicking the mouse button once in the box or pressing **Alt/L**

4. TYPE   **1991**

5. CHOOSE   **Create**

 6. CHOOSE   2nd Y

 7. CHOOSE   Legend

 8. TYPE   1992

 9. CHOOSE   Create

10. CHOOSE   Done

11. PRESS   Shift/F10

The chart appears. It now contains a legend at the bottom of the screen showing a box for each year, 1991 and 1992, representing each of the bars for the boats.

12. PRESS   **ESC** when through viewing

You are still in Chart mode.

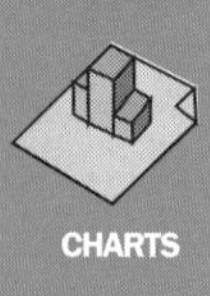

CHANGING OR DELETING A LEGEND

Use the **Legends** command in the **Data** menu to change or delete legends. For now, the legends created for this chart will remain the same. Removing or changing a legend could be done with the following steps.

CHANGING OR DELETING A LEGEND

1. READ   through the legends in the Legends dialog box from the **Data** menu

To delete a legend

In the **Series** box, select the series to be deleted.

In the **Legends** box, select the text for the legend.

Press the **Delete** key on the keyboard.

Choose **Create.**

Choose **Done.**

To change

In the **Series** box, select the series to be changed.

In the **Legends** box, type the new text for the series.

Choose **Create** or edit the existing text.

Choose **Done.**

2. PRESS   **Esc** to leave this dialog box

ADDING CHART TITLES

This chart and others can be enhanced further by adding titles. Titles can be added as chart titles, subtitles, X- and Y-axis titles, and Right Y-axis titles. Usually, the more information that can be added to a chart, the easier it is to interpret. A chart title and X- and Y-axis titles will be used on the present chart. Right Y-axis titles are used to identify values appearing on the right side of a chart. This is a format that is used when two values, such as Total and Individual sales, will be shown on the chart. The Total sales amounts would then appear on the left side with individual breakdowns on the right. This is an unusual format with which you can experiment later.

ADD CHART TITLES

While still in **CHART** mode,

1. CHOOSE **Titles** from the **Data** menu

The dialog box shown in Figure 15-6 appears.

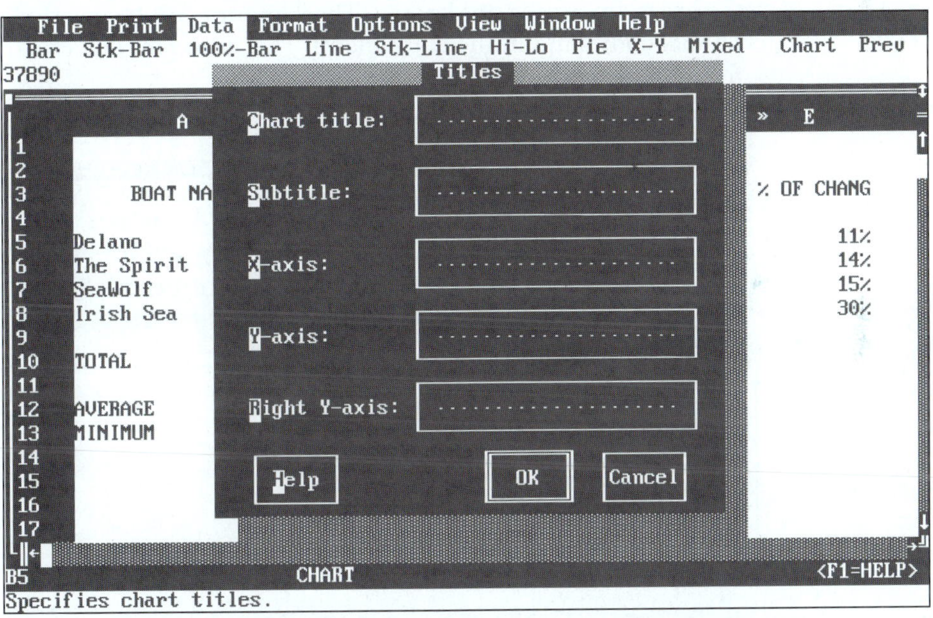

This dialog box shows text boxes for entering the **Chart title, subtitle, X-axis title, Y-axis title,** or the **Right Y-axis title** (discussed later). Titles may contain up to 37 characters, and any figure or character may be included.

2. TYPE **1991 AND 1992 SALES COMPARISON** in the **Chart title** text box

3. PRESS the **Down Arrow** key once

4. **TYPE** **Puget Sound Charters** as the subtitle
5. **PRESS** the **Down Arrow** key once
6. **TYPE** **Boat Name** as the X-axis title
7. **PRESS** the **Down Arrow** key once
8. **TYPE** **Total Sales** as the Y-axis title
9. **CHOOSE** **OK** or press Enter
10. **PRESS** **Shift/F10** to view the chart

The chart now gives much more information about what the bars are showing and about the dollar values and boat names appearing on the Y and X axes.

ADDING DATA LABELS

Data labels add even more information to a chart. In a bar chart, the exact value of each of the bars can be shown. As the bar chart now appears, each of the bars can represent only an estimate of the value. For example, look at the Delano sales. The 1991 sales show an amount that is somewhere above $35,000.00; however, the exact amount is not known. That amount can be inserted using the **Data Labels** command in the **Data** menu. This command inserts the exact dollar value from the spreadsheet.

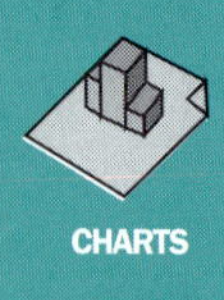

ADD DATA LABELS

1. **PRESS** **ESC** to return to **Chart** mode
2. **SELECT** the values in the first four rows of the spreadsheet, showing the sales amounts for each of the boats for 1991 as follows:

$37,890.00
$35,550.00
$38,950.00
$41,250.00

3. **CHOOSE** **Data Labels** from the **Data** menu

The dialog box shown in Figure 15-7 appears.

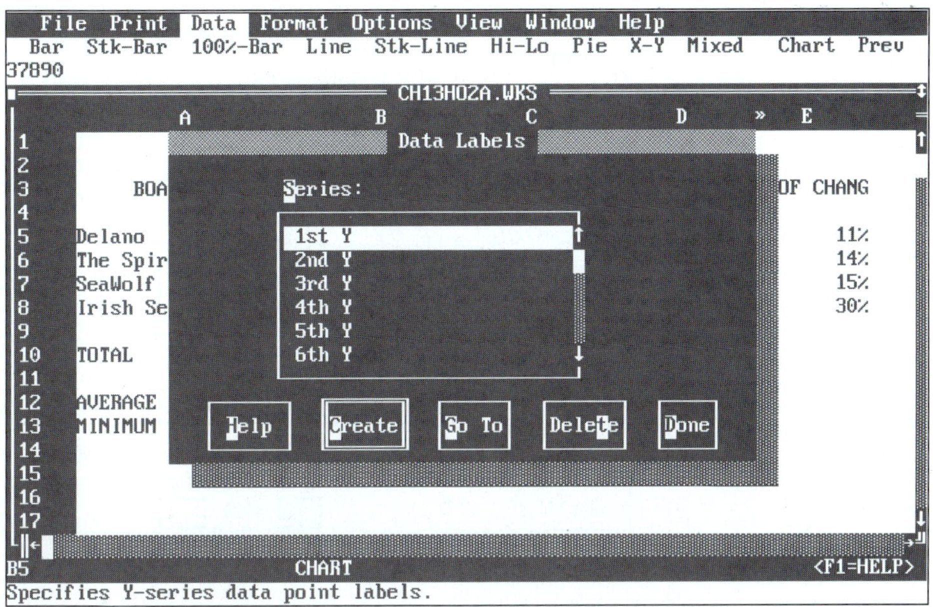

FIGURE 15-7
DATA LABELS
DIALOG BOX

4. **CHOOSE**   **1st Y** in the **Series** box

5. **CHOOSE**   **Create**

6. **SELECT**   the second series of **Y-axis** values for the boats as follows:

$42,520.00
$41,236.00
$45,800.00
$58,695.00

7. **CHOOSE**   **Data Labels** again from the **Data** menu

8. **CHOOSE**   **2nd Y** in the **Series** box

9. **CHOOSE**   **Create**

10. **PRESS**   **Shift/F10** to see the **Y-axis** series values inserted above each bar in the chart

A chart similar to that shown in Figure 15-8 appears.

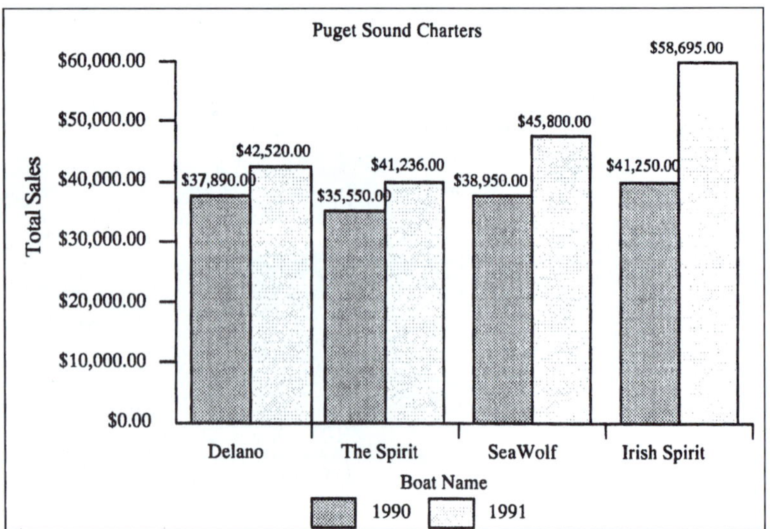

FIGURE 15-8
MODIFIED BAR
CHART

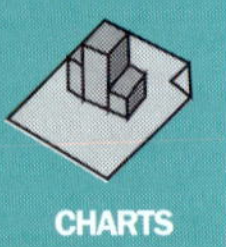

CHARTS

11. PRESS   **ESC** when finished viewing the chart

NAMING A CHART

When the chart is complete, it is a good idea to name it. Works has already named this chart, CHART1. If you were experimenting with creating many variations of charts on a single spreadsheet, Works would create each one as CHART1, CHART2, and so on. Each chart is then added to the **View** menu so that any chart can be quickly retrieved for viewing. It is optional to change the name that Works assigns to a chart; however, as with any document, a name given by you, the user, often makes it easier to identify.

NAME A CHART

While still in **CHART** mode,

1. CHOOSE   **Charts** from the **View** menu

The dialog box shown in Figure 15-9 appears.

294

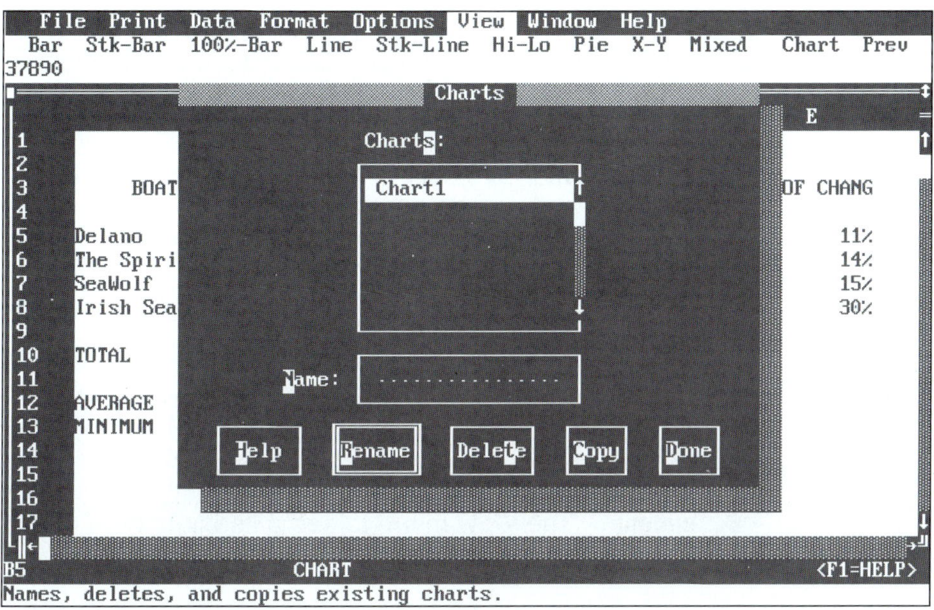

FIGURE 15-9
CHARTS DIALOG BOX

From this box the charts can be renamed, deleted, and copied. Copying a chart is like making a backup copy of a file. This option is covered next.

2. **SELECT**   **Chart1** in the **Charts** box (if necessary — this should be the only chart at this time)

3. **CHOOSE**   the **Name** box

4. **TYPE**   **Sales91_92** as the name of the chart

5. **CHOOSE**   **Rename** and **Done**

6. **CHOOSE**   the **View** menu to see the change in the name of the chart

7. **PRESS**   **ESC** or click the mouse button on the spreadsheet

COPYING A CHART

Copying a chart has two primary functions: (1) it creates an automatic backup of a chart, and (2) it allows the user to make changes and experiment with a chart without changing the original. For example, you could make a copy of the current chart, Sales91_92, and experiment with deleting some of the labels or legends or changing the type of chart. The original chart would remain intact.

COPY A CHART

1. CHOOSE   **Charts** from the **View** menu

With the **Sales91_92** chart selected in the **Charts** list box,

2. CHOOSE   **Name**

3. TYPE   **Sales2** as the name of the second copy of the **Sales** chart

4. CHOOSE   **Copy**

The **Charts** list box now shows the names of two charts.

5. CHOOSE   **Done**

6. CHOOSE   The **View** menu to see a listing of both of the charts

CHANGING THE CHART TYPE

Sometimes it is useful to change the chart type to see if another format will give more information or be easier to interpret than the standard bar chart format. You can use the same cells selected in a chart or choose different cells to view information in a new chart format.

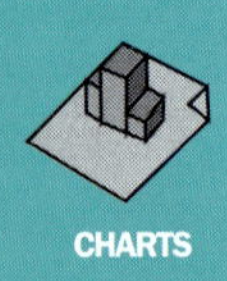

CHANGE THE CHART TYPE

1. CHOOSE   **Sales2** from the **View** menu to make the copy of the **Sales91_92** chart current

2. PRESS   **ESC**

3. CHOOSE   **Stacked Bar** from the **Format** menu

    Note: *All possible chart formats are listed in the **Format** menu. At any time, you could experiment with various types of charts. Some values, however, are better suited than others to specific chart formats.*

4. PRESS   **Shift/F10** to view the new chart

A chart similar to that shown in Figure 15-10 appears.

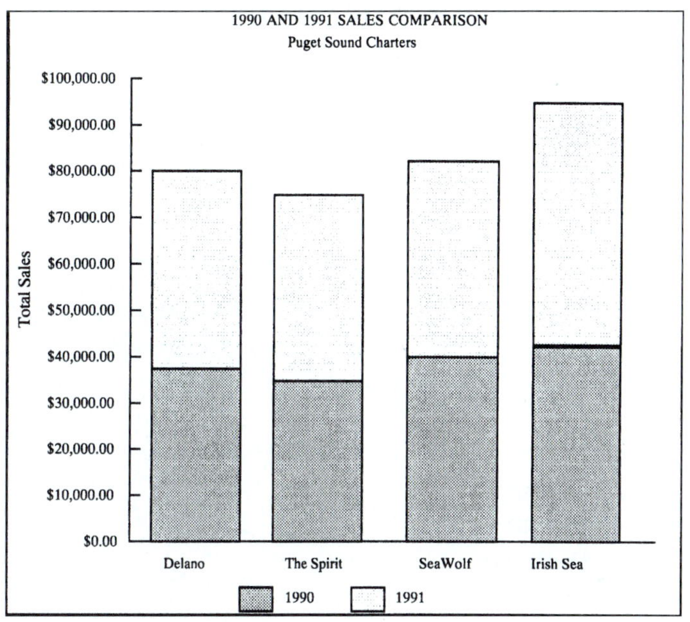

**FIGURE 15-10
STACKED BAR
CHART**

> **5.** PRESS **ESC** to return to the spreadsheet

REMOVING DATA LABELS

Data labels add more information to a chart. If, however, the chart is to be changed from one type to another, it is sometimes necessary to remove the data labels so that the chart does not become overly cluttered.

REMOVE DATA LABELS

1. CHOOSE **Sales91_92** from the **View** menu

2. PRESS **ESC** after viewing the chart

3. CHOOSE **Data Labels** from the **Data** menu

4. SELECT **1st Y** in the **Series** box

5. CHOOSE **Delete**

6. SELECT **2nd Y** in the **Series** box

7. CHOOSE **Delete**

8. CHOOSE **Done**

9. PRESS **Shift/F10** to view the bar chart without the data labels

10. PRESS **ESC** when finished

CREATING A PIE CHART

A pie chart is best demonstrated by selecting a single category. It shows an individual percentage of a group of values, such as what percentage one boat's sales is of all boats' sales combined. Choosing the **Pie** command in the **Format** menu will change the current chart to a pie chart or choosing **New Chart** in the **View** menu will create a new chart on selected cells.

CREATE A PIE CHART

1. SELECT the values under the **Change** column for each of the boats as follows:

$4,630.00
$5,686.00
$6,850.00
$17,445.00

---

2. CHOOSE **New Chart** from the **View** menu

3. PRESS **ESC** to leave the default bar chart

4. CHOOSE **Pie** from the **Format** menu

5. PRESS **Shift/F10** to view the basic pie chart

At this time the chart is broken down only into the individual percentage categories for each of the boats. The order of the breakdown is from the first boat to the last in the selected range of cells on the spreadsheet. Delano appears first, beginning in the 12:00 position on the pie. The Spirit appears in the second position, and so on. Now, additional features can be added to it to give more information to the reader.

6. PRESS **Esc** to leave the pie chart

ADD A MAIN TITLE

Use the **Titles** command from the **Data** menu to create a main title for the pie chart.

1. CHOOSE **Titles** from the **Data** menu

2. TYPE **PERCENTAGE OF CHANGE** in the **Chart title** box

3. PRESS **Enter** or choose OK

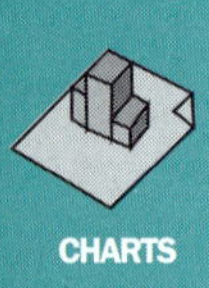

To add category titles

The chart now contains sections of the pie for each boat; however, the boat names are not identified, so the pie chart is still difficult to interpret. The **X-series** command in the **Data** menu is used to assign labels to sections of the pie chart.

ADD CATEGORY TITLES

1. **SELECT**   the cells containing the names of all four boats
2. **CHOOSE**   X-series from the **Data** menu
3. **PRESS**   Shift/F10 to view the current pie chart

The chart now gives complete information about each of the sections showing the percentage of change and the boat name.

4. **PRESS**   ESC to return to the spreadsheet and **CHART** mode

CHANGING THE DATA FORMAT

The format of a pie chart can be changed so that individual sections of the pie give the reader more information.

CHANGE THE DATA FORMAT

1. **CHOOSE**   Data Format from the **Format** menu

The dialog box shown in Figure 15-11 appears.

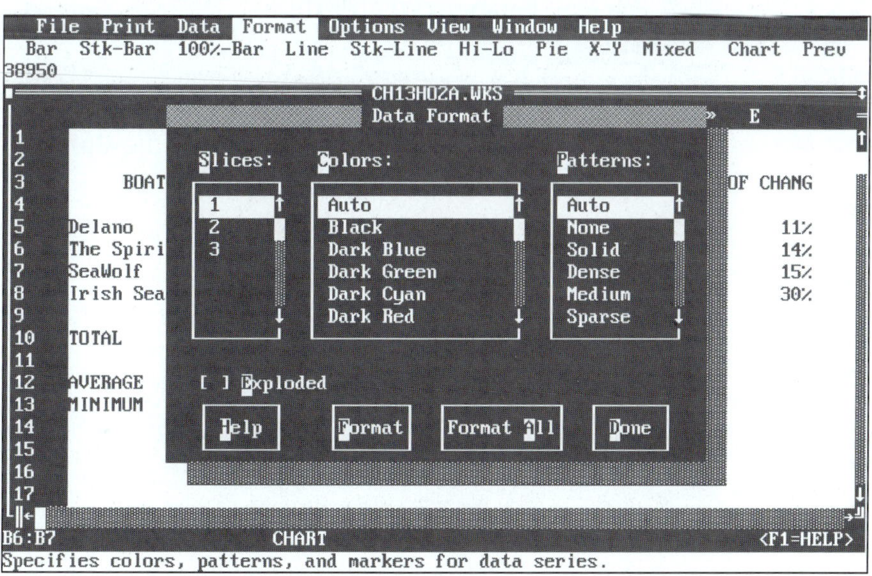

FIGURE 15-11
DATA FORMAT
DIALOG BOX

This dialog box contains the options listed in table 15-1 for changing the appearance of a pie chart.

<u>Slices:</u>

This list box shows numbers for each of the slices in the current pie chart. In this case, each slice represents a boat in the Puget Sound Charter business.

<u>Colors:</u>

This list box gives options for changing the color or shading of each section of the pie.

<u>Patterns:</u>

The Patterns list box contains options for changing the pattern in the pie sections from a solid color, to light shading, and in between.

<u>[   ] Exploded:</u>

The Exploded box allows for exploding all slices of the pie. For example, displaying the pie sections with space between each one.

The options at the bottom of the dialog box include formatting a single section of the pie <Format>, formatting all sections of the pie in the options chosen <Format All>, and leaving the dialog box with the selection made <Done>.

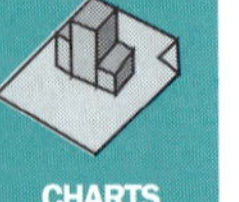

CHARTS

TABLE 15-1
DATA FORMAT
OPTIONS

2. CHOOSE **1** in the **Slices** list box

One (1) is the slice for Delano, the first in the list on the spreadsheet.

3. CHOOSE **Gray** in the **Colors** box (scroll to the selection) or press G

4. CHOOSE **Sparse** in the **Patterns** list box

5. CHOOSE **Format**

6. CHOOSE **2** in the **Slices** list box (the section of the pie for The Spirit)

7. CHOOSE **Dark Gray** or another color in the **Colors** list box (choose a color if your monitor displays colors)

8. CHOOSE **Medium** in the **Patterns** box

9. CHOOSE **Format**

10. CHANGE the colors and patterns of the other two sections of the pie chart. Be sure to choose **Format** when finished with each. Explode the pie section for Slice number 4, Irish Sea.

11. CHOOSE **Done** when all selections are made

12. VIEW the chart (**Shift/F10**). It should appear similar to that shown in Figure 15-12

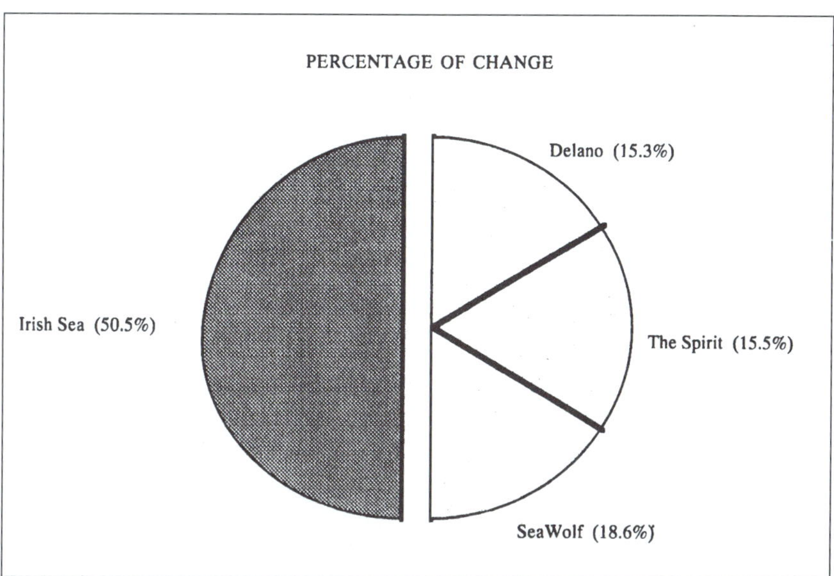

**FIGURE 15-12
FORMATTED
SECTIONS OF A PIE
CHART**

13. **PRESS**   **ESC** when finished

14. **RENAME**   this chart, chart 1, to **Change** (**Charts** from the **View** menu)

CREATING LINE CHARTS

Line charts are best used to make comparisons of multiple values over a period of time. They demonstrate increases and decreases in numeric values and show trends as no other chart form can.

In the following steps, you will also use the Toolbar to access some of the chart functions. By looking at the Toolbar, you will see that the bar styles are shown on the bar. They include bar, stacked bar (Stk-Bar), 100%-Bar, Line, stacked line (Stk-Line), Hi-Lo, Pie, X-Y, and Mixed. These are discussed in more detail at the beginning of this chapter. Also available on the Toolbar are the commands Chart and Prev (Preview). These two may be used to view quickly the current chart and to preview the chart prior to printing.

CREATE LINE CHARTS

**INSTRUCTOR'S
DATA DISK**

1. **RETRIEVE**   the spreadsheet **CH13PR1.WKS** which you created in Chapter 13; or retrieve it from the instructor's data disk.

2. **SELECT**   cells **A11** through **E14** (all text and values in the EXPENSES category, with the exception of Averages)

3. **CHOOSE**   **New Chart** from the **View** menu

4. **PRESS**   **ESC** when the bar chart appears

5. **CHOOSE**   **Line** from the **Format** menu or click **Line** on the Toolbar

6. **PRESS**   **Shift/F10** to view the graph or choose **Chart** from the Toolbar

A line chart similar to that shown in Figure 15-13 appears.

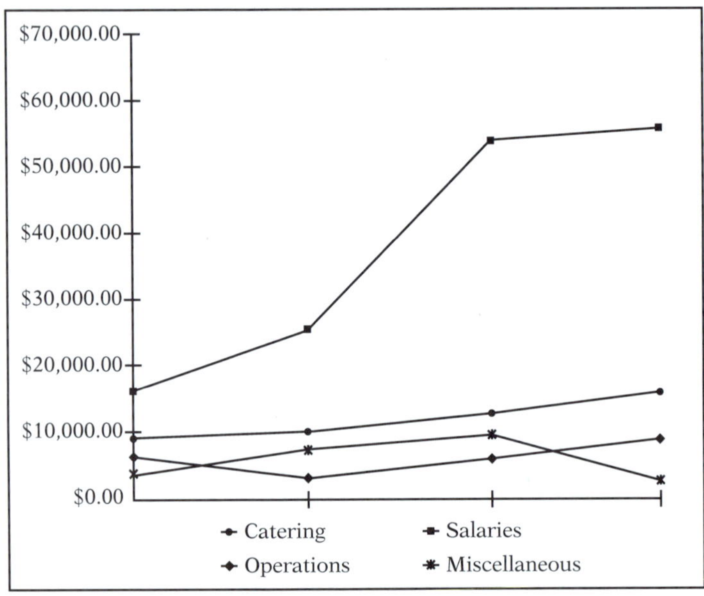

FIGURE 15-13
LINE CHART
SHOWING INCREASES
AND DECREASES IN
VALUES

CHARTS

7. **ADD**   appropriate titles, legends, and values to this line chart to enhance its appearance and increase the information found on it.

8. **RENAME**   the chart as **LINE**

INCLUDING GRIDS ON A CHART

Grids can be included on a bar or line chart. They are light, dashed lines that extend horizontally across the X-axis and vertically along the Y-axis. They assist the reader further in gathering information from the chart as they extend directly from the values on the Y-axis and up from the X-axis.

INCLUDE GRIDS ON A CHART

1. **CHOOSE**   **Hi-Lo-Close** from the **Format** menu or choose **Hi-Lo** from the Toolbar

2. **CHOOSE**   **chart** from the Toolbar

This chart shows the range of values found in each of the EXPENSES categories. Each dot on the vertical line represents the beginning through ending values for each item as shown in the legend at the bottom of the screen.

3. **PRESS**   **ESC** to return to the spreadsheet

4. **CHOOSE**   **X-Axis** from the **Options** menu

5. **CHOOSE**   **Grid lines** (or press **Spacebar** or click with mouse to put an X in the box)

6. **PRESS**   **Enter** or choose OK

7. **CHOOSE**   **Y-Axis** from the **Options** menu

The dialog box shown in Figure 15-14 appears.

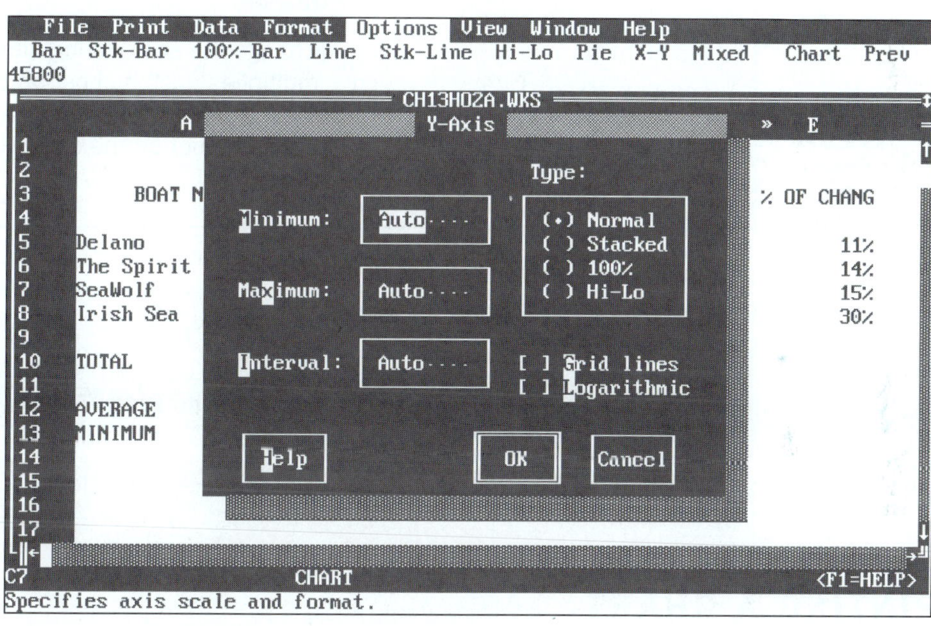

FIGURE 15-14
Y-AXIS DIALOG BOX

This dialog box gives you the options (not all of which will be used in this exercise) shown in Table 15-2.

CHOOSE THIS OPTION	TO DO THIS
Minimum:	Set a minimum value to begin the lowest value on the Y-axis.
Maximum:	Set a maximum value to appear as the highest value on the Y-axis.
Interval:	Set the desired interval along the Y-axis.
	For example, you could set a minimum of 10, maximum of 500, at intervals of 50.
Type:	Select the type of chart being used. The options include Normal (bar chart), Stacked (bar), 100% (bar), and Hi-Lo (bar).
Grid lines:	Attach grids along the Y-axis to assist the readers.
Logarithmic:	Change the scale to logarithmic. Works then multiplies each number on the scale to determine the next number. Works normally adds each number on the scale to determine the next.

TABLE 15-2
OPTIONS FOUND IN THE Y-AXIS DIALOG BOX

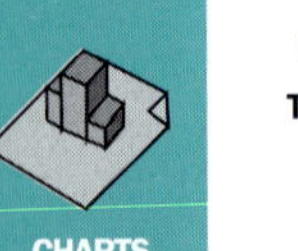

CHARTS

8. **CHOOSE** **Grid lines**

9. **CHOOSE** **OK** or press Enter

10. **CHOOSE** **Chart** from the Toolbar or press **Shift/F10** to see the grid lines on the current chart

11. **PRESS** **Esc** and then **F10** to leave CHART mode

PRINTING A CHART

When you are ready to print a chart, choose the appropriate chart from the **View** menu. A list of all charts created will be shown in the menu.

Note: *A chart is saved with a spreadsheet. The chart must be viewed when the spreadsheet is open.*

PRINT A CHART

With the **CH13PR1.WKS** spreadsheet still active,

1. CHOOSE   **Line** from the **View** menu

The chart appears.

2. PRESS   **ESC** to return to the spreadsheet in CHART mode

3. CHOOSE   **Page Setup & Margins** from the **Print** menu

 Note: *This works the same as in other Works' tools in that it may be used to make changes to the way the document will appear on the page.*

4. CHOOSE   **Landscape** (it should be selected) so that the chart will print horizontally on the page

As needed, you can also change other margin settings using this dialog box.

5. CHOOSE   **OK** or press Enter

6. CHOOSE   **Line** again from the Toolbar

7. CHOOSE   **Preview** from the **Print** menu or choose PREV from the Toolbar

8. CHOOSE   **Preview** again

9. PRESS   **P** to print

Be sure you are on line to the printer and that the printer is in **Ready** mode if necessary.

10. SAVE   the spreadsheet again, and **quit** or **continue** to the Tutorial

GUIDED TUTORIAL

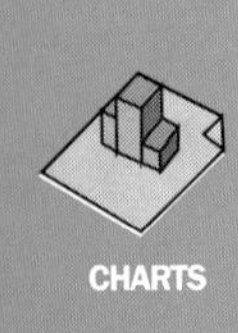

CHARTS

WHAT YOU'LL DO

- Create pie, line, and bar charts.
- Modify charts to include legends, titles, and data values.
- Preview and print charts.

HOW TO DO IT

1. **OPEN** the spreadsheet **CH13HO2B.WKS**. Change the format of all currency values so that they are whole numbers, no places to the right of the decimal.

2. **SELECT** cells **A5** through **C8**, the boat names, and the current and next year sales figures.

3. **CHOOSE** **New Chart** from the **View** menu to view the bar chart.

4. **PRESS** **Esc** when finished.

5. **CHOOSE** **Legends** from the **Data** menu.

6. **CHOOSE** **1st Y** from **Series** box.

7. **TYPE** **Current Year** in the **Legend** box and choose **Create**.

8. **CHOOSE** **2nd Y** from the **Series** box.

9. **TYPE** **Next Year** in the **Legend** box and choose **Create**.

10. **CHOOSE** **Done** when finished.

11. **CHOOSE** **Titles** from the **Data** menu.

12. **ENTER** the following titles for the chart.

    Chart title: SALES PROJECTIONS

    Subtitle: Current and Next Year Sales

    X-axis: Boat Names

    Y-axis: Dollars in Thousands

13. **CHOOSE** **OK** or press Enter when finished.

14. **SELECT** cells **B5** through **B8** or all values for the boats in 1991 (excluding the total, average, and minimum).

15. **CHOOSE** **Data Labels** from the **Data** menu.

16. **CHOOSE** **Create** to insert these cells as labels for the first series.

17. **SELECT** the four values under **1992**, **C5** through **C8**.

18. **CHOOSE** **Data Labels** from the **Data** menu again and choose **Create** for the **2nd Y-series**.

19. **CLICK** once on **Chart** on the **Toolbar** to view the chart again.

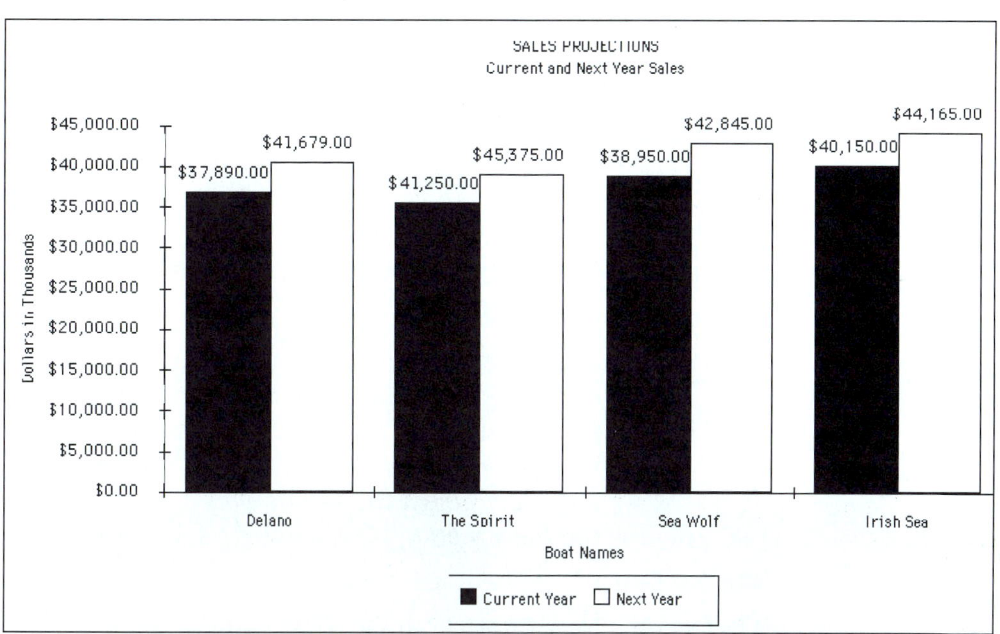

**FIGURE 15-15
BAR CHART WITH
DATA LABELS**

It should appear similar to the one shown in Figure 15-15.

20. PRESS	**Esc** when finished.
21. CHOOSE	**Charts** from the **View** menu.
22. TYPE	**CH15BAR** and choose **Rename**.
23. CHOOSE	**Done**.
24. PRESS	**F10** to switch to the spreadsheet mode.
25. SAVE	the spreadsheet again under a new name, **CH15TUT**. Saving the spreadsheet again will save all charts that have been created.
26. PRESS	**F10** to switch back to the chart mode.
27. CHOOSE	**PREV** from the Toolbar.
28. CHOOSE	**Preview** again.
29. PRESS	**P** to print.
Note:	*If the default font size is too large or too small on your printer, change the font through the Format menu.*
30. CHOOSE	for practice, each of the following on the Toolbar. Press **Esc** after viewing each chart.

    a. Click on **Stk-Bar** and choose **Chart.**

    b. Choose **Esc** when finished.

    a. Choose **Line** and then choose **Chart.**

    b. Choose **Esc** when finished.

        a. Choose **Mixed** and choose **Chart.**

        b. Choose Esc when finished.

31. CHOOSE   **Bar** again.

32. HIGHLIGHT   each of the **% of Change** values.

33. CHOOSE   **Pie** from the **Toolbar**.

34. CHOOSE   **Chart** from the **Toolbar** to view the chart or press **Shift/F10**.

35. PRESS   **ESC** when finished.

    Note: *You can change the type of chart you are looking at by simply choosing an option from the Toolbar or the Format menu. Doing so, however, will change the format of the current chart and will not create a new chart. If you wish to save both settings, you must select the values and then choose New Chart from the View menu.*

36. HIGHLIGHT   the percentage values again.

37. CHOOSE   **New Chart** from the **View** menu.

38. CREATE   a title as done for the bar chart.

39. HIGHLIGHT   the boat names in column A.

40. CHOOSE   **X-Series** from the **Data** menu to assign names to each of the pie sections.

41. CHOOSE   **Pie** and **Chart** from the Toolbar. Press **Esc**.

42. CHOOSE   **Charts** from the **View** menu and rename Chart1, **CH15PIE**.

43. SAVE   the spreadsheet again under the same name, **CH15TUT**.

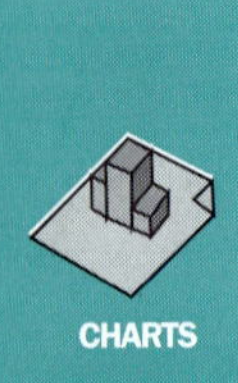

CHARTS

REVIEW QUESTIONS

1. List at least two ways to view a chart.

2. The _______________ command from the _____________ menu is used to add headings to a chart.

3. The _______________ command from the _______________ menu must be used when starting a new chart.

4. List the first step that must be taken prior to creating a chart.

5. Match each of the following to the correct term.

   _______ The values on the vertical axis

   _______ The labels along the horizontal axis

   _______ The component of a chart that identifies each unique bar or line

   _______ The identifying labels in a pie chart

   _______ The text in a chart that shows information about every bar or line

   a. X-series
   b. X-axis
   c. Y-axis
   d. legend
   e. data labels

6. The _______________ command from the _______________ menu is used to rename or delete a chart.

7. _______ Charts may be printed using both the **Print** command from the **Print** menu and the **Prev** command from the Toolbar.

HANDS-ON EXERCISES

EXERCISE 1

1. Open the spreadsheet **CH13HO2B.WKS** which you created in Chapter 13; or retrieve it from the instructor's data disk.

2. Create a bar chart that includes the **Current Year** and **Next Year Sales** amounts. Create an appropriate chart title and subtitle describing the chart. Include the Boat names on the X-axis.

3. Rename the bar chart **CH15BAR**.

4. Print a copy of the bar chart.

5. Create a second stacked bar chart on the five- and ten-year projections. Include the X-axis labels and titles. Also include main and subheadings.

6. Adjust the format of the bar by changing the patterns in each section.

7. Add a legend that identifies the five- and ten-year sections of the bar.

8. Add data labels to each of the bar sections.

9. Rename the chart **CH15SBAR**.

10. Print a copy of this second bar chart.

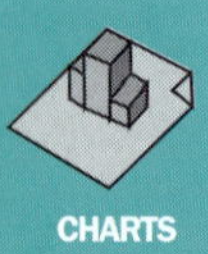

EXERCISE 2

Integrating a chart into a word processing document.

1. Open a new word processing document with the company logo at the top (the template called logo) or create the logo as shown in the following document if it is not at the top of the screen. Use borders from the format menu to add the double lines. Insert a blank line above the heading and select it, the heading, and a blank line below the heading before choosing the border option.

2. Type the following text two blank lines below the logo.

PUGET SOUND CHARTERS
West Lake Union Way
Seattle, WA 98108

PROJECTION REPORT

```
The following chart shows the five- and ten-year projection
for sales above the projected 10 percent increase in sales
for next year. We feel that this projection is a modest
one. It shows a 25 percent increase in sales beyond next
year's for a total 35 percent increase during the next six
years. Another 25 percent increase is projected for the
five years following. This averages to an approximate 58
percent increase in the next 11 years.
```

INSTRUCTOR'S DATA DISK

3. Open **CH13HO2B.WKS**.

4. Use the **Window** menu to move back to the word processing document.

5. Choose **Insert chart** from the **Edit** menu.

6. Choose **CH13HO2B** in the **Spreadsheets** list box.

7. Choose **CH15BAR** from the **Charts** list box.

8. Choose **OK** or press Enter.

The following line appears in the center of the document:

```
*chart CH13HO2B:CH15BAR*
```

This is the location at which the chart will be inserted. Notice that the message is stating the name of the spreadsheet and the name of the chart attached to it.

9. Save this document as **CH15HO2**.

10. Preview the document using **Preview** in the **Print** menu.

11. Print a copy of the document.

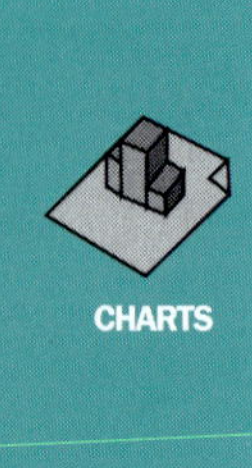

16 DATABASE DESIGN

Objectives

- Create a database.

- Understand database design.

- Create a record form.

- Enter data.

- Edit a database.

- Move through a database file.

- Copy field contents.

- Format a database.

PREVIEW ≫≫━▶

A database program is a system for using a computer to store information (data) in an organized fashion. Filing cabinets, address books, Rolodexes, and telephone books are all databases — they contain information in an organized format. This information is often sorted in alphabetical order and grouped in various categories. A database management program such as the Works tool operates in much the same way. The advantage of using a computer program for keeping data is that you can use the program not only to enter and store the information, but you can also use it to sort the information, to display it in forms, or to print it.

Any time that database design comes to mind, one usually asks the question: What kind of output is needed? It is important to know what you want from the database prior to creating and storing the data in it. For example, you might want a report that shows several characteristics of a general population group, and then you might want to see that data sorted by age groups. You need answers to these questions to best design the original database. In that way, the data you need is available and can be easily retrieved.

Once you know what information you need from a database, you can answer the second question: What data shall I put into the database? Suppose, for instance, that you want to start a database system for Puget Sound Charters. You have decided that you would like some information on the demographics of its clients: who they are, where they work, the company or home address, city, state, and so on. You compile a survey to collect this data into a database file called CLIENTS. From this data you can create reports or do sorts and queries to gather information about the kinds of clients you attract. This is the basis of good database design.

CREATING A DATABASE

As mentioned in the Preview, the first step in creating a database is to know what kind of file you want to create and what information you would like it to contain. One of the most commonly created files is one on the customers or clients of a firm. This information is critical in planning marketing strategies, creating mailing lists, and in analyzing the groups of people most attracted to your kind of service. In the case of Puget Sound Charters, it would be useful to know who most often books a charter. Is it businesses? Is it individuals? Is there a wide range of small groups that book?

The first file should be a simple file that is kept on each of the clients who book a trip. It could include:

    Name of the individual
    Name of the organization
    Address
    Telephone number

It is also advisable to include a unique identifier for each of the clients. This identifier could be a client ID number. The reason for this is to improve the accuracy of queries (searches for data characteristics) and to avoid replication of data (such as two or more identical records).

UNDERSTANDING DATABASE DESIGN

When creating a database file, information pertaining to each client (such as the list in the preceding paragraph) is called a record. Each individual item is called a field. Database files may consist of several records and each record may contain several fields. Each client is a single record. When entering field names, there is a limit to the number of characters that can be used in the field title. Each field name may contain up to 15 characters. A file may contain up to 32,000 records. Each record may contain 256 fields (although it would be unlikely), and each field may contain up to 256 characters. It is usually recommended that the fields be as brief and concise as possible since it makes them easier to work with.

The list of fields that are needed for the Client file could be abbreviated to read:

    CLIENT ID
    LNAME
    FNAME
    COMPANY
    ADDRESS
    CITY
    STATE
    ZIP
    PHONE

STARTING A NEW FILE

Starting a database file is the same as starting any other file in Works. The **Create New File** command is used in the **File** menu or the **Create a New File** option from the "quick start" box.

START A NEW FILE

1. **SIGN** onto Works and set the directory path (if necessary).
2. **CHOOSE** **Create New File** from the **File** menu or Create a New File from the "quick start" box
3. **CHOOSE** **Database**
4. **CHOOSE** **OK** or press Enter

A window similar to that shown in Figure 16-1 appears.

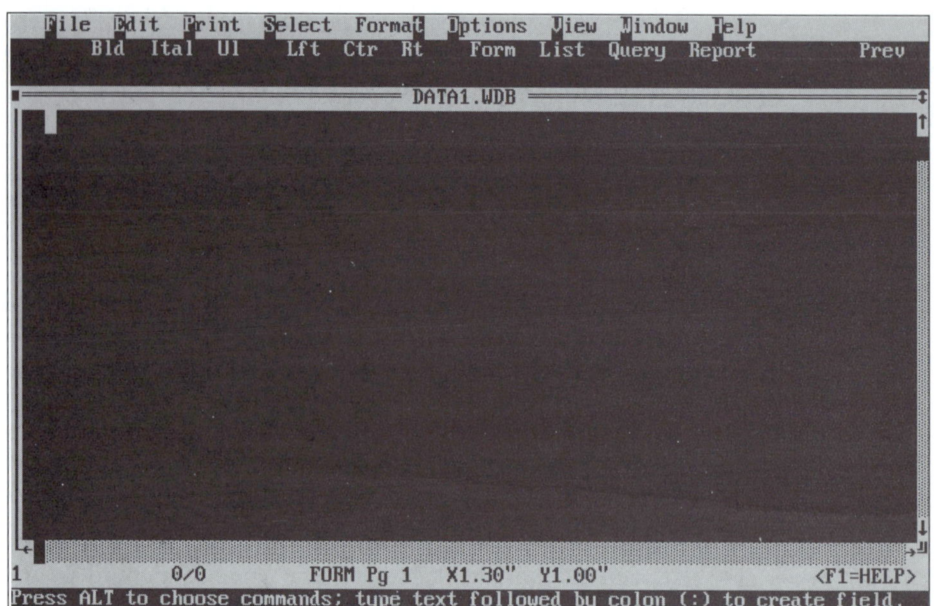

FIGURE 16-1
OPENING DATABASE SCREEN

This screen is similar to a word processing and spreadsheet screen. It contains the menu options at the top of the screen, the scroll bars at the right and bottom of the screen, and a status line at the bottom that gives information about what is currently on the screen and about the file size. The screen shows the total number of records displayed and indicates which record number is currently being viewed. It also shows the view in which you are presently working (FORM view is shown in this figure). Works opens the database file in the **Form** view. In **Form** view, you can create fields and insert field information; a single record appears on the screen at a time.

Records may also be displayed on the screen showing each record on a single line and displaying many records on the screen at a time. This mode is called **List** view. You can create fields and insert field information in either **Form** view or **List** view. When entering data, however, it is often easier to enter each record's data on its own **Form** screen.

DATABASE

CREATING THE RECORD FORM

Field names are created by typing them anywhere on the **Form** screen. All of the desired fields combined comprise a single record. After the basic record is designed, information on each client may then be typed into the record forms. As many records as needed may be called up.

At the bottom of the screen are position indicators. When the cursor is in the upper left corner of the screen, the indicators read, X1.30" Y1.00". When the cursor is moved, the indicators change. The X and Y are like X- and Y- axes on a spreadsheet chart. When the cursor is moved upward or downward, the Y setting changes; when the cursor is moved to the right or left, the X setting changes.

CREATE THE RECORD FORM

1. POSITION the highlight at **X1.80** and **Y1.33** using the **Down** and **Right Arrow** keys

2. TYPE **CLIENT ID:**

Note: *All field names are followed by a colon.*

3. PRESS **Enter**

A dialog box asking for the width and height of the field appears. The default width is 20 characters. The default height is 1 row. With each field, you can change the number of characters and change the number of rows involved as necessary. For example, if you wanted to include the address in a single field, you could call it LOCALE and make its height equal to four lines. However, if this were done, you could not later sort or do a query by city, state, or zip.

4. TYPE **5** in the **Width** box

5. LEAVE the setting of **1** for **Height**

6. PRESS **Enter** or choose OK

7. POSITION the highlight at **X1.80** and **Y1.67**

8. TYPE **LNAME:**

9. PRESS **Enter** and leave the default settings

10. CHOOSE **OK** or press Enter

11. COMPLETE the record by entering the following fields at the positions shown. Set the width as shown. Leave heights at 1.

Field name	Position	Width
FNAME:	X5.00" Y1.67"	9
COMPANY:	X1.80" Y1.83"	20
ADDRESS:	X1.80" Y2.00"	20
CITY:	X1.80" Y2.17"	20
STATE:	X5.00" Y2.17"	2
ZIP:	X6.20" Y2.17"	5
PHONE:	X1.80" Y2.33"	12

The finished form should look approximately as follows:

CLIENT ID:

LNAME: FNAME:
COMPANY:
ADDRESS:
CITY: STATE: ZIP:
PHONE:

The record form you have just completed is only an example for use in the following exercises. When designing your own record form, fields may be positioned anywhere on the screen.

SAVING THE FORM

In its completed form, the form is ready to be saved. Although the file has a name given by Works, it is best to rename the file to one that will be recognized quickly and easily for its contents.

SAVE THE FORM

1. CHOOSE	**Save As** from the **File** menu
2. TYPE	**CH16PR1** as the name of the file
3. CHOOSE	**OK** or press Enter

ENTERING DATA

It is now time to enter the field contents (also called the data) into the records. The record form can be used to enter as many client records as desired. If you make an error in a field entry, just select the field and retype the entry. The new contents will replace the old. Later, other methods of editing the fields are discussed.

DATABASE

ENTER DATA

1. HIGHLIGHT the field to the right of CLIENT ID by using the **Arrow** keys or by clicking the mouse button to the right of the field name

Note: *The highlight is as wide as the width setting given when the field was created.*

2. TYPE **101** as the first client ID number

3. PRESS the **Tab** key to move to the next field

Note: *You could also press **Enter** to enter the contents and remain in the field. Usually, the **Tab** key should be used to move to the next field.*

4. TYPE **Hammersmith** as the last name (LNAME)

5. PRESS **Tab**

6. TYPE **Michael** as the first name (FNAME)

7. PRESS **Tab**

8. TYPE **Software Unlimited** as the name of the COMPANY

9. PRESS **Tab**

10. TYPE **1984 Newton Road** as the ADDRESS

11. PRESS **Tab** and type **Seattle** as the CITY

12. PRESS **Tab** and type **WA** as the STATE

13. PRESS **Tab** and type **98102** as the ZIP

14. PRESS **Tab** and type **206 555-1297** as the PHONE

15. PRESS **Tab** again to move to the next blank record

Note: *The previous record was record 1. Notice that the lower left corner of the status bar shows a number 2 for the second record.*

16. CONTINUE entering records as shown below. Do not worry about errors at this time; however, if you wish, you may highlight a field and press F2 to edit as you did in the spreadsheet tool. We discuss this in more detail in the following steps.

102
Ho, Selena
The Northwest Bank
1900 Wilson Plaza
Bellevue WA 98004
206 455-7855

103
Baker, Charles
IMS Consultants
19451 N.E. 45th
Seattle WA 98107
206 296-1278

104
Schuster, Simon
CTech Corporation
2100 Plaza Center
Kirkland WA 98032
206 883-1129

319

105
Sills, Bonnie
CTech Corporation
East Hills Branch
Tukwila WA 98152
206 925-5500

106
Long, Robert
Long and Tukes
9800 Plaza Suite
Bellevue WA 98007
206 454-9825

107
Krogstad, Sandra
Krogstad and Company
5125 Compton Way
Woodinville WA 98042
206 821-9978

108
Judd, Thomas
Software Express
North Cromlin Blvd
Issaquah WA 98027
206 391-2857

109
Smith, Trisha
Julien's Computers
1001 South Plaza
Seattle WA 98108
206 284-9711

110
Grover, Douglas
Grover and Associate
123 4th Avenue N.E.
Seattle WA 98119
206 887-3455

111
Mills, Nevell
The Baldwin Co.
98 Baldwin Place
Seattle WA 98101
206 821-9942

112
Gonzales, Theodore
The Best Store
Century Plaza #20
Bellevue WA 98005
206 455-2396

17. SAVE the file again

EDITING A DATABASE

Now that all records are entered into the database, you can switch to **List** view to view a group of records at one time. **List** view is also a mode in which you can edit the records in a database. Because it shows multiple records on the screen at one time and makes it easier to proof the field contents, editing in this mode is often easier than in **Form** view. As with the spreadsheet tool, pressing the **F2** key when a field is selected will insert the contents into the **Edit** bar so that they can be changed without deleting the entire contents.

EDIT A DATABASE

1. PRESS **F9** to switch to **List** view, or use the View menu and choose List, or click List on the Toolbar

2. PRESS **Ctrl/Home** to move to the first record

List view shows all of the field names across the top of the screen. It also shows the contents of the fields. When the field contents are wider than the width shown on the screen, the contents overlap the next cell on the right if it is empty, or are truncated if the cell is occupied. However, when the highlight is in a field, the entire contents appear in the **Edit** bar at the top left of the screen.

3. SELECT the top cell in the **LNAME** field, **Hammersmith**

The full name, Hammersmith, appears in the **Edit** bar even though only part of the name appears in the selection.

CHANGING THE FIELD WIDTH

The default (automatic) field width in **List** view is 10. The advantage of having the width of the fields shortened is that more field names appear on the screen; however, when making editing changes, it might be easier to do so when all of the field contents are visible. The field width can be adjusted using the **Field Width** command in the **Format** menu.

With the highlight in the **LNAME** field,

CHANGE THE FIELD WIDTH

1. **CHOOSE**   **Field Width** from the **Format** menu
2. **TYPE**   **12**
3. **CHOOSE**   **OK** or press Enter

The field is widened and the entire contents are now visible.

4. **CHANGE**   the width of all other fields whose contents or whose field name are not entirely visible on the screen

It is suggested that in **List** view the field width be one character wider than the field name and/or the field's widest contents. This makes your database easier to read in **List** view.

Note: *You can also hide a field by entering a field width of zero (0). Sometimes it is desirable to hide a field when other users have access to a file. Any confidential data is then hidden. The width can be adjusted again at any time in **List** view. The hidden field is always visible in **Form** view .*

EDITING FIELD CONTENTS

With the entire contents of the fields visible on the screen, you can easily spot errors in the contents and make other editing changes. Press the **F2** key when making changes to the contents. If there is a major error in the contents, simply retype them when the field is selected.

When in the **Edit** bar, use the keys listed in Table 16-1 to aid in editing the field contents:

PRESS THIS KEY	TO DO THIS
Home	go to the beginning of the line
End	go to the end of the line
Left Arrow	go left one character
Right Arrow	go right one character
Backspace	remove the character to the left
Shift/Left or Right Arrow	select one or more characters to the left or right
Delete	remove a selected character

TABLE 16-1
ACTIONS IN THE
EDIT BAR

Use the cursor movements listed in Table 16-2 to move through a list of records.

<table>
<tr><td colspan="2">DO THIS IN</td><td></td></tr>
<tr><td><u>FORM VIEW</u></td><td><u>LIST VIEW</u></td><td><u>TO MOVE TO THIS</u></td></tr>
<tr><td>Left or Right Arrow keys in both</td><td></td><td>Left or right one field or cell</td></tr>
<tr><td>Up or Down Arrow keys in both</td><td></td><td>Down or up one record or row</td></tr>
<tr><td>Tab key in both</td><td></td><td>Next field</td></tr>
<tr><td>Shift/Tab in both</td><td></td><td>Previous field</td></tr>
<tr><td>Home in both</td><td></td><td>Leftmost field or cell</td></tr>
<tr><td>End in both</td><td></td><td>Rightmost field or cell</td></tr>
<tr><td>Page Down in both</td><td></td><td>Down one window</td></tr>
<tr><td>Page Up in both</td><td></td><td>Up one window</td></tr>
<tr><td>Ctrl/Home in both</td><td></td><td>First cell in first record</td></tr>
<tr><td>Ctrl/End in both</td><td></td><td>Last cell in last record</td></tr>
<tr><td>Ctrl/Pg Down</td><td></td><td>Next record</td></tr>
<tr><td>Ctrl/Pg Up</td><td></td><td>Previous record</td></tr>
<tr><td>Ctrl/Left</td><td>Ctrl/Pg Up</td><td>Left one window</td></tr>
<tr><td>Ctrl/Right</td><td>Ctrl/Page Down</td><td>Right one window</td></tr>
<tr><td></td><td>Ctrl/Arrow Keys</td><td>Up, Down, Left, or Right by one block of data</td></tr>
</table>

**TABLE 16-2
SELECTION
MOVEMENTS AND
SCROLLING**

EDITING FIELD CONTENTS

1. **PROOF** and make any necessary editing changes in the database records

2. **USE** the **F9** key to toggle between **Form** and **List** modes or click List or Form on the Toolbar

3. **SAVE** the file again when finished

COPYING IN *LIST* VIEW

To copy field contents

Sometimes it is useful to copy field contents rather than retype them. For example, if you know that you have new clients who live in Seattle and have the same zip code, you could copy the contents of the fields for the city, state, and zip code to the corresponding fields of another record.

In **List** view,

COPY FIELD CONTENTS

1. **HIGHLIGHT** the **City**, **State**, and **Zip Code** fields for record 7 (Woodinville WA 98042)
2. **CHOOSE** **Copy** from the **Edit** menu
3. **HIGHLIGHT** the **City**, **State**, and **Zip Code** fields in row 13 (the blank row at the end of the file) or select just the city field
4. **PRESS** **Enter**

The field contents are copied to record 13.

To repeat the copy command
You can repeat the insert of the copied fields as many times as needed.

REPEAT THE COPY COMMAND

1. **HIGHLIGHT** the **City**, **State**, and **Zip Code** fields for record 14 or just the city cell
2. **PRESS** **Shift/F7**

The same copied contents are inserted.

3. **ADD** the following information to complete the field entries. Stay in **List** view to do so. Use the Tab key to move from field to field.

```
113
Kimball, Elizabeth
Downtown Pets
23rd and Forest
206 832-8877

114
Bell, Pat
The Furniture Emporium
2525 16th Ave. N.W.
206 833-9000
```

4. **ADJUST** any column widths if necessary

To copy to adjacent fields
Field contents can be copied to adjacent fields using the **Fill Down** or **Fill Right** commands in the **Edit** menu. Suppose, for example, that the next four new clients were all from Woodinville. Since Woodinville is the city used in the last record in this database file, the city and state fields could be copied down to adjacent cells using the **Fill Down** command.

COPY TO ADJACENT FIELD

1. HIGHLIGHT   the **City** and **State** fields starting with row 14 (which contains the city name and the state name) and ending with row 17

2. CHOOSE   **Fill Down** from the **Edit** menu

The city and state are copied down to the adjacent rows.

MOVING IN *LIST* VIEW

Although it usually is not necessary to move records around in a file, it can be done. An entire record or individual fields in a record can be moved to another location.

In **List** view,

MOVE IN LIST VIEW

1. HIGHLIGHT   all of record **2** (all fields)

2. PRESS   **F3** or choose Move from the Edit menu

3. PRESS   **Home** to move the cursor back to the left margin

4. HIGHLIGHT   all of record 13 (or just the first cell)

5. PRESS   **Enter**

Record 13 is replaced by 2.

6. MOVE   **Record 2** back to its original location

7. ADD   record 13 again

113
Kimball, Elizabeth
Downtown Pets
23rd and Forest
Woodinville WA 98042
206 832-8877

DELETING A ROW OR COLUMN

To delete a row or column in the **List** view, use the **Delete Record/Field** command in the **Edit** menu. When specific fields are being removed, only the fields should be selected and then the **Field** option chosen in the dialog box. When a row is to be deleted, select the row or rows and then choose the **Row** option in the dialog box.

325

DELETE A ROW OR COLUMN

1. **HIGHLIGHT** the **City** and **State** fields in rows 15 through 17, which contain Woodinville WA

2. **CHOOSE** **Delete Record/Field** from the **Edit** menu

3. **CHOOSE** **Record** from the dialog box so that the records are deleted and not the fields

4. **CHOOSE** **OK** or press Enter

The three records are removed.

EDITING IN *FORM* VIEW

Using the **List** view mode is usually the fastest way to scan records and make editing changes by moving quickly from field to field. Using **Form** view, however, allows you to concentrate on one record at a time.

EDITING RECORDS IN FORM VIEW

You can move through records in **Form** view in the same way as **List** view. Use Table 16-2 to review the movements through records and fields in either mode.

EDIT RECORDS IN FORM VIEW

1. **SWITCH** to **Form** view (F9).

2. **PRESS** **Ctrl/Home** to move to the first record

3. **PRESS** **Ctrl/PgDn** until you reach Client 104

4. **HIGHLIGHT** the **Address** field

5. **PRESS** **F2** to edit this field

6. **USE** the **Arrow** keys and the **Delete** or **Backspace** key to change the number in the address to 2122.

7. **PRESS** **Enter** when finished

INSERTING A NEW RECORD

When initially entering the data into each record, a new record was inserted automatically at the end of the file when the **Tab** key was pressed at the bottom of the last record. Sometimes it is desirable to insert a new record in the middle of a file. This can be done using the **Insert Record** command in the **Edit** menu.

INSERT A NEW RECORD

1.	PRESS	**Ctrl/PgUp** or **Pg/Dn** until you reach Client 108
2.	CHOOSE	**Insert Record** from the **Edit** menu

A new blank record appears.

3.	PRESS	**Ctrl/PgUp** and note that the previous record is on Client 107
4.	PRESS	**Ctrl/PgDn** once to view the blank record
5.	PRESS	**Ctrl/PgDn** one more time to view the record for Client 108
6.	PRESS	**Ctrl/PgUp** to move to the blank record
7.	TYPE	the following data for the new Client 108. The old Client 108 has left town.

108
Jackson, Karen
Supermarkets, Inc.
South Perkins Blvd.
Issaquah WA 98027
206 392-5634

8.	PRESS	**Enter** after typing the phone number

DELETING A RECORD

Since there are two Client 108s at this time, the original one needs to be deleted from the file.

DELETE A RECORD

1.	PRESS	**Ctrl/PgDn** to move to Client 108, Thomas Judd
2.	CHOOSE	**Delete Record** from the **Edit** menu
3.	PRESS	the **Ctrl/PgUp** and **Ctrl/PgDn** keys to verify the change

MOVING TO A RECORD

You can position the highlight on a specific record quickly by using the **List** mode. When the highlight is positioned on a record in **List** mode, and the **F9** key is pressed to switch to **Form** mode, the highlight will be positioned on that particular record.

MOVE TO A RECORD

1. **PRESS**   **F9** to switch to **List** view
2. **PRESS**   **Ctrl/Home** to move to the first record (if necessary)
3. **PRESS**   the **Down Arrow** or click the mouse button on the last record in the file, client No. 114
4. **PRESS**   **F9** to return to **Form** view
5. Record 14, client No. 114, is on the screen.
6. **EDIT**   the name of the company so that the word **The** is removed. Use the **F2** key.
7. **PRESS**   **Enter** when finished

ADDING A LABEL TO A FORM

Labels can be added to a form to give additional information about the form contents. Labels are not part of the fields and do not affect the record contents in any way. They are typed anywhere on the **Form** view page and are entered as regular text and are not followed by a colon (:) as are field names.

ADD A LABEL TO A FORM

1. **POSITION**   the cursor at the top left of the screen in any one of the records in this file
2. **TYPE**   **Clients for Puget Sound Charters, Inc.** at the top of the page
3. **PRESS**   **Enter**

DATABASE

ADDING NOTES TO A FORM

Notes are similar to labels. The difference is basically in the content. **Labels** are used to add headings or titles to a form; **Notes** are used to make comments to yourself or other users about the form or its contents. **Notes** are inserted into a record in the form of a field. This field is a multiline field that can hold up to 256 characters.

INSERTING AN EXTRA FIELD

Inserting an extra field can be done at any time and uses the same method as when inserting fields when the file is initially created.

INSERT AN EXTRA FIELD

1.	POSITION	the cursor at **X1.80"**, **Y3.00"** at the bottom of any record in **Form** view
2.	TYPE	**NOTES:**
3.	PRESS	**Enter**
4.	CHOOSE	**20** as the width (it should be set there)
5.	CHOOSE	**4** as the Height
6.	PRESS	**Enter**

This will create a field that is 20 characters wide and four lines long. The maximum width of a field is 80 characters.

ADDING TEXT TO A NOTE FIELD

When entering text into a **NOTE** field, continuous text automatically wraps to the next line. If it is necessary to end a line and move to the next line, press **Shift/Enter**.

ADD TEXT TO A NOTE FIELD

1.	HIGHLIGHT	**record 9**, client 109, Trisha Smith (use Ctrl/PgUp or Ctrl/PgDn)
2.	HIGHLIGHT	the field to the right of **NOTES:**
3.	TYPE	**Requested additional information on charters**
	Note:	*Let the text wrap to the next line.*
4.	PRESS	**Shift/Enter** to move to the next line within the NOTE block
5.	TYPE	**11/92**
	Note:	*This is the date of the request.*
6.	PRESS	**Enter**
7.	USE	the **Arrow** keys to remove the highlight and move around in the record as needed.
8.	PRESS	**Ctrl/PgUp** and **Ctrl/PgDn** to view the **NOTES:** field on each record
9.	SAVE	the file again

FORMATTING A DATABASE

A database file can be formatted similar to a spreadsheet file or a word processing file. The margins can be adjusted, fields and forms can be protected, and page breaks added to any database file. You can also format numbers and create formulas in database fields. These and other topics are discussed in this and the next chapter.

FORMAT A DATABASE

1. **CHOOSE** **Create New** from the **File** menu and choose **Database**
2. **TYPE** the following fields at the locations shown

Field	Position	Width	Height
INVOICE NO:	X1.70 Y1.33	5	1
INVOICE DATE:	X1.70 Y1.50	8	1
CLIENT ID:	X1.70 Y1.67	5	1
BOAT NAME:	X1.70 Y2.33	20	1
DATE BOOKED:	X5.20 Y2.33	8	1
HOURS:	X5.20 Y2.50	2	1
DEPOSIT:	X1.70 Y2.67	6	1
TAX:	X1.70 Y2.83	6	1
BALANCE:	X1.70 Y3.17	6	1
NOTES:	X1.70 Y3.50	20	4

3. **TYPE** the following heading at position X3.10 Y1.00
      PUGET SOUND CHARTERS

The final format should appear approximately as follows:

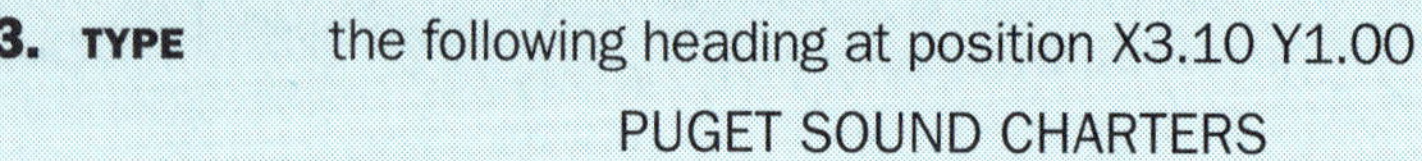

4. **SAVE**   the file as **CH16PR2**

5. **PRESS**   **F9** to switch to **List** view

6. **ADJUST**   the column width so that all field names are visible. Make the **Boat Name** field at least 12 characters wide.

ENTERING A SERIES OF VALUES

If it is known that a series of values will be entered into cells, such as 1 through 10 or 10/01/92 through 10/20/92, then the **Fill Series** command can be used in the **Edit** menu. This eliminates the necessity of typing each value individually. In the case of **Puget Sound Charters** invoices, the invoice numbers and dates can be entered using this command.

ENTER A SERIES OF VALUES

1. **HIGHLIGHT**   the first column in the **INVOICE NO** field in record 1

2. **TYPE**   **501** as the first invoice number

3. **PRESS**   **Enter**

4. **HIGHLIGHT**   rows **1** through **10**

5. **CHOOSE**   **Fill Series** from the **Edit** menu

The dialog box shown in Figure 16-2 appears.

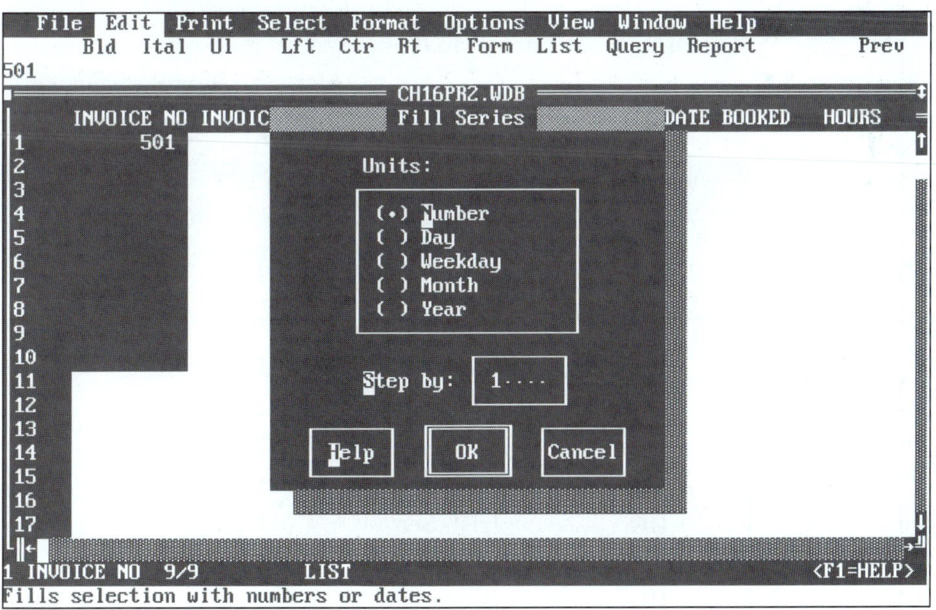

FIGURE 16-2
FILL SERIES DIALOG
BOX

From this dialog box, the type of series is selected and the increments on which to build the series is decided. Since the number 501 decided the format, the **Number** option is selected in the **Units** box. The only decision to make is the **Step by** option which decides the increments.

6. CHOOSE   **OK** or press Enter to accept the 1 in the **Step by** box

The series is filled, increasing by 1 in each row.

To fill a series of dates

FILL A SERIES OF DATES

1. HIGHLIGHT   the **INVOICE DATE** field in record 1

2. TYPE   **1/01/92** and press **Enter**

3. HIGHLIGHT   all **INVOICE DATE** fields in records 1 through 10

4. CHOOSE   **Fill Series** from the **Edit** menu

You now have the options of incrementing by **Day**, **Weekdays** only, **Month**, or **Year** in the date.

5. LEAVE   the setting at **Day** and **Step by** of **1**

6. CHOOSE   **OK** or press Enter

The days in the date format are incremented by 1.

To complete the file

COMPLETE THE FILE

1. COMPLETE   the file using the following data

Client ID	Boat name	Date booked	Hours	Deposit
105	Delano	1/20/92	3	100
113	The Spirit	1/25/92	4	200
102	Sea Wolf	1/15/92	4	500
109	Irish Sea	1/19/92	3	100
104	The Spirit	1/07/92	3	200
106	Delano	1/10/92	4	100
110	Irish Sea	1/27/92	3	200

111	Delano	1/28/92	3	100
114	Irish Sea	1/17/92	4	150
105	The Spirit	1/29/92	4	150

2. SAVE the file again.

CHANGING THE FONT AND SIZE

As with other tools in Works, you can change the character font and point size. The font and point selected change for the entire file as it does when changing the fonts in spreadsheets. To do so, use the **Font** command in the **Format** menu.

CHANGE THE FONT AND SIZE

1. CHOOSE **Font** from the **Format** menu

2. CHOOSE **Prestige 10** point in the dialog boxes or any other font different from the standard Courier

3. CHOOSE **OK** or press Enter

INCLUDING FORMULAS IN A DATABASE

Formulas are written into the cells, which will show the computed value. They are written using the same symbols for computing as those used in the spreadsheet functions (review that part if necessary). Field names are also included in formulas. As with spreadsheet formulas, all begin with the equals sign and can include the operands for division, addition, subtraction, and so on.

To insert a new field

New fields can be inserted at any time. Add them in **Form** view just as when creating the original record format. In this exercise it will be necessary to move some fields so that new ones can be inserted.

From **Form** view (click on the Toolbar),

INSERT A NEW FIELD

1. HIGHLIGHT the **TAX** field name

2. PRESS **F3** or choose **Move** from the **Edit** menu

3. PRESS the **Down Arrow** to move the highlight down one line (just above BALANCE:)

4. PRESS **Enter**

<table>
<tr><td>5.</td><td>PRESS</td><td>the Up Arrow to move the highlight up one line (just above TAX:)</td></tr>
<tr><td>6.</td><td>TYPE</td><td>TOTAL:</td></tr>
<tr><td>7.</td><td>PRESS</td><td>Enter</td></tr>
<tr><td>8.</td><td>TYPE</td><td>8 as the Width</td></tr>
<tr><td>9.</td><td>CHOOSE</td><td>OK or press Enter</td></tr>
</table>

To write the formulas

From **Form** view and the Invoice No. 501 record (press Ctrl/PgUp to reach it if necessary),

WRITE THE FORMULA

<table>
<tr><td>1.</td><td>HIGHLIGHT</td><td>the field to the right of TOTAL:</td></tr>
<tr><td>2.</td><td>TYPE</td><td>=HOURS*500</td></tr>
<tr><td>3.</td><td>PRESS</td><td>Enter</td></tr>
</table>

The cost per hour for the Delano is $500, which includes all catering and overhead.

<table>
<tr><td>4.</td><td>HIGHLIGHT</td><td>the field to the right of TAX:</td></tr>
<tr><td>5.</td><td>TYPE</td><td>=TOTAL*.08 and press Enter</td></tr>
<tr><td>6.</td><td>HIGHLIGHT</td><td>the field to the right of BALANCE:</td></tr>
<tr><td>7.</td><td>TYPE</td><td>=TOTAL+TAX-DEPOSIT and press Enter</td></tr>
</table>

DATABASE

To view all computed values

When the formulas are entered into a field for one record, they are automatically entered into the corresponding fields for all records in the file unless other data is entered in those fields. As with all formulas, they are then automatically computed.

VIEW ALL COMPUTED VALUES

<table>
<tr><td>1.</td><td>PRESS</td><td>F9 to switch to List view</td></tr>
<tr><td>2.</td><td>PRESS</td><td>Ctrl/Home and then the Right Arrow key to view all computed values in the TAX, BALANCE, AND TOTAL fields</td></tr>
</table>

FORMATTING DATA VALUES

Now that the formulas are entered and all records have computed data values, you can format them as currency values. When one value format is changed, all values in the same field are also changed.

In **List** view,

FORMAT DATA VALUES

1. **HIGHLIGHT** the **DEPOSIT** field in the first record
2. **CHOOSE** **Currency** from the **Format** menu
3. **ACCEPT** the decimal setting of **2** by pressing **Enter**

All values in the DEPOSIT field are changed.

4. **CHANGE** the values to **Currency** format for the TAX, BALANCE and TOTAL fields. Leave the decimal setting at **2** for each one.

   Note: *You can highlight two or more adjacent cells, such as TAX and BALANCE at the same time to change the format in a single command for both fields.*

5. **SAVE** the file again when finished

ADJUSTING FIELD WIDTH IN *FORM* VIEW

ADJUST FIELD WIDTH IN FORM VIEW

1. **PRESS** F9 to switch to **Form** view or click **Form** on the Toolbar

Notice that the fields in the form show a series of number signs (#########). You may recall from spreadsheets that the number signs indicate that the values in the field (cell) are too wide to fit into the width of the field. The width, therefore, needs to be changed. This is accomplished using the **Field Size** command in the **Format** menu.

2. **SELECT** the field opposite the label **DEPOSIT:**
3. **CHOOSE** **Field Size** from the **Format** menu
4. **TYPE** **8** and press **Enter**
5. **SELECT** the following fields and adjust the size as shown

Field	Size
TOTAL:	12
TAX:	8
BALANCE:	12

6. PRESS   **Ctrl/PgDn** to note the change in all records

7. RETURN   to record 1, invoice number 501 (Ctrl/Home)

8. SAVE   the file

9. QUIT   or **CONTINUE** to the tutorial

DATABASE

WHAT YOU'LL DO

- Create a database file.
- Adjust column width.
- Edit records.
- Format data.

HOW TO DO IT

1. **CHOOSE**   **Create New File** from the **File** menu or choose **Create a New File** from the "quick start" box.

2. **TYPE**   the following field names following by a colon in approximately the position shown in the box. You should decide on a good layout for each field.

> ID Number:
> Last Name: First Name:
> Membership Date:
> Dues Owing:

The field widths are:

ID Number:	9
Last Name:	12
First Name:	12
Membership Date:	6
Dues Owing:	4

The field height should remain at 1.

3. **SAVE**   the form as **CH16TUT**.

4. **WHILE**   still in **Form** view, enter the following records.

359345678	Randle, Colleen	1/2/92	3.25
329542198	Jones, Randall	1/3/92	2.95
295754444	Wilson, Richard	1/4/92	3.80
329951897	Costner, Jeremy	1/5/92	2.00

297882917	Mitchell, Sandra	1/4/92	4.00
278374758	Madsen, Olivia	1/3/92	3.00
278577611	Petrella, Harold	1/5/92	3.95
278574199	Ferrier, Karen	1/4/92	3.50
327899511	Jackson, Martha	1/3/92	3.60
547178594	McReynolds, Sally	1/2/92	3.70

5. PRESS **F9** to switch to **List** view and Ctrl/Home to move to the start of the file.

6. CHOOSE **Field Width** from the **Format** menu to change the width of the fields. All data and field names should be visible in the fields.

7. PRESS **Ctrl/End** to go to the last field in the last record.

8. HIGHLIGHT the date and dues fields of the last record, **McReynold's**.

9. CHOOSE **Copy** from the **Edit** menu or press Shift/F3.

10. POSITION the highlight in the date field below the last record.

11. PRESS **Enter** to copy the contents.

12. FILL in the remainder of this new record with the following information (stay in **List** view):

457882298	Newman, Julie

13. HIGHLIGHT all of the last record.

14. CHOOSE **Move** from the **Edit** menu or press **F3**.

15. HIGHLIGHT the first field in the row below this one.

16. PRESS **Enter.**

The last four rows of the file now appear similar to the following (shown through the Dues Owing field). Do not be concerned if your records are in a slightly different order.

DATABASE

9	327899511	Jackson	Martha	1/3/92	3.6
10	547178594	McReynolds	Sally	1/2/92	3.7
11					
12	457882298	Newman	Julie	1/2/92	3.7

17. MOVE the row back to its original location.

18. HIGHLIGHT the first and last names in the last row.

19. EXTEND the highlight to the next three rows (11 through 14).

20. CHOOSE **Fill Down** from the **Edit** menu.

21. HIGHLIGHT the data just filled in the last three rows (rows 12, 13, and 14).

22. CHOOSE **Delete Record/Field** from the **Edit** menu.

23. CHOOSE **Record** (if necessary) and **OK** or press Enter.

24. PROOF and save the file again.

25. PRESS **F9** to switch to **Form** view.

26. PRESS **Ctrl/PgUp** and **Ctrl/PgDn** to view the records.

27. MOVE to record **6** (watch the lower left corner of the status line).

28. CHOOSE **Insert Record** from the **Edit** menu.

29. ADD the following record:

238844768	Thiry, Jacques	1/5/92	4.50

30. SWITCH to **List** view.

31. FORMAT the **Dues Owing** field as currency.

32. HIGHLIGHT any record in the first field, ID Number.

33. CHOOSE **Insert Record/Field** from the **Edit** menu.

34. CHOOSE **Field** and **OK** or press Enter.

A new field is inserted in the database file.

35. PRESS **Ctrl/Home** to go to the first field of the first record.

36. TYPE **1** in the first record of this new field and press **Enter**.

37. SELECT the first field from record 1 through record 12.

38. CHOOSE **Fill Series** from the **Edit** menu and press **Enter** at the settings.

The first six fields of the file now appear as follows.

Field1	ID Number	Last Name	First Name	Membership	Dues Owing
1	359345678	Randle	Colleen	1/2/92	$3.25
2	329542198	Jones	Randall	1/3/92	$2.95
3	295754444	Wilson	Richard	1/4/92	$3.80
4	329951897	Costner	Jeremy	1/5/92	$2.00
5	297882917	Mitchell	Sandra	1/4/92	$4.00
6	238844768	Thiry	Jacques	1/5/92	$4.50
7	278374758	Madsen	Olivia	1/3/92	$3.00
8	278577611	Petrella	Harold	1/5/92	$3.95
9	278574199	Ferrier	Karen	1/4/92	$3.50
10	327899511	Jackson	Martha	1/3/92	$3.60
11	547178594	McReynolds	Sally	1/2/92	$3.70
12	457882298	Newman	Julie	1/2/92	$3.70

39.	SWITCH	to **Form** view.
40.	PRESS	**Ctrl/Home** to move to the first record (if necessary).
41.	HIGHLIGHT	the field name, **Field1**.
42.	TYPE	**MEMBER:** and press **Enter** to change the field name.
43.	HIGHLIGHT	the **Dues Owing** field.
44.	CHOOSE	**Yield Size** from the **format** menu.
45.	TYPE	**7** as the width and press **Enter** or choose **OK**.
46.	SAVE	this file again.

DATABASE

REVIEW QUESTIONS

1. _______ A field is made up of two or more records.

2. _______ A database may contain many records.

3. _______ Field names must always be followed by a colon (:) when creating fields in Form view.

4. List at least two features found on the status line of a database window.

5. The _________________ command from the _______________ menu is used to adjust the width of a field.

6. List two or more ways to move to and from List and Form views.

7. Match each of the following to the correct keystroke(s).

    _______ used to copy field contents
    _______ used to move field contents
    _______ used to repeat a copy command
    _______ used to move to the first field of the first record

   a. F3
   b. Shift/F3
   c. Shift/F7
   d. Ctrl/Home

8. List the keystrokes used to move to the previous and following records in Form view.

9. Briefly list the steps used to increment numbers or dates automatically when filling in fields.

10. Write a formula that will compute the tax on total pay and subtract that value from the total pay for a net value.

EXERCISE 1

Puget Sound Charters recently completed a survey to find out how customers heard about their services. This information will prove useful for developing future marketing strategies.

1. Create a database file for the following survey responses or retrieve **CH16HO1** from the instructor's data disk. The coding used is displayed at the top of the list. Fields should be included for the Survey number, the response, and the date of the response.

Customers heard about Puget Sound Charters through one of the following media:

N = Newspaper   **M** = Magazine   **C** = Current or previous client
P = Phone book   **O** = Other publication   **W** = Word of mouth   **T** = Other

2. Create in Form view

Survey Number	Response	Date
101	M	8/8/92
105	O	8/8/92
109	P	8/10/92
116	N	8/10/92
128	W	8/10/92
103	T	8/10/92
107	C	8/11/92
133	C	8/11/92
122	W	8/11/92
126	T	8/12/92
138	P	8/15/92
126	C	8/15/92
104	W	8/15/92
108	P	8/16/92
126	P	8/16/92
131	P	8/16/92
135	S	8/16/92
148	W	8/16/92
129	O	8/16/92
123	P	8/17/92
146	P	8/17/92
149	C	8/17/92
142	S	8/17/92

141	C	8/17/92
139	P	8/17/92
143	P	8/17/92
147	S	8/17/92
152	T	8/18/92
106	N	8/18/92
110	O	8/18/92

2. Save the file as **CH16HO1**.

3. Adjust the width of the fields in List view as necessary.

4. Format the date field so that it is in Long format showing the month, date, and year. (Use the **Time/Date** command from the **Format** menu.) What do the #####'s mean? What should you do?

5. Locate survey number 122 and change the response to T.

6. Insert a new field to the left of the survey number. Name the field **Response No**.

7. Fill in the new field with numbers, starting with the number 1. Be sure to use menu commands to fill in the numbers automatically.

8. Proof the records carefully and save the file again. Print a copy from List view.

EXERCISE 2

1. Create a database file to store the following payroll data.

Name	Rate	Hours	Total	Tax	Net
Kendall	15.50	45			
Wilson	15.00	42			
Randle	18.75	51			
Shepard	12.35	40			
Thiry	15.50	44			

2. Enter the data and save the file as **CH16HO2**.

3. Compute the total by multiplying the rate times the hours.

4. Compute the tax by multiplying the total times 20.2 percent.

5. Compute the net by subtracting the tax from the total.

6. Format all dollar values as currency.

7. Adjust the column width as appropriate.

8. Proof the file and save it as **CH16HO2**.

9. Print a copy from List view.

Objectives

- Sort records.

- Query a database.

- Query for more than one condition.

- Perform a search.

PREVIEW ▶▶▶

A database file can be sorted on any single field or on multiple fields in either ascending or descending order. When the client IDs are entered in a file for example, they may be out of order. If you wanted to see a list of all clients IDs in sequence so that you can identify the clients who made more than one booking, you could sort on the CLIENT ID field. The **Sort** command was also applied on spreadsheets, so you will recognize the **Sort Records** dialog box. You could also query the database field for all customers who made more than one booking and list specific fields on each one. Querying a database file means to search the file for specific characteristics. This is one of the most useful functions of any database management system since it gives valuable information to the user about what is occurring in the business.

SORTING RECORDS

As with the spreadsheet sort, you can sort on multiple fields at once or on a single field. When sorting on multiple fields, a sort is done within a sort. For example, you could sort on STATE, then CITY, then NAME in a file. All states would be sorted first, then the cities within each state, and finally the name within each city. Each field can be sorted in either ascending or descending order.

SORTING ON ONE FIELD

When sorting on one field, it is not necessary to select the field first. The name of the field is typed in the **Sort Record** dialog box. The choice of ascending or descending order is made for each field to be sorted, and the options are complete.

SORT ON ONE FIELD

1. **SIGN**   onto Works, if necessary

2. **OPEN**   the database file **CH16PR2** which you created in Chapter 16; or retrieve it from the instructor's data disk

3. **SWITCH**   to **List** view (F9), if necessary

It would be useful to see various fields in this file sorted. For example, it would be helpful to see on which dates the bookings are scheduled and which boats are scheduled. Although that information can be gathered by scanning the records, it would be much easier to see the fields grouped on **Date Booked** or on **Boat Name** or both.

4. **CHOOSE**   Sort Records from the **Select** menu

5. **TYPE**   DATE BOOKED in the **1st Field:** box (in upper- or lowercase lettering)

6. **LEAVE**   the setting at **Ascend**

7. **CHOOSE**   **OK** or press Enter

The **Date Booked** field is now sorted in ascending order. This information is useful in identifying the days that boats are booked.

SORTING ON MULTIPLE FIELDS

More useful information about the bookings of boats might be to sort on the boat name first and then on the date the boat is booked.

SORT ON MULTIPLE FIELDS

1. **CHOOSE**   **Sort Records** from the **Select** menu

2. **TYPE**   **BOAT NAME** in the **1st Field** box

3. **CHOOSE**   **Descend** for the **1st Field**

4. **TYPE**   **DATE BOOKED** in the **2nd Field** box

5. **CHOOSE**   **Ascend**

6. **CHOOSE**   **OK** or press Enter

The boat names are now shown in descending order and the date booked is shown in ascending order for each boat. Look at the three bookings for the Irish Sea, for example. Within the first sort, which produced a list showing all Irish Sea bookings together, is a list of the dates in ascending order — 1/17/92, 1/19/92, and then 1/27/92.

7. **PRINT**   a copy of this file using the **Print** command from the **Print** menu.

Note: *The **Print** commands are used the same as they were in word processing and spreadsheets, except that you have the additional option of printing the field and record labels.*

QUERYING A DATABASE

To query a database means to locate specific records for display. Locating the records is done through the use of the **Query** command in the **View** menu, the **Query** option on the **Toolbar,** or the **Search** command in the **Select** menu. Any of these two options allows you to look for records containing specific conditions. In this way, unnecessary information does not need to be displayed either on the screen or in a customized report (discussed in Chapter 18).

As an example, in the **CH16PR1** database file, which contains a list of client information, you could locate all clients who live in a specific city, or all of those who prefer to book a particular boat could be located by performing a query on the **CH16PR2** database file containing information on recent invoices.

STARTING A QUERY

In this first query exercise you will practice creating and implementing a query using **List** and **Form** views. Whichever view is used to start the query is the one to which you will return when the query is complete.

START A QUERY

1. OPEN   **CH16PR1** and keep **CH16PR2** open as well. You can retrieve **CH16PR1** from the instructor's data disk.

With **CH16PR1** active,

2. CHOOSE   **List** view from the **View** menu, click List on the Toolbar, or press F9, if necessary, to switch to List view

3. CHOOSE   **Query** from the **View** menu

A blank form like the one that would appear in **Form** view appears on the screen. It shows all of the fields in this file, but now they are empty. This is the form used to request information from a file.

USING COMPARISON FORMULAS

You can now enter the conditions that you would like to be met. One way to enter the conditions is through comparison formulas. Comparison formulas allow Works to locate records that match specific conditions. For example, you could locate all persons living in Seattle by using a formula written as

= "Seattle" in the **City** field.

Other comparison formulas and examples are given in Table 17-1.

<table>
<tr><td><u>USE THIS OPERATOR</u></td><td><u>TO LOCATE THESE RECORDS</u></td></tr>
<tr><td>Equal to (=)
Example: ="Seattle"</td><td>Those living in Seattle</td></tr>
<tr><td>Not equal to (<>)
Example: <> "Seattle"</td><td>Those not living in Seattle</td></tr>
<tr><td>Less than (<)
Example: < 12000</td><td>Amounts less than a specified amount</td></tr>
<tr><td>Greater than (>)
Example: > '10/11/91'</td><td>Amounts greater than a specified amount</td></tr>
<tr><td>Greater than or equal to (>=)

Example: >='10/11/91'</td><td>Amounts greater than or equal to a specified amount</td></tr>
<tr><td>Less than or equal to (<=)
Example: <=12000</td><td>Amounts less than or equal to a specified amount</td></tr>
</table>

Note: *All alphanumeric data values for which you are searching are enclosed in double quotes ("klklk"); all numeric values are not enclosed; dates are enclosed in single quotes (' ').*

TABLE 17-1 COMPARISON OPERATORS USED IN QUERY FORMS

ENTERING CONDITIONS IN A QUERY FORM

Suppose that you wanted to locate all persons living in Seattle using the current query form. Using the current form, you can locate one or more conditions.

ENTER CONDITIONS IN A QUERY FORM

1.	TYPE	="**Seattle**" in the **City** field (with quotation marks) and press **Enter**
2.	PRESS	**F10** or choose **List** from the **View** menu

A list of all records where the city is equal to Seattle are displayed on the screen. The quotation marks (" ") are used to identify alphanumeric text.

VIEWING ALL RECORDS AGAIN

With only a partial list on the screen (the query results), you can view all records again using the **Show All Records** command in the **Select** menu.

VIEW ALL RECORDS AGAIN

1.	CHOOSE	**Show All Records** from the **Select** menu

349

USING EXISTING QUERIES

When a query is defined in the query form, it can be reused quickly using the **Apply Query** command in the **Select** menu. With this command, the most recently created query condition can be reapplied. This would be useful when working with a long file into which you are adding records and rechecking the conditions of the query as you do so. You can create the query, add records or modify them, then use the query again to note the changes.

Create a second query,

USE EXISTING QUERY

1. **CHOOSE**   **Query** from the **View** menu or click Query on the Toolbar
2. **REMOVE**   the **Seattle** formula (highlight and press the Backspace or Delete key or use Clear from the Edit menu)
3. **TYPE**   **>105** in the **Client ID** field and press **Enter**
   Note: *No quotation marks are used with numeric values.*
4. **PRESS**   **F10** or choose **List** from the **View** menu

All records greater than Client ID 105 are displayed.

5. **CHOOSE**   **Show All Records** from the **Select** menu

All records are displayed again.

To apply the current query
With all records displayed on the screen,

DATABASE

APPLY THE CURRENT QUERY

1. **CHOOSE**   **Apply Query** from the **Select** menu

The conditions of the last query (all records above 105) are met again.

2. **CHOOSE**   **Show All Records** from the **Select** menu

MAKING CHANGES TO A QUERY FORM

When you are ready to create a new query or to make changes to the current one, you can delete the field contents one at a time by selecting them and then pressing the **Delete** key. You can also delete all query field contents and write a new query using the **Delete Query** command in the **Edit** menu (while in query mode).

MAKE CHANGES TO A QUERY FORM

1. CHOOSE   Query from the **View** menu or click Query on the Toolbar

The query form with the entries for the most recent queries (only the client ID entry at this time) is displayed.

2. CHOOSE   **Delete Query** from the **Edit** menu

You are now ready to enter new query conditions.

QUERYING FOR MORE THAN ONE CONDITION

You can search for more than one condition in a field using logical operators. The logical operators are shown in Table 17-2.

	AND	searching for one condition and a second one
Example:		>15000#AND#<200000
	OR	searching for one condition or another
Example:		=="Seattle"#OR#="Tukwila"
	NOT	searching for conditions not of a specific group
Example:		=#NOT#(="Seattle")#OR#<>"Seattle"

TABLE 17-2
LOGICAL OPERATORS

To query for two conditions

QUERY FOR TWO CONDITIONS

1. CHOOSE   CH16PR2 from the **Window** menu
2. OPEN   a query form (**Query** from the Toolbar or **Query** from the **View** menu).
3. TYPE   >1500#AND#<2000 in the **Balance** field and press **Enter**
4. PRESS   F10

The names of the five boats whose balance fell within the specified category appear.

To query for conditions on more than one field

You can apply conditions in as many fields as you wish. For example, suppose that you wanted to know the boats within the **Balance** category and booked on either 1/15 or 1/20/92.

QUERY FOR CONDITIONS ON MORE THAN ONE FIELD

1. **SWITCH** to Query view.

2. **TYPE** ==‘1/15/92’#OR#=‘1/20/92’ in the **Date Booked** field and press **Enter**.

   Note: *Dates are enclosed in single quotation marks. The OR operator begins with its own equal mark, separate from any equal mark in the condition and is entered using the OR symbol (#OR#).*

3. **PRESS** F10

The Sea Wolf and the Delano fell on one of the two dates and within the **Balance** category specified.

4. **CHOOSE** **Show All Records** from the **Select** menu

SEARCHING THROUGH A FILE

You can locate specific records using the **Query** command as discussed in the previous exercises. You can also search through a database file to locate specific records. There are many advantages to locating records of specific groups. For one thing, you do not need to scroll through a long file looking for records that meet certain criteria. For another, once the records are singled out, they can be used to create reports or to perform a mail merge operation (discussed in Chapter 18).

Searching through a database file using **List** view is extremely useful. It allows for searching through the entire database or only for specific fields. When searching in **Form** view, Works will display the result of the search one record at a time. For this reason it is probably most useful to search in **List** view.

PERFORMING A SEARCH

With the **CH16PR2** file active and in **List** view and the highlight in the first record,

PERFORM A SEARCH

1. **CHOOSE** **Search** from the **Select** menu

The dialog box shown in Figure 17-1 appears.

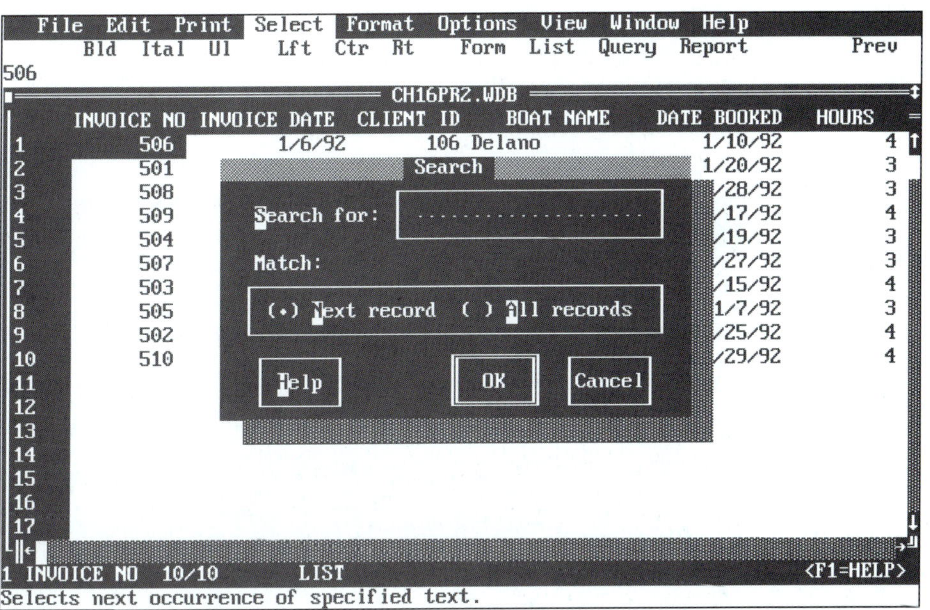

FIGURE 17-1
SEARCH DIALOG BOX

When the **Next record** option is selected, all records are displayed. The highlight
will be displayed on the first occurrence of the text for which you are searching.
When the **All records** option is chosen, only the records containing the search
condition will be displayed on the screen.

2. TYPE	**Delano** in the **Search for** text box
3. LEAVE	the **Next record** option selected
4. CHOOSE	**OK** or press Enter

The highlight is on the first occurrence of Delano in a record and all records
are displayed on the screen.

5. CHOOSE	**Search** from the **Select** menu
6. CHOOSE	**All records** from the **Match** options
7. CHOOSE	**OK** or press Enter

Only the records for the boat Delano are displayed on the screen.

8. CHOOSE	**Show All Records** from the **Select** menu

REPEATING A SEARCH

Sort the records
First, sort this file on the **Date Booked**.

START A SEARCH

1. **CHOOSE**   **Sort Records** from the **Select** menu
2. **TYPE**   **Date Booked** in the **First Field** box
3. **CHOOSE**   **Ascend**
4. **REMOVE**   the **2nd Field** contents.
5. **PRESS**   **Enter** or choose OK

The **Date Booked** data is now shown in ascending order.

Start a search

REPEAT A SEARCH

1. **CHOOSE**   **Search** from the **Select** menu
2. **TYPE**   **Delano** in the **Search for** box (it should be there)
3. **LEAVE**   the **Next record** match setting.
4. **PRESS**   **Enter** or choose OK

The first occurrence of a Delano booking is selected.

5. **PRESS**   **F7** to repeat the search
6. **PRESS**   **F7** again

Although all records are visible and the Delano records are easy to locate at this time, the advantage of using the **Repeat search** function is evident when the files are extremely large. By pressing the **F7** key, each record matching the search condition(s) is located one after the other. When the **F7** key reaches the last occurrence, it returns to the beginning of the file and locates the first occurrence in the file again.

WILDCARD SEARCHES

You can also search using wildcards. They are used as a substitution for unknown values in data variables. For example, suppose that you did not know the spelling of Woodinville, Washington. If the file were very large, Woodinville might be located anywhere. One approach would be to sort on the city, but suppose that you simply wanted to locate each occurrence.

To use a question mark (?)
With the **CH16PR1** file active and in **List** view,

<table>
<tr><td colspan="3">USE A QUESTION MARK (?)</td></tr>
<tr><td>1.</td><td>CHOOSE</td><td>Search from the Select menu</td></tr>
<tr><td>2.</td><td>TYPE</td><td>Wood? in the Search for box</td></tr>
<tr><td colspan="3">The question mark substitutes for the rest of the unknown spelling.</td></tr>
<tr><td>3.</td><td>LEAVE</td><td>the other settings in the box.</td></tr>
<tr><td>4.</td><td>PRESS</td><td>Enter or choose OK</td></tr>
<tr><td colspan="3">The first occurrence of Woodinville is located.</td></tr>
<tr><td>5.</td><td>PRESS</td><td>F7 to locate other occurrences</td></tr>
</table>

To use an asterisk (*)
You could also use the asterisk (*) to substitute for unknown characters in words. It stands for any number of characters in the same location in a word. For example, if you did not know the spelling of a client named Schuster, you could substitute the asterisk for unknown characters and all Schusters would be located.

<table>
<tr><td colspan="3">USE AN ASTERISK (*)</td></tr>
<tr><td>1.</td><td>CHOOSE</td><td>Search from the Select menu</td></tr>
<tr><td>2.</td><td>TYPE</td><td>S*ster in the Search for box</td></tr>
<tr><td>3.</td><td>CHOOSE</td><td>All records</td></tr>
<tr><td>4.</td><td>PRESS</td><td>Enter or choose OK</td></tr>
<tr><td colspan="3">Client 104 is located. If other names had been located that began with an S and ended with ster, they too, would have appeared.</td></tr>
<tr><td>5.</td><td>CHOOSE</td><td>Show All Records from the Select menu</td></tr>
<tr><td>6.</td><td>QUIT</td><td>or continue to the tutorial</td></tr>
</table>

GUIIDED TUTORIAL

WHAT YOU'LL DO

- Sort records.
- Practice query commands.
- Perform wildcard searches.

HOW TO DO IT

1. OPEN the database file **CH16TUT** which you created in Chapter 16; or retrieve it from the instructor's data disk.

2. SWITCH to **List** view if necessary.

3. HIGHLIGHT any record in the **Membership Date** field.

4. CHOOSE **Sort Records** from the **Select** menu.

5. TYPE **Membership Date** in the **1st Field** box.

6. CHOOSE **Ascend** if necessary.

7. CHOOSE **OK** or press Enter.

8. PRINT a copy of this database file by choosing **Print** from the **Print** menu as you would when printing any other Works documents.

9. CHOOSE **Sort Records** from the **Select** menu.

10. TYPE **Dues Owing** in the **2nd Field** box and choose **Descend**.

11. CHOOSE **OK** or press Enter.

The Membership and Dues Owing fields now appear similar to the following. The fields show a primary and secondary sort; first on Membership and within each group of "like" dates, the dues owing values are shown in descending order.

Membership	Dues Owing
1/2/92	$3.70
1/2/92	$3.70
1/2/92	$3.25
1/3/92	$3.60
1/3/92	$3.00
1/3/92	$2.95
1/4/92	$4.00
1/4/92	$3.80
1/4/92	$3.50
1/5/92	$4.50
1/5/92	$3.95
1/5/92	$3.00

DATABASE

12. What values appear in the **Dues Owing** field on all dates for **1/4/92**? Make a note of the answer

13. PRESS   **F9** to switch to **Form** view.

14. MOVE   to the **Dues Owing** field.

15. CHOOSE   **Field Size** from the **Format** menu.

16. TYPE   **8** as the new field size and choose **OK** or press Enter.

17. CLICK   once on **Query** from the **Toolbar** or choose **Query** from the **View** menu.

18. TYPE   **=='1/2/92'#OR#='1/4/92'** in the **Membership Date** field and press **Enter**.

The results show all dates that are either 1/2/92 or 1/4/92.

19. PRESS   **F10** to see the results of this query in List view.

20. PRINT   a copy of the results using the **Print** command from the **Print** menu.

21. CHOOSE   **Show All Records** from the **Select** menu.

22. SWITCH   to **Query** view again.

23. REMOVE   the old field contents in the data field.

24. TYPE   **>3.50** in the **Dues Owing** field and press **Enter**.

25. PRESS   **F10** to see the query results and print a copy.

The results show all values greater than 3.50.

26. CHOOSE   **Show All Records** from the **Select** menu.

27. CHOOSE   **Search** from the **Select** menu.

28. TYPE   **Ferrier** in the **Search** for box.

29. CHOOSE   the **All records** option to show only the Ferrier record(s).

30. CHOOSE   **OK** or press Enter.

The Ferrier record appears.

31. WHAT   amount does Ferrier owe?

32. CHOOSE   **Show All Records** from the **Select** menu again.

33. CHOOSE   **Search** from the **Select** menu.

34. TYPE   **M*R*nolds** in the **Search** for box (you are unsure of the spelling of a client named **McReynolds** or **MacReynolds**).

35. CHOOSE   **All records** and then **OK** or press Enter.

After viewing the record,

36. CHOOSE   **Show All Records** from the **Select** menu.

37. SAVE   the file again under the new name **CH17TUT**.

REVIEW QUESTIONS

1. Describe briefly the difference between querying and sorting a database file.

2. The _________________ menu is used to change the order of records.

3. The ______________ command from the ____________ menu is used to sort.

4. Which of the following is true about sorting on multiple fields?
   a. The order of both fields is changed equally.
   b. The order of only the first field changes.
   c. The order of the first field changes and then the second.
   d. The order of the second field changes and then the first.

5. What two options are available that determine the order of data when sorting a field?

6. Which of the following is true about the **Next** record option found in the **Search** dialog box?
   a. The results show only those records meeting the search conditions.
   b. The results show all records with the record(s) meeting the condition highlighted.
   c. The results show all records with the record(s) meeting the condition shown at the top of the file.
   d. The results show all records with the first record meeting the condition highlighted.

7. Which of the following is true about the **All records** option in the **Search** dialog box?
   a. The results show only those records meeting the search conditions.
   b. The results show all records with the record(s) meeting the condition highlighted.
   c. The results show all records with the record(s) meeting the condition shown at the top of the file.
   d. None of the above.

8. Which of the following shows the correct format?
   a. <"10/11/92"
   b. =<'10/11/92'
   c. '<10/11/92'
   d. =<"10/11/92"

9. Which of the following shows the correct format for meeting more than one condition?

    a. >15000AND<20000
    b. >15000#AND#20000
    c. >15000#AND#<20000
    d. >'15000'#AND#<'20000'

10. Which of the following shows the correct format for meeting one condition or the other?

    a. =="Seattle"#OR#="Everett"
    b. ="Seattle"#OR#="Everett"
    c. =='Seattle'#OR#='Everett'
    d. ='Seattle'OR'Everett'

11. _______ All values and text must appear in either single or double quotation marks within a query formula.

12. _______ Operators include AND, OR, and NOT.

13. _______ Logical operators are always surrounded by number signs (#).

14. _______ Only one condition at a time may be entered into a query form.

15. _______ A search always produces results that show only the records meeting the condition.

16. _______ The **Search for** box must contain the exact data for which you are searching.

DATABASE

17. List at least three query examples.

18. List at least three search examples.

19. List at least three multiple condition query examples.

20. What is the greatest advantage of a database system?

HANDS-ON EXERCISES

EXERCISE 1

1. Open the database file **CH16HO1** which you createdin Chapter 16.

2. Sort the file on the **Response** field in ascending order and print a copy.

3. Perform a query for each of the following. Print a copy of each of the results.
   a. All M responses
   b. All responses received on August 15 or 16
   c. All T or W responses
   d. All W responses received on August 10 or 11
   e. All C or N responses

   Remember that the date is treated as a date field even though it is in long format and contains text.

4. Sort the file by **Date** and print a copy.

5. Sort the file by **Survey Number** in ascending order and print a copy.

6. Save the file as **CH17HO1.**

EXERCISE 2

1. Create the following database file showing registration and licensing information on each of the vessels in Puget Sound Charters' ownership.

Boat Name	Reg. No.	Captain	Persons	License	Length	Tonnage	Beam	Speed
Delano	WN6655L	Randle	200	ILC	74	28	22	7.
The Spirit	WN6291L	Kennedy	225	LOC	130	74	34	14
Sea Wolf	WN3251J	Eiler	49	IC	62	29	24	11.5
Irish Sea	WN7210S	Brodie	150	LIC	90	60	28	12.0

2. Save the file as **CH17HO2**.

3. Include the following list as plain text. It explains the **License** information for each of the vessels. This information is defined as follows and should be added in Form view.

   I   Inland waters
   O   Ocean going
   C   Catering facilities
   L   Liquor license

   (Press **Shift/Enter** to move to a new line within the field.)

4. Sort the file by boat and print a copy.

5. Query for all boats licensed for inland waters (perform a wildcard search). Print a copy of the results.

6. Query for all boats that can carry more than 200 passengers. Print a copy of the results.

7. Query for all boats that can carry more than 200 passengers and that are licensed for ocean waters. What boat(s) are these? Write the query formula below.

8. **Locate** the names of all boats that can carry more than 200 passengers OR have a length greater than 90 feet. Write the formula you used. Print a copy of the results.

9. Save the file again.

DATABASE

18 REPORTS

Objectives

- Create a report.

- Customize reports.

- Switch from Report to List or Form view.

- Create report headings.

- Perform sorts.

- Insert field contents.

- Use formulas in reports.

- Name reports.

- Format reports.

PREVIEW »»➡

Reports give you a different way in which to present data. So far, you have printed copies of files as they appear in **List** view. You can also organize data so that it prints in report format. This format can group categories together, provide subtotals and totals to numeric fields, include main headings, and so on, into a presentable, businesslike format that is easier to read and more attractive to the eye.

Initially, Works creates a report for you. If you decide, for example, that you want to create a report using the **CH16PR2** database file, you can choose the **New Report** command in the **View** menu, and Works will display a dialog box that allows you to decide on the appropriate layout for the data and will give options for adding headings, and so on.

CREATING A REPORT

In this first exercise you will create reports using both the **CH16PR1** file and the **CH16PR2** file.

CREATE A REPORT

1. **LOAD**   Works and set the correct directory path (if necessary)

2. **OPEN**   both **CH16PR1** and **CH16PR2** database files

From the **CH16PR1** file,

3. **CHOOSE**   **New Report** from the **View** menu

A screen similar to the one shown in Figure 18-1 appears.

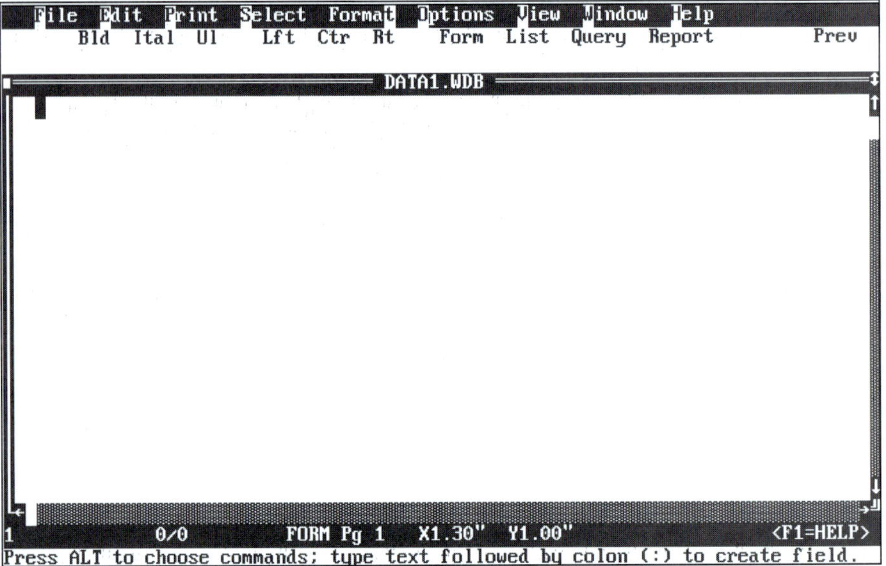

FIGURE 18-1
NEW REPORT
DIALOG BOX

This dialog box contains options for the basic layout of a report. Reports may contain any number of fields from the active database file and the fields may appear in any order on the report. Using the dialog box shown in Figure 18-1, fields are selected from the **Fields in database** list box and added to the report form using the **Add** button. As the fields are inserted into the report, they appear in the **Fields in report** box. A report title may also be included from this dialog box using the box at the top of the window.

CREATE A REPORT

1. **TYPE**   **CLIENT LIST REPORT** in the **Report title** box

2. **CLICK**   the mouse button once in the **Fields in database** list box or press Alt/S

3. **CHOOSE**   **Client ID** from the list

4. **CLICK**   **Add** or press Alt/A to add the field to the list

    Note: Do not press enter until all fields are added.

5. **ADD**   the following fields in the order shown

    LNAME

    FNAME

    COMPANY

    PHONE

6. **CHOOSE**   **OK** or press Enter when finished

The dialog box shown in Figure 18-2 appears.

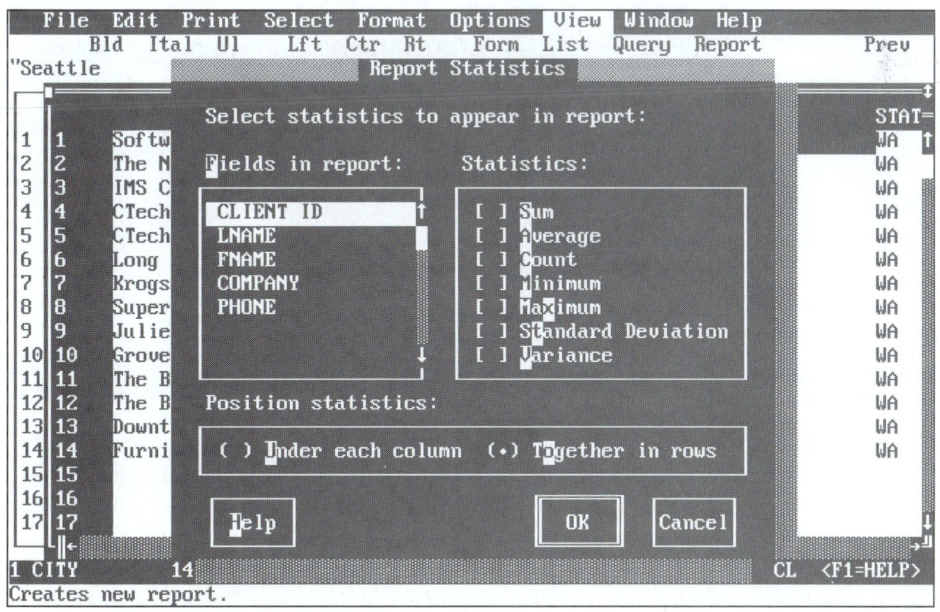

FIGURE 18-2 REPORT STATISTICS DIALOG BOX

This dialog box contains options to insert additional information into the report. Fields that contain numeric data, for example, may have a statistical function performed on them automatically by making a selection in the **Statistics** box. The statistics position will appear either under the column or together in a single row by making the appropriate selection in the **Position Statistics** option box. For example, if you wanted to know how many clients you have in this invoice file, you could count each of the records and have the result appear at the bottom of the report.

CREATE A REPORT

1.   CHOOSE   **Count** from the **Statistics** options

2.   CHOOSE   **OK** or press Enter

The report appears on the screen.

3.   PRESS   **Enter** again

The count for the total records in the file appears at the end of the report.

4.   CONTINUE   to press **Enter** until you reach the screen shown in Figure 18-3

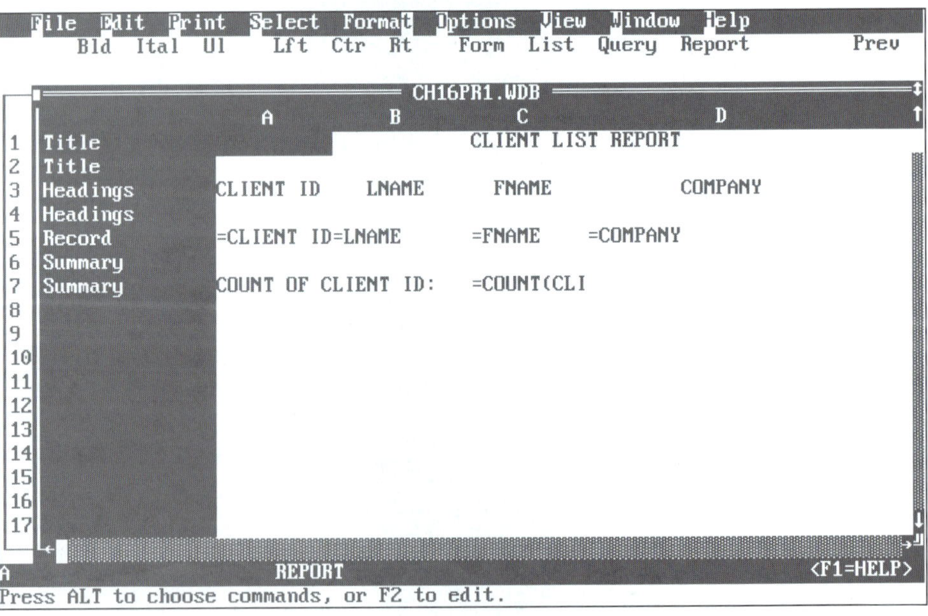

FIGURE 18-3
REPORT DEFINITION
SCREEN

This page is the **Report Definition** screen. It identifies the sections of the standard report format. Within each of the sections, additional rows could be added to increase the rows available for page and column headings or for report summaries, and so on. They are defined as outlined in Table 18-1.

THIS ROW	IS USED FOR
Title	Titles such as main and subheadings can be added on these two lines. If desired, the number of lines could be increased. The main report heading entered in the New Report dialog box appears here.
Headings	The database file field names appear as column headings. The names can be changed to any other names. These will be the final column headings of the report. The second Headings row is for adding a second line to column headings if desired.
Record	Formulas appear (such as =CLIENT ID=FNAME) for what will be the contents of the field in the final report. The equal sign (=) always precedes a formula in a cell on this definition page. =CLIENT ID is a formula that will insert the client ID data into this column.
Summary	Field summaries. If left blank, these rows will create groupings on like sets of data in fields, such as all persons living in Seattle. You can also define summary statistics, such as totals for the report in these lines. Statistics selections made in the New Report dialog box appear here.

TABLE 18-1
REPORT DEFINITION ROWS

CREATING A CUSTOM REPORT

The standard report format may not show all of the necessary information you would like to be shown in the final output. For example, a main heading and perhaps subheading, more detailed column headings, and even the use of separator lines would enhance this report and make it easier to read. The default column headings are the field names, and these names do not always clearly define the contents of the column. Sometimes field names are abbreviated for convenience and need further explanation in a report.

SWITCHING FROM *REPORT* TO *LIST* OR *FORM* VIEW

You can switch from **Report** view to **List** view or **Form** view (depending upon the view in use previously) by pressing **F10**. Use the menu to return to **Report** view.

SWITCH FORM *REPORT* TO *LIST* OR *FORM* VIEW

1. **PRESS**   **F10** to return to **List** view (if started from **List** view)
2. **CHOOSE**   **Report1** from the **View** menu to return to the report for this file
3. **PRESS**   **Enter** until you are at the **Report** definition screen as shown in Figure 18-3

CREATING MAIN REPORT HEADINGS

The main heading of a report is typed into the **Title** lines at the top of this report definition screen. It appears at the top of the report page. You can add one or two report heading lines.

Position the highlight in any cell in the **Title** line at the top of this screen or in the report title box when choosing the new report command.

Note: *Sometimes text will overlap into other cells. If this happens, continue typing. When the highlight is positioned in the cell, all contents will appear on the **Edit** line. When the report is output, the entire title will appear.*

CREATING COLUMN HEADINGS

The column headings are entered in the **Headings** rows of the report definition screen. The column headings can also be as many lines as you like. Usually, column headings are one or two lines long, and so this is the default. However, if you wished, you could add lines.

CREATE COLUMN HEADINGS

1. **HIGHLIGHT**   **Client ID** in column A
2. **PRESS**   **F2** to move to the **Edit** bar
3. **DELETE**   **ID** and press **Enter**
4. **PRESS**   the **Down Arrow** key once to move to the second heading line just below CLIENT
5. **TYPE**   **ID** and press **Enter**
6. **HIGHLIGHT**   **FNAME** in column B
7. **TYPE**   **FIRST**
8. **PRESS**   the **Down Arrow** key once
9. **TYPE**   **NAME** and press **Enter**
10. **CONTINUE**   entering the remaining column headings (in rows 4 and 5) as follows. Press the **Right Arrow** key to move to the other column in the report, which is not presently visible on the screen.

    LAST
    NAME   COMPANY   PHONE

Note: *When the cell contains data, press the **Delete** key to remove the contents or type new contents and press **Enter**. COMPANY and PHONE should appear on the second heading line as shown.*

CENTERING TEXT

Text may be formatting using either the **Format** menu or the **Toolbar**. The Toolbar options are for character and paragraph format, including Bold, Italic, Underline, Left align, Center align, and Right align. You may also use the Toolbar to switch views and to preview a file or report prior to printing.

CENTER TEXT

1. **HIGHLIGHT** all of the second **Headings** row
2. **CLICK** **Ctr** on the **Toolbar** or choose Center from the Format menu
3. **DELETE** any other formats (except Center) in the first heading line including bold or underline (highlight the row and click on the option in the Toolbar to turn it off)

INSERTING A NEW ROW

New rows can be added at any time in the report definition. For example, if you wanted to add a separator line to the **Headings** rows in the report, you could do so through options in the **Edit** menu.

INSERT A NEW ROW

1. **HIGHLIGHT** cell **A** in the **Record** row (it could be any cell in the row)

   Note: *The new row will be added above the selection.*

2. **CHOOSE** **Insert Row/Column** from the **Edit** menu
3. **CHOOSE** **Row**
4. **CHOOSE** **OK** or press Enter
5. **CHOOSE** **Headings** as the type of row to enter

Other selections in this dialog box include the other row types on the report definition screen. Inserting an extra **Heading** line will insert a blank line between the column headings and the body of the report. If the **Record** option were chosen, a blank line would be added between each record, giving the report a double-spaced appearance.

6. **CHOOSE** **OK** or press Enter

VIEWING A REPORT

VIEW A REPORT

1. **CLICK**   **Report** from the **Toolbar** or choose Report1 from the **View** menu

2. **PRESS**   **Enter** to reach the **Report Definition** screen (continue to press it until reached)

3. **CHOOSE**   **Preview** from the **Print** menu or choose **Prev** from the Toolbar and print the report

4. **PRESS**   **F10** to return to **List** view

CREATING A SECOND REPORT

This report will be created on the **CH16PR2** document.

CREATE A SECOND REPORT

1. **MAKE**   **CH16PR2** active

2. **CHOOSE**   **New Report** from the **View** menu

3. **ADD**   the following fields to the report form:

   INVOICE NO
   CLIENT ID
   BOAT NAME
   DATE BOOKED
   HOURS
   DEPOSIT
   TAX
   BALANCE
   TOTAL

4. **ADD**   a report title called **CHARTERS**

5. **CHOOSE**   **OK** or press Enter when finished

6. **CHOOSE**   **TOTAL** from the **Fields in report** box

7. **CHOOSE**   **SUM** from the **Statistics** options

8. **CHOOSE**   **OK** or press Enter

9. **PRESS**   **Enter** until the **Report Definition** screen appears or press **ESC**

10. **DELETE**   the extra word **TOTAL** in the **Summary** row in Column A

DATABASE

SORTING THE FILE

This report will be grouped by boat in ascending order. Within each boat group, the dates will be sorted in ascending order. This will give more order and meaning to the final report and will allow for a basis for grouping the report. It is important to sort a file prior to deleting columns. Reports do not always need to contain all of the columns shown in the original report or shown when viewing the records in **List** view. For this reason, columns are often changed after the initial setup.

SORT THE FILE

1. **CHOOSE** Sort Records from the **Select** menu

The dialog box shown in Figure 18-4 appears.

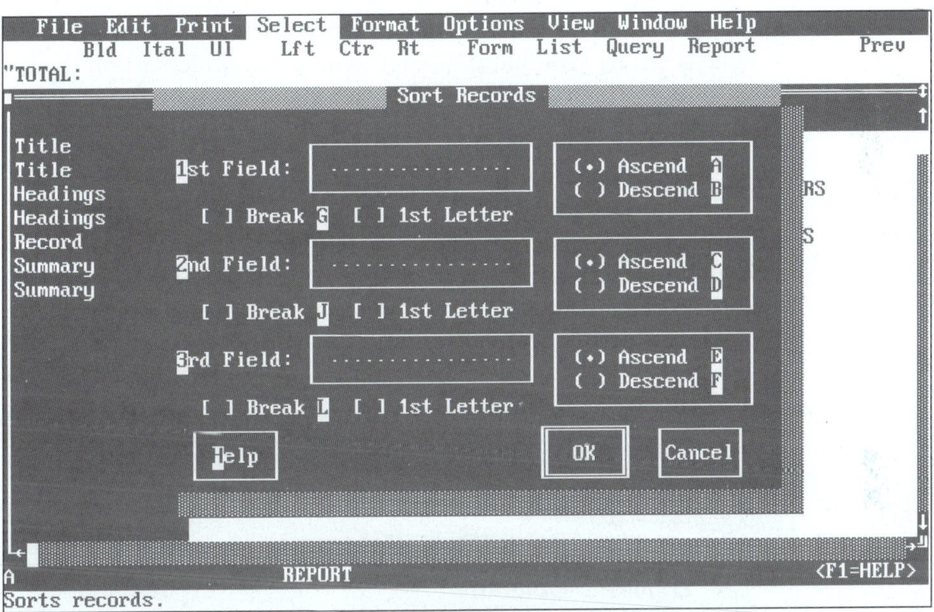

FIGURE 18-4
SORT RECORDS
DIALOG BOX (FROM
REPORT MODE)

2. **TYPE** **Boat Name** in the **1st Field** box and leave the selection at **Ascend**

3. **CHOOSE** **Break G** in the box below the **1st Field**

Making this selection tells Works that you want to break the report up in groups by **Boat Name** (the 1st Field). Making the other selection, **1st Letter**, will tell Works to start a new group when it sees any new character on the same line or the beginning of a new word. For example, making this selection would group the new boat, **Irish Spirit**, in with **Irish Sea**. In some cases this type of grouping would be okay. In this case you need to see all of the boats in separate categories. Therefore, this selection should not be made.

4. TYPE	**Date booked** in the **2nd Field** box
5. CHOOSE	**Descend**
Note:	*Do not make any other selections about groupings. Generally only one grouping is done on each report. Any additional grouping commands would make the report disorganized and confusing.*
6. CHOOSE	**OK** or press Enter

A new summary line is added to the report that reads, **Summ BOAT NAME**. This line is telling you that the report is now set up to sort on the boat name and that a summary report is defined that will group each boat name into separate categories.

REMOVING A ROW OR COLUMN

Suppose that you have decided that you will not need all of the information provided in this database report. You would like to view only the key information needed at this time. Any unwanted rows or columns can be deleted using the **Delete Row/Column** command in the **Edit** menu.

DATABASE

REMOVE A ROW OR COLUMN

1. HIGHLIGHT	any cell in column **B**, Client ID.
2. CHOOSE	**Delete Row/Column** from the **Edit** menu
3. CHOOSE	**Column**
4. CHOOSE	**OK** or press Enter
5. REPEAT	this procedure to delete the column for **Invoice Number**.
6. CHANGE	the title in the first row. Edit the title to read:
	REPORT ON CHARTERS

Insert rows or columns using the same procedure. If you wanted to insert new rows in this report, you would choose **Insert Row/Column** from the **Edit** menu.

INSERTING FIELD CONTENTS

You can add field contents anywhere in the report form. If you added a new column, for example, you could insert the contents of an existing field from the database file. Keep in mind as you are working with reports that they are attached to the original database file. All fields used in the active file are now available for use in this report. Refer to Figure 18-6 if necessary to see how the report should look after the insertion.

INSERT FIELD CONTENTS

1. **HIGHLIGHT**   cell **A** in the **Record** row (=BOAT NAME)
2. **PRESS**   the **Delete** key to remove the cell contents and press **Enter**
3. **CHOOSE**   **Insert Field Contents** from the **Edit** menu
4. **CHOOSE**   **BOAT NAME** as the contents to be inserted again in this first column
5. **PRESS**   **Enter** or choose OK

ADDING MORE INFORMATION TO THE REPORT

Information can be added to this report to tell the reader more about its contents. Things such as counting the number of entries in columns or summing values will give more information about the sales. Text, numbers, dates, and formulas can be inserted into any cell in the report.

You can also perform sorts on the database file, and the sorted order will affect the order of the data in the final report. For example, if you wanted to group this report by boat, you would first sort the file by boat, then create a formula for grouping or adding the total for each individual boat.

INTERPRETING REPORT FORMULAS

Reports should contain only the necessary information or fields. This report now contains formulas that will sum or count many of the fields listed in the report. When the sort command is put into effect, fields are summarized automatically. It is easy to remove the formulas from fields where a count or sum will not be necessary.

INTERPRET REPORT FORMULAS

1. **HIGHLIGHT**   cell **A** in the **Summ BOAT NAME** row (=COUNT(BOAT NAME))
2. **PRESS**   the **Delete** key
3. **HIGHLIGHT**   cell **D** in the **Summ BOAT NAME** row

This formula reads **=SUM(DEPOS**. It is shown only partially due to the width of the column. The formula is shown in its entirety in the **Edit** bar in the upper left corner of the screen. The formula, as written, will sum all values in the **Deposit** column. Since this is a currency field, this is a good use of the formula. You could write this formula as shown in the **Edit** bar or have it entered automatically when a sort command is given (as you did this time). You can also use **Insert Field Summary** from the **Edit** menu. A dialog box appears with a list of fields and with a list of available statistical functions. Using the **Insert Field Summary** command is useful when the names of fields are unknown or have been forgotten. The names of fields must always be exact when appearing in a formula.

4. SELECT   each of the remaining cells in the same row and read the formulas in the **Edit** bar

Each one of the formulas in this report will sum the values found in the corresponding columns. The formulas will show various totals for all of the sales on this sheet.

Other formula options are shown in Table 18-2. You will recognize many of these from the Spreadsheet tool.

USE THIS STATISTICAL FORMULA	TO DO THIS
SUM	Total each group in a report
AVG	Average each group
COUNT	Count the total items in a group
MAX	Locate the largest number in a group
MIN	Locate the smallest number in a group
STD	Calculate the standard deviation of a group
VAR	Calculate the variance of a group

TABLE 18-2
FUNCTIONS USED IN DATABASE FORMULAS

DATABASE

VIEWING A REPORT

There may be some additional things that could be added to this report; however, now is a good time to see the progress made in the report design.

VIEW A REPORT

1. CHOOSE   **Report1** from the **View** menu

Note: ***Shift/F10*** *could have been used; however, this command allows you to view the report but returns you to **List** view or **Form** view without seeing the **Report Definition** screen.*

A report similar to the one shown in Figure 18-5 appears.

```
                      REPORT ON CHARTERS

     BOAT NAME      DATE BOOKED   HOURS    DEPOSIT      TAX

 Delano              1/28/92        3     $100.00    $120.00
 Delano              1/20/92        3     $100.00    $120.00
 Delano              1/10/92        4     $100.00    $160.00
      Total Summary:              10     $300.00    $400.00

 Irish Sea           1/27/92        3     $200.00    $120.00
 Irish Sea           1/19/92        3     $100.00    $120.00
 Irish Sea           1/17/92        4     $150.00    $160.00
         Total Summary:           10     $450.00    $400.00

 SeaWolf             1/14/92        4     $500.00    $160.00
         Total Summary:            4     $500.00    $160.00

 Page 1                    REPORT
 Press ENTER to continue, ESC to cancel.
```

FIGURE 18-5
FIRST PAGE OF A
CUSTOM REPORT

2. PRESS **Enter** to see each of the pages of the report

When you view the report, it shows the breakdown of each grouping.

3. KEEP pressing **Enter** until you return to the definition screen

MAKING FINAL CHANGES IN APPEARANCE

Although the report looks okay and is fairly easy to interpret in its present format, it could be enhanced further. Text could give an explanation of each of the subtotals shown. Space could be added between each of the groupings and after the column headings, and the main heading could be shown in bold print.

MAKE FINAL CHANGES IN APPEARANCE

1. HIGHLIGHT cell **A** in the **Summ BOAT NAME** row

2. PRESS the **Spacebar** five times to indent this line

3. TYPE **Total Summary:**

4. PRESS **Enter**

5. HIGHLIGHT cell **A** in the first **Summary** row

6. CHOOSE **Insert Row/Column** from the **Edit** menu

7. **CHOOSE** **Row** and press **Enter** or choose OK

8. **CHOOSE** **Summ BOAT NAME** from the list of row types

9. **CHOOSE** **OK** or press Enter

10. **CHOOSE** **Report1** from the **View** menu or click Report on the Toolbar and press **Enter** until you return to the **Report Definition** screen

CHARACTER FORMAT TEXT

1. **HIGHLIGHT** the main heading **row 1**

2. **CHOOSE** **Style** from the **Format** menu

3. **CHOOSE** **BOLD** (if necessary)

4. **PRESS** **Enter** or choose OK

The final report should appear similar to the one shown in Figure 18-6.

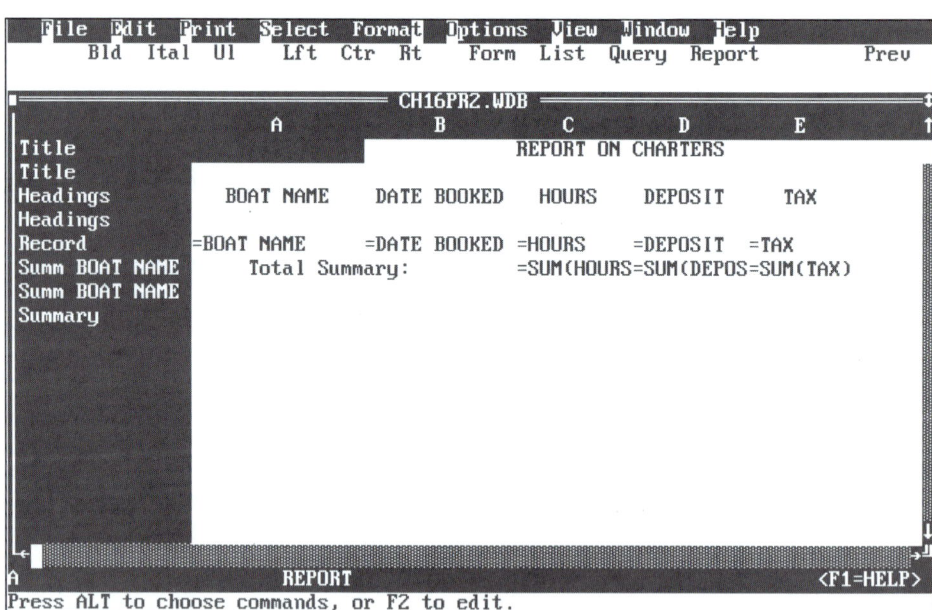

FIGURE 18-6
REPORT DEFINITION
SCREEN

5. **PRESS** **Shift/F10** to view the report again

RENAMING THE REPORT

If you look in the **View** menu, you will see a report called **Report1**. As you create additional reports, they will be named **Report2**, **Report3**, and so on, and will be listed in the **View** menu. The **Window** menu still shows only the names of the active database **files,CH16PR1** and **CH16PR2**. The reports listed in the **View** menu can be renamed using the **Reports** command.

RENAME THE REPORT

1. **CHOOSE**   **Reports** from the **View** menu
2. **HIGHLIGHT**   the name of **Report1** in the **list** box
   Note: *Additional names will appear as you create more reports.*
3. **MOVE**   to the **Name** box (Alt/N or click the mouse button).
4. **TYPE**   **CH18REP2**
5. **CHOOSE**   **Rename**

Other options in this dialog box include **Delete** and **Copy**. You could make a copy of this report with the **Copy** command. You could also delete it using the **Delete** command.

6. **CHOOSE**   **Done** and save the file again
7. **SWITCH**   to the database file **CH16PR1**
8. **USE**   the **Reports** command from the **View** menu to rename the **Report1** created in that file to **CH18REP1**

PRINTING THE REPORT

As long as the report is active, printing is the same as with other Works' tools. If the report is not active, use the **View** menu to make it so.

PRINT THE REPORT

1. **MOVE**   back to **CH16PR2**
2. **CHOOSE**   **CH18REP2** from the **View** menu
3. **PRESS**   **Enter** to move to the **Report Definition** screen
4. **CHOOSE**   **Print** from the **Print** menu
5. **MAKE**   any selections desired
6. **CHOOSE**   **Print** again
7. **SAVE**   the file
8. **QUIT**   or **CONTINUE** to the tutorial

GUIDED TUTORIAL

WHAT YOU'LL DO

- Create, modify, and print a report from a database file.

HOW TO DO IT

INSTRUCTOR'S DATA DISK

1. **OPEN** the database file **CH17TUT** which you created in Chapter 17; or retrieve it from the instructor's data disk.
2. **SWITCH** to **List** view if necessary.
3. **CHOOSE** **New Report** from the **View** menu.
4. **INSERT** the following fields into the report.

   ID NUMBER
   LAST NAME
   FIRST NAME
   DUES OWING

5. **CREATE** a report title that reads:

   MEMBERSHIP DUES OUTSTANDING

6. **CHOOSE** **OK** or press Enter.
7. **SUM** the **Dues Owing** field.
8. **CHOOSE** **OK** or press Enter.
9. **CONTINUE** to press **Enter** until you reach the **Report Definition** Screen.

The report definition screen now appears similar to the following.

DATABASE

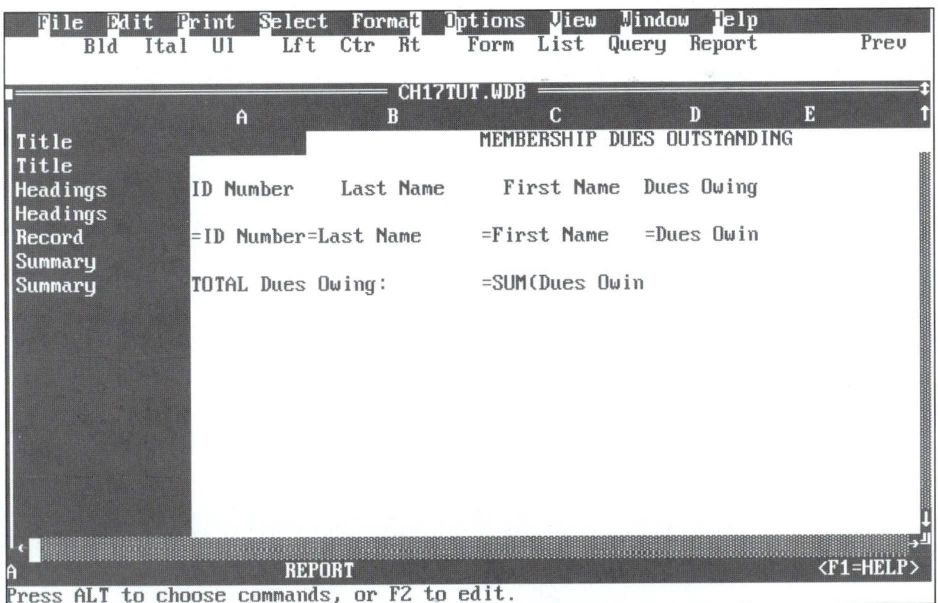

FIGURE 18-7
THE REPORT
DEFINITION SCREEN

10. POSITION   the highlight in column **A** on the second **Headings** row.

11. CHOOSE   **Insert Row/Column** from the **Edit** menu.

12. CHOOSE   **Row** and then **OK** or press Enter.

13. CHOOSE   **Headings** from the next dialog box (it should be selected).

14. CHOOSE   **OK** or press Enter.

15. EDIT   the **Heading** lines so that they appear as shown below. They should be inserted in the first and second heading lines.

ID NUMBER	LAST NAME	FIRST NAME	DUES OWING

16. CENTER   and underline the second heading line. Center the first heading line and remove any other formats.

17. CHOOSE   **Sort Records** from the **Select** menu.

18. TYPE   **Dues Owing** in the **1st Field** box.

19. CHOOSE   **Break G** to break this field into groups in ascending order and press **Enter**.

20. HIGHLIGHT   the **Summ Dues Owing** cell in column A.

21. DELETE   the contents.

22. DELETE   the contents in this row for columns B and C — **First Name** and **Last Name**. Leave the **SUM** formula in the **Dues Owing** column.

23. HIGHLIGHT   any field in the **Record** row.

24. **CHOOSE** Insert Row/Column from the **Edit** menu.

25. **CHOOSE** Row.

26. **CHOOSE** OK or press Enter.

27. **CHOOSE** Record (if necessary) and press Enter.

28. **VIEW** the report using **Report1** from the **View** menu or the Toolbar.

29. **PRESS** Enter until you return to the **Report Definition** screen.

The report definition screen should now appear similar to that shown in Figure 18-8.

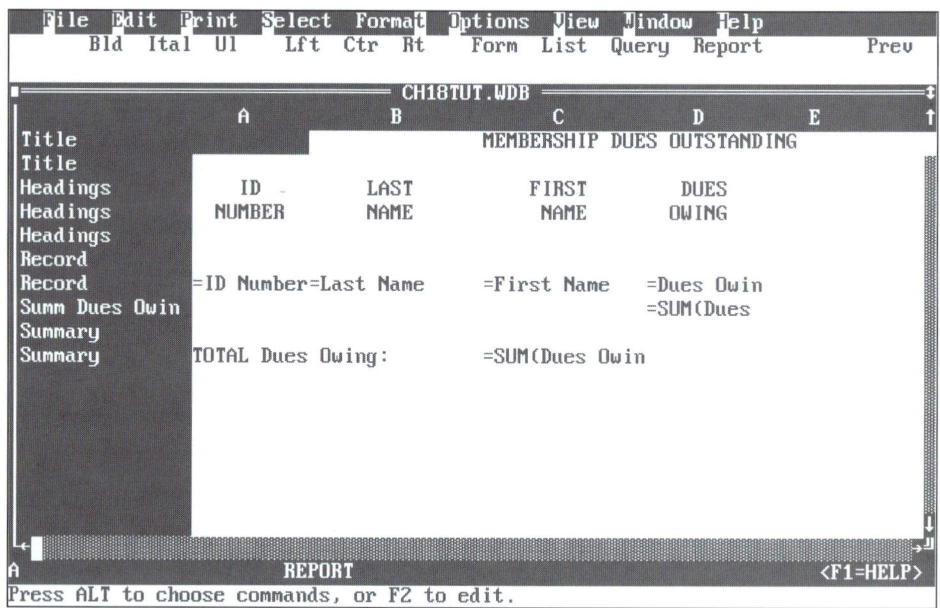

FIGURE 18-8
THE FINAL REPORT DEFINITION SCREEN

DATABASE

30. **PRESS** F10 to return to **List** view.

31. **CHOOSE** Reports from the **View** menu and select **Report1**.

32. **TYPE** CH18REP in the **Name** box.

33. **CHOOSE** Rename and then press **Enter** or choose OK.

34. **CHOOSE** Print from the **Print** menu to print a copy of the report.

35. **SAVE** this file again as **CH18TUT** and exit Works or continue to the next exercises.

REVIEW QUESTIONS

1. The ______________ command from the __________ menu is used to create a report.

2. Field names are added to a new report form using the ______________ dialog box.

3. List two locations where the report title may be entered.

4. Briefly state the features found in the **Report Statistics** dialog box.

5. The ________________ command from the ______________ menu is used to add rows or columns to a report definition.

6. The Report Definition screen is best described as which of the following?

    a. the final report structure
    b. the report and all data from the database file
    c. a summary of calculations to be performed
    d. the report titles and field names

7. The record row in a report does which of the following?

    a. shows the report titles
    b. shows the names of the fields from the database file
    c. shows calculations that will be made in the report
    d. shows the main report title

8. The summary row in a report does which of the following?

    a. shows the report titles
    b. shows the names of the fields from the database file
    c. shows calculations that will be made in the report
    d. shows the main report title

9. ______ The **Sort** dialog box contains options for dividing records into groups.

10. ______ The **Sort** dialog box contains options for dividing records into groups based on the first initial.

11. ______ Sorts may be performed on one or two fields at a time only.

12. ______ Field contents may be inserted from the **Report Definition** screen.

13. The ______________ command from the ______________ menu is used to change the name of a report.

14. Describe briefly the connection between a report and a database file.

15. How are reports printed?

HANDS-ON EXERCISES

EXERCISE 1

1. Open the database file **CH17HO1** which you created in Chapter 17; or retrieve it from the instructor's data disk.

2. Sort the file by **Response** in descending order and a second field sort on **date** in descending order.

3. Create a report that includes the following:

   Report heading: SUMMARY RESULTS

   Fields: Survey Number
                            Date
                            Response

   Count the total responses in the **Response** field.

4. Change the sort to **Grouped** on response with dates shown in **ascending** order within each grouping. Do this in Report Form view.

5. **Center** and **bold** the column headings. Put any two line word column headings on two lines. Leave a blank line after the column headings.

6. Insert a blank line between the groups after the subtotal line.

7. Preview the report and print a copy using **Print Preview**.

8. Name the report **CH18HOR**.

9. Save the file as **CH18HO1**.

EXERCISE 2

1. Open the database file **CH17HO2** which you created in Chapter 17; or retrieve it from the instructor's data disk.

2. Create a report with the following features:

   Report Heading: CHARTER BOAT STATISTICS

   Fields: Reg No
   Boat Name
   Length
   Persons
   License

   - A **count** of the number of boats in service.
   - A **grouping** on Persons, sorted on Persons.
   - Headings **underlined** and **centered**.
   - A blank line after the column headings.
   - Column width adjusted as necessary.
   - A blank line after each grouping.

3. Name the report **CH18HO2R** and save the file as **CH18HO2**.

4. Print a copy of the report.

19 FORM LETTERS AND MAILING LABELS

Objectives

- Create a form document.

- Merge and print a form letter.

- Create mailing labels.

PREVIEW ➤➤➤

A form letter (or other form document) is one that can be sent to many different people when merged with records from a database file. Using the word processing tool and the database tool, many different names and addresses (or other fields) can be merged with a single form document to produce standard letters, mailing labels, or other types of forms.

In this chapter you will produce a letter that will be sent to the clients in the **CH16PR1** database file. You will then create mailing labels to accompany the letters. Creating a form document is very simple. It is typed like any other document, and the locations for the fields are inserted by inserting the field name, which is enclosed in brackets. This is accomplished by making menu selections.

CREATING A FORM DOCUMENT

The form document for this exercise will be a form letter. Keep in mind, however, that you could create any type of document with the word processing tool. All you need to merge it with a database file is the inclusion of the field names within the body of the document. The field names shown in brackets (<< >>) are called placeholders.

Since the database document that will be used with this exercise is already created (**CH16PR1**), you will not need to create a new one. You will need to create the form letter.

CREATE A FORM DOCUMENT

1. **SIGN**   onto Works and set the directory path (if necessary)
2. **OPEN**   the database file **CH16PR1**
3. **OPEN**   a new word processing file
4. **BEGIN**   the document shown in the following box (start approximately five lines from the top of the document)

```
Today's date
```

With the cursor approximately five lines below the date,

5. **CHOOSE**   **Insert Database Field** from **Edit** menu

The dialog box shown in Figure 19-1 appears.

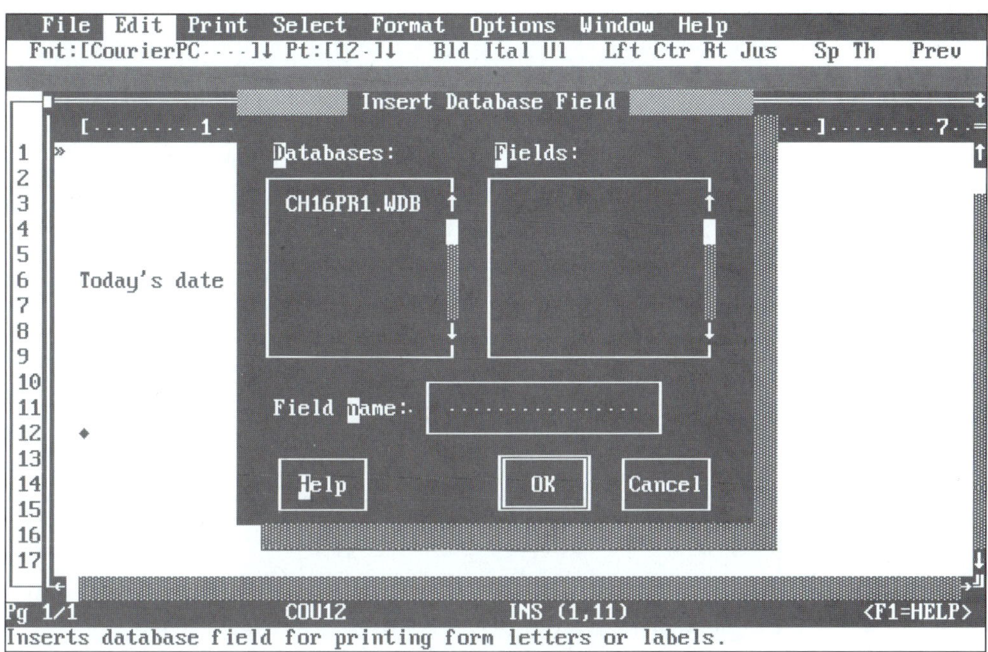

FIGURE 19-1
INSERT DATABASE
FIELD DIALOG BOX

6. **SELECT** the database file name, **CH16PR1**

Since **CH16PR1** is open, it is the database file name appearing in the Database list box. You can now select any one of the field names to be inserted into the form letter from the **Fields** list box. You could also type the name in the **Field name** box.

7. **CHOOSE** **FName** as the first field to be inserted at the cursor position

8. **CHOOSE** **OK** or press Enter

The field name appears in brackets «**FNAME**» as a placeholder in the document.

9. **PRESS** the **Spacebar** once to insert a space after the placeholder

10. **CHOOSE** **Insert Database Field** from the **Edit** menu

11. **CHOOSE** **LNAME** from the **Fields** list box

12. **CHOOSE** **OK** or press Enter

13. **PRESS** **Enter** again to insert a return after the placeholder

14. CONTINUE typing the remainder of the form letter and inserting field place-holders as shown in the following box. Leave the following spaces as you do so:

a comma and one space after city
two spaces after the state
three returns after the zip code
three returns after SUMMER PROMOTION
four returns to the closing, PUGET SOUND CHARTERS

Do not type the hyphens. Let text wrap on right margin as you normally do in a word processing document.

```
Today's date


«FNAME» «LNAME»
«COMPANY»
«ADDRESS»
«CITY», «STATE» «ZIP»


SUMMER PROMOTION


This summer season begins early for the boat charter busi-
ness. May begins a busy time that usually continues through
mid-October.

This year we are offering 25 percent off all tickets pur-
chased by corporations prior to May 1, 1992. This includes
tickets for any of our cruises - lunch, weekend brunches,
and evening dinners.

If you are interested in receiving this once-a-year offer,
please call our office for further details. Hope to see you
on board!



PUGET SOUND CHARTERS
```

15. RUN a spell check

16. SAVE the letter as **CH19PR1**

MERGING AND PRINTING THE FORM LETTER

Before merging a database file and the word processing form document, it is necessary to have both documents open. It is also necessary for the word processing form document to be the active one. Deciding who gets a form letter may result in not wishing to use the entire contents of the database file in the merge. It is possible that you would only want the form letter to go to the customers in the state of Washington or customers who live in Bellevue. When you wish to send to selected customers, you perform a query on the database file first and then a merge using the query results. For example, you might run a query on those living in the city of Bellevue by writing ="Bellevue" in the city field of the query form. The results of this query could be saved as a separate database file with the **Save As** command.

MERGE AND PRINT THE FORM LETTER

With the form letter active,

1. **MAKE** the database file, **CH16PR1**, active

2. **CHOOSE** **Query** from the **Toolbar**

3. **TYPE** ="Bellevue" in the **City** field and press **Enter**

4. **PRESS** **F10** to see the query results

5. **SAVE** the results as **CH19CITY**

6. **MAKE** the form letter active. Leave the database file open

7. **CHOOSE** **Print Form Letters** from the **Print** menu

8. **CHOOSE** the **CH19CITY** database file from the list (it should be active)

9. **CHOOSE** **OK** or press Enter

10. **LEAVE** all settings in the next **Print** dialog box

    Note: *In this dialog box you could decide on the number of copies to print, on the specific pages, and other options as discussed in detail in Part 2.*

11. **CHOOSE** **Print**

The documents are merged and printed.

CREATING MAILING LABELS

Creating a mailing label form is just like creating a form letter or other form documents. You insert the field placeholders in the correct positions, save the document with the placeholders, and then choose the correct print command from the **Print** menu.

The changes in creating labels occur when choosing print options. It is necessary to set the height and width of the labels and to adjust the margins on the page of labels as needed.

CREATE MAILING LABELS

1. BE SURE   that the **CH19PR1** document is open and that it has been saved

2. BE SURE   the database file, **CH16PR1**, is also open

With the form document active,

3. DELETE   any blank lines prior to the first field name, «FNAME»

4. LEAVE   the field names in the inside address in place and move to the blank line below the last line in the address («CITY» . . .)

5. DELETE   all lines below the last line of the address

6. SAVE   this revised document as **CH19PR2**

It should appear as shown in the box below.

```
«FNAME» «LNAME»
«COMPANY»
«ADDRESS»
«CITY», «STATE» «ZIP»
```

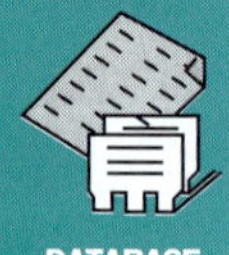

PRINTING MAILING LABELS

Printing mailing labels is done through the **Print Labels** command in the **Print** menu. Prior to creating the labels, it is necessary to know whether you are printing them down a single line, two across the page, or three across the page. It is also necessary to know the width of the paper. Usually, labels come on standard-size paper, which is approximately 8 1/2 inches by 11 inches. You need to leave a small margin along all edges of the label page, although the margins along the sides of the page should be narrower than they are in a standard word processor document.

PRINT MAILING LABELS

1. CHOOSE   **Print Labels** from the **Print** menu

A dialog box similar to the one in Figure 19-2 appears.

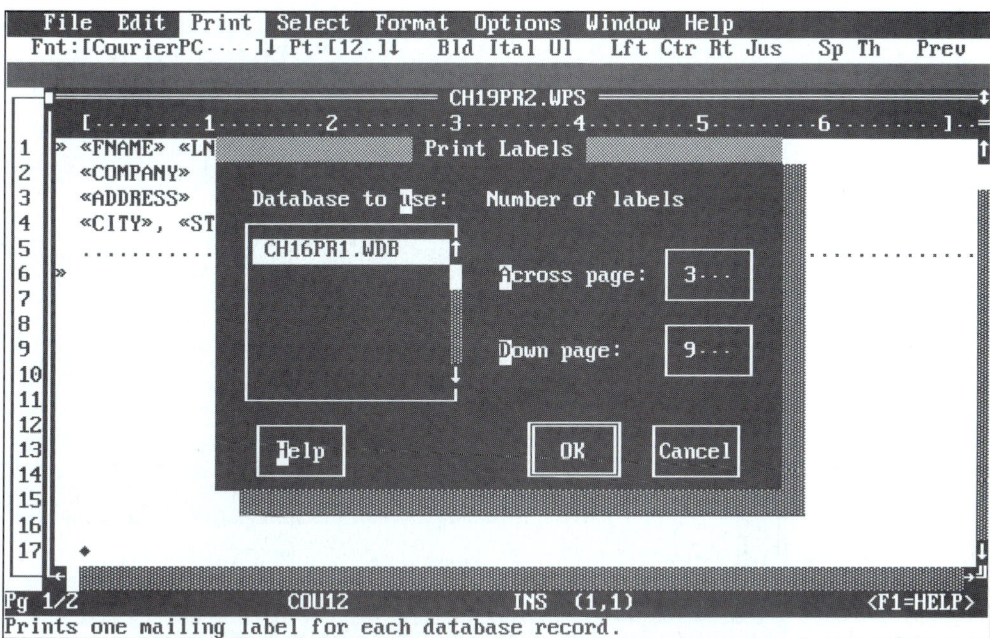

**FIGURE 19-2
PRINT LABELS
DIALOG BOX**

Since the client database, **CH16PR1**, is open, it is in the **Database** list box. You can now set the number of labels to appear across and down the page.

2. **TYPE**   **2** in the **Across page** box

Note: *Because the width of this address is wider than would be practical for mailing labels printing three across the page, a two across form will be practiced. You could, however, change the font to adjust the width if needed.*

3. **LEAVE**   **9** in the **Down page** box

4. **CHOOSE**   **OK** or press Enter

A dialog box similar to the one shown in Figure 19-3 appears.

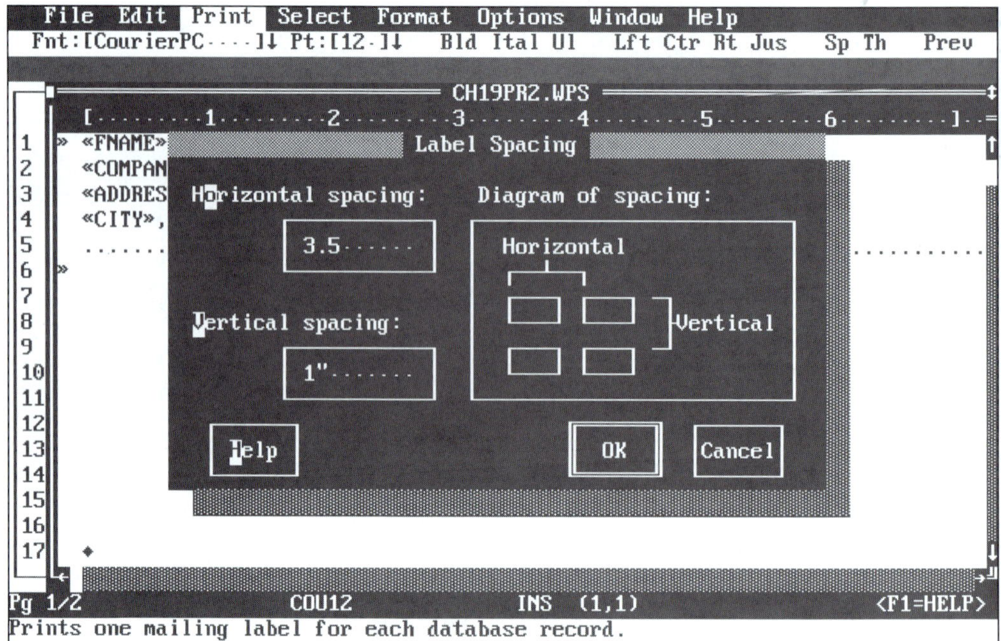

FIGURE 19-3
LABEL SPACING
DIALOG BOX

These settings depend on the mailing labels you are using. The label spacing settings are the distance from the beginning of one label to the beginning of the next (horizontal) and the top of one label to the top of the next (vertical). A standard label size is 1 inch high and approximately 3.5 inches (for two labels per page) or 2.5 (for three labels per page) from one to the other across. Unless your labels are marginally different, you can leave the settings in the **Vertical** and **Horizontal** boxes.

5. **CHOOSE** **OK** or press Enter to accept the settings

The box shown in Figure 19-4 appears.

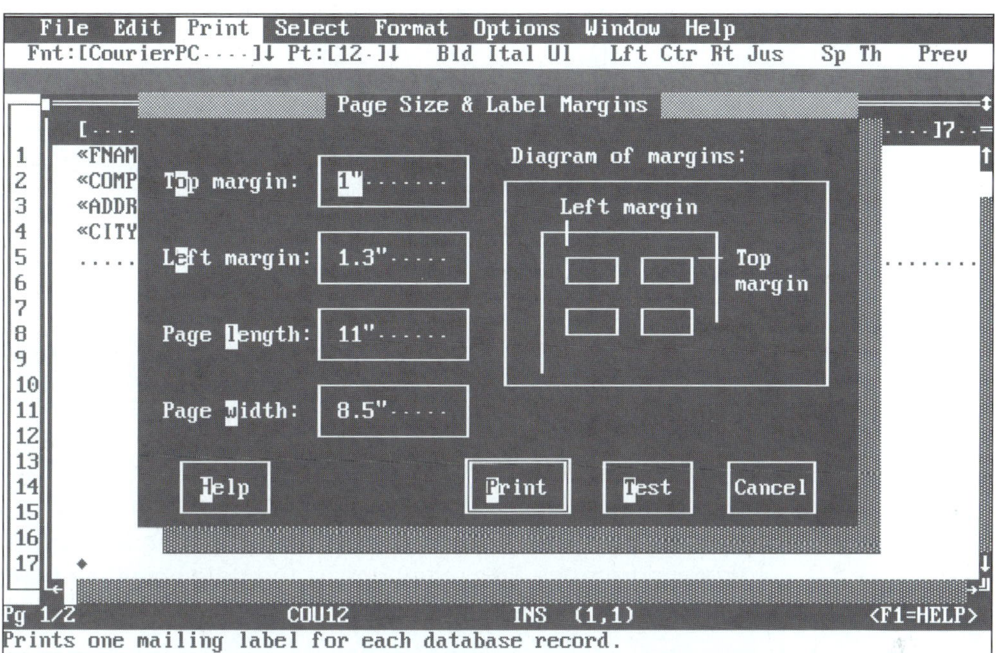

FIGURE 19-4
PAGE SIZE & LABEL
MARGINS DIALOG BOX

Here the margins of the label sheet may be changed. The information you would need for correct settings should appear on the label box you are using. For this exercise, you will print on a regular sheet of paper and the settings will remain as they are shown in the dialog box.

6. CHOOSE   **Print**

7. CHOOSE   **Print** again

Note: *When the Test option is chosen, the printer will print one row of mailing labels, in this case, two across. Works will then prompt you to either print all labels, reprint test labels, or cancel. Verify that the mailing labels are being printed. If they are, choose Print.*

If your printer has a problem printing at the edge of the page, you may receive a message on the screen saying to adjust the margins. If so, adjust the margins so that they are wider or narrower as needed and try the print command again. Notice that the labels in your document take up approximately 3 inches on the ruler line. The standard sheet of paper is 8 1/2 inches. Take into account the width of the page you are using and all margins included in the settings.

8. QUIT   or **CONTINUE** to the tutorial

GUIDED TUTORIAL

WHAT YOU'LL DO

- Create form documents including letters and mailing labels.
- Merge form and data documents.

HOW TO DO IT

1. **OPEN**   the clients database file **CH16PR1**.
2. **CREATE**   the following word processing form document.

As you do so, insert the fields as shown using the **Insert Database Field** command from the **Edit** menu. Insert the date using the **Insert Special Character** command from the **Edit** menu.

DATABASE

(today's date)

<<FNAME>> <<LNAME>>
<<COMPANY>>
<<ADDRESS>>
<<CITY>>, <<STATE>> <<ZIP>>

To the attention of: <<FNAME>>

This letter is to thank you for your continued support of Puget Sound Charters. You have been an outstanding client for the past few years and your company, <<COMPA-NY>>, has served us as an excellent public relations representative.

We at Puget Sound Charters like to reward good customers. We would like to offer you and six top employees from <<COMPANY>> complimentary dinner tickets any night during the next month.

Please contact us within the next week to set up a time and confirm reservations.

Again, thank you for your continued support. We look forward to serving your company in the years to come.

Sincerely,

P. J. MacRannall
President

---

3. **SAVE** the form letter as **CH19TUT**.

4. **CHOOSE** **Query** from the **Toolbar**.

5. **TYPE** **=98042** in the **Zip** field and press Enter.

6. **CHOOSE** **List** from the **Toolbar** to view the results.

7. **CHOOSE** the form letter from the **Window** menu.

8. **CHOOSE** **Print Form Letters** from the **Print** menu.

9. **HIGHLIGHT** the database file name if necessary and choose **OK** or press Enter.

10. **CHOOSE** **Print** again.

11. **DELETE** all parts of the form letters except the inside address containing the name, company name, address, city, state, and zip.

12. **SAVE** the revised document as **CH19TUTL**.

13. **CHOOSE** **Print Labels** from the **Print** menu.

14. **TYPE** **3** in the **Across page** box.

15. **TYPE** **9** in the **Down page** box (it should be set at 9).

16. **CHOOSE** **OK** or press Enter.

17. **TYPE** **2.6** in the **Horizontal** spacing box to give the space from the left edge of the first label to the left edge of the second, and so on.

18. **LEAVE** the vertical spacing setting.

19. **CHOOSE** **OK** or press Enter.

20. **LEAVE** a top margin of **1**.

21. **TYPE** a left margin of **0.2**

22. **LEAVE** other settings.

23. **CHOOSE** **OK** or press Enter.

24. **SAVE** changes and **QUIT** or **CONTINUE** to the Review Questions.

REVIEW QUESTIONS

1. A form document is created using the _________________ tool in Works.

2. A data document is created using the ________________ tool in Works.

3. The _______________ document is always the active one when merging.

4. The ________________ document and the _____________ document must be open prior to using a merge command.

5. Fields are inserted in a form document using the _________________ command from the _______________ menu.

6. Match each of the following to the correct menu, command, or option.

   ______ Used to merge a form letter with a data document

   ______ Used to merge mailing labels with a data document

   ______ Used to change label margins

   ______ Used to set the number of labels per page

   a. Print Merge
   b. Print Labels
   c. Print Form Letters

DATABASE

7. Space settings (for labels) are concerned with which of the following?
   a. The top edge of a label to the top edge of the next label
   b. The top edge of a label to the bottom edge of the same label
   c. The left edge of a label to the right edge of the same label
   d. None of the above

8. Top, bottom, left, and right margins settings are concerned with which of the following?
   a. The margins of the label
   b. The margins of the form document
   c. The margins of the page
   d. None of the above

HANDS-ON EXERCISES 

EXERCISE 1

1. Open the database file **CH16PR2**.

2. Create the following word processing document. Enter tab settings to align the headings (Management, Captain Eiler, and Vessel Statistics). Use the **Insert Special Character** command to insert the date.

(Today's date)

MEMORANDUM

TO: Management
FROM: Captain Eiler
SUBJECT: Vessel Statistics

Following is a summary of the activity for each of our boats during the last few months. This is a summary of bookings for the three- and four-hour cruises only.

    Let me know if you have any questions after looking over the list.

---

3. Save the document as **CH19HO1A.**

4. Create the following short-form document in a new word processing document space. Tab so that fields are placed approximately as shown.

<<BOAT NAME>>   <<HOURS>>   <<BALANCE>>

---

5. Do not enter a page break after the fields. The field names should appear as the only line in the document.

   Use the following guidelines as you merge this document. Use **Print Labels** to merge the document.

   a. One across the page
   b. Ten down the page
   c. Horizontal spacing at 3.5
   d. Vertical spacing at 0.5
   e. Top margin at 0.1
   f. Left at 0.5

6. Save the form document as **CH19HO1B**.

7. Proof and print a copy of the memo **CH19HO1A**.

8. Merge the short form document, **CH19HO1B**, with the database document, **CH16PR2**.

9. Attach the printout of the form document to the memo.

10. Quit or continue to the next exercise.

DATABASE

EXERCISE 2

1. Open the database file **CH18HO2** if necessary; or retrieve it from the instructor's data disk.

2. Create a word processing form document as follows. Insert the field names wherever you see the backets << >>.

Dear Prospective Client,

This letter is in response to your request for information on our boat, «Boat name», now in service with Puget Sound Charters. We are happy to provide you with the following specifics about the boat and its services, and we look forward to seeing you aboard in the future.

If you have any questions in addition to the information provided below, please do not hesitate to call. We believe that we offer the finest and most experienced private charter service in the region.

The boat, «Boat name», is captained by Captain «Captain». It is licensed for «License» and can carry a maximum of «Persons» persons. Its length is «Length» feet.
This vessel is captained by a licensed Merchant Marine captain with a minimum of five years' experience. The boat licenses are defined as follows.

    I   Inland Waters
    O   Ocean Going
    C   Catering Available
    L   Liquor License on Board

Inland waters are considered the lakes in the greater Seattle area and include Lake Union, Lake Washington, and special trips to Lake Sammamish. Ocean-going waters are all waters in the greater Puget Sound region, including the South Sound and the San Juan Islands. Overnight accommodations are available on some of our vessels.

---

3. Run a spell check and then save the document as **CH19HO2**.

4. Merge the form document with the database file.

DATABASE

20 APPLYING COMMUNICATIONS FUNCTIONS

Objectives

- Communicate with an information service.

- Copy information to another Works tool.

- Communicate with another computer.

PREVIEW »»—▶

This chapter will review the options that are available using Works communications tool. If you have communications capabilities, you can use this chapter as a general guideline for using communications. It is more of a reference tool than an instructional, practice tool as with other chapters in this text. The communications capabilities will vary with individual systems; therefore, this chapter should be a reference that can be applied in your unique situation.

Communications allows you to collect data from another computer or send information to one or more computers. In other words, it allows you to share information from one system to another. Through the communications system, you can access mainframe computers, other personal computers, or get access to bulletin boards (information data banks).

BEGINNING COMMUNICATIONS

There are several ways in which you can receive or send data from one location to another in a computer environment. One way is to communicate with another computer. Another way is to receive information or communicate with an information service. Information services offer packages such as banking services, stock exchange information, airline reservation services, world news bulletins, and information about technology news, such as public domain (or free) software available for microcomputer users, and so on. Communicating from one computer to another is a way to send letters and other documents or to send messages through an electronic mail system. You can also access programs and files stored on mainframe computers. Often these programs are too large and require faster and more complex processing capabilities than available on a microcomputer.

GETTING STARTED

The first step in communicating with any other computer system is to make sure that the settings on your computer match those with the computer you are calling. When communicating with another microcomputer, for example, it is important to know that the computer is on and that it is ready to receive and/or transmit messages in response to your communication. Usually mainframe computers in large organizations or on campuses are on 24-hours a day and so the communication time is not a problem. Check to make sure of the cost (if one is involved). Sometimes it is less expensive to communicate after prime-time hours (8 a.m through 5 p.m.). You also need to know what type of terminal you are contacting so that you can make the necessary selections in the **Terminal** dialog box.

COMMUNICATING WITH AN INFORMATION SERVICE

These instructions assume that this is the first time you have communicated with another computer. Check with your instructor or other system manager to make sure that the steps apply in your environment.

COMMUNICATE WITH AN INFO SERVICE

Sign onto Works and then,

1. **CHOOSE**   **Create New File** from the **File** menu
2. **CHOOSE**   **Communications**

At this time, if you need to make selections pertaining to communications and terminal specifications, access the **Terminal** or **Communications** dialog boxes from the **Options** menu as shown in Figures 20-1 and 20-2.

Making terminal settings

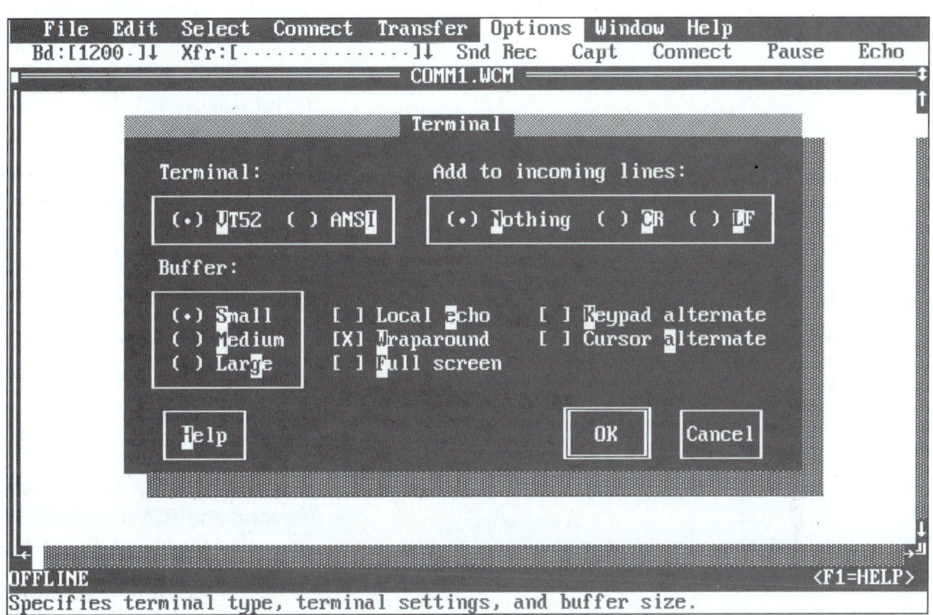

FIGURE 20-1
THE TERMINAL
DIALOG BOX

This dialog box and its settings determine how your computer receives data from another system. The default settings as shown in the dialog box are usually correct for communicating with another microcomputer. Normally, the only step necessary at this point is to type the phone number in the **Phone** dialog box. However, it is important to review this **Terminal** dialog box for those who might need to make special settings when just entering the telephone number in the **Phone** box does not work.

The settings are defined in Table 20-1.

THIS SETTING	IS USED TO
Terminal	Emulate the type of computer from which you are receiving information. If you are not sure, leave the selection at VT52.
Add to incoming lines	Insert a hard return or carriage return (CR) or a line feed (LF) to the end of each line of incoming text. If these lines are already displayed in the text being sent, do not change the setting. Leave at Nothing.
Buffer	Temporarily store incoming information. The buffer information can be viewed in the Communications screen and then copied to another Works document space, such as a word processing document. Move through the buffer document screen as you would any other document. Decide on a small (100 lines), medium (300 lines), or large (750 lines) buffer size depending upon whether you are receiving single page information (small), multiple pages (medium), or very large and complex documents with complex formatting (large).
Local echo	View the characters you are typing on the screen. When you and another personal computer are using Works, both of you should have Local Echo turned on.
Wraparound	Automatically wrap incoming text that reaches beyond the 80 space line. Much like the word wrap feature in word processing. Any text reaching the right margin will wrap to the next line.
Full screen	Remove the menu options and status line information on the communications screen. With this option on, the screen will be completely blank and ready for you to type or receive information. Turn the option off to have the menus reappear.
Keypad alternate	Switch to numbers on the numeric keypad when the NumLock key is pressed (on).
Cursor alternate	Switch to the use of the cursor or Arrow keys when the NumLock key is off.

TABLE 20-1
DESCRIPTION OF THE OPTIONS IN THE TERMINAL DIALOG BOX

Making communication settings

As with the terminal settings, do not adjust these unless you are certain that your environment is different from the standard ones set in Works. The **Communication** dialog box from the **Options** menu is shown in Figure 20-2 and described in Table 20-2.

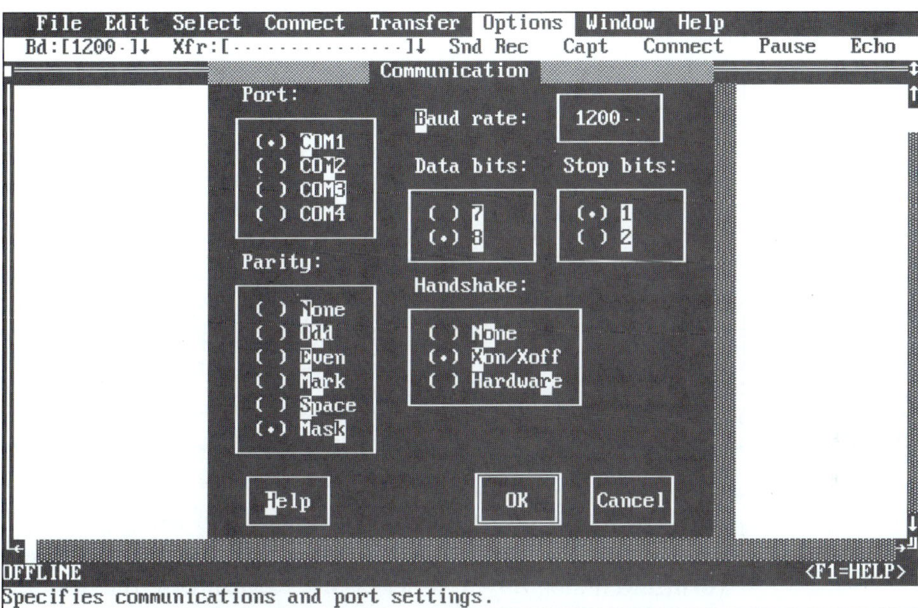

FIGURE 20-2
THE COMMUNICATION
DIALOG BOX

THIS SETTING	IS USED TO
Port	Determine the correct port from which your computer modem is working. Some microcomputers have more than one communications port. Usually they have only one so Works' default setting for this option is 1. For more detail on your ports, check with the lab administrator, your instructor, or the computer manual.
Baud rate	Determine the speed at which information is received and transmitted. The higher the setting, the higher the speed. Check the modem manual or check with the lab manager or your instructor. Often microcomputer modems are set at 1200 or 2400 baud. The baud rate cannot be higher than the highest baud rate supported by either modem.
Data bits	Set the number of bits that are equal to one character. Normally the number of bits is 8.

Stop bits	Set the number of bits between characters or where one ends and the other begins. This is normally 1 bit.
Parity	Determine the type of parity set a computer is using. If the Mask option is selected, Works will accept information regardless of the type of parity in use by the other computer. This is generally a good setting at which to leave the Parity option.
Handshake	Ensure that information is not lost when it is travelling from one computer to another. The Xon/Xoff setting is the one commonly used when communicating with another computer. The hardware option is used when there is a direct cable connection between your computer and another.

TABLE 20-2
THE
COMMUNICATION
DIALOG BOX

Continuing the communication

When the necessary changes have been made in the **Communication** and **Terminal** dialog boxes (if necessary), continue to the next step.

CONTINUE THE COMMUNICATION

3.	CHOOSE	**Phone** from the **Options** menu
4.	TYPE	the phone number of the service
5.	CHOOSE	**OK** or press Enter
6.	CHOOSE	**Connect** from the **Connect** menu

As soon as a connection is made, the OFFLINE message in the lower left corner of the status line at the bottom of the screen changes to begin counting the time elapsing during the connection.

Depending upon the service you are using, you will now need to follow the procedures for accessing that service. This will vary from service to service, so it cannot be outlined in detail here.

The information you receive will be stored in the communications buffer area.

To copy information to another Works' tool

Copy information from the communications tool to another Works' tool using **Pause** from the **Connect** menu. Then choose **Copy** from the **Edit** menu and open a new or already created file and copy to it as you would in any other tool.

To logoff and disconnect

Log off from the service you are using by entering that service's logoff command. Once you have done so, you can discontinue Works' communication service by choosing **Connect** from the **Connect** menu. This command both activates and deactivates the communication service in Works.

To save a communications file

Save a file by choosing **Save** from the **File** menu as you would in any other Works tool.

COMMUNICATING WITH ANOTHER COMPUTER

You can communicate with another computer in much the same way as you would a computer service. Usually user identification and passwords are used on your computer. You will need to know that the other computer is on and is ready to receive information from you or send information to you. Generally, follow the steps listed below.

COMMUNICATE WITH ANOTHER COMPUTER

1. CHOOSE **Create New File** from the **File** menu
2. CHOOSE **Communications**
3. ADJUST the terminal and communications settings as necessary and as discussed in detail in the previous instructions on communicating with a service
4. CHOOSE **Phone** from the **Options** menu
5. TYPE the phone number in the **Phone number** box
6. CHOOSE **Connect** from the **Connect** menu

Wait until the other computer responds.

7. TYPE your user identification number and password (if necessary)

You are now ready to type text, copy information from one Works tool to the other computer, receive information from the other computer, or transfer text or binary codes.

To copy information to another computer

You can copy part or all of a file from your computer to another computer once you are on-line to each other as stated in the previous steps. To copy information from one Works' tool to the other computer do the following:

COPY INFORMATION TO ANOTHER COMPUTER

With the computers connected,

1. **OPEN**   the document from the tool (word processor, spreadsheet, or database).

2. **SELECT**   all of the text you want to send

3. **PRESS**   **Shift/F3** or choose **Copy** from the **Edit** menu

4. **CHOOSE**   the **Communications** file from the **Window** menu

5. **PRESS**   **Enter** to copy the document into the communications window

   Note: *At the time you press* **Enter**, *the selected document will be passed to the computer to which you are signed on.*

To receive information from another computer

You can receive information from another computer using the **Receive File** command from the **Transfer** menu.

Be sure you have communicated with the other user so that both of you have your computers on and the sender has sent the document or information to your computer.

RECEIVE INFORMATION FROM ANOTHER COMPUTER

1. **CHOOSE**   **Receive File** from the **Transfer** menu

In the **Receive File** dialog box, selections are made for the incoming document using the guidelines in Table 20-3.

SET THIS OPTION	TO DO THIS
Save file as:	Give the incoming file a name.
Directory of C:\Works	Set the current directory. If the directory is different or you are saving to a subdirectory, change the directory path using the Directories box.
Directories:	Change the current directory or path.
Format:	
<u>Binary</u>	Receive a formatted Works' file, a software program, or another formatted file.
<u>Text</u>	Receive a file in ASCII format (text).

COMMUNICATIONS

TABLE 20-3
DESCRIPTION OF
THE RECEIVE FILE
DIALOG BOX

2. TYPE   the name of the incoming file into the **Save File As** box

3. SELECT   **Binary** or **Text** format

4. CHOOSE   **OK** or press Enter

Wait while the file is being transferred. When it is complete,

5. CHOOSE   **OK** or press Enter

To cancel a transfer

You can cancel a file transfer at any time. To do so,

CANCEL A TRANSFER

1. PRESS   the **ESC** key

2. CHOOSE   **OK** or press Enter to confirm the cancellation

To copy information received to a Works' tool

You can also copy the information received from another computer into any of the Works' tools. This same procedure should be followed if you are copying from a service.

COPY INFORMATION RECEIVED TO A WORKS TOOL

With your computer connected to a service or to another computer,

1. OPEN   a word processor, spreadsheet, or database file

2. BE SURE   the information is received and stored in the buffer (it should appear on the communications screen)

3. CHOOSE   **Pause** from the **Connect** menu

4. SELECT   all of the information you want to transfer to another file

5. PRESS   **Shift/F3** or choose **Copy** from the **Edit** menu

6. CHOOSE   the file into which you will copy the information from the **Window** menu

In the Works document space,

7. PRESS   **Enter**

8. CHOOSE   **OK** or press Enter

To resume communications after a copy

You can resume communications with the other computer or service after copying information.

<table>
<tr><td colspan="3">RESUME COMMUNICATIONS</td></tr>
<tr><td>1.</td><td>CHOOSE</td><td>the communications file from the Window menu</td></tr>
<tr><td>2.</td><td>CHOOSE</td><td>Pause from the Connect menu</td></tr>
<tr><td></td><td>Note:</td><td>The Pause command both starts and ends a pause during the communication.</td></tr>
</table>

To send a complete file to another computer

Previously, the steps were reviewed for sending parts of selected text to another computer. When that function is used, the text appears on the other computer's communications screen. The user receiving the text can then save it as a file. There are other ways to send information. You can send an entire file. When you choose the **Send File** command from the **Transfer** menu, a screen appears that is similar to the **Open Existing File** command in the **File** menu. It shows a list of all of your stored files. You can then select one and send it to another computer. The receiving computer must, however, be turned on and ready for your file. You may use these steps to send a file to another computer, an information service, or to a bulletin board. Sending a file with this series of commands sends the complete file and not just blocks of text. Therefore, when the person at the other end receives the file, it is in file form when received. In other words, the entire file is copied to his or her computer system. It is not just a block of text as with previous instructions in this chapter. The person at the other end has a new file that is saved to disk and can be opened and saved to his or her directory.

<table>
<tr><td colspan="3">SEND COMPLETE FILE TO ANOTHER COMPUTER</td></tr>
<tr><td>1.</td><td>BE SURE</td><td>you are connected with the system that will receive the file</td></tr>
<tr><td>2.</td><td>CHOOSE</td><td>Send File from the Transfer menu</td></tr>
<tr><td>3.</td><td>CHOOSE</td><td>the correct directory path from the Directories box (if necessary)</td></tr>
<tr><td>4.</td><td>CHOOSE</td><td>the file name you wish to send from the Files list box</td></tr>
<tr><td>5.</td><td>CHOOSE</td><td>Binary or Text format</td></tr>
<tr><td></td><td>Note:</td><td>Binary is used when the file being sent is formatted as a Works file, a software program, or any other formatted file. A Text file is one that is sent in ASCII (text) format.</td></tr>
<tr><td>6.</td><td>CHOOSE</td><td>an End-of-line option</td></tr>
</table>

> *Note:* The **End-of-line** option controls what will happen at the end of a typed line. Line endings with microcomputers are usually CR for carriage return (meaning that the **Enter** key was pressed). The LF endings, or line feed endings are more common with mainframe and mini computers. Make a selection here that will match those being used by the receiving computer. If you are uncertain, use the CR & LF option.

7. CHOOSE   **OK** or press Enter

Wait as the file is being transferred.

8. CHOOSE   **OK** or press Enter when the file transfer is complete

To send text (ASCII) to another computer

You can also send text to another computer. When you choose this option, you are sending text that you have in a stored file (it has already been typed) to another system. The text is not, however, received by the other system as a file. It is instead received as text. The dialog box used for this type of transfer is the **Send Text** dialog box accessed through the **Transfer** menu. It is similar in appearance to other **Send** dialog boxes. Use the following series of steps to send the block of text.

SEND ASCII TEXT TO ANOTHER COMPUTER

1. BE SURE   the other computer is ready and waiting to receive the text

2. CHOOSE   **Send Text** from the **Transfer** menu

3. CHOOSE   the correct file and the correct directory path

4. CHANGE   the **Delay** as necessary.

> *Note:* The **Delay** box is used to delay the time it takes to transmit a single line of text to the other system. Sometimes this is almost instantaneous, other times the other system is slower to receive incoming information. It is set at 0, which means no delay when the dialog box is first opened. Changing the setting to 1 would delay the time between lines by 1/10th of a second; 2 by 2/10ths, and so on.

5. CHOOSE   **OK** or press Enter

To receive calls automatically

You can receive calls automatically when your computer is on and you are away from it. This option is usually used when you are waiting to receive information from another personal computer.

RECEIVE CALLS AUTOMATICALLY

1. **CHOOSE** **Phone** from the **Options** menu

2. **CHOOSE** **Automatic answer**

3. **CHOOSE** **OK** or press Enter

4. **CHOOSE** **Connect** from the **Connect** menu

Any incoming files or text will now be received from other systems. Choose **Connect** again from the **Connect** menu to discontinue the automatic answering service.

5. **QUIT** or **CONTINUE** to the suggested practice exercises for this chapter.

COMMUNICATIONS

GUIDED TUTORIAL

There will not be any formal reinforcement exercises introduced in this chapter since your communications environments will vary dramatically from one to another. If you are networked, have access to information databanks, are linked to other computers through modems, or have other communications capabilities, it is recommended that you try any of the following.

1. Sending blocks of text to another computer.
2. Receiving blocks of text from another computer.
3. Accessing a mainframe computer or information databank.
4. Transmitting and receiving stored files to and from other systems.

416

21 INTEGRATED DOCUMENTS

Objectives

- Transfer information among Works tools.

- Use each Works tool.

- Create macros.

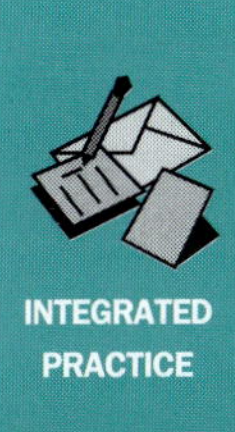

PREVIEW ➤➤➤

This part contains several integrated documents. The documents use word processor and chart tools, spreadsheet tools, and database tools. It is suggested that you practice using communications tools if possible in your own computer environment. Prior to starting the documents, read through the following instructions, which give guidelines to transferring information from one Works tool to another.

Also included in this section are macros. Macros allow you to store keystrokes so that they may be played back by pressing one or more key combinations. Macros are extremely useful. After using them in the first integrated document, practice creating other macros on other integrated documents and on those you may be creating on your own. The more you use macros, the more uses you will find for them.

TRANSFERRING INFORMATION AMONG TOOLS

Information is most often transferred to the word processor tool because the word processor tool is easiest to work with. Information and additional text can easily be added, the Draw tool used to enhance a document's appearance, and borders added quickly. Therefore, the most frequent transfer of information is into a word processing document space.

COPYING INFORMATION BETWEEN ANY TWO TOOLS

The following instructions may be used to copy information from one document to another.

With both documents open,

COPY INFORMATION BETWEEN ANY TWO TOOLS

1. **SELECT** the material to be copied
2. **CHOOSE** **Copy** from the **Edit** menu
3. **SELECT** the document to which the copy will be made from the **Window** menu or create a new file or open an existing document
4. **POSITION** the cursor at the desired location for the incoming selection
5. **PRESS** **Enter** to complete the copy

COPYING INFORMATION INTO A WORD PROCESSING DOCUMENT

When copying spreadsheet or database information into a word processing document, some characteristics of the document may be changed. For example, the columns in a spreadsheet document are separated by tab positions when copied to a word processing document space. The fields in a database document are also separated by tab positions. Therefore, the alignment will change when copied.

When all or part of a spreadsheet is copied to a word processing document, select all columns and reset the tab positions to realign them. When the spreadsheet is wide, it may be necessary to adjust the margins to accommodate all of the columns or to continue the spreadsheet on a new page. Use the same procedure with copied database fields. When the Copy command is used, values and labels will be copied exactly as they appeared at the time of the copy command. Any formulas used in a spreadsheet or data entered in a database file will no longer be in effect in the word processing document. In other words, you will not be able to change values in the spreadsheet and have the automatic recalculation feature in effect in the word processor tool.

Inserting placeholders into a word processing document

If changes are expected to a spreadsheet or database file after they are copied into a word processing document, you may insert placeholders instead of copying the entire document. Placeholders have a some advantages. They save space in the word processor file since the actual spreadsheet, chart, or database file does not appear in its entirety, and changes made to the placeholder file are automatically updated in the word processor file. A placeholder searches for the filename and inserts the requested information at the time of printing, and therefore inserts the latest revision of the document. To insert a placeholder for a chart, spreadsheet, or database field, use the **Insert Database Field, Insert Spreadsheet Range**, or **Insert Chart** commands from the **Edit** menu. Be sure the file to be used in the placeholder is open and that the word processing document is active.

For all of the exercises in this part, spreadsheets charts and database information will be copied into a word processing document. If you wish to transfer information in other directions within Works, check the Works user's manual.

INTEGRATED PROJECT 1
The Premium Art Gallery
Part 1

OBJECTIVES

- Create a database.

- Create a macro.

- Query a database.

- Create a merge document.

- Create a spreadsheet.

- Create a chart.

PREVIEW

You are to set up the basic word processing, spreadsheet, graphic, and database structures for a small art gallery. This gallery, The Premium Art Gallery, is located in LaConner, Washington, a small riverfront tourist town. The town shows works of local artists in the Pacific Northwest and Alaska. The owners would like you to set up form letters to send to regular customers and residents of the community on their mailing list. The letters will contain several variables. In addition, they would like a short newsletter format to be saved into which they can insert dates of shows, new artists, and other special announcements. They also want a database of all customers and information about their customers. The owners want to be able to create mailing labels from the database records. They need a database on the artists whose works they regularly show, as well. At this time, these are their only requirements for permanent storage. The manager, Sally Rutherford, has also asked to see results of the last six months' sales in both spreadsheet and chart format.

DATABASE

1. Create a file that includes the following information about each customer. Create separate fields for the customer ID (the four figures at the top of each name), artist ID shown below each customer (1, 2, 3, and 4), first and last names, street, city, state, zip, and telephone number.

1123
Sara Rinehard
8975 N.E. 124th St
Carnation WA 98014
(206) 785-1222
1

1124
Susan Beach
South Temple Drive, #45
Amanda Park WA 98526
(206) 278-1122
4

1125
Jane and Ray Ignacio
17858 22nd N.W.
Seattle WA 98133
(206) 888-1983
4

1126
Fred Hyland
4th N and Broadview
Bellevue WA 98007
(206) 877-2975
5

1127
Frances Kohler
2204 Cremona W.
Seattle WA 98122
(206) 785-5202
3

1128
Jeffrey Ladd
578 North Bend Road
LaConner WA 98257
(206) 785-8717
1

1129
Margaret and Howard Levitz
South Beach Drive, #27
LaConner WA 98257
(206) 777-5786
2

1130
D. D. Goodwin
1112 S. 78th St.
Mt. Vernon WA 98273
(206) 999-2785
3

1131
Mary Gordon
7502 N. Carmin
Bellingham WA 98225
(206) 445-9918
1

1132
Daniel and Trudy Cawthorne
1560 N. 115th
Carrolls WA 98609
(206) 554-1278
2

1133
Eleanor Rudine
27 North Mountain Drive
Burlington WA 98233
(206) 555-1785
5

2. Save the file as **CH21DB1**.

3. Create the following file and save it as **CH21DB2**.

As you are setting up the fields, create separate fields for the artist ID (at the top of each name), the first and last names, street, city, state, zip, and a field called specialty. The specialty field may contain more than one specialty, so the width should be set at least three spaces wide. The codes for the specialty field are as follows:

S   for sculpture

W   for woods

T   for watercolor

O   for oils

C   for ceramics

P   for pottery

1
Patrick Randle
817 12th N.E.
Onalaska WA 98570
sculpture, woods

2
Jean Hiebert
18972 37th N.W.
Vancouver WA 98682
watercolor

3
Don Day
1234 1st South
Seattle WA 98101
watercolor, oil

4
Marlene Beebe
24 Deep Freeze Drive
Saldotna AK 99662
ceramics, pottery

5
Bill Winkles
3000 3rd N.
Seattle WA 98133
watercolor, oil

4. Add a NOTE field that explains each of the specialties.

5. Create a short report on **CH21DB2** to show the artist's names and each of his
    or her specialties. Include an appropriate report heading, column headings
    and formatting, as well as the NOTES field. Rename the report as
    CH21DBR1. Print a copy of the report.

6. Query the **artists** file, **CH21DB2,** and the **customer** file, **CH21DB1**, for the following and send the results of each to the printer.

   a. All artists whose medium includes watercolor
   b. All customers who live in Seattle or Bellevue
   c. All customers who are interested in artist 1
   d. All customers who are interested in any artist except 3
   e. All artists whose medium is sculpture

7. Print a list of all customers living in Mt. Vernon or LaConner who are interested in artist number 1 or 3.

8. Sort both database files in ascending order by last name and print a copy of each.

9. Adjust the width of the fields in List view.

10. Query the appropriate database file for all customers living in LaConner or Mt. Vernon and print a copy of the results.

11. Query the database files as appropriate for the following information. Print copies of each result. You may choose to print the results in report format.

    a. All customers interested in artists 1 or 2.
    b. All customers living in Bellevue or LaConner.

CREATING A MACRO

Macros store a series of keystrokes in a single key or in a combination of keystrokes (usually no more than 2). The most important step in creating any macro is first to list all of the keystrokes used in the procedure you wish to store. For example, in this exercise you will create a macro that will play back all of the keystrokes, mouse actions, and menu selections used to create the logo shown in the form document. The steps you will use are listed below.

   a. Give the center command to position the cursor.
   b. Give the bold command to bold the text.
   c. Assign font and size changes to the text.

The full steps you will use to create the logo are:

   a. Press Ctrl/C for center.
   b. Choose Font & Style from the Format menu.
   c. Choose Bold and Helvetica 14 from the Styles, Fonts, and Sizes list boxes.
   d. Choose OK.
   e. Type the first line of the logo.
   f. Press Enter.
   g. Choose Font & Style from the Format menu.
   h. Turn off Bold, choose Italics and Times Roman 10.

    i.   Choose OK.
    j.   Press Enter.
    k.   Type the remainder of the header.
    l.   Press Ctrl/L to return to the left margin.
    m. Press Enter twice to move down in the document.

These are the steps you will want to record in the macro.

To begin the recording

Before beginning, run through the steps once for practice in a blank document space without recording them in a macro. Make certain that all of the steps are accurate and in the correct sequence. If the fonts listed are not available with your system, choose any other fonts. Position the cursor at the top of a blank document space. When ready, use the following steps to record the logo in a macro.

1. Position the cursor at the top of a blank word processing document space.

2. Press **Alt /** (hold down the Alt key and press the slash key (/)).

The dialog box shown in Figure 21-1 appears.

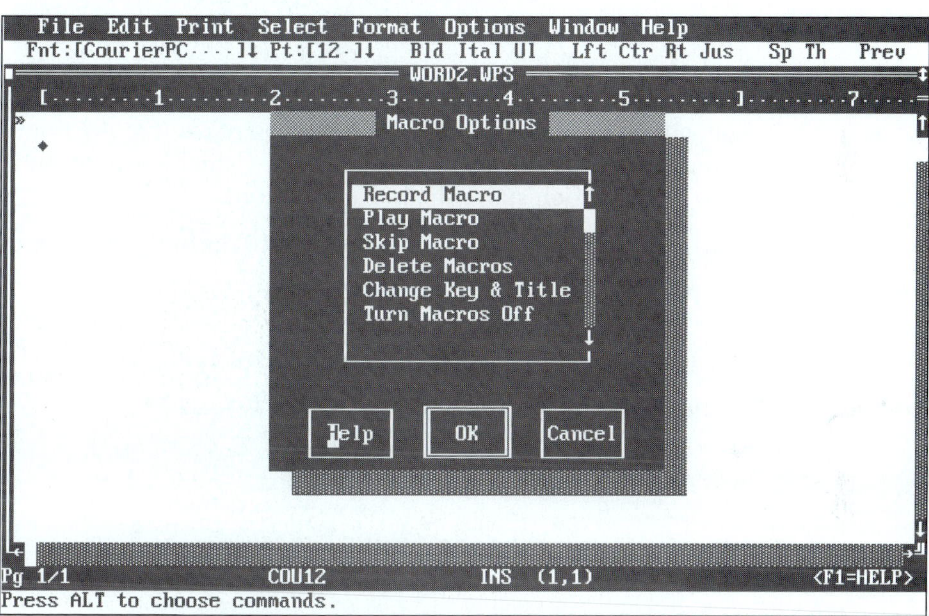

FIGURE 21-1
MACRO OPTIONS
DIALOG BOX

3. Choose **Record Macro** to show the dialog box in Figure 21-2.

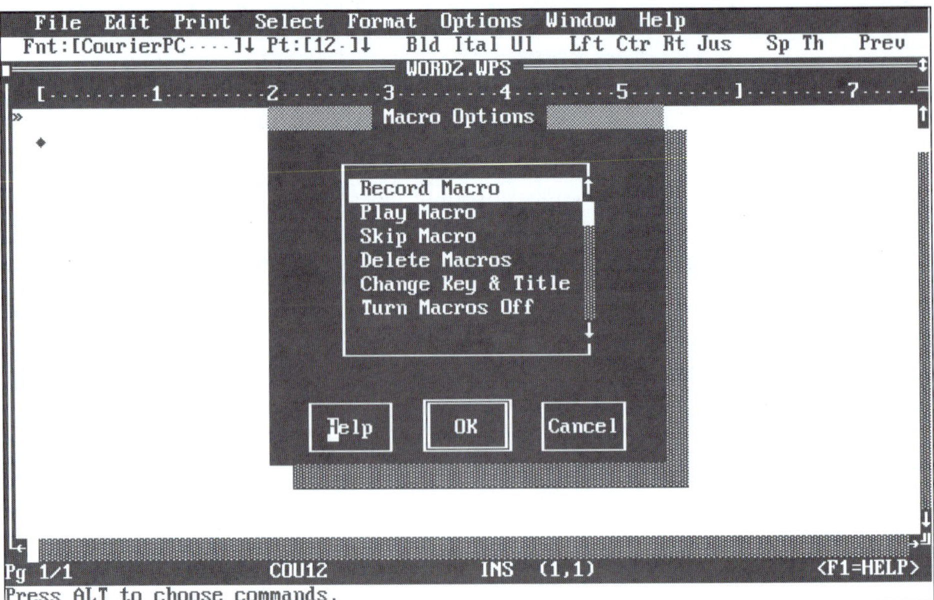

**FIGURE 21-2
RECORD MACRO
DIALOG BOX**

The Playback key is any single key or key combination that will be used to play back the recorded steps after the macro is saved. This key can be one of the function keys, such as F2, or a combination of keys, such as Ctrl/Q. For this exercise, you will use Ctrl/Q. Be careful to use keystrokes that are not used for other commands in Works, such as Ctrl/L or Ctrl/C (which move to the left and center of the line) or F3 (which starts the move function).

For this exercise you will store the keystrokes in the keys Ctrl/Q.

4. Press **Ctrl/Q** (Hold Ctrl down and then press the Q).

Works displays <ctrlq> in the **Playback** key box.

5. Press the **Tab** key to move to the **Title** box.

6. Type **Company logo** in the **Title** box.

This box is optional; however, it gives additional information about the function of macros that may be helpful later.

7. Choose **OK.**

The word RECORD appears in the lower right corner of the Works' message line. You are now ready to enter the keystrokes.

8. Enter the following actions and keystrokes.

    a. Press **Ctrl/C**
    b. choose **Font & Style** from the **Format** menu
    c. choose **Bold** & **Helvetica 14** from the **Styles**, **Fonts**, and **Sizes** list boxes

(or another font if not available)

   d.   Choose **OK**

   e.   Type **The PREMIUM ART GALLERY** and press **Enter**

   f.   Choose **Font & Style** from the **Format** menu

   g.   Turn off **Bold**, choose **Italics** and **Times Roman 10**

   h.   Choose **OK**

   i.   Press **Enter**

   j.   Type **47 North Mountain View Drive**
             LaConner, Washington 98257
             (206)555-1234 and press **Enter**

   k.   Press **Ctrl/L** to return to the left margin

   l.   Press **Enter** twice to move down in the document

   m. Turn off the italic and bold by clicking on the Toolbar or by pressing Ctrl/Spacebar.

9. Press **Alt/-** [Alt and then the minus (-) key] to end the recording.

10. Close this document space without saving it.

11. Position the **cursor** at the top of a new word processing document space.

12. Press **Ctrl/Q** (the keystroke combination holding the recorded macro).

   The logo is inserted.

Note: *When recording the macro, it is possible that an error could be made. If this happens, there are two choices. You can make the correction while the macro is being recorded. When the macro plays, it will follow the correct sequence of steps as you entered them. The playback of a macro is very fast, so it does not matter how many corrections you make during the recording process. You may also wish simply to start over. Press Alt/- to stop, and then start the process over as listed above.*

To use other macro options

Other macro options are listed on the macro menu by pressing Alt /. This dialog box was also used to reach the Record Macro option.

1. Press **Alt /** to access the menu.

The dialog box shown in Figure 21-3 appears.

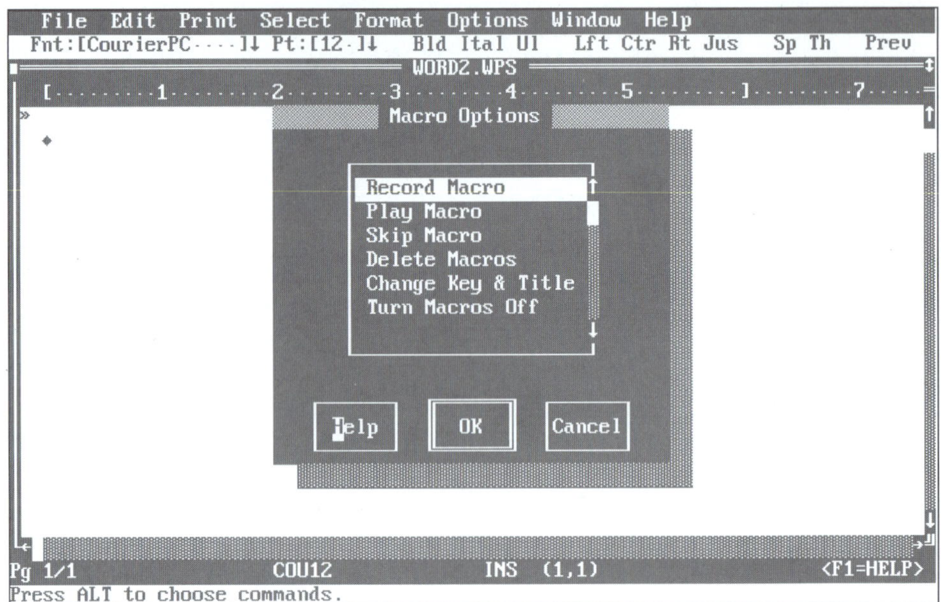

FIGURE 21-3
MACRO OPTIONS
DIALOG BOX

This dialog box may be used to begin the macro recording instead of using the playback keystrokes. The options listed here do the following:

Record Macro: Start the recording process.

Play Macro: Play a macro from a list of all stored macros.

Skip Macro: Ignore the macro keystrokes temporarily when using a standard Works' function key. For example, the F5 key is normally used as the GoTo key in Works. You could, however, assign a macro to that key. Pressing the accent grave key (`) prior to using F5 would ignore a macro stored there and the F5 key would function as normal.

Delete Macros: Show a list of all macros so that any may be removed.

Change Key & Title: Show a list of macros so that keys and titles may be changed.

Turn Macros Off: Turn all macros off temporarily so that they will not be played. This is useful when many of the keys also contain regular Works' instructions.

2. Choose **Cancel.**

FORM DOCUMENT

1. Open a new word processing document space. Press **Ctrl/Q** to insert the logo created as a macro.

2. Type the remainder of the form letter as shown in the following box. Decide on appropriate margins and font styles.

3. Insert the appropriate fields from **CH21DB1,** the customer file.

4. Retrieve the paragraphs asked for in the brackets from the instructor's data disk. They are **CH21WP2** and **CH21WP3.** These documents are shown on the following pages.

5. Save the letter as **CH21WP1.**

The PREMIUM ART GALLERY
47 North Mountain View Drive
LaConner, Washington 98257
(206)555-1234

(type current date)

<<first name>> <<last name>>
<<street address>>
<<city>>, <<state>> <<zip>>

Dear <<first>>:

This is to let you know that we will be holding a special preview of the works of artist Don Day from next Thursday through Sunday from noon to 5 p.m. [Insert paragraph on artist, Don Day from CH21WP2]

As you will probably remember, we are located at the corner of Spring and 2nd Avenue in downtown LaConner. [Insert paragraph on seasons from CH21WP3]
We look forward to seeing you soon.

Sincerely,

Sally Rutherford
Manager

6.   Merge the document with the database file, **CH21DB1.**

<u>Artists:</u>

1

Patrick graduated from the University of Washington with a degree in Fine Arts. Since his graduation 15 years ago, Patrick has been widely recognized in his field. He has done extensive work in oils and sculpture, and for several years completed large graphic designs for medical clinics around the country. His present focus is in sculpture, including woods and glass. His craftsmanship is finely tuned and varied — depicting soft shapes that hint at life, and sharp edges showing force and a driving nature. Most pieces range in size from small tabletop objects to larger cityscape and garden abstracts. Wherever they appear, they evoke a presence within nature that demands that we rethink our own perceptions of what we see.

2

Jean has been painting in watercolor medium for over thirty-five years. She is widely recognized in this country and Japan. Jean's subjects often contain various floral environments, from still life, to Northwest woods, to English and American garden surroundings. Her compositions are bold, colorful, and intricate in detail.

3

Don is truly a unique artist. His art leans toward modernist impressionism in the watercolor medium. His works are original, lively, colorful, and moving. They sweep in moods of reflection or assault the senses with vivid images and colors that evoke moods of introspection and searching. His work has often been compared to the moods and intensity of a young Van Gogh.

4

Marlene is an accomplished ceramist and potter. Her vases and bowls have been displayed at numerous art galleries throughout Washington and Alaska. Marlene is an Alaska native whose influence in pottery and ceramic design came in part from the use of color and texture in native art. Many browns, reds, and blues are brought into rough-hewn bowls often molded into the shapes of baskets, canoes, and even human shapes reflecting native culture. These are truly original, beautiful pieces.
5

Bill is an experienced oil and watercolor artist. He depicts nature in its extremes — cold, white-capped mountains; dark, moss hewn forests; and streams and ponds filled with cattails. The scenes reflect the mood - cold and majestic, dark and tropical, spacious and filled with the hope of a new season. The moods are varied showing the varied range of the artist himself. Bill's style is impressionism mixed with abstraction. The reality comes through with the viewer's own perceptions and ideas and seems to change with the next glance.

<u>Seasons</u>

Winter

Winter brings a light snowfall on LaConner and the Skagit valley. The weather, however, is still mild and the skies frequently sunny. This is a beautiful time of the year and has the added advantage of quieter street-side walks and supper meals.

Spring

The tulips and daffodils are in season. Plan to come prepared to purchase bulbs at an extremely reasonable price and to buy cut flowers at any of the many roadside stands. The valley is its most striking this time of the year, showing an array of brilliant colors covering hundreds of acres. This is a scene that should not be missed. Call ahead if you want reservations for overnight accommodations.

Summer

LaConner is warm and at its most resort-like during the summer months. Once again, it is often very crowded (especially on weekends). If you plan to stay overnight, call ahead for reservations. During this time of the year, however, the valley is beautiful, the farmlands lush, the skies sunny, and the atmosphere relaxed. It is truly a time to vacation and feel the release of the winter blahs.

Fall

The summer harvest turns to gold and the trees to rust. The air is crisp and the sky a mix of white rolling clouds and deep blue sky. There is a freshness in the air and it is time to bring out the woolen sweaters. Many shops display arrangements of dried Skagit valley wildflowers and leather goods. Sip warm coffee and watch the fishing boats go up river and head out to the San Juan Islands. It is a time to enjoy the shopping and then warm up in any one of our fine restaurants.

MAILING LABELS

1. Create a form for mailing labels for each of the customers using **CH21DB1**. Save this file as **CH21LAB**.

2. Merge and print copies of the labels showing three across a page.

SPREADSHEET

1. Create the spreadsheet in the following box. Enter the values as whole numbers. Do not worry about centering the heading exactly as shown.

PREMIUM ART GALLERY
STATEMENT OF SALES
SIX MONTH PERIOD
ENDING JUNE 1992

	January	February	March	April	May	June
Randle	1300	1200	1560	1240	3579	1450
Hiebert	1200	570	900	1540	1980	2470
Day	270	240	580	970	520	480
Beebe	980	800	1700	1200	1340	2100
Winkles	740	1430	1970	540	2200	1950

2. Total the sales for each month.

3. Create a Total column next to June and total the sales for each artist.

4. Create an Average column to the right of the Total column and average the monthly sales for each artist.

5. Average the sales for each month at the bottom of the worksheet below the monthly totals.

6. In an appropriate cell, compute the grand total of all sales. Give this total an appropriate label, as well.

7. Format all sales amounts in currency format with two places to the right of the decimal point. Format the column labels as right justified. Adjust column width as necessary. Save the spreadsheet as **CH21SS1**.

8. Create a bar graph showing the total sales for each artist per month. Add the total amount to the worksheet. Create appropriate labels and headings for the graph and print a copy. Name the chart **CH21BAR1**.

9. Create a line graph that compares the average sales for each artist. Create appropriate labels and print a copy. Save as **CH21LINE1**.

10. Save the spreadsheet again.

INTEGRATION

1. Create a word processing document that will explain to all members of the staff the contents of the spreadsheet document **CH21SS1**. Make the document in memo format as follows. Save the document as **CH21WP4**.

	MEMO
TO:	All employees
FROM:	Sally Rutherford
SUBJECT:	Sales Report

2. Copy the spreadsheet into the word processor memo. Copy half of the spreadsheet at a time. Take all rows through April first, then the rows for May through Average (in the rightmost column). Insert the second half below the first half in the word processing document.

3. Insert the chart **CH21LINE1** so that it is shown below the spreadsheet in the word processing document. To do this, use the **Insert Chart** command from the **Edit** menu. Choose the spreadsheet name and then the name of the chart. A line will appear in the position of the chart that reads

    Chart CH21SS1.WKS:CH21LINE1

    This is the position where the chart will print. Use **Print Preview** to view the document.

4. Adjust margins and tabs as necessary. Save the document again and print a copy.

INTEGRATED PROJECT 2
The Premium Art Gallery
Part 2

1. Create the following spreadsheet showing purchases made by various customers

The Premium Art Gallery
Customer Purchases
by Artist
July through December

	Randle	Hiebert	Day	Track	Winkles
Rinehard	1240.23	45.89			
Beach			488.24	89.12	
Ignacio				872.54	
Hyland					1233.00
Kohler			432.32	12.50	1200.00
Ladd	1580.00				
Levitz	589.00	800.12			
Goodwin		1200.24	3424.00		
Gordon	340.32				540.80
Cawthorne		345.98			
Rudine			589.20		490.12

2. Sum the totals for each of the customers in the column to the right of Winkles. Create an appropriate heading.

3. Write a formula to insert the highest sale for each artist at the bottom of the worksheet and create an appropriate label for this amount. (Hint: use =Max.)

4. Write a formula to insert the minimum purchase made and insert this amount in the row below the highest sales. Create an appropriate label.

5. Save the worksheet as **CH21SS1B** and print a copy.

6. Create a bar graph comparing the total purchases for each customer. Name the graph **CH21BAR1B**.

7. Calculate the grand total of all purchases. Calculate the percentage of the grand total for each customer's purchases (customer total divided by grand total) and insert this amount to the right of the total column (the rightmost column on the spreadsheet). Make the grand total cell address absolute in the formula. Format two places to the right of the decimal.

8. Create a pie chart showing the Percentage of Total values for each customer. Print a copy of the pie chart with necessary labels. Name the graph **CH21PIE1B**.

9. Format the spreadsheet and save it again.

DATABASE

1. Create a database file showing the purchases made in the spreadsheet. The file should include a field for the Customer ID and the Artist's ID as well as numerical fields for net amount, tax, and total amount as follows:

Customer ID

Artist's ID

Net Amount:

Tax: (Net Amount * 0.08)

Total Amount: (Net Amount + Tax)

Note: *The customer IDs are numbers 1123 through 1133, beginning with Rinehard, Beach, and so on. The artist IDs are Randle (1), Hiebert (2), Day (3), Track (4), and Winkles (5).*

2. Fill in the data values from the spreadsheet. Save this file as **CH21DB1B**.

3. Query the file for all sales by artist number 1 and print a copy of the results.

4. Create a report showing total sales by artist and the customer ID. The report should show totals where appropriate. Include the artist ID, net, tax, and total amounts. Include modified headings and a report main heading. Name the report **CH21DBR1B**.

5. Query the files to locate total sales made during this period that were greater than $500.00. Organize the file so that all amounts greater than $500.00 are shown in descending order, and print a copy.

WORD PROCESSING

1. Create the following document using font and point sizes as similar to those shown as possible. Press Ctrl/Q to execute the logo macro. Use the **Border** command for the borders surrounding the page.

2. Save the document as **CH21WP1B.**

The PREMIUM ART GALLERY
47 North Mountain View Drive
LaConner, Washington 98257
(206)555-1234

NOW SHOWING

Artist: Patrick Randle

Featuring:

Northwest sculpture, stained glass, and fine wood carvings

through March 30

Next artist:

Jean Hiebert

April 1 through June 30

9 - 5 daily

INTEGRATED PROJECT 3
Northwest Fund Raisers

OBJECTIVES

- Create database files.
- Query database files.
- Create a spreadsheet.
- Create newsletters.
- Copy from one tool to another.
- Create charts.

PREVIEW

This project includes setting up several documents, database files, and spreadsheets for a local fund-raising organization, Northwest Fund Raisers. NFR is a general-purpose fund-raising organization that raises thousands each year for local charities, including the children's hospital, the symphony, the city theater group, and others. Its primary purpose is to reach as many target population groups as possible for donations, as well as to keep in touch with current donors about NFR success stories so that they will continue to donate to the organization.

DATABASE

Your first task for this company will be to set up the database files. They are shown as follows. You should decide on the appropriate field length and name. The address, city, state, and zip fields should remain consistent from file to file. When creating this database, use separate fields for the first and last names. These files are also on the data disk. They are CH21DB1C, CH21DB2C, and CH21DB3C.

The status field will have responses of Y or N for current or not current. The members who are not current are kept on the mailing list for a period of one year before being deleted.

The Members file contains all persons who contribute a set amount either monthly or yearly. The Donors file contains names of persons who have contributed single sums from solicitations in the mail or directly as tax deductions. The Donation file contains the amounts donated during a period of time. Members may or may not be donors. The donations file identifies all donors and members and the date of the contribution. When a donor is not a member, a new donor number is assigned.

438

Database File 1, CH21DB1C

MEMBERS

memid	name	address	city	state	zip	status
29847	Leo Castillo	808 E. Elm	Seattle	WA	98123	Y
10985	K. R. Bender	703 Bellevue E.	Bellevue	WA	98004	Y
00287	E. B. Bell	25 W. Highland S.	Seattle	WA	98102	Y
23771	Kathy Agar	7053 32nd N.E.	Seattle	WA	98102	N
00785	R. Aiken	500 Wall Street	Seattle	WA	98101	Y
20127	John Higley	8300 Earl N.W.	Seattle	WA	98145	N
24758	Ken Higgins	2132 S.W. Mercer	Seattle	WA	98107	Y
19275	Y. Kwon	326 N. W. 32nd	Lynnwood	WA	98036	Y
12377	M. Williams	6306 Greenwood	Seattle	WA	98135	Y
12388	Gene McNeal	8307 39th S.	Seattle	WA	98102	Y
15849	Andy Phillips	12209 Marine Dr. W	Seattle	WA	98110	N
00589	Sharon Pettit	3832 22nd E.	Bellevue	WA	98005	Y
12340	Elaine Seaton	1601 8th N.E.	Bellevue	WA	98004	Y
18323	B. Heather	98477 112th S.W.	Kent	WA	98031	Y
28755	J. Shelley	611 S.W. 140th	Auburn	WA	98003	Y
19855	Bea Conners	4031 48th N.E.	Edmonds	WA	98020	N
23006	David Collwell	1541 S. Mt. Drive	Issaquah	WA	98027	Y
24112	A. Gladwell	731 N. 75th	Issaquah	WA	98027	Y
26002	P. Axtell	3608 S. 5th	Kirkland	WA	98032	Y
00623	S. Lehwalder	602 N. Bell	Lynnwood	WA	98037	N

Database File 2, CH21DB2C

DONORS

memid	donid	name	address	city	state	zip
00785		R. Aiken	500 Wall Street	Seattle	WA	98101
15849		Andy Phillips	12209 Marine Dr. W.	Seattle	WA	98110
12340		Elaine Seaton	1601 8th N.E.	Bellevue	WA	98004
	178	J. Ing	2004 Alki Way	Seattle	WA	98022
	179	May Keith	4504 N.E. 70th	Lynnwood	WA	98037
	180	F. Ebsworth	323 N. Olympic	Bothell	WA	98011
24758		Ken Higgins	2132 S.W. Mercer	Seattle	WA	98107
	181	Rhonda Leigh	47 6th South	Tukwila	WA	98102
	182	D. Macintyre	3911 Terrace Dr.	Edmonds	WA	98020
19855		Bea Conners	4031 48th N.E.	Edmonds	WA	98020

Database File 3, CH21DB3C

DONATIONS

memid	donid	amount	date	cause
00785		500.00	09/12/91	PG
15849		50.00	09/12/91	CT
12340		200.00	09/13/91	CH
	178	400.00	09/14/91	CH
	179	1500.00	09/14/91	CT
	180	250.00	09/15/91	FG
24758		150.00	09/15/91	FG
	181	2000.00	10/1/91	CH
	182	2500.00	10/1/91	PG
19855		250.00	10/2/91	SO

In the **cause** category, the abbreviations stand for the following organizations:

PG	Policeman's Guild
CT	City Theater
CH	Children's Hospital
FG	Fireman's Guild
SO	Symphony Orchestra

1. Use the plain text format to enter the information about the organizations into a record in Form view.

THE SPREADSHEET AND GRAPHS

Northwest Fund Raisers would like to see the results of recent donations. They are about to hold a fund-raising drive and would like to ask members and donors who have contributed in the past to contribute again during this fund-raising drive.

1. The manager, Ralph Hornsby, has asked to see a spreadsheet containing the following information. Obtain this information from the database files for this project.

   a. A list of all member names.

   Note: This may be copied from the database file to the spreadsheet file. Copy first and last names. Show the last name in column A, the first in column B.

   b. The amount of the donation
   c. A cell showing the highest donation received
   d. A cell showing the average of all donations combined

    e.   A cell showing the total of all donations

    f.   A column showing the percentage that each donation is of the total amount

    g.   Format as currency (two places) and percent (three places)

2.   Mr. Hornsby would then like to see a pie chart showing the results of step f. Save as **CH21PIE1C**. Save the spreadsheet as **CH21SS1C**.

3.   He would also like a comparison of all donations shown in a bar chart. Use data labels and appropriate titles. Save as **CH21BAR1C**.

NOTE: You should include appropriate headings and labels for all charts and the spreadsheet and print copies of each. Remember, the percentage for each donor is computed by dividing the total percentage into each individual donor amount. Create a separate column for the individual percentages.

WORD PROCESSING

As mentioned earlier, a fund-raising campaign is about to begin. On the next few pages, you will be creating various word processing documents in connection with the campaign. Save the file as **CH21WP1C**.

1.   You are to design an eye-catching flyer to be mailed to all members, donors, and the general public that contains the following information. It should be designed so that all information fits on one 8 1/2- by 11-inch sheet of paper so that it attracts attention and shows off key phrases. Use your imagination in deciding font and point sizes, character formatting, and paragraph formatting. Use borders.

heading: THANKS TO YOU

brief paragraph:

Donors from our last campaign helped to assist our local organizations to:

Supply additional emergency care equipment at the Children's
    Hospital
Buy a new computer for the City Theater
Increase the resources for anti-drug programs through the
    Policeman's Guild
Buy emergency supplies for the Fireman's Guild
Add new furniture and props to the Symphony Orchestra's
    inventory

THANKS TO YOU

These organizations can continue to operate as a service and as an asset to the community.

PLEASE CONTINUE YOUR GENEROSITY!

It is time once again to let your favorite organization know that your support is on-going and that you realize the need for continuing support.
Check whichever box is most appropriate at this time and mail your check today.

_____ $ 50.00
_____   100.00
_____   150.00
Other: _____ amount:_______

I am:

a new contributor: _______
a continuing member: _______   member id: ___
a regular contributor: _______   contributor id: ___
interested in becoming a member:_____
membership dues enclosed: _____ ($50.00)
send more information: _____

Name and address: For office use only:

____
___________________________   new member id:______
___________________________   donor id:______

Daytime phone: _________________

2. Print a list of mailing labels to all donors and members from the database files. Query the file containing both member and donor names for the donor names only. This will avoid duplication of members who are both donors and members. Save the label form as **CH21LB1C.**

3. Create and save the following logo for Northwest Fund Raisers as a macro. Make it as close to the example as possible.

NORTHWEST FUND RAISERS
a nonprofit organization
1245 North Mt. View Rd.
Mercer Island, WA 98042
(206) 555-1238

4. Create the following form letter, which is also a part of the fund-raising efforts, to be sent to all members. Insert fields from the database file, **CH21DB1C.** Save the form letter as **CH21WP2C.**

(date)

(first) (last)
(address)
(city), (state) (zip)

Dear Member:

    Northwest Fund Raisers would like to take this opportunity to thank you for your generous support during the past year. Your donation has been a significant amount of all funds raised to assist our local public organizations to continue their efforts to both entertain and serve the public. Whatever cause you support, it is a contribution to the well-being of a community—your community, and that is one of the best things you can do to improve the quality of life in your city.

    Writing letters requesting additional generosity on your part is always a difficult thing to do. But once again, it is time to solicit funds for the requirements of the coming year. As a past donor, you already know how necessary community assistance is to public organizations. You also know that without this assistance, many wonderful services and great entertainment and talent would be missed.

    Thank you for your continuing support. A form and a copy of our latest newsletter are enclosed for your convenience.

Sincerely,

(your name)
Northwest Executive Assistant
Encl.

---

5. Insert the logo at the top of the letter using the macro.

6. Merge the letter with the member database, **CH21DB1C**.

7. Create the following newsletter to be enclosed with the fundraising letter just created. The newsletter should be designed as closely as possible to the one that follows and should fit on one 8 1/2- by 11-inch sheet of paper. Create the newsletter in a single column instead of two.

    Insert the logo macro at the top of the newsletter. Save the newsletter as **CH21WP3C**.

NORTHWEST FUND RAISERS
a nonprofit organization
1245 North Mt. View Rd.
Mercer Island, WA 98042
(206) 555-1238

Volume 3, No. 2   April 1993
**Fund-raising Campaign in
Full Swing**

This year's fund-raising campaign is expected to be the most successful to date. Over $200,000 has been raised through the second week of the campaign. The target for the end of the month is $300,000. It is expected that this amount will be exceeded due to the generous donations given by new and continuing donors and members.

This year's contributions will assist the same organizations as last year. They include:

The Children's Hospital
The Symphony Orchestra
The City Theater
The Policeman's Guild
The Fireman's Guild

Through last year's efforts many new programs and equipment were acquired by the organizations. The contributors greatly assisted in maintaining the continued services and pleasures these organizations bring to the community.

SEND IN CONTRIBUTIONS THIS MONTH!

OPEN HOUSE ON MAY 1st!!

We're Moving!!

The Northwest Fund-Raisers are moving to new quarters. We have managed to increase the size of our volunteer staff by five this year. With the addition of the volunteers, we have the need for a space with more elbow room. Our new address is:

2400 North Plaza, Suite 103
Seattle, WA 98101

The telephone number will remain the same. Please feel free to drop by any time to visit, see the new facilities, or talk about projects and the needs of the organizations we support.

Change of Address? Let Us Know!

Cut out and return the form below:
____

name_______________________________________
new address_________________________________
city_________________state____zip____________
new phone________________
member or donor id __________

____

Thanks for helping!!

FINAL REQUESTS

1. Print a list of all members from **CH21DB1C**. Include the Member ID, name, and city only.

2. Query the database files for all donors or members who live outside Seattle. Print a copy of their names and addresses sorted by city in descending order. Save as **CH21DB4C**.

3. Query the database files for all donors who contributed $500.00 or more to the Children's Hospital. They will be given a complimentary lifetime membership with Northwest Fund Raisers. Perform a combined query in the Amount field. The format is equal to or greater than 500 AND cause equals CH.

INTEGRATED PROJECT 4
King County Environmental Support Group

OBJECTIVES

- Create databases and a report.

- Query a database.

- Create a spreadsheet containing @IF functions.

- Create other functions in a spreadsheet.

- Create a multipage word processing document with footnotes.

- Create charts.

- Copy information between the Works tools.

PREVIEW

The King County Environmental Support Group is made up of all concerned citizens who wish to join in the support and preservation of greenbelts and public park systems. It meets regularly to discuss and review possible developments that may be planned that would infringe upon the greenbelts. It also looks for public support to improve park maintenance, and it draws attention to the beauty and necessity of the greenbelts within a large metropolitan area.

This organization is in the process of computerizing its paperwork. They need several reports entered, a database created, form letters written, spreadsheets developed for analyzing population growth, and numerous other projects. You have been hired to initiate some of these projects.

WORD PROCESSING

Your first word processing document will be the following manuscript and footnotes.

1. Double space the report.

2. Use appropriate top, bottom, and side margins (2-inch top and 1-inch margins on all other sides).

3. Enter footnotes as shown using the **Footnote** command.

ENVIRONMENTAL UPDATE

Introduction

This is a report on the current status of several greenbelts within greater King County. As many of you are aware, the King County Environmental Support Group has been concerned with the well-being and preservation of our county's greenbelts for the past seven years. KCESG was formed by Bill Marks, a concerned citizen, then living next to a greenbelt on Capital Hill. That particular greenbelt was unfortunately lost to development, but it motivated Mr. Marks to become involved and to involve other citizens in preventing unnecessary destruction of greenbelts within a metropolitan area. His efforts in protecting areas within a metropolitan area were so successful, and the community support so strong, that KCESG expanded its efforts to include all areas of King County.1

Involvement

With the population growth on a rapid incline over the past several years, and with the population growth predicted to double in the next decade, many citizens have become increasingly aware of the need to protect and preserve natural wildlife habitats as well as natural greenbelts and city parks. Public awareness has increased and the support of the activities of KCESG is now strong.2

KCESG has been responsible for the preservation of the following greenbelts since its establishment in 1984:

The Lakefront Legacy
The Marshall Legacy
Madison and Leschi Parks
Magnolia Drive
Mt. St. Helens Park
The Seattle Hill Park

In addition, KCESG has helped to keep wildlife preserves intact, including those located in West Seattle, on Harbor Island, Lake Washington Blvd., and in Steward Park.3

Yet, there have been failures, too. The fight was lost last fall to save the preserve in east King County along the Snohomish slough. While a small section of the Snohomish preserve was saved, biologists have already noticed a decrease in the numbers of deer and eagles, as well as other fowl and ground animals in the area. A large riverfront park and condominium complex is under development there and much of the preserve has been lost.[4]

Membership and Support

The membership began with a few concerned citizens and has grown to include a coalition of citizens as well as politicians supporting actions in legislature. Because of this expanded support, KCESG has a good success record. KCESG, however, would like to have an excellent success record. It plans to show a 100 percent success in the next annual report.[5]

To improve the success rate in supporting the preservation of parks and greenbelts, KCESG realizes that it needs additional public support and support in the legislature. It is now in the process of a large mail promotional campaign in which it will discuss its successes and failures openly and encourage local citizens to attend support meetings in their neighborhoods and to contribute financial support if possible. With an additional community support growth of 10 percent, KCESG feels it can accomplish its goal of 100 percent success in all upcoming issues in the next year.

Summary and Focus

KCESG has continued to win its campaigns against over development. It is also a realistic group of persons who recognize that the problems will only become more serious and the struggle to protect greenbelts and parks more difficult as the fight over remaining land within the city and county becomes tougher.[6]

Continued efforts in soliciting funds and assistance from concerned citizens will remain a primary focus of the group. In addition, it will be necessary to increase the staff size at headquarters in Seattle, computerize the mailing lists and files, and essentially create an efficient operation that functions to reach the greatest segment of the population.

[1]Jordon, Charles, <u>Seattle Journal of Environmental Affairs</u>, June 1988, p. 92.

[2]Anderson, Nancy, <u>KCESG Monthly Magazine</u>, Vol. 7, No. 2, March 1990, p. 34.

[3]<u>The Seattle Reporter</u>, Vol. 26, No. 1, January 1991.

[4]Edison, Judith, "Gains and Losses," <u>The Environment Today</u>, May 1990, p. 180.

[5]Parks, Mark, <u>KCESG Quarterly Report</u>, Vol. 8, No. 2, March 1991, p. 52.

[6]"An Editorial on Public Concerns," <u>Seattle Journal of Environmental Affairs</u>, April 1990, p. 142.

INTEGRATED
PRACTICE

448

4. When finished, save the document as **CH21WP1D**. Be sure that the manuscript (not the footnotes) is double spaced.

5. Run a spell check on the manuscript. Check all hyphenation. Apply hyphenation at any point in the manuscript where there is a greater than six-space difference between the longest and shortest line on the right margin.

6. Underline all subheadings. Center the main heading and set in bold.

7. Create a header for the document to appear on all pages with the exception of the first. It should read as follows:

<u>King County Environmental Support Group</u>   <u>2</u>

Note: *Use a header paragraph for the header format shown. Use the **Insert Special** command to add the Page Number on the right margin.*

8. Print a copy of the document.

9. Create an appropriate cover for the report. Save as **CH21WP1D.COV.**

DATABASE

KCESG needs many database files created. Its first priority, however, is a set of related database files to keep track of the number of published articles, authors who write articles for KCESG, dates of published articles, and a listing of specialties and the active status of KCESG on particular topics.

You are to create the following database files. Use one field for the full name.

Database File 1, CH21DB1D.

AUTHORS						
Author ID	fname	address	city	state	zip	spec
101	J. Perkins	1200 N. Elm St.	Redmond	WA	98052	P
102	A. Sanders	1812 43rd Ave. E	Seattle	WA	98118	W
103	B. Barnes	12145 N. 42nd St.	Seattle	WA	98132	B
104	R. Rooks	985 4th Ave. N.E.	Kirkland	WA	98032	PR
105	M. Gregory	45785 N.E. Mt. Rd.	Issaquah	WA	98027	F

The last column contains abbreviations on each author's area of specialty. Use a note field to identify these. The abbreviations are:

P	Parks and Greenbelts
W	Wilderness
B	Biology
PR	Preserves
F	Forests

Database File 2, CH21DB2D

PUBLISH

Author ID	Publisher ID	Publication Date
105	22345	1/15/91
102	24689	1/01/91
103	1785A	2/15/91
104	85784	3/01/91
102	34785	3/15/91
101	24689	4/15/91
105	1785A	6/24/91
103	34785	7/01/91
101	85784	7/01/91
102	87578	8/01/91
102	22345	9/15/91
101	22345	10/15/91
103	1785A	11/20/91
105	34785	12/30/91

In this table, the following abbreviations apply:

22345	Seattle Journal of Environmental Affairs
1785A	KCESG Quarterly Report
34785	KCESG Monthly Magazine
87578	The Seattle Reporter
85784	The Environment Today
24689	A Biological Balance

Database File 3, CH21DB3D

This file should contain separate fields for each of the specialist categories, P, W, F, and so on. Descriptions for each of these is given following database document 1. As each of the specialties applies, respond with Y or N in the field.

PUBS

PID	spec	dead-line	circ	address	locale
1785A	P	30	PN	1234 Lake Drive	Seattle, WA 98144
22345	W, F	30	PN	14577 1st South	Seattle, WA 98101
34785	P, W	15	PN	1234 Lake Drive	Seattle, WA 98144
87578	P, PR	15	PN	407 Westlake Drive	Seattle, WA 98107
85784	B, W	30	N	14 & Broadway	New York, NY 10001
24689	B, F	30	N	Oceanview Road	Los Angeles, CA 90301

The deadline for articles submitted for publication in this file is the 15th or 30th of the month. The circulation is either the Pacific Northwest (PN) or national (N).

KCESG would like you to provide them with the following information from the three databases.

1. Print results of each action and include appropriate information with the output.

   a. Sort on author ID for any file containing this field.
   b. Locate all publications outside Seattle (use not equal to) from **CH21DB3D**.
   c. Locate the number of articles published by a KCESG publication (PID 1785A and 34785) from **CH21DB2D**.
   d. The publications that publish outside the Pacific Northwest. Circulation equal to N from **CH21DB3D**.

2. Create and print a report using **CH21DB1D** to include the following information:

   a. Specialties listed in ascending order
   b. Publication ID numbers
   c. Author ID number
   d. Author name
   e. Author city
   f. Deadline
   g. Circulation

3. Give the report an appropriate heading. Group by specialty and save as **CH21REPD**.

SPREADSHEET

1. Create the following spreadsheet. Save as **CH21SS1D**. Center the column headings and the main heading. Do not worry about the alignment of other values.

<table>
<tr><td colspan="9" align="center">AUTHOR PUBLICATION RECORD
January 1991 through December 1991</td></tr>
<tr><td>Author
Name</td><td colspan="4" align="center">Publication Dates</td><td>Amount
Earned (each)</td><td>Times
Published</td><td>Total
Earned</td></tr>
<tr><td>Perkins</td><td>4/15</td><td>7/01</td><td>10/15</td><td></td><td>$450.75</td><td>3</td><td></td></tr>
<tr><td>Sanders</td><td>1/01</td><td>3/15</td><td>8/01</td><td>9/15</td><td>$580.12</td><td>4</td><td></td></tr>
<tr><td>Barnes</td><td>2/15</td><td>7/01</td><td>11/20</td><td></td><td>$425.50</td><td>3</td><td></td></tr>
<tr><td>Rooks</td><td>3/01</td><td></td><td></td><td></td><td>$430.00</td><td>1</td><td></td></tr>
<tr><td>Gregory</td><td>1/15</td><td>6/24</td><td>12/30</td><td></td><td>$612.40</td><td>3</td><td></td></tr>
</table>

2.   Compute the Total Earned. Be sure that all dollar amounts are formatted as currency values.

3.   Add a column on the right that uses an IF-THEN-ELSE formula to compute bonus points earned. This formula should read that if the Times Published is equal to or greater than 3, then insert 2 bonus points, else insert 0 bonus points earned. Create an appropriate column heading.

4.   Compute all totals for Amount Earned, Total Earned, and bonus points.

5.   Format appropriately.

GRAPHICS

Print copies of each graph.

1.   Create a bar chart comparing the amount earned by each author. Be sure to include appropriate headings and labels. Save as **CH21BAR1D.**

2.   Create a line chart comparing the Amount Earned by each of the authors. Include appropriate labels. Save as **CH21LINE1D.**

3.   Create a pie chart showing the breakdown of the times published as a percentage of the whole (the total times published by all authors). Again, use appropriate labels. Save as **CH21PIE1D.**

FINAL REQUESTS

This exercise combines the spreadsheet and word processing documents.

1.   Add the following paragraph to your word processing document, **CH21WP1D**, prior to the summary paragraph.

<u>Statistics:</u>
Following is a spreadsheet and several graphic representations of articles published this year in local and national publications to draw attention to our cause (the graphics are attached.) A group of local writers, working with KCESG but writing articles for other publishers as well, has done an excellent job in keeping the public informed of the efforts of KCESG as well as other pertinent issues concerning the environment both locally and nationally.

2.   Insert the spreadsheet after the paragraph. Adjust the tab positions. Underlin the last figure in the third, fourth, and fifth columns prior to the totals.

INTEGRATED PROJECT 5
Hobby Shop

OBJECTIVES

- Create, save, and use styles.

- Assign various point and font sizes within styles.

- Create database files and reports.

- Predict future trends on a worksheet.

- Index multiple fields or columns of a database file.

- Perform queries.

PREVIEW

This project concerns the activities of a local hobby shop. The hobby shop is a small single-owner operation. The owner, Patrick MacRannall, would like you to set up a database, make predictions about future growth using a spreadsheet program, and create a flier to be sent to neighborhood residents.

DATABASE

1.   Create the following database files on inventory and sales. Decide on appropriate field and file names.

Database File 1, CH21DB1E

INVENTORY

No.	Description	Price	Quantity on Hand
201	R/C Airplanes	12.00	12
202	R/C Transmitters	8.00	8
301	Ship Model	59.00	10
302	Ship Model	69.00	
303	Ship Model	79.00	8
304	Ship Model	89.00	6
401	Brass Engine	200.00	7
501	Kite	5.00	30
502	Kite	15.00	15
503	Kite	20.00	20
601	Scale Rocket	8.00	12
701	R/C Car	120.00	3
801	Steam Engine	49.00	1
901	Dollhouse	99.50	3
902	Miniature Furniture	6.50	23
1001	Dremel Tools	89.00	3
1002	Dremel Saws	110.00	1
2001	Spray Paint	1.99	134
3001	Balsa Wood	.49	2
4001	Model Magazines	1.50	40
5001	Paintbrushes	1.39	73
		1043.37	*418

2.   Switch to List view. Adjust field width, edit, and print a copy.

3.   Print the results of each of the following actions.

   a.   The cost of the total inventory on hand (create a total field). Multiply the Price times the Quantity. Print a list of the revised database.
   b.   A count of the total number of items in each category (such as all items in the 100 category, all in the 200 category, and so on).

4.   Create a report that shows items grouped by category (all 100s together, all 200s, and so on — sort first). Save the report as **CH21REP1E**.

5.   Query the database for the following information.

    a.   Any inventory items that show three or fewer items remaining in stock.
    b.   Any inventory items that show a cost of greater than $40.00 but less than $100.00 for each item.

6.   Sort on the Description field in ascending order. Answer the following questions.

    a.   How many descriptions begin with R/C for remote control? (Hint: Use the wildcard formula, ="R/C *".)
    b.   How many brass engines are on hand?
    c.   Search for the total number of remote control airplanes on hand.
    d.   Search for the remote control transmitters if they are fewer than 12 in quantity.

SPREADSHEET

1.   Create the following spreadsheet as shown. Save as **CH21SS1E.**

THE HOBBY SHOP
Sales Report

Description	Sold This Month	Price Each	Total Sales This Month	Sold Last Month	Total Sales Last Month	Percentage of Increase/Decrease This Month
201 R/C Airplanes	4	$12.00		3		
202 R/C Transmitters	2	$8.00		1		
301 Ship Model	1	$59.00		2		
302 Ship Model	1	$69.00		1		
303 Ship Model	0	$79.00		1		
304 Ship Model	1	$89.00		1		
401 Brass Engine	1	$200.00		0		
501 Kite	8	$5.00		4		
502 Kite	6	$15.00		4		
503 Kite	3	$20.00		2		
601 Scale Rocket	10	$8.00		12		
701 R/C Car	1	$120.00		0		
801 Steam Engine	2	$49.00		3		
901 Doll House	0	$99.50		1		
902 Miniature Furniture	24	$6.50		30		
1001 Dremel Tools	1	$89.00		1		
1002 Dremel Saws	0	$110.00		1		
2001 Spray Paint	52	$1.99		47		
3001 Balsa Wood	74	$0.49		92		
4001 Model Magazines	30	$1.50		25		
5001 Paint Brushes	43	$1.39		20		

Total Sold This Month
Total Sold Last Month
Total Sales This Month
Total Sales Last Month
Projected .05 Increase
Projected .10 Increase

2.   Compute the Total Sales for this month and last month.

3.   Create the labels shown at the bottom of the worksheet, and compute each of the values.

4.   Compute a 5 percent increase in sales over this month. Compute a 10 percent increase (Total Sales * 1.05 and 1.10).

5.   Compute the percent of increase or decrease in sales from this month to last next month. Divide the Total Cost for last month by the total for this month. Format as percent (three places). Delete any ERR or 0.00 messages in the cells. This is due to no sale of some items.

6.   Print a copy of the worksheet using horizontal format (if possible) or print on two pages.

WORD PROCESSING

1.   Create the following flier to be sent to residents in the neighborhood. Use the same or similar fonts and point sizes. Since this format will be used for future fliers, the owner would like you to save them in styles to be retrieved quickly as needed. Save each of the unique paragraph and character formats shown as a style, including:

   a.   The logo (this one is 12-point Times; use London or any other you have — experiment).
   b.   Save the trains as a glossary entry or use a style. These images were achieved using 12-point Cairo. Use any characters or symbols to come up with an attractive design. Save the format as a style.
   c.   The list of items is done in 12-point Helvetica, bold, italics. Save this format as a style.
   d.   The remainder of the text is shown in 10- and 12-point Helvetica. Use it or another font and save each as a style.
   e.   The images at the bottom of the flier are combinations of 10-point upper- and lowercase Cairo and Mobile fonts. Again, use graphic images, other fonts, or simply keyboard symbols to substitute. Save the format as a style.

MACRANNALL'S HOBBIES
1807 North Shore Drive
Edmonds, WA 98020
(206) 555-1988

ΔΔΔΔΔΔΔΔΔΔΔΔΔΔΔΔΔΔΔΔΔΔΔΔΔΔΔΔΔΔΔΔΔΔΔΔΔΔΔΔΔΔΔΔΔΔΔΔΔΔΔΔΔΔΔΔΔΔΔΔΔΔ

TRAINS
PLANES
REMOTE CONTROL
KITES
DOLLHOUSES
MODELS
COLLECTOR'S ITEMS
KID'S TOYS

Come to MacRannall's Hobbies. Located on North Shore Drive. Enjoy a view of Puget Sound while you view a magnificent collection of antique and new toys and models.

SALE

Begins Tomorrow Ends on the 1st!

Every item in stock 10 to 15 percent off.

VISIT US TODAY!!

MacRannall's Hobbies
A hobby store for letting your imagination run free!

§§

2. Add a border to the flier. This one is a double-line border. Use it or a single-line border if available. If lines and/or borders are not available, use an underscore at the top and bottom of the flier.

3. Save the flier as **CH21WP1E**.

INTEGRATED PROJECT 6
Perennial Plant Shop and Information Center

OBJECTIVES

- Create a multipage document.

- Create headers.

- Create an income statement.

- Create charts.

- Create and query database files.

PREVIEW

This company is both a plant shop and a horticulture information center. It sells a variety of perennial plants and provides information on plant care to the public. It also regularly holds plant workshops.

The manager of the company, Margaret Shepard, would like you to set up a few database files concerned primarily with organizing data on plant names, zones in which they may be grown, and zones within Pacific Northwest states. She would also like the income statements set up on a spreadsheet program and the information from them graphically represented for an upcoming presentation to the company owners.

In addition, the shop has been sending out a monthly newsletter. They would like the newsletter set up so that the main heading and general format may be used for each of the newsletters going out every month.

SPREADSHEET

1. Create the partial worksheet shown in the following box. Center all column headings, center the main heading, left align the main side headings, and indent the side headings under a main topic two spaces to the right. Decide on appropriate column widths and placement.

Perennial Plant Shop & Information Center
Income Statement
1st Quarter 1991

	Jan	Feb	Mar	April
SALES	7527.00	8237.00	8528.00	9432.00
COST OF GOODS	1340.00	1492.00	1780.00	2142.00
NET SALES				
EXPENSES				
Equipment	540.00	130.00	170.00	142.00
Supplies	1230.00	1421.00	2100.00	2500.00
Payroll	2400.00	2400.00	2400.00	2400.00
Miscellaneous	400.00	420.00	400.00	430.00
TOTAL EXPENSES				
NET INCOME				
PERCENTAGE OF				
NET INCOME TO				
GROSS SALES				

2. Compute the **Net Sales** (**Sales** less **Cost of Goods**). Compute the **Total Expenses** and the **Net Income** (**Net Sales** less **Total Expenses**).

3. Compute the **Percentage of Net Income to Sales** (**Sales** into **Net Income**) for each of the months.

4. Format all dollar values as currency and all percentages two places to the right of the decimal. Adjust the column width as necessary.

5. Print a copy of the spreadsheet. Print another copy showing the formulas (choose **Show Formulas** from the **Options** menu). Save it as **CH21SS1F.**

GRAPHICS

With each of the charts, show appropriate main headings, labels, and other information to clearly demonstrate the meaning of each chart. Print copies of each chart.

1. Create a bar chart showing a comparison of all expenses for each month. Include X- and Y-axis labels and appropriate titles. Rename as **CH21BAR1F.**

2. Create a bar chart showing a comparison of the **Sales** for each month. Rename as **CH21BAR2F.**

3. Create a line chart showing the increase or decrease in **Net Sales** over all months. Rename as **CH21LINE1F.**

4. Create a bar chart showing the percent of net income to Sales. Save as **CH21BAR3F.**

5. Create a pie chart showing the percent of net income to gross sales. Save as **CH21PIE1F.** Why doesn't this pie chart work as well as the bar chart?

DATABASE

1. Create each of the following database documents. Use appropriate database names, field names, and data variables to closely represent the information given.

2. Create a separate field for each of the states. When a state applies answer Y; when it does not, answer N.

Database File 1, CH21DB1F

Zone	State	Minimum Temperature
1	AK	-51 and below
2	AK	-50 to -40
3	ID MT AK	-40 to -30
4	OR ID MT AK	-30 to -20
5	OR ID MT AK	-20 to -10
6	WA OR ID MT AK	-10 to 0
7	WA OR ID MT AK	0 to 10
8	WA OR ID MT AK	10 to 20
9	WA OR ID MT AK	20 to 30
10	WA OR ID MT AK	30 to 40

Database File 2, CH21DB2F
The Zone field in this file shows the zone containing the minimum temperature in which the plant can survive.

No	Latin Name	English Name	Zone
01	Acanthus Mollis	Bear's Breach	8
02	Achilia Filipendulina	Fernleaf Yarrow	7
03	Alchemilla Vulgaris	Lady's Mantle	3
04	Anchusa Azurea	Italian Bugloss	3
05	Aquilegia	Columbine	8
06	Belamcanda Chinensis	Blackberry Lily	5
07	Caltha Palustris	Marsh Marigold	3
08	Chrysanthemum Coccineum	Painted Daisy	2
09	Chrysanthemum Superbum	Shasta Daisy	5
10	Dicentra Spectabilis	Bleeding Heart	5
11	Digitalis Pupurea	Foxglove	4
12	Gaillardia Grandiflora	Blanket Flower	2
13	Hibiscus Moscheutos	Rose Mallow	6
14	Iris Kaempferi	Japanese Iris	4
15	Kniphofia Uvaria	Torch Lily	7

Database File 3, CH21DB3F

3. Enter a formula in the tax field that multiplies the net cost times the 0.06 to compute the tax. Enter a formula in the total cost field that computes this amount by adding the net cost to the tax amount.

No	net cost	tax	total cost
01	3.25		
02	5.50		
03	3.50		
04	7.25		
05	5.50		
06	9.50		
07	3.25		
08	3.25		
09	5.50		
10	3.25		
11	4.00		
12	7.50		
13	10.50		
14	12.50		
15	12.50		

Database File 4, CH21DB4F

This table shows the minimum temperature zone within each state.

State	Zone
WA	6
OR	4
ID	3
MT	3
AK	1

4. Query the appropriate files for the following information. Print copies of the results. First sort the state in **CH21DB4F** in descending order, and the zone in **CH21DB2F** in descending.

    a. All states in zones 4 and below. List the zone and the states. Use **CH21DB1F.**
    b. All plants that can survive in zones 1 through 3.
    c. The minimum temperature in zones 1 through 3.
    d. A list of all plants by Latin name that can survive in Alaska (AK). What did this query show?
    e. A list of all plants that can survive in zones 1 through 5. Sort by Latin name in ascending order.

5. Create a report using **CH21DB3F**. Use appropriate main and column headings. If a numeric or real field is used, be sure the column containing that value is subtotaled and a grand total is shown if the report is grouped into categories. Print a copy of the report. Rename the report **CH21REP1F.**

WORD PROCESSING

1. Create the following newsletter using a single column. Use Insert Picture and then choose Clipart from the Edit menu to add one or two designs to the newsletter. Choose the designs from the Files list box in the Clipart Directory. A placemarker will be inserted at the position of the cursor. Use Preview to view the clipart placement. Center all headings.

2. Print and group all of the documents done for this company together and create an attractive cover for them.

PERENNIAL PLANT SHOP AND INFORMATION CENTER
Monthly Newsletter

Volume 3 No. 2   February 1992

WORKSHOPS

Monday and Saturday

3:00-4:00 p.m.
When to Plant Perennials
Location: The Garden Room

A workshop concerning the best time to plant this year's perennials for best long-term results. Garden experts will be on hand to introduce some of the heartiest varieties of perennials for the Pacific Northwest. A color slide presentation will be given. Topics of discussion will include starting perennials from seedlings, the right time for planting perennials outdoors, fertilizing for maximum plant growth, and winter care.

Tuesday

7:30 - 8:30 p.m.
The Daisy Family of Perennials
Location: The Sun Room

This workshop discusses all members of the daisy family, including Chrysanthemum Coccineum and Chrysanthemum Superbum, the Painted Daisy and the Shasta Daisy, two Pacific Northwest favorites. It will include the numerous varieties of daisies that are available to PNW gardeners. Most varieties are very hearty, grow rapidly, and make beautiful shrubs that bring color from summer through fall.

XXXXXXXXXXXXXXXXXXXXXXXXXXXXXXXXXXXXXXXXXXXXXXXXXXXXXXXXXXXXXX
Thursday

2:00-3:00 and
7:30-8:30 p.m.
Ferns of the Northwest
Location: The Garden Room

Well over 30 varieties of ferns will be discussed and over 100 slides shown during this hour-long presentation of ferns of the Northwest. This presentation will be presented by The Fern Garden, a shop in Woodinville specializing in fern growth and ferns within the landscape. Hints will be given on blending groups of ferns together, displaying ferns with other perennial and annual plants, and caring for ferns.

SALE

All perennials 15 - 20 percent off!!
Sale runs through this weekend and includes

   Bear's Breath
   Lady's Mantle
   Columbine
   Shasta and Painted Daisies
   Bleeding Heart
   Foxglove
   Japanese Iris

2- and 4-inch pots ready for planting in March.

ΩΩΩΩΩΩΩΩΩΩΩΩΩΩΩΩΩΩΩΩΩΩΩΩΩΩΩΩΩΩΩΩΩΩΩΩΩΩΩΩΩΩΩΩΩΩΩΩΩΩΩΩΩΩΩΩΩΩΩΩΩΩ

Perennial Plant Shop and Information Center   February 1991, Page 2

History

Perennials are plants that live more than two years. Perennials include trees, shrubs, and bulbs. Commonly, however, perennials are thought to be flowering plants or herbaceous plants, meaning that they have soft and fleshy stems rather than woody ones such as trees and bushes have.

Any herbaceous perennial survives varying degrees of cold weather. Whether or not they may survive depends on the strength of their root system. The root systems of perennials are generally stronger and more vigorous than those of annuals. In harsh weather, the perennial greenery dies down due to the cold, but the deep root system remains protected beneath the ground's surface in a dormant sate.

Perennials often survive in this life cycle for years — sometimes longer than human life spans. Perennials such as peonies, bleeding heart, and hosta are examples of some of the extremely hearty ones.

Having perennials in the garden saves the gardener time and money in the long run, for generally the perennials reseed and spread and often become heartier with each passing year.

The Importance of Design

A strong design or structure prior to developing your perennial garden may make the difference between a garden that is presented with beautiful style and one that is disorganized and difficult to maintain. Even though perennial gardens are often their most beautiful when they are profuse in the cottage garden sense, even these gardens must begin with a serious plan in mind. The way in which plants are grouped and the colors displayed makes all the difference.

Steps in Good Garden Design

*   Determine from which point the garden will most often be viewed.
*   Consider the design of the present year - its shape and topography.
*   Consider all existing plants. Can some be moved? Which are permanent?
*   Decide whether you really prefer a formal garden or an informal one. Do you like straight lines and pathways or curved lines and a natural look?
*   Decide how much yard you want and whether you want your perennials to be primarily on a border and/or within beds.
*   Read gardening books and magazines and visit nurseries to determine which plants you prefer. Look at color and texture.

Perennial Plant Shop and Information Center   February 1991, Page 3

Transplanting Tips

*   Wait until seedlings have produced a second set of leaves.
*   Move seedlings to individual containers from flat trays.
*   Use good-quality packaged soil mix thoroughly soaked prior to transplanting.
*   Never allow seedlings to dry out.
*   Keep in a protected environment.

Lecture Series

Due to the popularity of our lecture series in the past, we are happy to announce that Dr. Jennifer Rose will be giving a three-day lecture during April entitled, "Herbaceous Garden Designs for Beginners."

As some of you may be aware, Dr. Rose is a renowned landscape architect and professor at the University of the Pacific Northwest. She has written numerous articles on horticulture studies and designs, is a contributor to the Journal of Landscape Design, and has written a book entitled Perennial Perfection. In addition, she is a dynamic and enthusiastic lecturer who always draws large crowds and leaves her audiences inspired. Further information on the exact time and location of the lecture will appear in next month's newsletter.

A thought for the gardener:

"What a desolate place would be a world without flowers? It would be a face without a smile; a feast without a welcome. Are not flowers the stars of the earth? And are not our stars the flowers of heaven?"

Clara L. Balfour

APPENDIX I
INSTALLING WORKS

INSTALLING ON A HARD DISK

If setting up Works for the first time, you will need:

- All of the Works disks

- Information on the type of video card you have

- The name and type of printer you will be using

- The name and type of mouse you will be using (if using one)

INSTALLING ON A HARD DISK

Then,

1. **TURN ON**   the computer
2. **INSERT**   the Works Setup disk into drive A
3. **TYPE**   **a:setup** at the DOS prompt
4. **PRESS**   **Enter**
5. **FOLLOW**   the instructions on the screen

INSTALLING AND USING WORKS WITH A DUAL-DISK SYSTEM

Before starting, make backup copies of all the Works disks. If you do not know how to make backup copies, check the DOS manual. Use the backup copies with the following steps. Store the original disks in a safe place.

If setting up Works for the first time, you will need:

- The DOS program disk that came with the computer

- The Works disks you purchased

- A blank, formatted floppy disk

- Information on the type of video card you have

- The name and type of printer you will be using

- The name and type of mouse you will be using (if using one)

INSTALLING ON A DUAL-DISK SYSTEM

Then,

1. **INSERT** the DOS disk into drive A
2. When the DOS prompt appears on the screen, remove the DOS disk and **INSERT** the Works Setup disk into drive A
3. **TYPE** **a:setup** at the DOS prompt
4. **PRESS** **Enter**
5. **FOLLOW** the instructions on the screen

When using Works, sign on as instructed in Part 2 of this book. You will have the Works program disk in drive A and a formatted data disk in drive B. The only time you should need to change disks is when a dialog box appears that lists files, such as Open, Save As, Copy File, or Delete File. You may also need to change disks when Works prompts you to do so with a message on the screen. The instructions on the screen will guide you through all of the necessary steps when using Works on a dual-disk system.

APPENDIX II
GLOSSARY OF TERMS

This appendix contains definitions for many of the terms used throughout this book, as well as some terms that are familiar to computer applications and environments. It should be used as a reference to questions you may have concerning the meaning of unfamiliar words. The definitions are taken from _Webster's New World Dictionary of Computer Terms_, (Englewood Cliffs, NJ: Prentice Hall).

ALPHANUMERIC

A general term for alphabetic letters (A through Z), numeric digits (0 through 9), and special characters [-, /, *, $, (,), +, etc.] that are machine-processable.

APPEND

To add on, for example, to add new records to a database or to add to the end of a character string or list.

APPLICATION

Task to be performed by a computer program or system. Broad examples of computer applications are computer-aided design, numerical control, airline seat reservations, business forecasting, and hospital administration. Word processing and electronic spreadsheet programs are examples of applications that run on microcomputer systems.

APPLICATION PROGRAMS

The programs normally written by programmers within an organization that enable the computer to produce useful work: for example, inventory control, attendance accounting, and so on.

ARITHMETIC OPERATOR

A symbol that tells a computer to perform addition, subtraction, multiplication, division, or raising to a power.

ATTRIBUTE

(1) A word that describes the manner in which a variable is handled by the computer. (2) A characteristic quality of a data type, data structure, element of a data model, or system.

BACKUP COPY

A copy of a file or data set that is kept for reference in case the original file or data set is damaged or destroyed.

BOLDFACE

A type font in which the main strokes of the letter are thicker than normal.

BOOT

To start or restart a computer system by reading instructions from a storage device into the computer's memory. It involves loading part of the operating system into the computer's main memory. If the computer is already turned on, it's a "warm boot"; if not, it's a "cold boot."

BUSINESS GRAPHICS
(1) Pie charts, bar charts, scattergrams, graphs, and other visual representations of the operational or strategic aspects of a business, such as sales versus costs, sales by department, comparative product performance, and stock prices. (2) The application programs that allow the user to display data as visual presentations.

CACHE MEMORY
A small high-speed memory for the temporary storage of information, usually used between a slower large memory and a fast central processing unit. Also called SCRATCHPAD.

CHARACTER
Any symbol, digit, letter, or punctuation mark stored or processed by computing equipment.

CHIP
A small component that contains a large amount of electronic circuitry. A thin silicon wafer on which electronic components are deposited in the form of integrated circuits. Chips are the building blocks of a computer and perform various functions, such as doing arithmetic, serving the computer's memory, or controlling other chips.

CLIPBOARD
A portion of the computer's memory set aside to store data being transferred from one file or application to another.

COLUMN
(1) The vertical members of one line of an array. (2) A position of information in a computer word. (3) A vertical division of an electronic spreadsheet. Together with rows, columns serve to form the spreadsheet matrix. Contrast with ROW.

NOTE: A column is also referred to as the "field" in some database programs, such as the column in a table. Example: Name, Address, City, State, Zip of a customer table.

COMMAND
Loosely, a computer instruction. Example: the commands given at the prompt in a database program.

COMPUTER GRAPHICS
A general term meaning the appearance of pictures or diagrams, as distinct from letters and numbers, on the display screen or hard-copy output device.

COMPUTER SYSTEM
A system that includes computer hardware, software, and people. Used to process data into useful information.

CONTINUOUS SCROLLING
Moving text, line by line, forward or backward, through a window.

CONTROL FIELD
A field in a data record used to identify and classify the record. Same as KEY.

CONTROL KEY

A special function key on a computer keyboard. Used simultaneously with another key to enter a command instructing the system to perform a task.

COPY

To reproduce data in a new location or other destination, leaving the source data unchanged, although the physical form of the result may differ from that of the source; for example, to make a duplicate of all the programs or data on a disk.

CRT

An abbreviation for "cathode ray tube," the picture tube of a video display terminal.

CURSOR

A moving, sliding, or blinking symbol on a CRT screen that indicates where the next character will appear.

CUT

The act of removing text or graphics from a document.

DATA

A formalized representation of facts or concepts suitable for communication, interpretation, or processing by people or by automatic means. The raw material of information. Individual pieces of quantitative information, such as dollar sales of carpets, or numbers of building permits issued.

DATABASE

A collection of logically related records or files. A database consolidates many records previously stored in separate files so that a common pool of data records serves as a single central file for many data processing applications.

DATABASE MANAGEMENT SYSTEM (DBMS)

The collection of hardware and software that organizes and provides access to a database. The computer program provides you with the mechanisms needed to create a computerized database file, to add data to the file, to alter data in the file, to organize data within the file, to search for data in the file, and so on. In other words, it manages data.

DATA DICTIONARY

A list of all the files, fields, and variables used in a database management system. A data dictionary helps users remember what items they have to work with and how they have been defined. Particularly helpful when writing a large number of linked procedures or programs that share a database.

DATA ELEMENT

One or more data items that form a unit or piece of information, such as the social security number in an employee payroll database.

DATA ENTRY

The process of converting data into a form suitable for entry into a computer system, such as by keying from a keyboard onto magnetic disks.

DATA FIELD
One column or consecutive columns used to store a particular piece of information.

DATA FILE
A collection of related data records that have been organized in a specific manner.

DATA IMPORT
The ability to use (read) information developed with another program. This is particularly important in the use of integrated software, where several programs will use the information gathered or used by one program.

DATA ITEM
An item of data used to represent a single value. A data item is the smallest unit of named data.

DATA PROCESSING
(1) One or more operations performed on data to achieve a desired objective. (2) The functions of a computer center. (3) A term used in reference to operations performed by data processing equipment. (4) Operations performed on data to provide useful information to users.

DATA RECORD
A collection of data fields pertaining to a particular subject. Part of a data file. Example: One customer entry, including name, address, city, state, and zip, would be one record in the customer file.

DATA STRUCTURE
The structure of relationships among files in a database and among data items within each file.

DATA TYPE
An interpretation applied to a string of bits, such as integer, real, or character.

DEFAULT
An assumption made by a system or language translator when no specific choice is given by the program or the user.

DESCENDING ORDER
Order that ranges from highest to lowest in numeric value or alphabetically.

DESCRIPTOR
A significant word that helps to categorize or index information. Sometimes called a KEYWORD.

DISK OPERATING SYSTEM (DOS)
An operating system in which the operating system programs are stored on magnetic disks. Typically, it keeps track of files, saves and retrieves files, allocates storage space, and manages other control functions associated with disk storage.

DOT COMMANDS
An approach to formatting in which a word processor records formatting instructions in the text but does not apply them to the text until it is printed.

DOT MATRIX

A technique for representing characters by composing them out of selected dots from within a rectangular matrix of dots.

DOUBLE DENSITY

Having twice the storage capacity of a single density disk or tape. The ability to store twice as much data in a given area on a disk or tape as on single density.

EDIT MODE

Available in many programs, this mode permits easy modification of cell contents, such as changing program lines or word processing text, without rekeying the entire entry.

ENTITY

An object that has meaning for a particular application. A computer system may be an entity; a job position, a company, or even a technique or concept could be an entity as well.

FIELD

A single piece of information, the smallest unit normally manipulated by a database management system. In a personnel file, the person's age might be a field. A record is made up of one or more fields.

FILE

A collection of related records treated as a basic unit of storage.

FILE STRUCTURE

The format of fields within a data record. For example: PART NAME in the first field of a record, PART NUMBER in the second field, PRICE in the third field, and so on, specify the structure of a file.

NOTE: The structure also contains information such as the width of a field, the type of field (such as character or numeric), and the number of decimal places (if numeric or real).

FORM

A preprinted document requiring additional information to make it meaningful. Also the format of program output.

FORM LETTER

A document consisting mainly of standard text into which selected pieces of personal information, such as a business name and address, have been inserted.

MEGABYTE

Specifically, 1,073,741,824 bytes or 230 kilobytes. More loosely, 1 billion bytes, 1 million kilobytes, or 1000 megabytes. Abbreviated GB.

GLOBAL CHARACTER

A character used in a searching routine that can stand for any character. It allows the operator to search for a character string of a specified length, by specifying only some of its characters and using global characters to stand for the others. Also called a WILD CARD.

GLOBAL OPERATION
In word processing, an operation performed throughout an entire file.

GLOBAL SEARCH AND REPLACE
In word processing, the ability to find a character string anywhere it appears in a document and to substitute another character string for it.

GRAPHIC-DISPLAY MODE
A mode of operation that allows the computer to print graphics on a the screen.

GRAPHICS
Any computer-generated picture produced on a screen, paper, or film. Graphics range from simple line or bar graphs to colorful and detailed images.

HARD COPY
A printed copy of machine output in readable form, such as reports, listings, or graphic images.

HARD DISK
A fast auxiliary storage device that is either mounted in its own case or permanently mounted inside a computer. A single hard disk has storage capacity of several million characters or bytes of information.

HARDWARE
The physical components or equipment that make up a computer system, such as a keyboard, floppy disk drive, and visual display.

HEAD
A device that reads, records, or erases data on a storage medium; for example, a small electro-magnet used to read, write, and erase data on a magnetic disk.

HEADER
(1) The top margin of a page. It is generally considered the area between the top edge of the paper and the first line of type. (2) The text that appears in the header, usually repeated on every page of a word processing document.

HIERARCHY
Order in which arithmetic operations within a formula or statement will be executed.

HIGHLIGHTING
The process of making a display segment more noticeable by causing flickering, blinking, bright-ening, or reversing the background and the character images (e.g., dark characters on a light background). Most video displays have software controls to accomplish this on a selective basis.

HOME
The starting position for the cursor on a terminal screen. It is usually in the top left-hand corner of the screen.

ICON
A tiny on-screen symbol that simplifies access to a program, command, or data file. For exam-ple, a wastebasket may represent the command to delete a file. It is activated by moving the cursor onto the icon and pressing a button or key.

474

IMPORT

To read a file created by one program into another. Such as importing a Lotus 1-2-3 file into a Works spreadsheet file.

INDEX

A symbol or number used to identify a particular quantity in an array of similar quantities; for example, X(5) is the fifth item in an array of Xs. Also a table of reference, held in storage in some sequence, that may be accessed to obtain the addresses of other items of data, such as items in a graphics or data file.

INDEXED ADDRESS

An address that is modified by the content of an index register prior to or during the execution of a computer instruction.

INDICATOR

A device that registers a condition in the computer.

INFORMATION PROCESSING

The totality of operations performed by a computer. It involves evaluating, analyzing, and processing data to produce usable information.

INPUT

The introduction of data from an input device or auxiliary storage device, such as a floppy disk.

INPUT DEVICE

A unit used to enter data into a computer, such as a graphics tablet, keyboard, or secondary auxiliary storage device, such as a floppy disk.

INSERTION POINT

The position at which text is entered into a document.

INTEGRATED SOFTWARE

A group of programs that may freely exchange data with each other, a software package that has a word processor, database manager, electronic spreadsheet, and communications program. Since the information from the electronic spreadsheet may be shared with the database manager and the word processor (and vice versa), this software is called "integrated." Examples are WORKSTM, APPLEWORKSTM, FRAMEWORKTM, and SYMPHONYTM

JUSTIFICATION

The alignment of text margins on both right and left sides. Justified text is both flush left and flush right.

KEY

Control field or fields that identify a record. Also the field that determines the position of a record in a sorted sequence.

MACRO

A single, symbolic programming-language statement that when translated results in a series of machine-language statements.

MEGABYTE

1,048,576 bytes or 1024 kilobytes, actually; or roughly 1 million bytes or 1000 kilobytes.

MEMORY

The storage facilities of the computer, capable of storing vast amounts of data.

MENU

A list of options within a program that allows the user to choose which part to interact with. Menus allow computer users a facility for using programs without knowing any technical methods. Menus are usually an on-screen series of program options that allow you to select the course of action you wish to take; for example, to print a report or to select a specific program stored on a disk.

MERGE

To combine items into one or more files with a form document. An example of merge is a form letter merged with multiple customer records in a database file.

MICROCHIP

A tiny silicon chip with thousands of electronic components and circuit patterns etched onto its surface.

NANOSECOND

One billionth of a second, one thousand-millionth of a second; abbreviated ns. Same as millimicrosecond. Light travels approximately 1 foot per nanosecond, electricity slightly less. The most powerful computers now being manufactured can carry out an instruction in less than a nanosecond. That is, such a machine can execute more than 1 billion instructions in 1 second!

NETWORK

A system of interconnected computer systems and terminals.

NUMERIC

Pertaining to numerals or to representation by means of numerals.

OFF-LINE

Pertaining to equipment, devices, or persons not in direct communication with the central processing unit of a computer. Equipment not connected to the computer. Contrast with ON-LINE.

ON-LINE

Pertaining to describing equipment, devices, and persons who are in direct communication with the central processing unit of a computer.

OPTICAL DISK

A high-density storage device that uses a laser to burn a pattern of holes into a tellurium film on a disk surface. A single optical disk can hold billions of bytes of data. In fact, one optical disk storage system can store the entire Encyclopedia Britannica.

OUTPUT

Data transferred from a computer's internal storage unit to some storage or output device. Also, the final result of data that have been processed by the computer.

PIE CHART

Graphical representation of information. A charting technique used to represent portions of a whole. Commonly used in business graphics.

QUERY

To ask for information. To make a request for information from a database system.

RAM

An acronym for "random access memory," a memory into which the user can enter information and instructions (write), and from which the user can call up data (read). RAM is the "working memory" of the computer, into which application programs can be loaded from outside and then executed.

RANGE

The span of values that an element may assume.

RELATIONAL DATABASE MANAGEMENT SYSTEM

A collection of hardware and software that organizes and provides access to a relational database.

RELATIONAL STRUCTURE

A form of database organization in which all data items are contained in one or more files and are linked together by a trail of logical pointers. The relationships between these data items can be altered at will, and the information can be obtained by interactive query or batch processing.

REPORT

Usually associated with output data; involves the grouping of related facts so as to be easily understood by the reader. A common means of presenting information to users. Most reports are on-screen display or printed listings showing selected information extracted from a database.

RESERVED WORDS

Certain words that because they are reserved by operating systems, language translators, and so on, for their own use, cannot be used in an application program. For example: READ, FOR, and LET in the BASIC programming language.

ROM

Read-Only Memory. A special type of computer memory, permanently programmed with one group of frequently used instructions. Read-only memory does not lose its program when the computer's power is turned off, but the program cannot be changed by the user.

ROW

The horizontal divisions of an electronic spreadsheet. Together with columns, rows serve to form the spreadsheet matrix.

NOTE: Rows are also the record in a table structure database program. A row may contain all of the information about one customer in a customer table, such as name, address, city, state, zip, and so on.

SOFTWARE

The programs or instructions that tell a computer what to do. Software may be built into the computer's ROM or may be loaded temporarily into the computer from a disk or tape.

SORT

To arrange records according to a logical system.

SPLIT SCREEN

A display screen that can be partitioned into two or more areas (called windows) so that different screen formats can be shown on the screen at the same time.

SPREADSHEET

Any one of a number of programs that arranges data and formulas in a matrix of cells.

SYNTAX

The rules governing the structure of a language and its expressions. All assembly and high-level programming languages possess a formal syntax.

TABLE

A collection of data in a form suitable for ready reference. The data are frequently stored in consecutive storage locations or written in the form of an array of rows and columns for easy entry. An intersection of labeled rows and columns serve to locate a specific piece of information.

VARIABLE

A unit of memory that can hold a given value.

VIEW

A way of presenting the contents of a database to the user, not necessarily the same as the way the fields and records are stored in the database. Different users or programs that call upon the database for information may have unique views of the data.

WINDOW

A portion of the video display area dedicated to a specific purpose. Special software allows the screen to be divided into multiple "windows" that can be moved around and made bigger or smaller. Windows allow the user to treat the computer display screen like a desktop where various files can remain open simultaneously.

WORD PROCESSING

A software system that lets you write, revise, manipulate, format, and print text for letters, reports, manuscripts, and other printed matter. Word processing is the most common use for personal computers in business and the home.

WRAPAROUND

The continuation of an operation, such as a change in the storage location from the largest addressable location to the first addressable location or a visual display cursor movement from the last character position to the first position.

INDEX

A

Absolute cell addresses, 227-28
Accessories
  alarm clock, 177-79
  calculator, 174-77
  Wizard tools, 179-80
Active cell, 193
Active drive, 16-17
Addition, 176
Addresses, cell, 214, 224-29
  absolute, 227-28
  relative, 224-26
  viewing, 228-29
Add-to-incoming-lines option, 406
Alarm clock, 177-79
Alignment, paragraph, 49-50
Alt/Backspace, 6
Alt key, 5
Application software, 2
Apply Query command, 350
Arrow keys (cursor movement
  keys), 5, 6, 34
ASCII characters, searching and/or
  replacing, 92
ASCII files, sending to another
  computer, 413
Assistance commands, 88
Asterisk (*), 18-19, 21, 355
Average, 215
AVG function, 215, 376

B

Backspace key, 6, 42, 46
Bar charts, 284-85, 287, 297
Baud rate, 407
Blocks of text. See under Text
Bookmarks, 144-47
Borders, 147-49
Buffer option, 406
Button, defined, 33

C

Calculator, 174-77
Cancel option, 33
Caps Lock key, 5
Caret (^), searching and/or replacing, 92
CD command, 13, 24
Cell(s). See also Spreadsheet(s)
  active, 193
  addresses, 214, 224-29
  absolute, 227-28
  relative, 224-26
  viewing, 228-29
  copying, 224-26
  date and time in, 259

editing, 201-3
  entering values into, 200-201
  highlighted, 194
  printing selected, 250
  range of, 228, 232
  selecting, 214-15, 230
  sorting contents of, 266-67
Centering headings, 68-69
Centering text, 45, 371
Central processing unit (CPU), 2, 3
Character formatting, 44, 52-53,
  240-44, 378
  copying, 115
  fonts, 240-41
  style, 241-44
Chart(s), 283-312
  bar, 284-85, 287, 297
  changing data format, 299-301
  changing types, 296-97
  copying, 295-96
  creating, 286-88
  data labels, 292-94, 297
  grids on, 302-4
  hi-lo-close, 285
  legends, 288-90
  line, 285, 301-2
  maximum number in spreadsheet, 284
  naming, 294-95
  pie, 285-86, 298-99
  printing, 304-5
  switching between spreadsheet
  mode and, 288
  titles, 291-92, 298-99
  X-Y, 286
Codes used in headers and footers, 135
Color monitor, 3
Column(s), 193
  changing width of, 199-200, 244-45
  deleting, 229-32, 325-26, 374-75
  headings, 127-29, 370
  inserting, 229-32
  locking, 227
Comma format, 246
COMMAND.COM, 18
Commands. See also specific names
  of commands
  assistance, 88
  DOS, 12-25
    active drive and, 16-17
    eternal, 19
    internal, 17, 20
    Works, 32
Communications, 403-15
  with another computer, 409-14
  copying information received to
  Works tool, 411-12

  receiving information, 410-11
  resuming, 412
  sending information, 409-10,
  412-13
  communication settings, 407
  copying information to another
  Works' tool, 408
  disconnecting, 409
  with information service, 404-9
  logging off, 409
  receiving calls automatically, 414
  saving communication file, 409
  terminal settings, 405-7
Comparison formulas, 348-49
Computer(s)
  communication with other, 409-14
  starting the, 10-11
  system components, 2-8
COPY, 17-19
Copy command, 226
Copying
  of blocks of text, 113-14
  of cells, 224-26
  of charts, 295-96
  of field contents, 323-24
  of formats, 115
  of formulas, 224-25
  in List view, 323-25
Copy Special command, 115-16, 229
COUNT function, 376
Create New File command, 315
Ctrl/Arrow keys, 6
Ctrl key, 5
Currency format, 246
Cursor, 4
Cursor alternate option, 406
Cursor movement
  with arrow keys, 5, 6
  in documents, 43-44
  making menu selections with, 34

D

Database(s), 313-63. See also
  Reports
  adding labels to form, 328
  adding notes to form, 328-29
  creating, 314-15
  data entry, 318-21
  editing, 321-28
    changing field width, 321-22
    copying in List view, 323-25
    deleting a row or column, 325-26
    of field contents, 322-23
    in Form view, 326-28
    moving in List view, 325
  formatting, 330-36
    of data values, 335

entering series of values, 331-33
field width adjustment in **Form** view, 335-36
font and point size, 333
formulas, 333-34
mailing labels, 391-95
querying, 347-52
changing query form, 350-51
comparison formulas in, 348-49
entering conditions in form, 349
for more than one condition, 351-52
starting, 348
using existing query, 350
record form, 316-18
saving, 318
searching, 352-55
repeating, 354
wildcards in, 355
sorting records, 346-47
on multiple fields, 347
on one field, 346-37
starting new file, 315-16
Data bits, 407
Data disk, 3
Data format, changing, 299-301
Data labels, 292-94, 297
Date, 94
in spreadsheets, 258-62
Delete key, 6, 42, 46
Delete Page Break command, 248
Delete Query command, 350
Delete Row/Column command, 229, 374
Deletion
of blocks of text, 112
of cell contents, 203
of footnotes, 144
of legends, 290
of page breaks, 248
of records, 327
of rows or columns, 229-32, 325-26, 374-75
Dialog box, 33-34
Bookmark Name, 146
Border, 148
Check Spelling, 97-98
Communication, 407-8
Data Format, 299-300
Data Labels, 293
Date/Time, 261
Fill Series, 263, 331
Fonts, 241
Font & Style, 77
Headers & Footers, 134
Indents & Spacing, 51, 131
Insert Special, 93
Label Spacing, 394
Legend, 289
Open, 55
Phone, 405

Print, 58, 149, 249
Printer Setup, 139, 140
Print Labels, 393
Range Name, 265
Receive File, 410
Replace, 90
Report Statistics, 367
Search, 89, 353
Send Text, 413
Setup & Margins, 122
Sort Records, 373
Sort Rows, 267
Styles, 242-43
Tabs, 125
Terminal, 405-6
Thesaurus, 101
Titles, 291
Wizard, 180
Works Alarm Clock, 178
Works Setting, 163-64
Y-Axis, 303-4
Dictionary, built-in, 96, 98-100
DIR, 12, 13-14, 22, 23, 24-25
Directory listing, 13-14
DISKCOPY, 19-20
Disk drives, 2, 4, 11
active, 16-17
changing logged, 16-17
configurations of, 11-12
Diskettes, 4, 14-15
Document(s), 39-64. See also Paragraph(s); Word processing
character formatting, 52-53
cursor movement in, 43-44
form, 388-91
inserting calculator results in, 177
line spacing in, 50, 51-52
opening existing, 55
previewing, 56-57
printing, 56-58
options for, 149-50
without previewing, 57
previewing before, 56-57
revising text, 111-20
copying blocks of text, 113-14
copying character and paragraph formats, 115
copying multiple paragraphs, 115-16
corrections, 46-47
moving blocks of text, 113
undoing text, 112-13
saving, 54, 75
screen and, 42
selecting blocks of text, 45-46
text entry, 42-43
DOS. See Operating systems
Double quote marks, 198
Drive(s). See Disk drives
Dual disk system
active drive on, 17
DISKCOPY on, 19-20

formatting in, 14-15
staring Works on, 31

E

Edit bar, 322
Editing
of cells, 201-3
of databases, 321-28
changing field width, 321-22
copying in **List** view, 323-25
deleting a row or column, 325-26
field contents, 322-23
in **Form** view, 326-28
moving in **List** view, 325
of documents, 111-20
copying blocks of text, 113-14
copying character and paragraph formats, 115
copying multiple paragraphs, 115-16
corrections, 46-47
moving blocks of text, 113
undoing text, 112-13
with F2 key, 202
of spreadsheets, 201-3, 223-38
absolute cell addresses and, 227-28
copying adjacent cells, 224-25
copying nonadjacent cells, 226
Copy Special command for, 228
inserting and deleting rows and columns, 229-32
moving range of cells, 228
relative cell addresses and, 224-26
removing range of cells, 232
of templates, 166
Edit menu, 112
Ellipsis, 32
End key, 6
End-of-line mark, 92, 93, 137
Enter key, 6, 42
Equals sign (=), 213
ERASE, 20-21
Esc key, 5
Exiting Works, 54
Exponential format, 246
Extensions, file, 13, 56
External DOS commands, 19
External (transient) files, 11
EXT mode, 230

F

F2 key, 202
F8 key, 230
False conditions, searching for, 21
Field(s), 315
changing widths of, 321-22
copying contents of, 323-24
editing contents of, 322-23
inserting, 328-29, 333-34
in reports, 375

NOTE, 329
query for conditions on more than one, 352
sorting on one or more, 346-47
width adjustment, 335-36
Field names, 316, 333
Field Width command, 321-22
File(s)
copying, 17-19
creating, 68
defined, 2-3
erasing, 20-21
external (transient), 11
internal (resident), 10-11
remote sending and receiving, 409-13
sorted, 373-74
File menu options, 32
Filenames, 13, 94
Fill command, 226
Fill Down command, 324
Fill Right command, 324
Fill Series command, 262, 331
Fixed format, 246
Font command, 333
Fonts, 76-78, 79, 240-41
in databases, 333
Font & Style command, 76
Footers. See Headers and footers
Footnote pane, 140-41
Footnotes, 140-44
closing footnote pane, 141-42
deleting, 144
reference marks, 142-44
inserting, 142-43
moving, 142
positioning cursor at, 143-44
Form. See Database(s)
FORMAT, 14-16, 23
Format menu, 50, 53
Formatting, 67-86
centering heading prior to typing text, 68-69
character, 44, 52-53, 240-44, 378
copying, 115
fonts, 240-41
style, 241-44
of data, 299-301
of databases, 330-36
data values, 335
entering series of values, 331-33
field width adjustment in **Form** view, 335-36
font and point size, 333
formulas, 333-34
of diskettes, 14-15
font changes, 76-78, 79
of hard disks, 15-16
of paragraphs, 44-47
copying, 115
indented, 71-76

of spreadsheets, 239-56
character, 240-44
headers and footers, 246-47
margins, 249
page breaks in, 247-48
for printing, 249-50
from toolbar, 193, 244, 245
values, 244-46
subscripts, 78-79
superscripts, 78-79
toolbar for, 79-80, 193, 244, 245
Form letters, 388-91
creating, 388-90
merging and printing, 391
Formula(s), 211-22
comparison, 348-49
for computing averages, 215
for computing percentages, 216-17
copying, 224-25
in database, 333-34
functions used in, 212, 217, 376
range names in, 266
in reports, 375-76
for searching for true or false conditions, 216
selecting cells for, 214-15
for subtraction, 213-14
for summing range of values, 214
viewing, 218
Formula bar, 213
Form view, 316, 326-28, 335-36, 369
Full screen option, 406
Function keys, 5
Functions, 212, 217, 376. See also Formula(s); names of functions

G

General formats, 246
Global (wildcard) character, 18-19, 21
Grids on charts, 302-4

H

Handshake, 408
Hanging indents, 73-74
Hard copy, 4
Hard disk drives, 2, 4, 11
Hard disk systems
active drive on, 16-17
formatting in, 15-16
starting Works on, 30
Hardware, defined, 2
Hardware components, 3-6
Headers and footers, 123, 133-40
codes used in, 135
multiline, 137-38
paragraph, 136-37
in spreadsheets, 246-47

standard (single line), 134-35
Heading(s)
centering, 68-69
column, 127-29, 370
main, 370
moving, 248
Help, invoking, 6
Hi-lo-close charts, 285
Home key, 6
Hyphen
non-breaking, 92, 93
optional, 92, 93, 94-95
searching and/or replacing, 92

I

IF-THEN-ELSE function, 216
Indentation, 71-76
all lines, 71-72
custom, 75-76
of first line of paragraphs, 48
hanging, 73-74
removing or changing, 72-73
Indicators, position, 316
Information service, communications with, 404-9
Insert Field Summary command, 376
Insertion
of date and time
in document, 94
in spreadsheet, 258-59
of fields, 328-29, 333-34
in reports, 375
of page breaks, 247-48
of records, 326-27
of reference marks, 142-43
of rows and columns, 229-32, 371
Insert Page Break command, 131, 247
Insert Record command, 326-27
Insert Row/Column command, 229, 231, 374
Insert Special Character command, 92-96, 137
Internal DOS commands, 17, 20
Internal (resident) files, 10-11

J

Justifying paragraphs, 48-49

K

Keyboard, 2, 4-6
manipulating windows using, 170-74
menu selections using, 32
for scrolling, 194-95
Keypad alternate option, 406

L

Labels
  data, 292-94
    removing, 297
  form, 328
  mailing, 391-95
    creating, 391-92
    printing, 392-95
Left indent option, 71
Legends, 288-90
Line charts, 285, 301-2
Line spacing, 50-52
List view, 316, 321, 352, 369
  copying in, 323-25
  moving in, 325
Local echo option, 406
Locking rows and columns, 227
Logical operators, 351
Long-date placeholder, 94

M

Magnetic disk, 4
Mailing labels, 391-95
  creating, 391-92
  printing, 392-95
Main headings, 370
Manual page-break mark, searching
  and/or replacing, 92
Manuscripts, creating, 40-42
Margins, 42, 122-24
  spreadsheet, 249
Match upper/lower case option,
  89
Match whole word option, 89
MAX function, 376
Memory, 3, 10
Menu(s). See also specific menus
  making selections, 32, 34
  to move from window to window,
  169
  spreadsheet, 193
Merging form letters, 391
Message line, spreadsheet, 193
Messages and prompts
  "Are you sure (Y/N)?," 21
  "File not found," 16
  "Format another (Y/N)?," 23
Microsoft Works
  exiting, 54
  starting, 30, 31
  viewing settings of, 163-64
MIN function, 376
Monitor, 2, 3
Monochrome monitor, 3
Mouse
  manipulating windows using,
  170-74
  menu selections using, 32
  scrolling through spreadsheet
  using, 194
Move command, 142

MS-DOS (Microsoft Disk Operating
  System), 10

N

Name(s)
  of charts, 294-95
  of files, 13, 316, 333
  of ranges, 264-66
New Chart command, 286
Non-breaking space, searching
  and/or replacing, 92
NOTE field, 329
Notes in databases, 328-29
Number(s)
  adding, 176
  changing sign of, 175
  clearing, in calculator, 176
  series of, 262-64
  subtracting, 177
Numeric keypad, 4-5
Num Lock key, 5

O

Open Existing File command, 412
Open read-only option, 56
Operating systems, 2, 9-28
  DOS commands, 12-25
    active drive and, 16-17
    CD, 13, 24
    COPY, 17-19
    DIR, 12, 13-14, 22, 23, 24-25
    DISKCOPY, 19-20
    ERASE, 20-21
    eternal, 19
    FORMAT, 14-16, 23
    internal, 17, 20
  drive configurations and, 11-12
  starting the computer, 10-11
Operators
  comparison, 349
  hierarchy of, 217
  logical, 351
Option box, 33
Options. See specific names of
  options
Options menu, 34, 46-47
Output devices, 3, 4

P

Page breaks, 131-33
  manual, 92, 131, 132-33
  removing, 131
  in spreadsheets, 247-48
  viewing, 131-32
Page design, 121-63
  bookmarks, 144-47
    creating, 146-47
    going to, 147
  borders, 147-49
  column headings, 127-29

footnotes, 140-44
  closing footnote pane, 141-42
  deleting, 144
  reference marks, 142-44
headers and footers, 123, 133-40
  codes used in, 135
  multiline, 137-38
  paragraph, 136-37
  standard (single line), 134-35
margins, 122-24
page breaks, 131-33
  manual, 92, 131, 132-33
  removing, 131
  viewing, 131-32
paragraphs, 130
tab settings, 124-27
  changing, 129-30
Page Down key, 6
Page layout, changing, 165-66
Page number placeholder, 94
Page Setup & Margins command,
  122
Page Up key, 6
Paragraph(s)
  adding new, 130
  copying, 115-16
  formatting, 44-47, 71-76, 115
  headers and footers, 136-37
  indentation, 71-76
    all lines, 71-72
    custom, 75-76
    first line, 48
    hanging, 73-74
    removing or changing, 72-73
  justifying, 48-49
  reviewing alignments, 49-50
  separating and merging, 47-48
Paragraph mark, searching and/or
  replacing, 92
Parity, 407-8
Pause command, 408
PC-DOS (Personal Computer Disk
  Operating System), 10
Percentages, 216-17
Percent format, 246
Pie charts, 285-86, 298-99
Pie command, 298
Point size, 333
Port, 408
Position indicators, 316
.PR1 extension, 56
PREV command, 249
Previewing
  documents, 56-57
  of spreadsheet, 247
Printers, 2, 4
Printer Setup, 138-40
Printing
  of charts, 304-5
  of documents, 56-58
    options for, 149-50

without previewing, 57
  previewing before, 56-57
  of form letters, 391
  of mailing labels, 392-95
  of reports, 379
  of spreadsheet, 249-50
  selected cells, 250
Print Labels command, 392
Print Preview, 131
Print Preview (Prev) tool, 79
Print Screen key, 6
Program disk, 2
Prompts. See Messages and prompts

Q

Query(ies), database, 347-52
  changing query form, 350-51
  comparison formulas in, 348-49
  entering conditions in form, 349
  for more than one condition, 351-52
  starting, 348
  using existing, 350
Query command, 347, 352
Question mark (?), 92, 355
Quick Start options, 31-34

R

Random access memory (RAM), 3, 10
Range(s)
  of cells, 228, 232
  names of, 264-66
  of values, summing, 214
Read only memory (ROM), 3
Receive File command, 410
Record(s), 315, 316-18
  deleting, 327
  editing in **Form** view, 326
  inserting, 326-27
  moving, 327-28
  sorting, 346-47
  viewing all, 349
Reference marks, 142-44
  inserting, 142-43
  moving, 142
  positioning cursor at, 143-44
Relative cell addresses, 224-26
  replacing, 88, 90-91
  of cell contents, 202
Report Definition page, 368
Reports, 365-86
  additional information in, 375
  centering text in, 371
  character format in, 378
  column headings, 370
  deleting rows or columns in, 374-5
  inserting field contents in, 375
  inserting new rows in, 371
  interpreting formulas in, 375-76
  main headings, 370
  printing, 379
  renaming, 379
  with sorted files, 373-74
  standard, 366-68
  switching between views, 369
  viewing, 372, 376-77
Report view, 369
Resident (internal) files, 10-11
Row(s), 193
  deleting, 229-32, 325-26, 374-75
  inserting, 229-32, 371
  locking, 227
Ruler, 126
Ruler line, 42, 76

S

Saving
  of communications file, 409
  of databases, 318
  of documents, 54, 75
  of spreadsheets, 203-4
Screen, 42
Scroll bars, 42, 193
Scrolling, 194-95
Scroll Lock key, 6
Search command, 347
Searching, 88-92
  of databases, 352-55
  special characters used in, 91-92
  for text, 88-90
  for true or false conditions, 216
Secondary storage, 4
Send File command, 412
Series of numbers, 262-64
Set Print Area command, 250
Shift key, 5
Show All Characters switch, 47
Show All Records command, 349
Show Footnotes option, 142
Show Formulas command, 218
Sign of numbers, changing, 175
Size box, 193
Soft copy, 4
Software, defined, 2
Sort command, 346
Sorting
  of cell contents, 266-67
  of records, 346-47
  on multiple fields, 347
  on one field, 346-47
  in reports, 373-74
Spaces, 92, 94
Spelling checking, 96-100
Spelling (Sp) tool, 79
Split bar, 193
Spreadsheet(s), 191-209. See also
  Cell(s); Chart(s); Formula(s)
  closing and exiting, 204
column width changes, 199-200
  creating, 192-93
  date and time in, 258-62
  calculating, 261-62
  changing time format, 260-61
  inserting, 258-59
  description of space, 193
  editing, 201-3, 223-38
  absolute cell addresses and, 227-28
  copying adjacent cells, 224-25
  copying nonadjacent cells, 226
  Copy Special command for, 229
  inserting and deleting rows and columns, 229-32
  moving range of cells, 228
  relative cell addresses and, 224-26
  removing range of cells, 232
  entering text in, 197-99
  entering values in, 197-99, 200-201
  formatting of, 239-56
  character, 240-44
  headers and footers, 246-47
  margins, 249
  page breaks in, 247-48
  for printing, 249-50
  from toolbar, 244, 245
  values, 244-46
  freezing titles, 259-60
  making selections in, 230-31
  maximum number of charts in, 284
  moving through, 194-96
  previewing, 247
  printing, 249-50
  range names, 264-66
  retrieving, 213
  saving, 203-4
  series, 262-64
  size of, 195-96
  sorting cell contents, 266-67
  switching between chart mode and, 288
Stacked bar chart, 285
Stacked line chart, 285
Status line, 42, 193
STD function, 376
Stop bits, 407
Storage, secondary, 4
Strikethrough, 77
Style, character, 241-44
Subheadings, 231
Subscripts, 78-79
Subtraction, 177, 213-14
SUM function, 214, 376
Sum tool, 244
Superscripts, 78-79
System software. See Operating systems

T

Tab key, 5
Tables, creating, 124
Tab mark, searching and/or replacing, 92
Tab settings, 124-27
  changing, 129-30
Templates, 165-67
  creating, 165-66
  editing, 166
  removing, 167
  using, 166
Terminal emulation, 406
Terminal settings, 405-7
Text, 111-20. See also Document(s)
  ASCII, sending to another computer, 413
  blocks of
    copying, 113-14
    deleting, 112
    moving, 113
    searching within, 88
    selecting, 45-46
  centering, 45, 371
  copying character and paragraph formats, 115
  copying multiple paragraphs, 115-16
  entering, 42-43
    into spreadsheet, 197-99
  in **NOTE** field, 329
  special commands in, 92-96
  undoing, 112-13
Text box, 33
Thesaurus, 79, 100-101
Time
  inserting in document, 94
  placeholder for, 94
  in spreadsheets, 258-62
Time/Date command, 260
Title(s)
  on charts, 291-92, 298-99
  freezing, 259-60
Title bar, spreadsheet, 193
Toolbar, formatting from, 79-80, 193, 244, 245
Transient (external) files, 11
True conditions, searching for, 216
True/False format, 246
Typing Replaces Selection command, 46-47, 114

U

Undo command, 112
Undoing text, 112-13

V

Value(s)
  entering into spreadsheet, 197-99, 200-201

formatting, 244-46, 335
  series of, 331-33
  summing range of, 214
  viewing all computed, 334
VAR function, 376

W

.WDB extension, 56
White space, searching and/or replacing, 92
Wildcard (global) character, 18-19, 21
  in searches, 355
Windows, 167-74
  arranging, 171
  expanding size of, 172
  maximum number of, 167
  moving between, 169, 173
  reducing size of, 169-71
  removing split, 173-74
  splitting, 172-73
Wizard tools, 179-80
.WKS extension, 56
Word processing, 39-190. See also Document(s); Formatting; Page design
  form letters, 388-91
  searching and replacing, 88-92
    special characters used in, 91-92
    for text, 88-90
  special commands in text, 92-96
    optional hyphens, 94-95
  spelling checking, 96-100
  thesaurus, 79, 100-101
Word wrap, 42
Works. See Microsoft Works
Worksheet, 192
Works Settings command, 163-64
.WPS extension, 56
Wraparound option, 406

X

X-series command, 299
X-Y charts, 286